D0850052

INDIA'S
INDUSTRIALISTS

India's Industrialists

Volume One

Margaret Herdeck—Gita Piramal

WASHINGTON, D. C.
THREE CONTINENTS PRESS, INC.

First Edition, Volume One, India's Industrialists
© 1985 Margaret L. Herdeck and Gita Piramal

Cover Design by Contour Advertising Pvt. Ltd., Bombay

ISBN: 0-89410-415-2 (Cased)
ISBN: 0-89410-474-8 (Deluxe Edition)
LC No: 83-50574

Three Continents Press, Inc.
1346 Connecticut Avenue, N.W.
Washington, D.C. 20036

For Gita

Dilip Piramal
Rahul Bajaj

For Margaret

Dev Raj Narang
Nitish Sengupta

Acknowledgments

Every creative work draws heavily on the encouragement and energies of the people who happen to be in the immediate vicinity of those involved in the creation. Aparna and Radhika Piramal cheered Gita on when she was down and pried her away from the manuscript when she labored too hard at it. Donald Herdeck kept the lamps of enthusiasm and good will lit to help bring this work to a conclusion. They were the sources for our inspiration and, thus, this book is really their book.

To the industrialists, their spouses and children who cheerfully met us and spent hundreds of hours submitting to our inquisitions. Their cooperation helped us achieve our goal of presenting their accomplishments in the context of the growth of a nation. They are:

Dhirubhai H. Ambani
Mathur Bajaj
Meenakshi Bajaj
Neeraj Bajaj
Rahul Bajaj
Ramkrishna Bajaj
Rupa Bajaj
Shekhar Bajaj
Shishir Bajaj
Aditya Birla
Amita Birla
Ashok Birla
Chandrakant Birla
Rajashree Birla
Arvind Doshi
Gouri Prasad Goenka
Harsh Goenka
Indu Goenka
Jagdish Prasad Goenka
Mala Goenka
Rama Prasad Goenka
Ajit Gulabchand
Bahubali Gulabchand

Gautam Khanna
S. L. Kirloskar
Atulya Mafatlal
Rasesh Mafatlal
Yogindra Mafatlal
Keshub Mahindra
Govind Mathrani
Bina K. Modi
Bina M. Modi
Bhupendra K. Modi
Devendra K. Modi
Krishan K. Modi
Mahendra K. Modi
Kedar Nath Modi
R.P. Nevatia
M.S. Oberoi
P.R.S. Oberoi
Kunti Shah
Viren J. Shah
B.R. Sule
J.R.D. Tata
Lalit Mohan Thapar
T.T. Vasu

We owe the following persons special thanks for providing us access to a vast amount of published and unpublished material, arranging interviews with industrialists in some cases and generally being available to provide the facts and figures which went into this book. Without them also this book could not have been written:

V.A. Adya, Vice President, Mafatlal Industries Ltd.; Ashok Advani, Publisher, *Business India*; Rusi Engineer, Editor, *Business India*; J.C. Jain, Director, Advertisement, Indian Express Newspapers (Bombay) Pvt. Ltd.; M.N. Jain, Joint President, Century Rayon; Nimesh Kampani, Managing Director, J.M. Financial & Investment Consultancy Services Pvt. Ltd.; K.K. Maheshwari, General Manager, Finance, Blow Plast Ltd.; A.G. Mathew, News Editor, *Economic Times;* Dr. Makrand J. Mehta, Professor & Head of History Department, Gujarat University; Manoj Nakra, Executive Assistant to Lalit Mohan Thapar, Managing Director, Ballarpur Industries Ltd.; Swarj Paul, Chairman, Caparo Group Ltd.; S.K. Saboo, Vice President, The Gwalior Rayon Silk Mfg. (Wvg.) Co. Ltd.; Ratna Sahai, Manager, Public Relations, Oberoi Hotels; Dhanpal Shah, Chairman, Dynamic International Trading Co. Pvt. Ltd.; Thakur Sharma, Director, International Marketing, Chemtex, Inc.; R.P. Swami, Manager, Public Relations, Modipon Ltd.; Aroon Tikekar, Reference Chief, *Times of India.*

The following persons took time to meet with us to share their views and insights on so many of the topics which we treated in this book:

J.J. Bhabha, Chairman, Tata Services Ltd.; Dr. S.S.M. Desai, Economic Advisor to S.L. Kirloskar; Allan Fernandes, Vice President, Marketing, Oberoi Hotels; Jankir Ganju, President, Public Relations International; J.N. Gurjar, Managing Director, Kirloskar Systems Ltd.; P.S. Kashyap, Vice President, Kirloskar Electric Ltd.; D.R. Pendse, Economic Advisor, Tata Industries; Sadanand Shetty, Managing Director, Fouress Engg (India) Pvt. Ltd.; Raj Sikka, Executive, Godfrey Phillips India Ltd.; Suresh Trivedi, Secretary to Yogindra Mafatlal.

We are especially grateful to some friends whose insight, knowledge, helpful comments, encouragement and criticism have enriched this book:

S.P. Bagla, Indian Administrative Service; Harry Cahill, American Consul General, Bombay; Patricia Erdman, Executive Director, India Chamber of Commerce of America, Inc.; the late S.M. Ghosh, Government of India; Promodh Malhotra, Senior Official, International Finance Corporation; Vijay Mehta, Consultant, McLean, Virginia; Kuldip Narang, philosopher, ambassador-at-large; Saloni Narang, writer; H.C. Pant, Government of India; M.R. Pai, Vice President, Forum of Free Enterprise; Dr. Mohanlal Piramal, Chairman, Piramal Spg. & Wvg. Ltd.; Robert Rosen, Attorney, Washington, D.C.; Devinder Sahi, Senior Commercial Advisor, American Embassy, New

Delhi; Sunanda Sengupta, Economist, World Bank, New Delhi; Mohan Shah, President, Minerva International, New York; Shehkar Shah; Partner, M.S. Textiles; Usha Singh, New York; Thomas Timberg, Economic Consultant, Washington.

Others have encouraged our endeavors and shared their experience and insight: Ashok and Samir Jain of Bennett Coleman (New Delhi); K.K. Jajodia (New Delhi); Sudhir Jalan, Chairman, Bells Control Ltd. (Calcutta); D.C., H.C., and P.D. Kothari, the Kothari Group (Madras); Avjit Mazumdar, Managing Director, Tractors India Ltd., (Calcutta); C.S. Pande, formerly Secretary-General, Indian Chamber of Commerce (Calcutta); D.H. Pai Panandiker, Secretary-General, FICCI (New Delhi); Dipak Narang, President, Narang Industries (New Delhi); K.S. Rangraj, Director, Kothari Group (Madras); Jughal Saraff, Chairman, Saraff Industries (Calcutta); Man Mohan Singh, Chairman, Frick India Ltd. (New Delhi); Arun Vakil, Secretary-General, Indo-American Chamber of Commerce (Bombay); Hasmukh Shah, U.S. India Enterprises, Washington, and his wife, Shoba.

To Daisy Lobo, P. V. Venkatesh, Norman Ware, Heidi Loomis, Wendy Weems, and everyone who helped physically to put the book together from the manuscript stage to printing or who chased down isolated pieces of information all hours of the day.

We are especially grateful to everyone at Contour Advertising of Bombay who designed the book cover which expresses the past, present and future of Indian industry. We are also grateful for their masterful work in restoring many old photographs to life to enable us to include them here. To Judith Smith of Studio de Soleil in Washington for the special effort she invested in designing our publication's announcement, and to Max Karl Winkler for design work.

Everyone we have come into contact with during the writing of this book has no doubt influenced us somewhat and caused us continually to re-evaluate what we had written. To them, we add our final thanks for taking time to share so many thoughts on a business environment which is undergoing so many exciting changes as we write.

G.P.   M.H.

Terms Used in Text

Rs: Rupee, the Indian currency; (Rs 12 equal U.S.$1.00 in 1985)
Cr: Crore, a unit of 10,000,000; (Rs 1 cr equals U.S.$833,000 in 1985)
Lakh: a unit of 100,000; (Rs 1 lakh equals U.S.$8,333 in 1985)
FICCI: Federation of Indian Chambers of Commerce and Industry

Contents

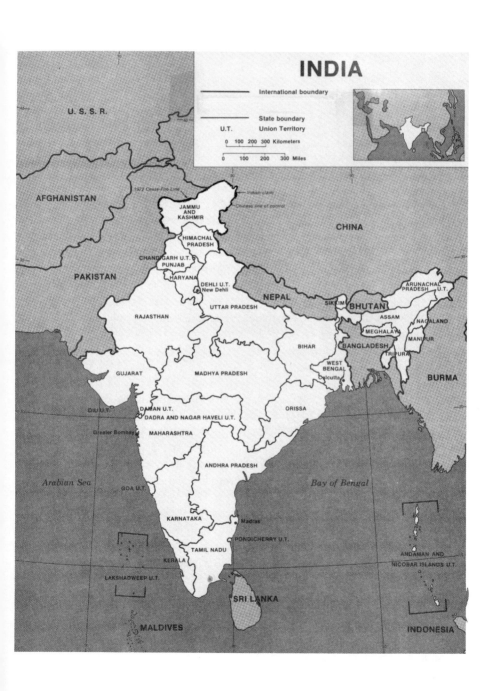

INDIA

——— International boundary

——— State boundary

U.T.   Union Territory

0   100   200   300 Kilometers

0   100   200   300 Miles

U. S. S. R.

AFGHANISTAN

1972 Cease-Fire Line

Indian claim

Chinese line of control

JAMMU AND KASHMIR

CHINA

HIMACHAL PRADESH

CHANDIGARH U.T.

PUNJAB

HARYANA

PAKISTAN

DEHLI U.T.
New Dehli

NEPAL

ARUNACHAL PRADESH U.T.

UTTAR PRADESH

SIKKIM

BHUTAN

ASSAM

RAJASTHAN

NAGALAND

MEGHALAYA

MANIPUR

BIHAR

BANGLADESH

TRIPURA

WEST BENGAL

GUJARAT

MADHYA PRADESH

Calcutta

BURMA

DIU U.T.

DAMAN U.T.

DADRA AND NAGAR HAVELI U.T.

ORISSA

Greater Bombay

MAHARASHTRA

ANDHRA PRADESH

Arabian Sea

Bay of Bengal

GOA U.T.

KARNATAKA

Madras

PONDICHERRY U.T.

TAMIL NADU

ANDAMAN AND NICOBAR ISLANDS U.T.

KERALA

LAKSHADWEEP U.T.

SRI LANKA

MALDIVES

INDONESIA

INTRODUCTION

This is the first of a three-volume study of some of India's leading industrial families, their founding fathers, dreams, foibles, successes and occasional failures . . . the hard early days, gradual expansion into large-scale enterprises, development of new technologies and their growing international images.

It is also a book about the origins of modern Indian industry, its current condition and its plans for the future. The profiles are set in the historical socio-economic context of pre- and post-independence India. Through a look at the founders of these groups, their successors, their business philosophies, their corporate performance and their contribution to society, the reader should gain an insight into the people whose vision and dynamism, shrewdness and hard work, have helped place India among the top 25 industrial countries in the world today.

We have written these profiles largely with the Western reader in mind, to provide him or her ready access to the industrial society of India. We felt there was no better way than to feature some of the leading business families, many of whom played roles as significant in India as the Carnegies, Mellons, du Ponts, Rockefellers, Fords and Watsons have in America.

We will treat a representative group of Indian industrial houses, covering a broad spectrum of industrial activities initiated by groups from every quadrant of India. Many of their names are household words in India, either for historical reasons or for some of their more recent streaks up the corporate performance charts. In these studies, we present 36 industrial families as they became ready for publication–there is no other order of ranking suggested. The readers should be aware, however, that hundreds of thousands of small, medium and large companies exist in India making every conceivable product from shoe laces to oil rigs and whose names are not mentioned here. Similarly the stories of India's public sector giants and those private sector corporations run by India's formidable professional managers yet remain to be chronicled in a similar format.

We have tried to stick closely to the chronology of events in each group's development, highlighting the various turning points and crises which challenged their single-mindedness and many times their scarce resources. We have kept the tone and style informal and personal, but business-oriented.

The material is based on scores of interviews with the business leaders themselves, many of their associates, discussions with experts from many disciplines, including government officials, materials provided by the firms themselves, stock exchange reports, media reports, autobiographies and biographies.

It has often been difficult to compress the knowledge so gained into a score of pages. The profiles on the Tatas and the Birlas have been especially difficult: they have a rich and varied history with many lessons to teach. Several people suggested that they be omitted or, conversely, that a separate volume be written on them. We have compromised by trying to pen the essence of the groups while providing a detailed bibliography for the interested reader.

For Gita Piramal, the challenge was to make her own countrymen appreciate the contributions made by the Indian entrepreneurial sector to the nation's wealth, by evaluating its performance on an international yardstick. For Margaret Herdeck, the goal was to discern the telling pattern–the significant thread–which would illuminate the traditions and personalities of these groups for Americans.

In our conversations and interviews with many of India's industrialists, we tested our theories about what makes their groups tick. We also provoked interesting silences and sighs. All the time we studied what attitudes and skills were developed to help them survive in the rough and tumble world of industry.

In India, a relatively young industrial country in the Western sense, business traditions had their beginnings thousands of years ago. Thus we find modern industry built by entrepreneurs who are by no means new to business. Yet the old exists frictionless next to the new. Tata trucks, Birla cars, Bajaj scooters still move and dart around the ubiquitous bullock-cart on city streets. Very little is cast aside in India. There is a great capacity to accept whatever is new and keep what can still be of use. You can check into a five-star Oberoi or Tata hotel, buy luxurious silks or comfortable cottons, smoke a Modi Chesterfield or Goenka Rothmans cigarette and still patronize the paanwalla on the street corner outside your highrise hotel overlooking the Arabian Sea.

Much of this progress has been undertaken indigenously. But India has never shut its doors on the world of international investment (though some felt it would have been justified in doing so). Since independence, foreign firms, in particular American firms, have played an important role in joining with Indian industry to build India's industrial base. No profile in these volumes lacks an example or two, if not many, of Indian industrialists collaborating with foreign firms to speed up the task of development so comprehensively conceived and articulated by India's national leaders.

We present a snapshot of the industrialists in Volume I:

The name *Ambani* is the story of a human dynamo who, instead of fighting a byzantine system of controls, perfected his knowledge and use of them to build a synthetic textile empire in less than two decades– one which exceeds the efficiencies of similar American and Japanese efforts, as they themselves admit.

The founder of the *Bajaj* group placed himself at the feet of Mohandas K. Gandhi, the lawyer from Gujarat who led India's organized struggle for independence. For 22 years Jamnalal Bajaj was treasurer of the Indian National Congress Working Committee which oversaw the work of the freedom movement. When Bajaj died in 1942, Gandhi had to appoint a small army of people to carry on the work Bajaj had undertaken singlehandedly. Yet Bajaj still had the energy to promote sugar and steel mills, almost always in partnership with other businessmen. Some of his companies have done exceedingly well in post-independent India, all the while maintaining the founder's belief in the importance of a moral basis for business activities.

The pride of the Marwari community, and one whose record every entrepreneur desires to emulate, the *Birlas* are one of India's largest and most dynamic business groups. Its founder, G.D. Birla, was a businessman first, last and always, but he was also an Indian who placed his now legendary skills at the helm of his country's ship of progress. As Gandhi's unofficial ambassador-at-large, Birla smoothed out many wrinkles in the way of gaining complete freedom for Indians. But freedom means something only if economic freedom is also attained. By producing a plethora of goods from cars, aluminium and cement to cheap cottons for the masses, the Birlas have made a dent toward achieving complete economic independence for India.

The *Goenka* name takes the reader back to the days when the British reigned supreme in India and Indians, though shrewder and more talented on the face of things, progressed only by acting as their middlemen. But the Indian's skill in doing so helped them acquire a prominence all their own in Indian business circles. Keshav Prasad Goenka, the son of a prominent businessman, built up an empire of jute mills, carbon black plants, textiles, cigarettes and tea–principally via acquisitions of existing operations which the owners, most often British, could no longer finance or manage. Toward the end of his life KP reacted strongly to the tensions building up among his sons over the business. One day he called in his first son, showed him a three-columned list of the group's companies and told him to choose one. Next, KP called in his middle son and gave him second choice. R.P. Goenka, KP's blue-eyed boy, got last choice. Each son multiplied his empire within a short time of the split. But RP has once again moved out ahead despite the seeming disadvantage at which KP had placed him.

India's first home-made iron plough was the creation of Laxmanrao *Kirloskar.* From ploughs to small diesel engines, power irrigation pumps to large diesel engines for industrial-size generators, from simple lathes to sophisticated numerically-controlled machine tools, the name Kirloskar is the name of one of India's industrial pioneers. Laxmanrao wanted to be an artist, a painter to be exact. Fortunately for his country he was color-blind and had to turn to mechanical drawing and tinkering with machines to channel his creativity. The rest is history. His sons and grandsons inherited his singular devotion to hard work and precision engineering. Like their father, the Kirloskar boys were talented engineers with a shrewd sense for timing, and an almost superhuman will to survive the bleakest of times.

Gagalbhai *Mafatlal,* from Gujarat, rose above his small trader's background to found one of India's largest cotton textile empires, expanding into manufacture of the machines which help make the cloth itself. At 57, to prove he still had what it takes to build a company from scratch, and in the face of protests from his sons, Mafatlal left for Calcutta to set up a highly profitable jute mill. It took him three years and he turned it over to his impressed progeny. Mafatlal was helped in his early days by generous patrons who admired his industry and ingenuity. He never forgot to return the favor by extending a helping hand to many young industrialists who wished to follow in his footsteps. He was a venture capitalist before the term became popular.

Mahindra means jeeps. After that, it means steel, light commercial vehicles, the engines to run them, tractors, precision control equipment and an interest in the development of human resources as well. Its founders traded in some of the products they eventually came to manufacture. Growing quietly and steadily, the Mahindra group has followed a genteel, but successful, path to corporate empire-building.

The *Modis,* a north Indian group whose business roots trace to Patiala in southern Punjab, rooted their industrial beginnings outside Delhi in the rich sugar-cane fields of Meerut. From flour to sugar, Gujar Mal Modi, the founder, moved his group into a host of money-spinning activities during World War II. Their first large-scale industrial endeavor involved the purchase of American textile equipment in 1948 when the British, war-weary, failed to supply the needed machinery. When his town was flooded and his plant and equipment under several feet of water, it was Gujar Mal who waded from home to home, plant to plant, to keep up the spirit of his workers and to save his industrial dreams.

The Modis are pioneers in attracting some of the most renowned names in world-wide technology to India's shores. Rohm & Haas, Xerox, Continental Gummi-Werke, Philip Morris are just a few of the names linked with the Modi group.

The first Indian to own a string of hotels in his own country was Mohan Singh *Oberoi.* He went on to become an international hotelier with a reputation for understanding the needs of business travellers. Oberoi's chain of more than thirty luxury hotels worldwide (there are always six or more on the planning anvil) started with his clerkship in a British-run hotel in Simla. Within two decades, he bought up the shares of the company which owned that same hotel and seven others. From then on, he never looked back. MS Oberoi says one should never look back unless it is to assess one's progress, not to worry over spilt milk. Oberoi was the first to hire women in the hotel business, causing a momentary scandal in India's still outwardly conservative society. He encouraged his three daughters to enter business as well. The roots of his progressive attitude are in his childhood. His father died when MS was only six months old, and it was left to his mother to provide for his well-being. She was MS's role model. The awards with which Oberoi has been showered in his life have placed him unquestionably in India's business hall of fame.

Tata. It is the name which will be synonymous with India's industrialization for a long time to come. Jamsetji Tata realized his dreams for his country to flower again industrially. India's first integrated steel mill, India's first luxury hotel, its first cement plant, life insurance company, first national airline–all are Tata monuments. As important to the Tata saga as the vision of the founder is the rigorous personnel training and development programs which are still unmatched in Indian industry. Almost every industrialist will say that human development is as important to his organization as is modernization of technology. The Tatas have institutionalized this philosophy from top to bottom in all their companies. Today most of the top Tata executives are not Tatas, but they are known as Tata men so pervasive is the impact which the Tata administrative service has had on the minds of the general populace.

Destined to rise to prominence in the coal business in and around Calcutta, the world of Karam Chand *Thapar* was initially not as blessed as that of Jamsetji Tata. A Punjabi hailing from Ludhiana, KC pushed off to the east after college to establish his own business when he realized that his future was limited in his home town. At first trading in the inferior coal which the British allotted Indian merchants in those days, it was not too long before the powerful personality of KC shook up the foreign-dominated coal scene of India. He demanded and received better coal at better prices than his fellow Indians had been used to getting. Through the entrepreneurial eye of one of his agents, the opportunity for diversification presented itself in the early 1930s. A local sugar mill which was buying coal from KC's firm was going under. KC's industrial imagination was sparked. From his first acquisition of the floundering sugar mill, KC entered the then infant paper industry, then textiles, chemicals, engineering products and services. He was a tough taskmaster who nonetheless inspired great loyalty from his organization. Despite the nationalization of the Thapar coal, banking and insurance properties after KC's death, his sons have multiplied the turnover of the group by more than eight times.

Walchand Hirachand, one of India's first general contractors, was catapulted into a leadership role in business when his two older brothers died in a plague which hit Bombay in 1897. Ignoring his elders' pleas that he manage the family's traditional money-lending activities, Walchand followed his dream to establish a construction/engineering firm. In partnership with L.B. Phatak, he bid on minor railway contracts at first as there was little competition from foreign firms. But later the Tatas put their financial muscle behind Walchand and together their new partnership constructed larger and larger projects in a timely and efficient fashion. He employed 30,000 people during his most active period when his firm completed the Bhor Ghats and Tansa Completion water works. The Walchand monuments continue to function and have undergone only minor repairs down the decades. In 1937, Walchand, already in the shipping business, joined fellow industrialist Gagalbhai Mafatlal to take on the battle of his life when the British shipping interests tried to squash their joint efforts to indigenize the shipping business.

We have saved the *TTK* group for last. It is special for two reasons. The founder of the group, T.T. Krishnamachari, broke with his Brahmin family tradition to enter business in Madras. He pioneered the marketing of international brand-name consumer products in India. His sons carried on the business, adding hosiery, kitchenware, condoms, and pharmaceuticals to their distribution network. After independence, they began to manufacture many of the products they had only distributed before then. Since the age of consumerism is coming to India only in the 1980s, we felt it appropriate to feature a group which long ago began catering to the needs of a consumer society. Perhaps more important, however, was T.T. Krishnamachari's political and administrative career during the 1950s and 60s in New Delhi when Indian industrialization took off under a dynamic and farseeing Nehru government. TTK was Minister of Commerce & Industries in the mid-1950s and then Minister of Finance. It is said that his word was all an industrialist needed to initiate a project. He was allergic to red tape and to those who found comfort in it. TTK and Indian industrialization are inextricable.

A few words about the concept of a business group. The prevalent form of corporate control in India by the middle of the nineteenth century was the managing agency system established by the British adventurers, a system which allowed them to control vast economic empires with a minimum of investment. While the shareholders of the managed companies sometimes had to wait years for a return on their investment, the agent/promoter was assured of a return via the managing agent's commission which was ordinarily on the basis of turnover or production, not profit. There was no need for the up and coming Indian entrepreneurial classes to organize their first industrial ventures in a different manner. In fact, the managing agency system was ideally suited to the Hindu joint family system in India which had operated on a limited liability basis in business for millenia. Family members could share in the general profits of the managing agency rather than become entangled in a division of the underlying assets of the managing agency empire which would not suit the joint family culture.

At best, the managing agency system could result in certain economic efficiencies by pooling administrative, marketing and some production operations. At its worst, it left shareholders of the operating company at the mercy of greedy agents who milked the companies dry. By 1970 the government had completely abolished the system. The Tata group, for all legal intents and purposes, ceased to exist, for example, as the Tata family members had long ago relinquished any controlling interests in the large industrial projects they promoted. Investment companies with cross shareholdings sprang up in the managing agency's place to help shelter income or conceal ultimate ownership. This also helped keep the businesses under the control of the joint family. Though internal family pressures have caused many groups to divide their assets among family members in recent years, the concept of business groups continues because the individual family member, upon receiving his share of the business, is quick to start multiplying his inheritance to pass on to his children and his grandchildren. The cycle continues. Even with the dissolution of the Tata group of companies in 1970, for instance, a Tata family member continues to act as the leader of the Tata group of companies. Indians have clung to their family ties.

In India, business is fascinating precisely because it is still identified with the people who do it. In America, successful entrepreneurs who are overnight successes rarely consider keeping the business in the family, if they have one at all. One many times promotes a company with the idea of spinning it off as fast as possible to the highest bidder, usually a large conglomerate. And so that cycle continues and T. Boone Pickens becomes a folk hero in part because he has assaulted the impersonal monolith of the "widely held corporation" managed by people attached to golden parachutes. In the end, we all like to attach a human face to our institutions. We have tried to do that here.

A few technical points. We have used a U.S. dollar/rupee rate of 1 to 12, but any historical figures given in the text obviously reflect a greater value than that of the present day. In the case of group or individual company's sales, we have used the latest information available. In referring to the industrialists in the text, we have often used their first two initials after introducing them. This is in keeping with how many of them are addressed by their friends or in written references.

In a work of this kind, there are bound to be some shortcomings in fact and interpretation. We invite readers to inform us of any errors we have made unwittingly. We will include any corrections received in the next edition. The logistics of putting this book together have naturally been complicated by the complexity of the task as well as by the time and physical distance between the two authors. But we feel confident that we have bridged many of these distances in our collaboration. As S.L. Kirloskar told us in our recent meeting with him, budgets and economic policies come and go, but a collaboration can only be successful if the right two people meet and work out a fair deal. Our collaboration falls in line with the Kirloskar formula. We are, therefore, especially grateful that Rupa and Rahul Bajaj took an interest in suggesting that we combine forces in what began as independent initiatives to tell the story of India's industrialists.

Gita Piramal–Bombay   Margaret Herdeck–Washington

1985

Ambani

Polyester filament yarn
Synthetic textiles
Petrochemicals

Sales
Rs 605 crore
($504 million)

Headquarters:
Maker Chambers IV
222, Nariman Point
Bombay, India 400 021

Head of Group
Dhirubhai H. Ambani

Dhirubhai H. Ambani

AMBANI

In a cool, modernly furnished meeting room just off the spacious reception area of Reliance Textile's corporate headquarters in Maker Chambers in Bombay's Nariman Point sits Dhirubhai Ambani on the edge of his soft-cushioned chair. His ankles are slightly crossed, his head slightly cocked as he waits for the interviewers' questions the way a tennis pro awaits an opening serve. If the question has a spin to it, Dhirubhai attacks it frontally. If it is a lob, Ambani answers quietly. If the question suggests a certain admiration for the extraordinary success of Reliance Textile Industries and its chairman, he will sit back slightly in his chair. What Dhirubhai Ambani has touched so far has turned to gold. Yesterday, synthetic textiles. Today, petrochemicals. Tomorrow is only in the mind's eye. One thing is certain. If Dhirubhai gets involved, it will be big.

The story unfolds as an industrial phenomenon in 1966 with the registration of Reliance Textile Industries Ltd. and as a human story with the birth of Ambani in 1933. Both beginnings were small and quiet. Ambani's first manufacturing operation was capitalized at Rs 15 lakh ($125,000) and first year sales were a little under a million dollars. Plant and equipment consisted of four warp-knitting machines and a small dyeing section and 70

> *Ideas are no one's monopoly; those who criticize me and Reliance's growth are slaves to tradition.*
>
> *Most Indian companies do not understand the workings of the bond market and its advantages.*
>
> *It is necessary to modernize men as well as plant and equipment.*
>
> *God is kind to me. I don't ascribe everything to my ingenuity. God is kind.*
>
> *It is a leader's role to inspire. My job is to motivate my people. We can buy the technical expertise we need to do anything new. But leadership makes the difference.*
>
> Dhirubhai H. Ambani

employees. By 1984, employees numbered nearly 9000 and sales touched Rs 604 crore ($504 million). Expansion into petrochemicals announced by Ambani in 1984 envisions a capital outlay of another half billion dollars before 1988. Petrochemicals is an industry with vast potential in India, according to Dhirubhai.

In mid-1984, a journalist noted: "Whatever else one may say about Reliance's dangerously fast growth, it is unquestionably the one company that has always something new and elegant to offer—both in fabrics and in finance. VIMAL fabrics are as much a draw with the elite consumers as Reliance 'convertibles' with discreet investors." He might have added: "Whatever one may say about Dhirubhai Ambani, he has shown that successful industrial development can be the result of one's man vision and energy anywhere in the world."

The story starts in the tiny village of Chorwad near Porbander, Mahatma Gandhi's birth place, in the Suarashtra area of Gujarat. Born Dhiraj Ambani, Dhirubhai H. Ambani is the son of a school teacher, though the future whiz kid was not to pursue higher education. Even as a boy, Dhirubhai seemed to exhibit a restless brightness which his contemporaries remember being a characteristic peculiar to Dhirubhai. When his brother began work in a factory in his home area, observers say that Dhirubhai knew instinctively that he would not follow a similar path. The observations were accurate because in less than twenty years of establishing his first factory, Ambani challenged the growth rates of India's industrial pioneers like J. N. Tata, Walchand Hirachand and G. D. Birla. Moreover, while most Indian business houses have grown through a proliferation of companies in a variety of industries, Ambani has promoted one company and expanded by vertical integration in one sector, synthetic fibers.

At sixteen, Ambani left India. A friend found him a job clerking in a French-owned, Indian operated export-import firm in Aden, still a British crown colony when Dhirubhai arrived in 1949. It had been administered by the British as part of India from 1839 to 1937. After eight years of learning the tricks of trading, Ambani became restless. He wanted, he said, to do something on his own. So he designed his own job and moved back to India in 1958, not to Gujarat, but to the business crucible of Bombay. He set up his own trading firm there, Reliance Commercial Corporation, which traded in profitable commodities such as nylon, rayon, cashews and pepper. The contacts he had established in Aden became important buyers of Ambani's exports. It no doubt helped that Ambani began life as a member of a successful trading community in Gujarat. But such roots were fortified by his Aden experience and even more so by the confidence gained from being on his own in Bombay.

Reliance spinning unit

Ambani has been criticized along the way for many things. Some comment that Dhirubhai has not developed an industrial ethos, that he still has a trader's mentality. For Ambani, however, it is not possible to separate the two concepts. If you manufacture a product, you have to be able to market it, he says. It matters little from which angle you approach the business of business. The move into industry was easy for Dhirubhai because of his ability to lead his people to dizzying heights of performance. Quality of product is ensured through constant technical innovation. The criticism of Ambani's trading mentality grows dim as the total picture of his growth emerges.

When Ambani started up his trading firm in Bombay after his return from the Gulf, he immediately noticed the potential in yarns, especially synthetic yarns like nylon. By the mid-1960s several Indian business groups had begun the manufacture of rayon, but nylon continued to be imported to be sold at premiums ranging from 100 percent to 300 percent. On one occasion, it even touched 700 percent. Ambani also took note of a government export promotion scheme whereby imports of nylon fiber were permitted against exports of rayon fabrics. Energized by these high returns, Ambani soon became one of the biggest exporters in the country to ensure his ability to import the 'golden fiber.'

Other traders could not match his performance, not because they were unaware of the opportunities in the situation at hand, but because of the difficulties they met in selling poor quality synthetic fabrics in a competitive global market. They waspishly watched as Ambani's exports fetched him replenishment licenses which he used to import yarn which then sold at a premium and assured his company of huge profits. What they failed to see was that Ambani was willing to sell his materials abroad cheaply, even at a loss, for such losses incurred in exports would naturally be offset by yarn entitlements.

After eight years of highly successful trading activities, Ambani decided to begin to manufacture the money-spinning synthetic fabrics himself. In the process, he crystallized two key corporate concepts which his company continues to follow even today: produce the best quality goods possible and diversify into related fields, preferably vertically (and generally downward). Thus in February of 1966, Dhirubhai established a textile mill in Naroda, near Ahmedabad, Gujarat, one of India's historic textile centers. It was a miniscule unit with just four imported warp-knitting machines and a small dyeing section. But it initiated Ambani in industrial management and, more important, it enabled him now to trade in his own products. He continued his trading activities as well and this still remained the most profitable avenue of business for him. The four warp-knitting machines were to proliferate rather quickly, however.

The business environment never remains static in any country, and 1971 ushered in several changes in India. In order to bolster the nation's foreign exchange reserves, the government introduced the high unit value scheme which would hopefully boost exports. This time the government would permit the import of polyester filament yarn against exports of art silks (mainly nylon fabrics). It was a game whose moves Ambani had already mastered. Some saw the deft hand of Dhirubhai in the promotion of the scheme itself. Polyester played a key role in the Indian textile industry in the 1970s similar to the role nylon played in the 1960s. Moreover, this time Ambani had the further advantage of being a producer of finished fabrics himself. He could ensure their quality and would no longer be at the mercy of other producers.

He possessed several other advantages as well. Ambani was among a handful of organized manufacturers of art silks, the rest being small-scale units. He had also built up a formidable directory of international contacts

Naroda facilities

and thus had a clear advantage even over other organized units. He was able to import yarn to use in his company's sophisticated crimping and texturizing division and turn out products whose quality would command even higher values in the international markets, in turn earning him higher import allotments. His competitors could not keep up. Soon over 60 percent of the exports undertaken under the high unit value scheme were Reliance products.

Within a decade of its beginnings, Reliance Textile's sales climbed from $600,000 to $68 million. Ambani was just getting started. In November of 1977, Reliance Textile went public and the lucky shareholders were not disappointed. Within three years the value of their shares appreciated over fifteen times. Expansion continued with the support of an excited public.

As the Reliance phenomenon began to overshadow all previously set records of corporate growth, rumors about how Dhirubhai was managing all of this began to trade as furiously as Reliance shares. Some alleged that his superb relations with everyone in a high or low position of authority were the real roots of his success, not business acumen or honest hard work. Many others already believed that the high unit value scheme of 1971 was a creation of Dhirubhai, by Dhirubhai and for Dhirubhai. They pointed at Reliance's extremely healthy profits. Ambani dismissed the charges with a toss of his head, saying he did not need to wait for an invitation to make profit as others apparently did. Ambani's advantage is that he has the ability to move into a situation quickly, reap the initial benefits and move on to greener fields before his competitors can call a board meeting. In Ambani, there is no hesitation between thought and action. They appear to be one and the same.

Reliance's 1977 expansion projects were completed by the last quarter of 1978. It included expansion of the Naroda facility's filament yarn twisting

Naroda facilities

capacity, crimped yarn twisting capacity and expansion of weaving capacity from 125 to 450 looms. Printing capacity was expanded by installation of additional rotary and flat bed printing machines and the processing department was expanded by installation of imported and indigenous machinery such as Stenters and jet dyeing machines. Expansion of the utilities capacity was also undertaken.

By 1979 Reliance was adding 12,500 spindles for the manufacture of man-made fibers on the worsted system adjacent to its existing mills at Naroda, funded in part by the floating of convertible debentures of Rs 7 crore, a form of financing popularized by Reliance. Completed by the end of 1979, the company had also installed a computer, diesel generator and effluent treatment plant at the existing mill at Naroda. 1980 saw the installation of 154 Sulzer and Saurer looms and further replacement and modernization of existing plant and equipment with a Eurodollar loan of $18 million and issuance of $11 million more in convertible debentures. Sales in 1980 were $262 million, up from $68 million just four years earlier. Reliance also entered the polyester fabric export market in 1980 and exports totalled $7.5 million.

Controlling the costs of inputs translates into certain profits, more so than increasing sales. Ambani noticed that the wide gap between demand and supply for polyester filament yarn in India was ripe for narrowing. In 1980 alone demand for the raw material was more than double installed capacity. It was expected to double again by 1985. Ambani moved to secure a license from the government to put up a 10,000 ton per annum capacity polyester filament yarn plant. The $90 million plant was set up on 30 acres of land outside Bombay at Patalganga. It was Reliance's biggest project yet. The Industrial Credit & Investment Corporation of India, known as ICICI, managed a public issue of $24 million convertible debentures to assist Reliance. Du Pont of the USA supplied the technology and equipment for the project which represented the first time the American firm had ever parted with the particular polymerization process provided Reliance. Chemtex, Inc. of New York arranged the deal between Reliance and du Pont. The plant was also designed to operate on dimethyl terethalate (DMT) or purified

Reliance Textile's Patalganga Facilities

terepthalic acid (TPA), the principal raw material in PFY production. While most PFY plants in India use DMT, Ambani planned from the beginning to switch to TPA and to manufacture it himself.

The Patalganga plant was a watershed in the Ambani corporate saga. It propelled the Ambanis into the big leagues. Never satisfied with today's success, Reliance moved to obtain approval to expand the 10,000 ton plant to 35,000 tons soon after the first project was up (in 1981, du Pont's own aggregate worldwide capacity for PFY was 280,000). With this one plant, India's planned capacity for PFY for the period of the Sixth Five Year Plan (1980-85) was filled and ensured a complete import substitution of the product. In spite of this important factor, however, Reliance had to agree to export production of fabrics equal to two times the value of capital goods imported for the project over a five year period in order to obtain government approval.

The Patalganga project also focused attention on Dhirubhai's eldest son, Mukesh, a chemical engineer from Bombay University with an MBA from Stanford. Just as the high unit value scheme of the early 1970s had made Dhirubhai's reputation, so the success of the Patalganga operations established Mukesh's bona fides on the industrial scene. Camping out at the project site, outlawing the use of memos to address problems, Mukesh and his staff managed to erect the plant in a record 18 months. This was accomplished in a milieu in which project delays and cost overruns are the norm, not the exception. Even du Pont International's director attested to the Patalganga phenomenon by stating that in America it would have taken not less than 26 months to put up a similar plant.

Mukesh Ambani, Dhirubhai's son

Once the Patalganga plant was operating—and there were no hitches here—the duty on imported polyester filament yarn moved from Rs 564 to Rs

900 per kilo. Competitors reliant on imports now had to purchase from Dhirubhai or face being priced out of the market. There were new complaints about Dhirubhai's talent for obtaining the edge over his competitors.

While the Patalganga plant was getting under way in 1981, Reliance took over the operation of a bankrupt or "sick" mill at Sidhpur, Gujarat, the Sidhpur Mills Co. Ltd. which had an installed capacity of 38,368 spindles and 490 looms. Losses carried forward on Sidhpur's books were $2 million at the time Reliance moved to acquire the mill. An additional half million dollars in accumulated depreciation added to Reliance's own credits for the year. Moreover, the takeover of a sick unit in India makes it eligible for concessionary loans from government financial institutions and Reliance secured $8 million in such loans for new machinery to assist in the $12 million modernization plans Reliance had for Sidhpur.

Early in 1982 Reliance's authorized capital was increased from $20 million to $60 million to fund its across-the-board expansion plants. Not only was the PFY plant at Patalganga going up, and the Sidhpur Mills being renovated, but the Naroda facility was being expanded to the tune of $61 million. Basically a modernization and balancing move, the Naroda plant imported twisting, coning, dyeing and other related equipment for producing higher value-added yarn to improve the quality of its product which would further enhance sales and profitability. In the meantime, Dhirubhai keeps trading in cloth. He buys grey cloth from producers at cut-rate prices, processes it in his plants and sells it for much more than the original producer could have. In late 1982, the Patalganga plant reached full operating capacity within 96 hours of its start-up. Reliance stepped onto a new plateau.

The Raid on Reliance Shares

The growing excitement, both positive and negative, over Ambani's successes climaxed in 1982. With two large debenture issues just having come on the market to fund the new plant and modernization of the existing ones, Reliance's shares were thought by analysts to be overpriced. A downward slide in the price was anticipated and investors (some say Ambani's competitors) began to sell Reliance shares short. Some parties (some say Ambani himself) began buying up every share which came up for sale. The parties went further and demanded delivery of the shares on the settlement day, contrary to general practice. The short sellers could only come up with one third of the shares. Chaos broke out on the Bombay Stock Exchange in the biggest crisis since its opening in 1875. The unfortunate bear marketeers scoured every market to cover their positions and in the midst had pushed up the share prices of Reliance even further. The market in Reliance shares finally settled down.

Two years later, however, the controversy surrounding the stock manipulation of Reliance shares reared its head again. In a takeover attempt of two well-known New Delhi firms, Escorts and DCM, a question was raised as to the source of funds for the share purchase by non-resident, London-based industrialist Swarj Paul. The uproar which the Swarj Paul affair caused in industrial and political circles provoked a scrutiny of other offshore deals. Among them was the funding of the controversial purchase of almost a million shares of Ambani's Reliance Textile by eleven investment companies registered in the Isle of Man. Suspicion was further aroused by the unlikely names of the companies, Fiasco Investments and Crocodile Investments, among others. Questions began to be raised in Parliament. Although nothing was conclusively proven, most people were convinced that Fiasco and Crocodile were only two of the images still fresh in the mind of the man whose company had survived the competitors' long knives just two years earlier.

Further questions were raised in Parliament about an apparent violation of the non-resident investment rules when it was learned that Ambani's company had negotiated a price with the offshore companies which was 20 percent less than the prevailing market rate. Rules stipulated that non-residents had to buy their shares on the open market, not in privately negotiated deals. In the cock fight which broke out over the raid on Reliance, however, few would have failed to predict the winner as the man who made Reliance.

Where Growth Is a Way of Life, the Reliance Motto

In 1984 Ambani announced plans for expansion into petrochemicals and other high technology sectors. Initial projections put the costs of the expansion at $450 million and would require Reliance to seek massive new funding. Naturally Dhirubhai had a plan for raising the needed funds. In any event, he said, a project in the petrochemical sector costs $200 to $300 million, just "a drop in the bucket compared to what needs to be done in this area."

He announced as part of his scheme a new $150 million debenture issue, subject to approval by the government. It was to be the biggest issue thus far in the private sector. To make way for the government's positive nod and shareholder acceptance of the scheme, Ambani devised a means to tidy up Reliance's debt to equity ratio. Current holders of the Series I-IV debentures would be given the opportunity to convert all the outstanding non-converted portion of the debentures to equity at a rate which would hopefully yield a profit if such shares were subsequently sold on the market. The success of the plan would mean retirement of Rs 88.2 crore ($73.5 million) of liabilities. The resultant increase in the company's reserves would also make a one for one bonus share possible. For Ambani, the plan also meant his possible ascendancy to the number one spot on the corporate chart with a net worth for Reliance exceeding that of Tata Iron and Steel, Gwalior Rayon or Century Spinning, the former a Tata company and the latter two owned by the Birlas, India's top two industrial families.

Reliance set about in early August 1984 to open more than 50 centers nationwide for the purpose of enabling existing debenture holders to convert their interests into equity. Before the closing date, which had to be extended, more than 95 percent of those holding debentures had converted.

Dhirubhai's Management Family

Ambani insists that along with his constant modernization of Reliance's plant and equipment, it is also necessary to modernize the men who must work side by side of the modern machines. To accomplish this Ambani believes in large doses of delegation of authority to his managers, all the while projecting an unsurpassed image of a leader in easy control of his empire. Many of the Reliance general managers have been around a long time. A man who was handling $4 million in turnover now handles four or five times that. The fast pace of the Reliance growth has burned some managers out. A visit to Ambani's corporate offices in Maker Chambers at Nariman Point will leave few in doubt that burnout can be a hazard of working with Dhirubhai. Everyone is breathless, moving, edgy and always pressed for time. And everyone seems to have one eye and ear permanently cocked for the commands from the chairman's office. There is also little indication that they would rather be anywhere else.

Most corporate watchers had at first felt that Reliance's one man show would conclude almost as suddenly as it had opened. But the entry of Dhirubhai's sons, Mukesh and Anil, in Reliance's operations helped in part to quell those fears. While Mukesh manages the Patalganga facility, Anil is understudying Dhirubhai's brother and joint managing director, Ramniklal, to assume management of the Ahmedabad operations. Ramniklal's son, Vimal, for whom the company's textiles trade logo is named, is likely to assume a post in the industrial empire as well. The two sons of Dhirubhai's younger brother, Natwar, are also waiting in the wings. Though still studying, they will in due course no doubt find themselves a niche in this flourishing empire.

It is Mukesh who is Dhirubhai's right hand. Immediately after receiving his MBA from Stanford, Mukesh directed the Patalganga project. It is thought that he will gradually take over the role of chief executive of Reliance as Dhirubhai concentrates on general corporate strategy. Mukesh was named one of India's 50 future leaders by *Gentleman* magazine in 1985. His priorities included putting Indian industry on the world map by making it more self-reliant. He sees all of Reliance's expansion plans as part of a campaign to cut down India's imports by producing raw materials and finished products at home. Mukesh says that Reliance "holds the interests of its consumers, shareholders and the nation on par with, if not above, its own business interests."

The relationship between Dhirubhai and his brothers, Ramniklal and Natwar, is one of mutual support. With Dhirubhai as the undisputed head of the group and family, the others have always deferred to their brother when it

Patalganga plant: interior

comes to any interaction with the public. They have little interest in the spotlight, preferring to remain typical Ahmedabadi managers. While it is clear that Dhirubhai is to remain front and center, the chairman is careful to include his family in his busy life. Though he is state-of-the-art when it comes to technology and industrial performance, Dhirubhai remains close to his country's traditional values.

Phase II: Petrochemicals

Dhirubhai's eyes light up when he talks petrochemicals. When Reliance was incorporated as a public company in 1966, its purposes included manufacture of petrochemicals as well as textiles and related products. The $30 million acquisition of Union Carbide's petrochemical plant in Chembur in 1984 was the opening shot in Reliance's major diversification plans. With 14 factories spread over six states, Union Carbide had pioneered the manufacture of batteries, plastics, electrodes and pesticides in India starting with the meager import of dry cells worth $50 in the mid 1930s. The deal which Reliance struck with Union Carbide, including transfer of new technology from Union Carbide, will help Reliance in its half billion dollar petrochemical diversification scheme. Reliance plans include establishment of new plants to produce a raw material for polyester, monuethlenegycol, linear alkyl benzene for the production of synthetic detergents, and possible forays into photographic chemicals, acrylics, papers and fibers—even offshore oil drilling has been mentioned—all should rival its first two decades of success.

The company's expansion plans also mean a continuing piling up of tax concessions and credits available on the purchase of new plant and equipment, location of plants in industrially "backward areas," and plenty more tax breaks for big risk-takers. For over a decade, consequently, Reliance did not pay "a paisa" in tax. The government finally instituted a minimal tax on profits as more and more companies toted up zero tax liabilities.

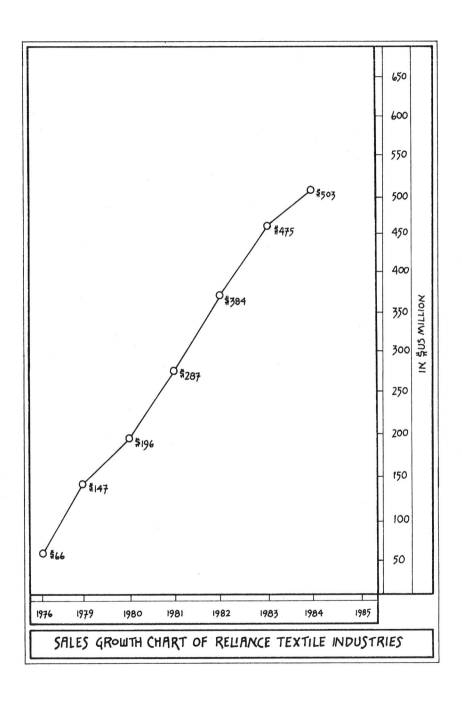

SALES GROWTH CHART OF RELIANCE TEXTILE INDUSTRIES

Beyond Reliance's aggressive financing techniques and tax planning, it is the unstinting quality of the final product which keeps its dealers ordering even in times of low demand. Most owners of shops which sell Reliance textiles are shareholders as well, although no preference is apparently given to shareholders for the sought-after franchises. While Reliance does not charge the dealers for the franchises, it expects them to buy more goods than they would have done otherwise had a franchise fee been levied. Reliance tends to deal more with its retailers than with wholesalers, but the latter are part of the aggressive marketing scheme of Reliance as well. To push its products, Reliance continuously devises new campaigns for its dealers. Famous people from all walks of life grace VIMAL fabric ads to sell the latest styles. To keep his export performance on the rise, Ambani wines and dines international buyers during textile shows to the almost total exclusion of his competition. Even the Japanese have admitted that Ambani's performance would be difficult to match in Japan.

Ambani keeps a close watch on the marketing operations of Reliance. Some of the top posts are not filled with the leading lights from the Indian Institute of Management, but with colleagues from Ambani's days in Aden. The technical posts, however, are filled by graduates of the best schools and many are lured away from rival firms with well-kept promises. Reliance managers are also shareholders of the firm.

Ambani also cultivates shortage situations. He has in the past pressed for import liberalization, immediately imported the goods, then along with others who acted similarly, called for a closing of the import window. Ambani has not cornered the market in import/export techniques by any means, but his success has stemmed in large part from his knack for beating his competition to the punch.

Ambani speaking at shareholders' meeting

John Maynard Keynes would have approved of Reliance's motto "Where Growth Is a Way of Life," and its chairman. Supporting large scale deficit financing to overcome recession and to spur growth, Keynes' belief that the ends will justify the means shocked conservative minds as much as Ambani's bold borrowing challenged ancient taboos against debt. Ambani's justification is straightforward. If Reliance is to meet international competition, it must do so with the latest marketing and financial tools available, not to mention the latest technology as well.

Today Ambani has become as much an integral part of the Bombay establishment as the Oberoi Towers hotel on Nariman Point. Both were high rise acts which received an initial cool reception from the status quo-conscious society of Bombay.

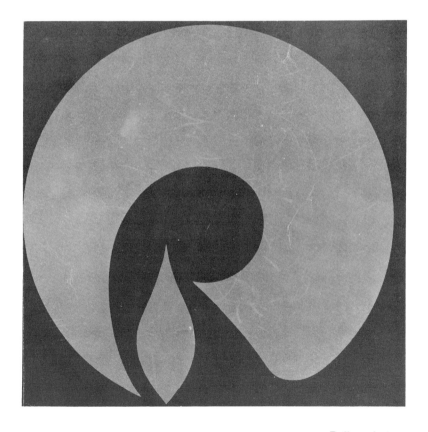

Reliance's logo

Bajaj

Scooters
Three-wheelers
Motorcycles
Steel
Alloy castings equipment
Sugar
Cement
Engineering services
Electricals (industrial and consumer)
Material handling equipment
Switches, motor controls
Trading
Ayurvedic medicines

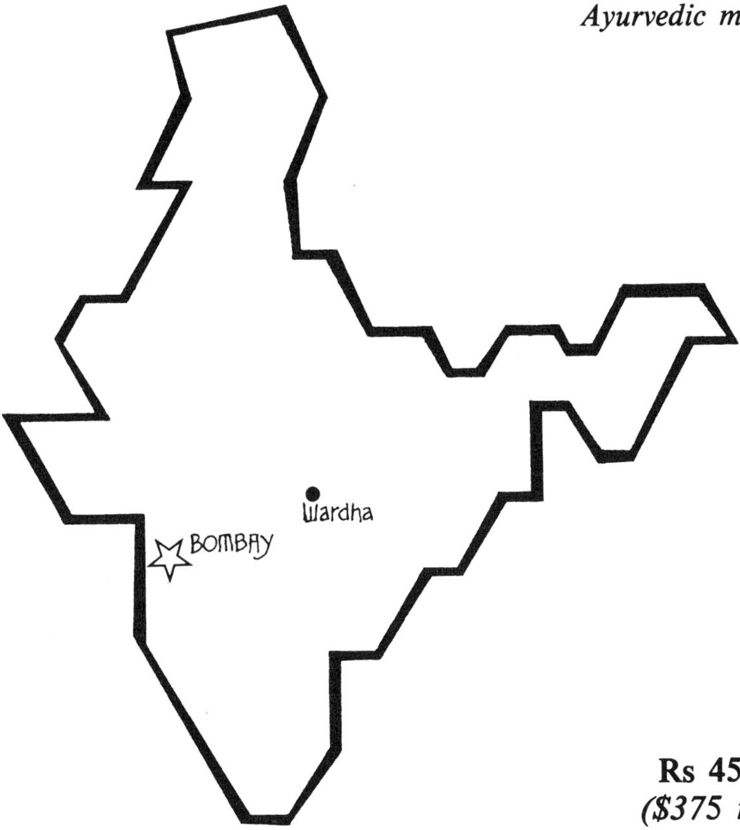

Wardha

☆ BOMBAY

**Sales
Rs 450 crore
($375 million)**

Headquarters:
Bajaj Bhavan
226, Nariman Point
Bombay, India 400 021

Head of Group
Ramkrishna Bajaj

Jamnalal Bajaj (1889-1942)

BAJAJ

In 1920, having distinguished himself in the family business of cotton ginning and pressing as well as indigenous banking, the founder of the Bajaj industrial group, Jamnalal Bajaj allied himself with Mohandas K. Gandhi. Though deeply involved in the freedom movement throughout the next twenty-two years of his life, Bajaj undertook the establishment of industrial projects while continuing the family's traditional businesses.

In 1932, Bajaj's company founded one of the first sugar mills to be set up as a result of the colonial government's decision to provide a protective tariff for local sugar development. The Hindusthan Sugar Mills Ltd., managed for fifty years by Jamnalal's son-in-law, R.P. Nevatia, organizer of northern India's modern sugar industry, is one of the largest and most efficient mills today. In 1937, on a suggestion from Gandhi, Bajaj and fellow businessman, Jeewanlal Motichand of Calcutta, acquired a faltering steel rolling mill in Lahore and expanded its facilities. The plant was lost when the subcontinent was partitioned, but the company, Mukánd Iron and Steel Works Ltd., was successfully reorganized in Bombay after independence. Today Mukand is the second largest privately-owned steel company in the country behind Tata Iron and Steel Company initiated in the early 1900s by another leading industrialist, Jamsetji Tata.

The Bajaj group is a pioneer in the fields of product quality, industrial efficiency and fair business practices. Ramkrishna Bajaj, Jamnalal's younger son, was a founding member of the Fair Trade Practices Association in 1966 and was elected president of the Federation of Indian Chambers of Commerce & Industry in 1984. The Gandhian philosophy espoused by the founder and his sons has given way to more modern approaches to business in third generation Bajajs, but the group's traditions of fair play and social responsibility continue and have placed it among the most respected of India's industrial families.

Jamnalal's elder son, Kamalnayan, headed the group after his father's death. Under his chairmanship the group expanded into production of two and three-wheeled vehicles as well as the marketing of a wide variety of consumer and industrial electrical products. Bajaj Auto Ltd. has long held the number one place in India for production of scooters and is number three in the world. Bajaj Electricals Ltd., looked after by Shekhar Bajaj, has provided hundreds of small producers of electrical goods with a nationwide outlet for their products. The group also went into production of cement, engineering goods and services and medicines as well as other activities.

Jamnalal Bajaj with Mahatma Gandhi, from oil painting

The major growth of the group has occurred in Bajaj Auto Ltd. under the chairmanship of Rahul Bajaj, Kamalnayan's son, and in Mukand Iron & Steel Works, headed by industrialist/politician Viren Shah, son of Jeewanlal

Motichand, one of Mukand's founders. The Bajaj group has concentrated on expansion of its major industrial undertakings rather than diversifying into a wide variety of sectors typical of many business houses in India. As domestic competition in the scooter and motor cycle sector increases over the next five years, however, and the outlook for sugar and steel remains uncertain at best, any significant long-term growth in the group's profitability may depend on its expansion into new products and services. Given a less conservative approach to risk-taking, the group's financial, managerial and technical resources enable it to undertake large projects with a high technology base in related fields of activity as well as new sectors.

Jamnalal Bajaj

Seth Bachhraj, a successful businessman from Wardha in central India, returned to his family home in 1894 in the then princely state of Jaipur. Bachhraj was accompanied by his wife Sadibai when they visited the small village of Kashi-ka-Bas, a ward of Sikr, Rajasthan, in search of an heir to adopt, as their only son had died childless. Sadibai naturally paid a visit to the local temple and on her way caught sight of a spirited boy who immediately impressed her. Inquiries led the visitors to the house of Kaniram and Birdibai Bajaj and it turned out the two women were old acquaintances.

Jamnalal, the village couple's second son, entered the room and Sadibai recognized him as the boy she had spotted earlier that day. Some innocent remarks by the boy's mother in response to Sadibai's inquiry about Jamnalal led Seth Bachhraj's wife to believe her search for a child had ended happily. Birdibai's unwitting remarks of common courtesy thus resulted in the separation of Jamnalal, aged five, from his family and his village as his parents did not wish to go back on their word, however innocently spoken.

The adoption of a poor village boy by a wealthy couple might have alleviated many a parent's sorrow over such a loss. But Jamnalal's parents, when pressed to accept some compensation from Seth Bachhraj, would only request that a well be sunk in the village to provide clean water to his community. The well still exists today. The future founder of the Bajaj industrial group, Jamnalal never severed his ties with Jaipur and spent the last seven years of his life working for the liberation of its citizens from the feudal politics of the time.

Naturally bright and inquisitive, qualities Sadibai had noticed on her visit to the village temple in Kashi-ka-Bas, Jamnalal received only four years of formal education before his apprenticeship to the aging Seth Bachhraj began. Jamnalal quickly absorbed the requisite business skills for managing and expanding the already successful business, but he missed his formal studies and looked for ways to expand his general knowledge.

His interest led him into philanthropy. Lokmanya Tilak, Indian nationalist and editor of a daily newspaper published in Marathi, *Kesari,* wanted to publish his newspaper in Hindi as well to give his ideas wider circulation. Jamnalal heard about the project and sent in his contribution to Tilak, helping the idea to be realized. His willingness to support causes he believed in, and which were tied inevitably to his desire for greater personal development, came to full fruition when he joined Gandhi and put his considerable personal and financial resources behind the independence movement.

Jamnalal was married at the not unusual age of thirteen to Janaki Devi, nine years old, daughter of a wealthy merchant, Gudharlal Jajodia, who had made his fortune in the opium trade. The Jajodias were a conservative Hindu family where the women lived in purdah, a practice Jamnalal and his wife were to campaign against from the time they joined Gandhi. A few years after his marriage, at the age of seventeen, Jamnalal repudiated his family fortune and left home after a quarrel with his adopted father who felt the young man was not sufficiently appreciative of his privileged position in society. Jamnalal determined to follow the life of a sanyasi, but old Seth Bachhraj, filled with remorse over his treatment of the sensitive teenager, found Jamnalal and convinced him to return to Wardha. When Bachhraj died six months later, he left Jamnalal in control of the family business.

Jamnalal Bajaj as boy   Jamnalal as young businessman

Jamnalal's insistence on honest business practices did not prevent him from multiplying the earnings of his companies with the help of his managers, nor did his more spiritual nature dull his ability to take up profitable business opportunities. It was not be unexpected that he would split with his firm's partner, Hiralal Ramgopal, when a dispute arose involving a charitable contribution Jamnalal had made on behalf of the firm in Ramgopal's absence. Since Seth Bachhraj's wealth had come in great part from his acquisition of a share of Ramgopal's successful trading operations, the decision to separate would be the first test of Jamnalal's ability to establish himself as an independent businessman. It was Jamnalal's business which continued on successfully under the name of Bachhraj Jamnalal in Bombay, while his former partner's business floundered. Jamnalal was to come to Ramgopal's aid later on when the latter faced financial difficulties.

Jamnalal's company had to weather some storms. Depressions in the cotton business led many of the cotton merchants to falsify the weight of their cotton bales by watering them. Facing a loss position at the time, Jamnalal nonetheless refused to follow suit and it was not long before the initials 'B.J.' came to stand for a guaranty of pure cotton, eventually commanding higher prices and increased sales at home and abroad.

The young businessman also showed an early interest in looking out for his colleagues. It was the general practice in the cotton warehousing trade, for instance, not to pass on the profits made from the sale of merchants' samples deposited with the warehouse for display. Seeing this, Jamnalal asked his managers to devise a system by which the profits could be passed back, and merchants doing business with Bachhraj Jamnalal & Company soon received a return on their samples in proportion to the amount of their goods sold by Bajaj's company.

It was around 1919 that Bajaj saw the need for an indigenous insurance industry and convinced the Tatas, a leading industrial family, to join him in floating the New India Assurance Company. It would underwrite fire, marine and general insurance. He later sold his share in the company when the Board of Directors wanted to introduce certain commission practices with which he did not agree. His fearlessness in withdrawing from a situation if it did not agree with him, or in supporting a cause which could well result in material loss, earned him the respect of his community. The British government in India had even honored him with the title of Rai Bahadur. But the British were to become increasingly overbearing in their scrutiny of Jamnalal's growing friendliness with the leaders of the independence movement. Bajaj eventually found it impossible to serve two masters, as was the case with a growing number of Indians. He was to cast his lot formally with Gandhi and the freedom struggle in 1920.

The Indian National Congress held its now historic annual meeting at Nagpur, in Jamnalal's adopted home area, and he was elected chairman of the Reception Committee. It was at this meeting that Gandhi's proposal or non-cooperation with the British government was put to formal vote and carried unanimously by the Congress delegates. The events of the preceding two years, including the slaughter of innocent women and children at Amritsar by General Dyer's troops on April 13, 1919, had convinced Gandhi that an organized campaign of non-cooperation was the only solution to gaining freedom. The goal of the Congress now became complete independence rather than a heretofore vaguer 'dominion status'. Gandhi now was clearly the movement's leader.

Jamnalal's role at the Nagpur conference, attended by more than fourteen thousand Indians from across the subcontinent, took on special significance. The movement for total freedom would need money and skilled managers. At first hesitant to accept the chair of the Reception Committee because of his lack of formal education and his little knowledge of English, Jamnalal was urged by Gandhi, fast becoming a father figure to the young businessman, to take his rightful place at the Nagpur session. In his address to the assembled, Jamnalal therefore put himself in direct opposition to anything British and challenged his fellow businessmen to do the same.

"Whatever we have earned under British rule," he said, "has been earned not by enriching our country or countrymen, but by making our motherland and her children poorer . . . Fellow businessmen, our trade, industry and commerce will flourish a hundredfold by our participation in the great national endeavor for swaraj."[1] Of particular challenge to his colleagues was the policy of swadeshi or boycott of foreign goods which was adopted at the Nagpur conference. Many in the trading community held back, but some well-known business leaders such as G. D. Birla, along with Bajaj, followed this initiative. It was an initiative which soon appealed to the Indian business community for it promised a market for any goods they could produce at home.

Jamnalal had been following Gandhi's crusade for some time before the Nagpur conference. He felt that his involvement in the freedom movement could only have real meaning if he had a personal connection with the charismatic Gandhi who came closest to Jamnalal's ideal of a spiritual father. It was soon after the successful events at Nagpur that Jamnalal offered himself to Gandhi as a "fifth son." Gandhi responded positively and Bajaj's life and that of his family merged completely with the business of Gandhi & Company.

The entire Bajaj family was eventually caught up in the freedom struggle. They initiated satyagrahas, burned all foreign-made cloth and goods in their possession, promoted khadi to revive village industries, campaigned against separation of women from society, advocated opening temples to untouchables, supported Hindu-Muslim solidarity and contributed sizable sums to the many causes spawned by the independence movement.

In 1924 Jamnalal spent nearly a year in jail for his involvement in the first great flag satyagraha in which he led hundreds of volunteers through the streets of Nagpur to fly the national flag in defiance of a ban on such activities. When he was released, he began a tour throughout India to promote the sale of home-spun cloth to support tens of thousands of village producers. By 1947, when independence was achieved, sales of khadi had reached in the millions of dollars from a negligible amount in 1925 when Bajaj commenced his tour.

At the meeting of the Indian National Congress in Nagpur in 1920, Bajaj had also been made Treasurer of the Congress Working Committee which was set up to oversee the business of the Congress throughout the year. Before 1920, the Congress had met only on an annual basis with little intervening activity. Thus, his increasing involvement with the Gandhian program for freedom and his responsibilities as Treasurer of the Working Committee left him little time for his own business. He gradually disassociated himself from the Bajaj company activities.

Day to day activities of the cotton business and the group's other lines were looked after by his managers. Keshavdeo Nevatia joined the management of Jamnalal's firm at the latter's urging in 1926. It was

Keshavdeo Nevatia (1888-1960), Managing Director, Bachhraj & Co.

Keshavdeo, a close friend of Jamnalal in public life and, like him, a Marwari from Rajasthan, who became managing director of Bachhraj & Company Ltd., the parent company. Nevatia played a large role in the establishment of the sugar mill, Hindusthan Sugar Mills Ltd., the group's first industrial undertaking. The actual setting up and operation of the mill was the responsibility of Nevatia's nephew and Jamnalal's son-in-law, Rameshwar-prasad (RP) Nevatia. RP went on to become the country's leading advisor to and spokesman for the sugar industry.

When the group acquired a small steel rolling mill in 1937, it was Jeewanlal Motichand, Jamnalal's partner in the project, and a fellow freedom fighter from Calcutta, who was to manage that company with the help of others, especially Rameshwar Agarwal, a distant Bajaj relative.[2] As to other opportunities for expansion, the Bajaj family decided not to enter the lucrative textile mill sector because of its involvement in the promotion of khadi. Further, because of Gandhi's espousal of prohibition, Jamnalal declined to set up production of potable alcohol, an activity engaged in by most sugar mill owners. No other industrial projects were begun by the group until after independence at which time the founder's sons were able to devote themselves to business. But the period of 1939 to 1947 was to see most of the Bajaj family in jail at one time or another, their sentences sometimes crossing. V. Kulkarni writes in *A Family of Patriots:* "Bajaj's wife and children and even his sister, cousins and nephews, joined him so that at one stage most of the adult members of his family found themselves behind prison bars in the cause of Indian freedom."[3]

Jamnalal Bajaj (far right) with national leaders

February of 1939 was the beginning of the end for Jamnalal. He entered Jaipur State in defiance of a ban placed on his entrance by the local authorities. He was arrested and jailed at Moransagar, a hill fort about forty miles from Jaipur. The accommodations were not health-inducing to say the least, but Jamnalal was permitted to take walks in the area. It was on these walks that he fell into conversations with local villagers whose cattle and lives were threatened daily by the panthers which were allowed to roam freely in the area which served as a game reserve for the maharaja and his friends. Typically ignoring his own deteriorating health, Jamnalal composed a letter to the maharaja imploring him to consider the plight of his people. "I am sure your heart will melt when you come to know that behind your back the poor subjects are suffering a great deal of harm from these wild beasts," he wrote.

Jamnalal continued to organize local villages in Jaipur to help them gain some degree of political freedom, but shortly after his release he was forced to seek treatment in Poona for his deteriorated condition. While he was to take up his political work in Jaipur for a short while after his stay in Poona, it was not long before he felt the need to lead a less intense existence, one in which he could renew his quest for greater personal and spiritual growth. After consultation with Gandhi who instinctively understood Jamnalal's need for a more contemplative existence, he decided to take on the cause of cattle preservation. Conferences were organized and Jamnalal called in experts in animal husbandry to promote the welfare of India's vast cattle wealth. But he had never fully recovered from the debilitating incarceration at Moransagar. Jamnalal died suddenly on February 11, 1942 of a cerebral hemorrage. He had noted his severe headaches in his diary in the days leading up to his death but had mentioned them to no one, according to his daughter-in-law, Savitridevi. When he died at the young age of 53, Jamnalal's country was still five years away from independence and the Quit India movement was yet to be launched.

The list of causes to which he had given his life and at least five times the amount of his original inheritance was so long that Gandhi had to call a meeting of a large number of friends, including G. D. Birla, to divide up responsibility for the projects Bajaj had undertaken. In a letter addressed to Jamnalal's friends, Gandhi said:

You are aware how intimate was the relationship between Jamnalal and myself. There was no work of mine in which I did not receive his fullest co-operation in body, mind and wealth. Neither he nor I had any attraction for what is called politics. He was drawn into it because I was in it. My real politics was constructive work, and so too was his. I had hoped that after me he would fully carry on those works of mine which would be regarded as of special importance.[4]

Kamalnayan Bajaj

Jamnalal left modest assets of approximately Rs 13 lakh when he died in 1942, much of which was given over to the creation of charitable trusts in his memory under the direction of Gandhi himself. His widow, Janaki Devi, carried on many of Jamnalal's causes and his first son, Kamalnayan, became heir to the business. Although himself involved in freedom movement activities from childhood, Kamalnayan deliberately avoided occasion for arrest over the next five years in order to look after his many relatives and fellow freedom fighters who were in jail or in the underground during the most intense years of the freedom movement. Consequently, it was only after 1947 that a Bajaj was able to take up the role of industrialist once again.

When Kamalnayan, with the help of his group's trusted managers, began to rebuild the family business, his philosophy was not to differ from that of his father. Echoing the words of Jamnalal Bajaj at the Nagpur Congress in 1920, Kamalnayan once said in an interview:

I am of course anxious that the various industries with which I am connected should generate profits, but if any move on our part goes against national interest, I would condemn it and would not be a party to it even if it meant a loss in the bargain. Whatever we industrialists do should be primarily in the interests of our country and only secondarily in our own interests.[5]

Kamalnayan was raised in an ashram near the family home of Wardha under the spiritual and cultural guidance of Archaya Vinobe Bhave, the Bajaj family guru. Strict discipline was observed and six hours of manual labor was part of the typical day's activities. He learned to spin, weave, cook, plough and 'keep cattle spic and span.' At the age of fifteen, ill with fever, he joined Gandhi for part of the now famous salt march in defiance of British law. Unlike his father who did not wish to travel outside the country, Kamalnayan desired to study abroad and went first to Sri Lanka and then to Britain to study at Cambridge. In 1937, he married Savitridevi Poddar, a member of a prominent Calcutta family. (Savitridevi's sister, Vimla, was later to marry Kamalnayan's younger brother, Ramkrishna.)

India's business leaders shared Prime Minister Nehru's sense of urgency about their country's need to establish a modern industrial and scientific base as quickly as possible. Kamalnayan was no exception. Reliance on outside powers for life's basic necessities for too many hundreds of years had given every Indian a fierce desire for self-reliance. Though many industrialists were to feel betrayed by the Nehru government's downplaying of their role in India's industrial development, they joined the race. They continued to look abroad for the latest technology and, in some cases, new foreign partners, to step up the process of industrialization. But Indian industrial policy never veered from the goal of self-reliance. Technology would be imported, but adapted by local business. The Bajaj group, under Kamalnayan's leadership, entered into joint ventures or technical collaborations with leading companies such as Philips of Holland for electricals and Piaggio & Company of Italy for the manufacture of scooters. The steel company which had to be completely reorganized and recapitalized after independence also sought new technology

Kamalnayan Bajaj (1915-1972), head of group (1942-1972)

to improve its steel-making processes. Believing it a national duty to strengthen the industrial and entrepreneurial bases of his country, Kamalnayan undertook to share his group's technologies with other Indian companies.

Though conservative in his approach to growth, preferring to plough back profits for expansion rather than borrow heavily, Kamalnayan did not hesitate to break new ground for Indian industry. In the 1960s, for example, he took Mukand Iron and Steel into the export market despite a strong domestic market at the time. When recession hit the steel market in the late 1960s, Mukand's annual export earnings of $12 million tided the company over a difficult period. More importantly, Mukand's products became known internationally for their quality and proved that the newly industrializing country was ready to compete worldwide.

According to family members, Kamalnayan's manner of decision-making was totally detached and objective. He was also a strict taskmaster, according to his son Rahul, in whose presence it was difficult to remain casual or careless. "Your every action and word were being observed." It was a trait which Rahul inherited as well. Kamalnayan's love for his work and dedication to the task of nationbuilding left him little time for the home. An occasional game of bridge or small parties with close friends apparently were the extent of his relaxation. His unshakable self-confidence and strong will, honed by men such as his father, Gandhi and Vinobe Bhave, no doubt made it difficult for those around him to live up to his expectations. But he respected the stubbornness and independence in others and he was not one to impose his will once he believed in the seriousness of another's decision. He was tall like his father, affable, and a great host as his father had been to most of India's great nationalist leaders and workers. He played the role of peacemaker in political disputes and was usually successful because of his ability to subordinate his personal interests when it came to solving problems.

He believed businessmen should involve themselves in politics and, following independence, he won a seat in the Lok Sabha (Lower House). He served on many government commissions and delegations at home and abroad. He eventually lost his seat in Congress, having failed to join the new Congress coalition put together by Indira Gandhi in 1969 whose party won the elections. Disappointed over his perhaps predictable loss (Kamalnayan had rejected the offer of a safe constituency from which to contest the election), Kamalnayan continued to serve his country in a variety of capacities after his defeat.

Kamalnayan cultivated an interest in modern art toward the latter part of his life. He took special interest in the preparation of his company's reports and many were to win national awards for excellence in printing and layout.

Kamalnayan died suddenly at the age of 57 in May of 1972 during a visit to his sister's home in Ahmedabad. In the 25 years he had headed the Bajaj family and the Bajaj group of companies, Kamalnayan had built a considerably stronger and diversified portfolio of business activities than he had inherited.

Ramkrishna Bajaj

After Kamalnayan's death, his younger brother, Ramkrishna, became head of the group. Any conversation with Ramkrishna leads one immediately to perceive that his role as head of the Bajaj group is more ceremonial than operational. As author of numerous works on business and government, administrator of the formidable group of family trusts, promoter of Gandhian ideals within the business community and spokesman for many causes, Ramkrishna would indeed seem to have little time to tend to company matters. Yet no major decision in any of the group's 22 companies is taken without him, according to Rahul Bajaj, Kamalnayan's elder son, who along with Ramkrishna, oversees the management of the group's activities. Ramkrishna's role as head of the joint family as well as of the group has itself merged successfully and provided a strong central focus among the varied activities of the large group of companies. The day to day management of the companies, however, is in the hands of the respective chief executives or managing directors, leaving Ramkrishna more time to oversee the spending of the money that the others are responsible for generating.

Jailed off and on for four years between 1940 and 1945 for his role in the independence movement, Ramkrishna grew up in Gandhi's extended family. In 1940, at the age of 17, he sought Gandhi's permission to join Nehru and Vinobe Bhave in offering individual satyagraha for which Gandhi had called in part to protest India's being pulled into World War II. Gandhi was at first reluctant to subject young people to the rigors of imprisonment, but relented under pressure from Kamalnayan that the independence movement should not discriminate on the basis of age. Young Bajaj was to represent the student community, it was finally determined, and Gandhi addressed a letter to the Deputy Commissioner in Ramkrishna's hometown of Wardha announcing Ramkrishna's intention to defy the local authorities. The letter was brief:

> *Sevagram,*
> *Wardha (C.P.)*
> *12-4-41*

Dear Sir:

Shri Ramkrishna Bajaj, ex-student, son of Seth Jamnalal Bajaj, will offer C.D. [Civil Disobedience] on Tuesday 15th instant at 8 a.m. from Gandhi Chowk, Wardha, by reciting the usual anti-war slogans.

> *Yours sincerely,*

> *M.K. Gandhi*

Ramkrishna was arrested. In anticipation of this event, Gandhi had also drafted a special statement for Ramkrishna to read at his trial. Ramkrishna had reviewed the statement carefully with Gandhi as the latter wanted to make certain that the 'ex-student' agreed with it before its delivery in court. Ramkrishna's statement at the trial was the mature and disciplined voice of

Ramkrishna Bajaj with Gandhi   Ramkrishna Bajaj with Gandhi

one who had been deeply affected by the sacrifices which colonialism, war and patriotic duty had imposed. "I felt," he said at his trial, "that the practical experience I should gain in the pursuit of freedom would be of far greater value than the ordinary schooling which every schoolboy knows is conceived not so much in the interest of the masses as that of the rulers." When he was sentenced to prison, he joined his father, Jamnalal, and Vinobe Bhave in Nagpur jail. Ramkrishna related that the atmosphere was so surcharged with the cause of freedom that there was little occasion to feel abandoned by his family. Every person who wanted had a role in the movement and waited only to be called on to perform it.

Ramkrishna's adherence to Gandhian ideals seemed impractical to many. His advocacy of self-regulation for business has proven especially difficult for the business community to absorb. Unless business acts responsibly, however, Ramkrishna feels it cannot protest if government becomes more and more involved in its daily life and society takes an adversarial view of business. This enlightened self-interest is followed in the Bajaj group and Ramkrishna says the group has benefitted from such a philosophy because ultimately a business runs on prestige.

Ramkrishna's involvement in business did not begin until after independence and, even after that, it was his older brother, Kamalnayan, who took charge of the family businesses, leaving Ramkrishna the time to develop a variety of interests outside of business. Nevertheless, Ramkrishna serves on many of the boards of the Bajaj companies as well as on those of unrelated companies. The training and wisdom gained at perhaps too young an age under the tutelage of such disciplined men as his father and Gandhi gives him an instinctive appreciation for hard work, efficiency and positive results. Ramkrisha's quiet confidence that the younger generation of Bajajs will succeed through adherence to these family attributes explains his importance to the family as well as to the group. Such confidence creates an atmosphere in which the younger generation is given the space to grow personally as well as to meld as a corporate group.

Bajaj Auto Ltd. Executive Meeting: Rahul Bajaj, Chairman and Managing Director

When N. D. Tiwari, India's Minister of Industries at the time, visited Bajaj Auto Ltd. in October of 1983, he wrote the following words in the company's guest book:

> *I have no doubt that in Bajaj Auto Ltd. we have in our country one of the best managed, maintained & quality-oriented undertakings. I congratulate Sri Rahul Bajaj & his colleagues, & also all the technicians & workers of the Plant for giving solid results & manufacturing vehicles comparable to international standards. I hope excellence in quality & productivity will continue to be the watchword of Bajaj products.*

In a few words, Tiwari summed up the elements of Bajaj Auto's success story. It is not the saga of one individual pulling others after him, but of technology, management, engineering talent, concentration on productivity and quality and concern for the consumer's pocket coming together to produce one of India's best run business enterprises. Under the direction of Kamalnayan's elder son, Rahul Bajaj, since 1968 when sales were about $7 million, Bajaj Auto's sales climbed to nearly $200 million in 1984. Pre-tax profits were a healthy $33 million. A major expansion being carried out in Aurangabad and Agra will more than double the company's scooter capacity, as well as its production of three-wheelers and motorcycles.

In 1960, in keeping with its practice of seeking technology from abroad, Bajaj Auto Ltd., established that year as a public company out of a small trading concern, Bachhraj Trading Company, entered into an agreement with Piaggio & Company of Italy for the manufacture of the Vespa scooter. Prior to this the trading company had been importing parts for assembly and sale. The major shareholders in the new company were the Bajaj family and the Firodia family, a leading industrial group from Pune. Both families were involved in the management of Bajaj Auto until the late 1960s when the Firodias left to take up the full-time management of Bajaj Tempo, India's largest moped manufacturer. Each group holds a minority interest in the other's company, but cool relations between the two families since the split over Bajaj Auto management ensures that neither family interferes in the other's operations.

From 1960 to the early 1980s, Bajaj Auto enjoyed a virtual monopoly of the two-wheeler market, the equivalent of the car industry in most Western countries. Because of its competitive advantage resulting from its economy of scale, consistent quality and reasonable price, the Bajaj scooter will maintain its edge in the market for a while to come despite the entry of a host of new two wheeler producers. In a country where the key factor for the middle class consumer is the lowest price for the highest possible quality, Bajaj scooters are assured of a steady market.

In 1978 when the government permitted Bajaj Auto to expand its licensed capacity over the objection of some competitors, it noted that "despite their dominant position, the Bajaj . . . scooter is the cheapest compared to other brands . . . the company has not tried to take undue advantage of its dominant position and consumer preference." Under no legal obligation to hold the price line on the ubiquitous scooter, Bajaj Auto made it a policy to pass along to consumers the savings resulting from its highly efficient operations. The fact that a used Bajaj scooter or three-wheeler will command one and a half to two times its original price is a testament to their durability. Fellow businessmen agree that Bajaj Auto is one of the most progressive companies in terms of productivity and quality. Attention to detail and giving value for money, trademarks of Jamnalal Bajaj's business practices, have been successfully carried on by his sons and grandsons. A prolonged strike by Bajaj Auto workers in the early 1980s was called mainly because of management's hard-driving production schedules. Though it ended amicably, production schedules never slackened thereafter.

Rahul Bajaj, Bajaj Auto's chairman, studied economics and law at the university and took an MBA from Harvard in 1964. He admits the workload at Harvard was heavy, but the business theories were not too daunting to one who grew up with business in his blood. As with all the Bajaj boys, Rahul underwent an apprenticeship—his was at Bajaj Auto when his father was chairman. The training was rigorous and gave him an exposure to what was

BAL Executives with N.D. Tiwari (former Minister of Industries), on visit to Pune Plant, 1983

happening on the shop floor and the board room. By the time he was expected to take the reins of Bajaj Auto in 1968, Rahul had been sufficiently steeped in the Bajaj traditions of hard work and disciplined application of time and money. The subsequent growth of the firm's sales and profitability speaks for itself. A share in Bajaj Auto, worth $10 in 1967, was worth over $830 in the stock market in 1983.

Spread over 160 acres of prime industrial property outside Pune, southeast of Bombay, Bajaj Auto's manufacturing complex consists of machine, heat treatment, press, body, paint and assembly shops. A new $2 million cafeteria for the workers was added in 1983 and the company is also expanding its machine tool manufacturing capabilities. The expansion under way in Aurangabad will mirror the current operation and an assembly plant is being set up in Agra as part of the overall expansion. A deal with Kawasaki of Japan for new motorcycle technology was signed in 1983 and was approved by the government in 1984. Bajaj Auto also arranged to purchase a new design for the body of the Bajaj scooter in 1983 from Industria Prototipi and Serie of Italy.

A major export thrust by Bajaj Auto in the early 1970s was so successful that its former collaborator, Piaggio, took legal action in the early 1980s to halt Bajaj's export activities. Exports of Bajaj scooters were halved to a little under $2.5 million from the previous year. They recovered in 1984 to $4 million. But foreign exchange remittances earned from the program which permits release of Bajaj scooters and motorcycles within India against inward payments from Indians living abroad, increased from $3.5 million in 1983 to $4.3 million in 1984. In the meantime, Piaggio linked up with other Indian companies to produce the latest line of its two-wheelers, giving Bajaj competition on its home ground. Trying to feel its oats in the global marketplace has had its costs. More important for Bajaj Auto is the domestic competition which is coming on stream. Adoption of the Kawasaki motorcycle technology, upgrading its scooters and completing its ambitious expansion will keep Bajaj Auto busy for some time.

While it is a combination of hands-on management, a cooperative labor force, skilled technicians and satisfied customers, which make Bajaj Auto a successful enterprise, management's regard for its technical managers on a level equal to that given to administrative or marketing personnel is an essential ingredient in that success. Where the product is everything, the men who make it deserve the credit.

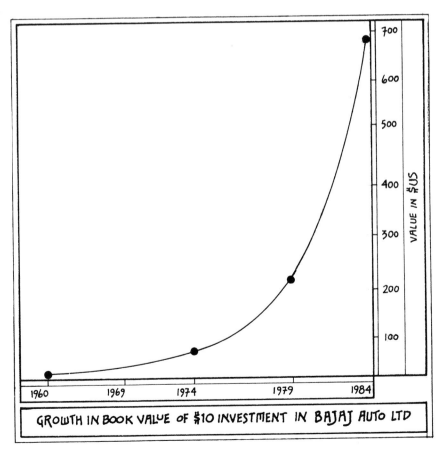

GROWTH IN BOOK VALUE OF $10 INVESTMENT IN BAJAJ AUTO LTD

Chart: growth and value of investments in Bajaj Auto Ltd.

Rahul Bajaj family (l. to r.: Rajiv, Rupa, Rahul, Sunaina, Sanjiv)

The chairman, Rahul Bajaj, lives in Pune with his wife, Rupa, and three children, preferring to keep a close watch on his group's principal profit-making company. While some fault him for an apparent hesitancy to delegate the smaller details of running a large company, it is difficult to dispute the profitable results of Bajaj Auto. He meets his executives often to check on production schedules, budgets and progress on expansions. His large and simply furnished office is one floor above one of the plant floors which can be observed through one long, continuous glass window stretching the length of the plant itself. Visitors waiting to enter the chairman's office at the Pune headquarters can read the latest edition of *The Economic Times* and simultaneously check up on the efficiency of Bajaj Auto's employees.

A local citizen with political connections hopes to jump ahead on the waiting list for a Bajaj scooter and, after a suitable wait, has access to the chairman. He is politely turned away, but not before receiving a gentle chide for having offended the secretary with his impatient persistence. The informality which can exist at all levels in what is often seen as a very structured and status conscious society is disarming. While the business of Bajaj Auto is high speed, high quality production of India's most popular vehicle, there appears to be time in the chairman's day for meeting local citizens in a long wait for a scooter, or taking time to talk with foreign visitors about the people who built Bajaj Auto and keep it running on its road to further success.

Bajaj Electricals Ltd.

Bajaj Electricals Ltd. was established in 1938 and was originally known as Radio Lampworks Ltd. It markets lamps, flourescent lights, appliances, diesel engines, pump sets and electric motors, among other goods. It has shareholdings in two product-related companies, Matchwel Electricals (India) Ltd., established to manufacture fans in 1946 in Pune, and Hind Lamps Ltd., established in 1951 in Shikohabad, to manufacture lamps and flourescent tubes. Bajaj Electricals buys its products from about 100 small-scale industries which manufacture the products under strict quality control and supervision of the company. Sixty Bajaj sales and service centers, 3500 dealers and 20,000 retail outlets all over India market Bajaj Electricals' products.

As with other Bajaj group companies, responsibility to the consumers is taken very seriously. Consumers of Bajaj Electricals' products are invited periodically to come together in public fora to discuss their satisfaction or dissatisfaction with Bajaj products and to make suggestions for improvements.

Day to day operations of the 1000 worker strong company are looked after by Shekhar Bajaj, Ramkrishna's son, who has been Chief Executive of the company since 1980. Shekhar attended Poona University and took an MBA from New York University in the USA in 1974. He started in business as Chief Executive of Bachhraj Factories Ltd., the cotton ginning and pressing company established by his grandfather, Jamnalal, in 1926. Shekhar has also been involved with the Bajaj group's export activities carried on by Bajaj International Pvt. Ltd. which exports chemicals, electrical products, jute and imports chemicals and engineering products.

Marketing firms' sales are subject to more volatility than those of manufacturing or retail units. Once a manufacturing concern feels that there is a market for its goods, it is reluctant to go on sharing the profit margins with the marketing agent. And some manufacturers feel the margins are pretty thin. Bajaj Electricals is as vulnerable to this phenomenon as all the others. Over the past three years or so Bajaj Electricals' sales have been as high as Rs 60 crore ($50 million) and as low as Rs 46 crore ($38 million).

The Hindusthan Sugar Mills Ltd.

The Bajaj group established its first industrial enterprise with the incorporation on November 23, 1931 of The Hindusthan Sugar Mills Ltd. (HSM). In 1930, under great pressure from local sugar interests which were threatened with extinction by cheap sugar imports, the British colonial government was compelled to impose a protective tariff in favor of indigenous producers. The number of sugar mills consequently increased from 31 to more than 130 shortly after imposition of the tariff. Nearly every Indian businessman with industrial yearnings went into sugar in the 1930s.

The site selected for the mill was Golagokarannath in the Lakhimpur Kheri district of the Terai region in Uttar Pradesh, an area rich in sugar cane. Jamnalal Bajaj's son-in-law, Rameshwarprasad Nevatia (b. 1907), was given the task of organizing and managing the new mill. Nevatia's uncle, Keshavdeo Nevatia, a social reformer as well as businessman, had been persuaded by Jamnalal to look after the cotton ginning business in 1926. As managing director of the parent company, Bachhraj & Company, Keshavdeo also had a direct hand in overseeing the affairs of the new Bajaj sugar mill. But it was RP, his nephew, and Jamnalal's son-in-law, who pioneered the success of the first Bajaj industrial venture. RP's mild manner belies a sharp business sense which led him to organize India's sugar industry in the north at a time when the disorganization threatened its development.

HSM began with $500,000 in capital. Its initial 400 ton per day cane-crushing capacity was eventually expanded to 4,800 tons by 1984. A power alcohol distillery was added in 1944 and a subsidiary, Udaipur Cement Works Ltd., was set up in 1970. A second sugar factory, Sharda Sugar & Industries Ltd., about 70 kilometers from HSM's facilities, was established in 1972. Sales in 1984 from the sugar and cement operations of the group reached Rs 52 crore ($43 million).

HSM's beginnings were difficult. In 1933, sugar mill operators faced the problem of ensuring adequate supplies of sugar cane for processing. It was RP Nevatia who organized the mill owners to find a solution. Up to this time, the cane growers were selling their produce for production of gur, the price being offered by the middlemen for sale of cane for sugar production being lower. Focussing on the issues quickly, RP approached the cane growers directly, bypassing the middlemen. He promised a fair price for the cane, and RP's 'Zoning System' which consisted of a statutory minimum cane price to ensure production, was born. Allocation of specific growing areas to each sugar factory was also part of the scheme. At first adopted voluntarily by the sugar factories, when a popularly-elected government came to power for the first time in 1937 in Uttar Pradesh, the principles of the Zoning System were adopted as part of the U. P. Sugar Factories Control Act of 1938.

RP had also promoted the 'Gola System' which became part of the Sugar Factories Act. After two years of operations, it had become apparent to RP that the usual practice of cane growers hauling their cane to the gates of sugar factories without prior notice resulted not only in long waits, but in deteriorating products as the bullock carts stretched along the road, waiting off-loading. Nevatia saw the inefficiency in such a system and set up a system where the factory would go to the farm, an order would be placed, with preference being given to the small grower, and a time for delivery was set. Costly waiting periods were eliminated and an equitable distribution of cane purchases among the growers throughout the crushing season resulted from RP's initiatives. RP's moves established an immediate credibility between the new sugar factories and the growers. RP's talent for satisfying the needs of the growers and HSM's workers kept delays in deliveries and crippling strikes to a minimum, safeguarding the shareholders' interests and winning him the respect of his community.

Rameshwar Prasad Nevatia (b. 1907), Managing Director of Hindusthan Sugar Mills

Hindusthan Sugar Mills

Sharad Nevatia,

Shishir Bajaj

From its inception, HSM's board of directors included names from other leading industrial families of India. R.D. Birla, one of four founders of the Birla group, was HSM's chairman for 27 years, guiding it during a long period marked by steady growth. His grandson, Ashok Birla, serves on the present-day board. As was Jamnalal Bajaj's practice, he enlisted the support of other well-known industrialists, the Ruias and Pitties, to realize the group's first industrial undertaking.

HSM has spent large sums over the years on a cane development program which included substantial loans to cane growers, many of them refugees from Pakistan. Production in crushed cane rose from 60,000 tons in 1932-33 to 1.2 million tons in 1981-2, sugar production having increased from 5,500 tons to 112,000 tons during the same period.

Projects in housing, irrigation, veterinary medicine and demonstration plots for improving new protein-rich varieties of fodder have been implemented by HSM. Training of local citizens in cottage industries such as carpet-weaving, tailoring and repair works, has been undertaken by HSM and previously isolated villages have been linked through construction of roads and the food for work program.

The group's 80,000 ton per annum cement factory was inaugurated in 1970 in Bajajnagar (formerly Dabok), 22 miles from Udaipur in Jamnalal's home state of Rajasthan, and is looked after by RP's son, Sharad. When Sharda Sugar & Industries was established two years after Udaipur Cement, it was primarily to assist the cane growers of the area by locating closer to the source of cane. Forty-nine percent of the initial subscribed capital was given to the cane growers in accordance with the terms of the industrial license.

HSM's philosophy of continuous modernization and expansion over the years has helped it weather the worldwide downturn in the sugar industry. At home, the Indian government's policy of increasing support prices to growers while holding the selling price of sugar down has added to the inevitable crippling losses of the industry. Given its strong performance from the beginning, however, HSM will undoubtedly maintain its industry leadership. RP has been on the scene for more than 50 years. Kamalnayan Bajaj's younger son, Shishir, as Executive Director of HSM today, has been overseeing the day to day management of the sugar operations. He has learned the business from the ground up, having lived for several years with his wife Meenakshi (of the well-known Calcutta business family of Jalan) at Gola. He completed his MA in Finance from New York University and travels abroad frequently to keep up with the latest industry technology. Shishir has an eye for new opportunities and is keenly aware that the Bajaj group must diversify and take bigger risks if it is to maximize its growth potential in an increasingly competitive environment. HSM's horizons should expand under Shishir.

Mukand Iron & Steel Works Ltd.

Prior to the twentieth century, there were seventeen attempts to establish iron works based on Western techniques. All but one failed and the company, The Bengal Iron Company, manufactured pig iron for export, its attempts at manufacturing steel also having failed. Iron ore, plentiful and easily exploitable, had been smelted in simple furnaces throughout the subcontinent for more than 3,000 years. After the commencement of British rule and the collapse of Maratha and Sikh power during the first half of the nineteenth century, however, demand for the highly regarded indigenous armaments disappeared. The demand for more sophisticated iron and steel products necessitated by increased trade and industrial activity between the colony and Britain left the local artisans out of the picture altogether. It was the smashing of the indigenous small-scale industrialist which left the future of Indian industry in the hands of the trading classes.

Five years after the establishment of the sugar mill at Gola, Gandhi persuaded Jamnalal Bajaj and his friend, Jeewanlal Motichand of Calcutta, to take over the operation of a modest and faltering steel re-rolling mill and foundry in Lahore, now in Pakistan. The owner of the mill, Lala Mukand Lal, who had set up the mill in 1922 to produce steel from scrap was anxious to divest his operations in order to devote himself full time to the freedom movement. Despite their own preoccupation with their country's independence, Jamnalal and his colleague acceded to Gandhi's wish and purchased it from the owner for less than $50,000. Today Mukand is the largest steel concern using the electric arc furnace technology and has the largest steel foundry in the non-government sector.

Jeewanlal Motichand, Founder-Director, Jeewan Ltd.

Jeewanlal Motichand, along with a distant Bajaj relative, managed the company in the first ten years from 1937, but Jamnalal Bajaj served as chairman until shortly before his death in 1942. Jeewanlal, a long time friend of Bajaj, was offered shares in all the Bajaj undertakings. He declined a share in Hindusthan Sugar Mills in 1933 when he gave up business and retired to his farm in Suarashtra, his first love. Although he had worked hard for his money, his son Viren, chairman of Mukand today, says he gave it all to the freedom movement without hesitation. Jeewanlal supported all the Gandhian causes. The Mukand proposition was to bring him back to the business world, however.

On June 17, 1939, the new owners met in Bombay to present the first annual report to the shareholders. In the period ending March 31, 1939, two new rolling mills were erected in Bombay, a steel furnace was added to the Lahore facilities and new land was purchased and improvements carried out in the factories. A small profit was also reported. The thirteen page annual report of 1939 also noted that "owing to the shortage of suitable raw materials, the mills could not be worked to their full capacity. Keen competition had also to be faced both from Tatas and local mills at Lahore."

When it became increasingly clear that India would be partitioned and facilities not owned by residents of the newly created countries lost, R. P. Nevatia, a director of the steel company, sought advice from another leading industrialist, Lala Shriram, as to whether the Bajaj group should move the assets of the Lahore facilities to salvage part of the operation before partition. Shriram, according to Nevatia, did not share the sense of urgency and, moreover, felt that the new government of Pakistan was going to be more favorably inclined toward business than India. Its market also beckoned. Shriram's advice was heeded by the Bajaj group. It is not clear if in the general environment of conflict which led up to partition the group could have transferred the assets, but the property was lost after partition as Nevatia had anticipated. Hopes that adequate compensation would be paid were dashed when the new leaders of India and Pakistan met and Pakistan's new President, Mohammed Ali Jinnah, did not care to discuss what must have seemed an insignificant agenda item at the time. But the Bajaj group was given a small re-rolling mill in return for the lost Lahore facilities. The firm, BECO, is now a subsidiary of the Bombay company.

Though Mukand had increased its sales to about $6 million in 1946 from $1.8 million in 1939, the post-war slump made it unlikely that the company could survive with the small production facility it had established in Bombay. This combined with an overall deteriorated financial position of the Bajaj group in 1947 caused the group's executives to consider whether to stay in the steel business at all. Moreover, the new government's industrial policy reserved the integrated steel mill sector for public enterprise concerns and promised to reassess the status of private firms in the steel sector in ten years time. It was thus in the face of slack demand for steel products, diminished assets, crushing overheads and an uncertain government policy over the medium term that the Bajaj group, headed by Jamnalal's son, Kamalnayan, then 32, set about to rebuild the steel company in Bombay.

In 1950, on the strength of personal guaranties put up by Bajaj executives, including R. P. Nevatia, the group obtained a loan of $220,000 from the Industrial Finance Corporation for a new steel foundry and rolling mill to be located on twenty acres of land at Kurla, on the outskirts of Bombay. Viren Shah recalled that the group bought a second-hand bulldozer to prepare the uneven land for the plant. Shah lived in a thatched hut on the factory site as the construction was under way. In the early years of operation, when the company was short of cash, Shah invited a Scottish banker with the Allahabad Bank to a cocktail party to work up to requesting a very necessary loan. Shah recalls he wore a black tie with a brown suit that day. While he did not realize his lack of color coordination until quite a while later, he did establish a fruitful rapport with the banker and Mukand received a $300,000 overdraft shortly thereafter.

As with all the Bajaj family and associates, Shah was deeply involved in the freedom movement. The intensely nationalistic winds which were blowing when Shah grew into his teens could not help but attract the strong-willed and fearless young man. He attended the G. S. College of Commerce in Wardha where he stayed with the Bajaj family while attending classes. Coming of age during the Quit India movement launched in 1942, Shah joined in student agitations at his school and boycotted further English education. Then only 16, and disillusioned by the turmoil around him, he went off to work on his father's farm in Suarashtra. Returning to Bombay in 1945, he began his apprenticeship in Mukand's facilities there. But in 1946 he was arrested for taking part in a procession banned by the police. Out of jail, he went to Lahore to work in Mukand as a day laborer. When Muslim-Hindu clashes broke out in Lahore, he defied curfews to help those in need. When Shah left Lahore for Suarashtra in 1947, it was never to return. While many doubted the group could begin its steel business again, Shah joined in to accomplish the task. In 1954, he was appointed a director of the company as he became increasingly influential in directing the company's growth.

Shortly after Mukand's Kurla operations were established, Shah recalls having to face down an executive from Associated Cement which was contemplating establishing its own foundry rather than continue to buy products from Mukand. Faced with a potentially crushing withdrawal of an important customer, Shah convinced the executive, then at least twice his age, to rethink the decision in favor of continuing to buy Mukand's products. He was successful. He continued to imprint his risk-taking style on the company. He pushed the sometimes conservative board of directors to take on a large order for rolled steel which meant purchasing enough raw materials to fulfill the order. This in turn would soak up a great part of the company's cash resources of the time. But Viren pushed ahead, bought the steel billets required at a favorable price and Mukand executed the order in record time. This move helped the company reach an important plateau.

Expansion continued through the late 1950s with an emphasis on sales of rolled products. Its casting facilities were expanded in the early 1960s. A license for production of steel billets was increased from 45,000 tons to 135,000 tons per year in the early 1960s. In 1983, Mukand secured additional government approval to double the capacity to 270,000 tons. Special steel billet production technology was imported from Sweden in 1964 as well as technology for high speed manufacturing of wire rods. The technology, not yet successfully tried in Europe, was nonetheless adapted to local conditions and Viren's decision as chief executive to import the new

Mukand Iron & Steel Works

Viren Shah, Chairman, Mukand
Iron & Steel Works Ltd.

technology paid off. The new system, since updated with French technology, consolidated the many steel billet-making operations into one.

It was in the early 1970s that Mukand's policies of technology adaptation began to pay off and sales jumped 40 percent between 1972 and 1973 and a further 28 percent in 1974 to $34 million. In the next decade, sales advanced on the average of 11 percent annually, among stiff competition from both public and private sector firms.

A $12 million expansion program was begun in 1981 in part with the issuance of $7 million in convertible debentures, representing the first time in the company's then 43-year history that it approached the general market for financing. Being a closely held corporation with over 40 percent of its shares held by the original shareholders, it was felt by some that Mukand could have grown much faster if it had gone to the market earlier. But Mukand grew nonetheless and its growth has been attributable in large part to its policy of continual product innovation.

Mukand has a technical collaboration in special and alloy steels with Société des Aciers de L'est of France. The foundry, which provides castings for India's railways, automobile, earth-moving equipment, defense and shipyard industries, as well as those of power, sugar and cement, benefitted from technology from Amsted Industries International of the U.S. and Hitachi of Japan. Mukand's fabrication in the early 1960s of electric overhead travelling cranes for its own operations led to the formation of its machine building division, an increasingly important part of Mukand's capabilities. It has designed industrial equipment for chemical, petrochemical, fertilizer, cement and metallurgical industries, carrying out turnkey projects in many of these. It joined with Peiner of West Germany for the design and manufacture of port cranes.

Mukand's chairman is well aware that the future of Mukand is tightly wound up in India's own economic development. New roads, housing, new factories, power transmission systems, nuclear energy, oil exploration, updated ports—all are areas of growth in India and potentially for Mukand. The firm's survival as a medium-sized, diversified steel and engineering entity among the public sector giants is indicative of its strong roots in the beginning years of India's independence.

Mukand survived a six-month strike in the late 1970s and in 1983 was again hit with a crippling series of slowdowns and labor demands at one of its plants. Datta Samant, the feared leader of Bombay's industrial labor community, represented the Mukand workers and shut down the Kalwe plant for thirteen months and the Kurla plant for six months. Shah would not back down. With his own activist background, and his ability to deal directly with his workers, he was able to win a court ruling in 1984 to hire new employees to take up the work of the striking laborers. While sales plummetted by almost one third to below Rs 100 crore in 1983-84, production had begun to pick up at the crippled plants in late 1984 when the workers themselves deserted Datta Samant to form two new trade unions. Viren relates:

Datta Samant is no longer our Union President, in fact, that Union has ceased to exist. A local lady social worker has become the President of the new Union with mostly new Committee members. A good settlement, from everybody's point of view was signed and as of today the results seem to be satisfactory. This unfortunate event has given us a setback not only in terms of profits and cashflow but in terms of our losing valuable time in introducing new technology processes and offering better products in the market. But these are the wages of modern industrial society.[6]

Shah keeps an active interest in all aspects of his country's development. He writes frequently to government officials suggesting ways to improve services to India's 750 million citizens. Mistreatment of a citizen on a street corner by a policeman will be enough to motivate the busy chairman of Mukand to dash off a letter of protest to the chief of Bombay's police asking that he take care to instruct his officers to treat people in a more kindly fashion.

It was in 1966 that Shah took up the challenge to defend business against increasingly antagonistic politicians. He felt that if business did not establish its right to exist and grow in India's pluralistic society that it would sink into 'servile insignificance.' Never one to simply comment from the sidelines, Shah decided to run for a seat in the Lok Sabha in 1967 under the Swatantra Party banner. He defeated his Congress Party rival by more than 11,000 votes. His successful campaign was the result of applying the latest management techniques to a solid political instinct. After his elections, he visited each of the 600 villages in his constituency and followed up more than 17,000 letters received from his constituents. It was not enough apparently to get him re-elected in 1971, but Shah never lost his interest in advising those in power, just as Kamalnayan Bajaj had not upon his defeat in the same elections.

Viren Shah campaigning during 1971 elections

After his defeat, Shah set about to streamline Mukand's operations to place it on a sounder footing for growth in the next decade. But by the mid-1970s, Shah was again involved in politics. He was elected to the Rajya Sabha by the Janata Alliance from the state of Gujarat. He used his seat to launch a stinging criticism of the State of Emergency which had been declared by Prime Minister Indira Gandhi on June 25, 1975 which had resulted in the jailing of most of the opposition. His friendship with many of the opposition leaders and his almost solitary voice of protest against the suspension of freedoms eventually landed him in jail as well in 1976. Management of Mukand was turned over to his associate and friend in the Bajaj group, Rahul Bajaj. When the Emergency ended and elections were called, the Janata Party coalition overwhelmed the Congress Party and Shah naturally became a close adviser to the new leaders.

The "Baroda Dynamite" Gang

Those accused in the 1977 "Baroda Dynamite" case. All were liable to be sentenced to life imprisonment or ten years of hard labor. Viren Shah is in second row, fourth from left; his son, Sukumar, is in third row, fourth from left. On Viren Shah's right is George Fernandes, Minister of Industries under the Janata government (1977-79).

Whether Mukand Iron's performance has suffered because of the chairman's activism is not easily analyzed. For it is Shah's dedication to his country, his belief in the value of business's contribution to society and his own innate dynamism which helped build Mukand Iron & Steel Works. At the same time, there was never a question as to whether Shah would speak out on issues which he felt vital to his country's political and economic survival. Without an hospitable respect for business's role in society, Shah knew Mukand's future was not secure in any event.

Viren's eldest son, Rajesh, is now in charge of Mukand's day to day operations. Sukumar Shah, a political activist like his father, also joined the management of Mukand recently in addition to managing his own pharmaceutical company. It was Rajesh who played a key role in bringing about a satisfactory end to Mukand's labor strife in 1984. As his sons take over more and more responsibilities, Viren is increasing his public activities.

I am inaugurating the annual convention of the Institute of Indian Foundrymen; . . . in Delhi the new Minister of Steel has invited me to attend a Round Table to discuss the steel industry for the next decade. As I am President of the Indian National Committee of the International Chamber of Commerce for 1984-85, I will be heading the Indian delegation to Seoul for the 6th annual conference.[7]

Birla

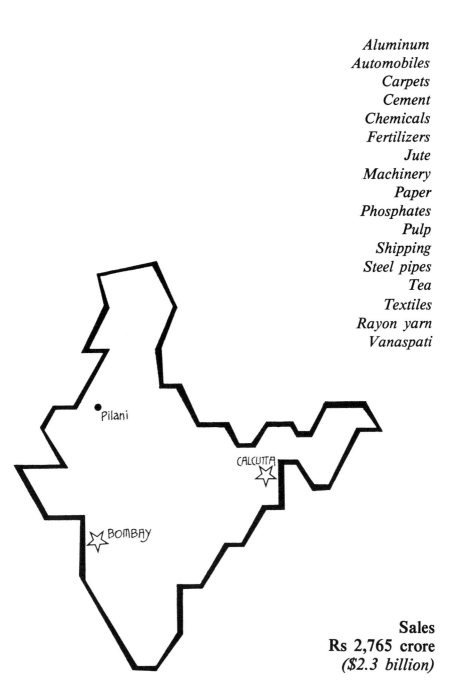

Aluminum
Automobiles
Carpets
Cement
Chemicals
Fertilizers
Jute
Machinery
Paper
Phosphates
Pulp
Shipping
Steel pipes
Tea
Textiles
Rayon yarn
Vanaspati

Pilani

CALCUTTA

BOMBAY

**Sales
Rs 2,765 crore
($2.3 billion)**

Headquarters

Bombay:
Industry House
159, Churchgate Reclamation
Bombay, India 400 020

Calcutta:
Birla Building
9/1, R.N. Mukherjee Road
Calcutta, India 700 001

Heads of Group
L.N. Birla
K.K. Birla
B.K. Birla
G.P. Birla
M.P. Birla
Ashok Birla

The Four Founding Brothers (l. to r.): Jugal Kishore (1883-1967), Rameshwardas (1892-1973), Ghanshyamdas (1894-1983), Brij Mohan (1905-1982)

BIRLA

Now people talk only of people who've got money. They forget that if you read the puranas you do not find any history of some big landlord or a big merchant doing something. It is all about good people. Values have now changed. I don't like it myself.

G. D. Birla (1894-1983)

This seemingly incongruous statement from an acknowledged leader of India's industrial revolution is typical of the man who became a legend in his own lifetime. The industrial empire which G.D. Birla and his brothers built in seventy short years encompassed a vast spectrum of capital and consumer goods. Aluminum, textiles, chemicals, automobiles, jute, cement, tea, textile machinery, light engineering and a host of other products manufactured by their 175 or so companies keep the Birla group a dominant force in Indian industry.

No fewer than 30 of the group's companies are listed among the top 250 corporations in India's private sector. In the midst of the unbroken chain of corporate successes which the four Birla brothers chalked up in the twentieth century, the independence movement led by Mahatma Gandhi kept their undivided attention as well. Gandhi was joined early on in the movement by the Birlas who placed unprecedented financial resources at the feet of the man who led India to freedom. Independence would not be sacrificed for short-term profits. The Birla vision was all-encompassing and farsighted. They rode the crest of the wave of independence into the latter half of the twentieth century, remaining all the while one of the largest and the most consistently profitable industrial conglomerates in India.

The Exodus from Rajasthan

1857 is a year not easily forgotten by the Indian people. The year of "The Great Mutiny" or "The First War of Indian Independence" (depending on which side of the fence the historian is sitting) marked not only the end of the East India Company's governance of a nation, but also heralded a massive migration of the Marwari community from Rajasthan in western India to the new colonial urban centers. Among the first to leave was Shiv Narain Birla, a merchant from Pilani who rode on camel-back to Ahmedabad, and from there took a train to Bombay.

The timing could not have been better. The years 1861 to 1865 were some of the most prosperous ones in the history of Bombay. With the onset of the American Civil War, supplies of raw cotton to Lancashire textile mills dried up overnight. Desperate to keep their machines working, the mill owners scoured the world for raw material. They found a rich source in Bombay Presidency. With the increased demand, prices of raw cotton shot up. Fortunes were made as quickly as they were lost as another leading family, the Tatas, found to their loss. Shiv Narain, however, did well. He called his son Baldeodas from Pilani to join him in Bombay to help expand their trading activities. Soon the father-and-son team became fairly well-known traders, dealing in opium, silver and sugar as well as cotton. One record mentions that in Pilani during the last decade of the nineteenth century, a bullock-chariot was a luxury vehicle maintained especially by the well-to-do mainly for the ladies and the infirm. The Birlas now had two very good camels and a bullock-chariot.

From 1881 onwards, Bombay began to suffer from recurring incidences of plagues. The 1897 plague was possibly the worst in the annals of Bombay's history, so much so that the Birlas removed themselves to Calcutta (there are conflicting accounts as to whether the Birlas shifted to Calcutta in 1898 or 1901). There they found themselves a niche in the firm of Tarachand Ghanshyamdas, an enormously influential firm which helped the Birlas learn about the opium and jute markets of Calcutta. Soon the Birlas left Tarachand Ghanshyamdas to set up a firm of their own. It was in the opium futures trade that the Birla fortune was first made.

By the turn of the twentieth century, the four sons of Baldeodas, grandsons of Shiv Narain, were called to Calcutta to join the family business. The eldest son, Jugal Kishore Birla (1883-1967) became a reputed trader and speculator without peer in the business world of Calcutta. A financial wizard, he was able to keep track of the rapid oscillations in the opium prices which fluctuated wildly because of the changing value of silver–the commodity with which China paid for her opium–as well as the Chinese government's futile attempts to ban the import of the drug. Thus the instability of the opium market offered great potential for speculative coups. The Marwari community, with its cohesive clan mentality, had organized the opium trade as early as 1830. When the Birlas came to Calcutta, being Marwaris, they easily gained an entry into this trade. It would have been difficult to penetrate other avenues of business in any case since most of them were the well-guarded preserves of the European managing agency houses.

The jute and hessians market was also important, but not nearly so unstable. By 1915 the Birlas had established themselves in this field as well. As in 1861, so in 1914, circumstances favored them. World War I created boom times in India and the demand for gunny sacks spiralled. The Birlas, especially Ghanshyamdas (universally known as G.D.) Baldeodas' second son, were quick to fulfill these demands and were well-rewarded. It is estimated that the total Birla worth rose from Rs 20 lakh ($166,000) to Rs 80 lakh ($664,000) over the war years. With this capital accumulation, they began to shed their trading and speculative character and, between 1916 and 1922, they crossed over from trade to industry.

Apart from working with Tarachand Ghanshyamdas, the Birlas had also managed to become brokers (banians) to Andrew Yule quite soon after shifting to Calcutta. The experience gained from the association with a well-known British managing agency with wide industrial and trading interests helped the Birlas enter the cotton textile industry. In 1916 they took over a sick cotton mill in Delhi. This was to give them their first taste of industrial management. But the real thrust began in 1919 with the establishment of Birla Jute in Calcutta and Jiyajeerao Cotton in 1921 at Gwalior.

Until this time the Birlas had been carrying on business under the name of Baldeodas Jugalkishore. In 1918 they established a limited company for the first time, Birla Brothers, which was to become, along with Tata Sons,[1] the most well known Indian managing agency in colonial India. But in 1920, it was still touch and go. Birla Jute was established in defiance of the Scottish monopoly which had governed the entire jute industry from its inception. GD's project soon took on hues of a war between an Indian entrepreneur and the colonial establishment.

"It was very difficult for grandfather to establish this jute mill," recalls GD's grandson, Aditya Birla. "Whenever he would buy some land to establish this mill, the English and the Scots would buy land all around to prevent him from building the jute mill." But GD's determination matched that of his opponents. His intelligence, drive and gut feeling for business made a mockery of any obstacles others cared to put in his way.

Only once did GD falter. As Birla Jute's first Indian manager pointed out: "In those days financial institutions to promote industrial development did not exist. An aspiring industrialist had to invest almost his entire savings to promote his first venture and then expand it by mortgaging the assets of the

Baldeodas Birla

Seth Shiv Narain Birla

GD Birla as young boy

first undertaking to raise enough capital for the second. If one venture failed, a man could be ruined. Nationalized banks and sympathetic governments came much later. Those were not the times for the faint-hearted."

Because of the strong antagonism from the entire jute industry whose long arms reached far across the oceans to influence jute machinery makers in Britain, the costs of GD's project went up considerably. Generally a practical man, GD made an offer of sale to Andrew Yule, one of the largest British managing agency houses in India. But when he walked into the Andrew Yule offices to conclude the deal, a Scottish manager started criticizing him for having had the audacity to establish a jute mill. Stung, GD instantly withdrew his offer and made a resolution that come what may, he would break the foreign monopoly of the jute industry.

That GD succeeded is history. In 1923 the tables turned. The post-war depression forced Andrew Yule to sell a cotton mill, Kesoram Cotton, to the Birlas. In the same year, they set up a second managing agency, Cotton Agents Ltd. Though merely a trading concern at first, it soon acquired an industrial character. It took over C & E Morton, a confectionery company in 1928 and when sugar came under a protective tariff, the Birlas promoted, along with several other Indian business groups, a number of sugar mills. (Between 1931-33, they set up Bharat Sugar, New Swadeshi Sugar, Upper Ganges Sugar and New India Sugar.) During the 1920s they had also gone into publishing and, in a smaller way, soap and chemicals. All these investments paid rich dividends—especially sugar. They were also able to set up their first insurance company in 1933 and a paper company, Orient Paper, in 1936.

World War II provided the next stimulus for growth. At the beginning of the war, reputedly the Birlas were worth Rs 4 crore ($3.3 million). By the end of it, they had increased their assets to Rs 25 crore ($20 million). Progress after independence was even faster. Out of the approximately 175 companies run by the Birlas today, probably only 20 pre-date 1947. To some extent, the growth was helped forward by GD's political activities. Though the Birlas have never been accused of exploiting their relationships with national leaders for economic gain, there is no doubt that GD's close relationship with Gandhi, Sardar Patel, Nehru and others gave him a clear idea of the type of policies an independent India was likely to follow. Besides, the late 1940s and 50s were years of frenetic growth for the entire country, including business houses. The Monopolies Restrictive Trade Practices Act, licensing, and the industrial policy resolution were yet to come, and anyone who cared to, and had the resources, could build and grow. Those who had established themselves earlier, as the Birlas had, naturally got a head start.

After jute, cotton and sugar, the Birlas expanded into the manufacture of a well diversified range of products: textile machinery, automobiles, bicycles, ball-bearings, fans, non-ferrous metals, rayon, plastics, plywood, and vegetable

Birla Jute plant

oil. As they went into newspapers and aviation, acquired tea and coal companies and set up a bank, it seemed that no field of economic activity was left untouched.

While much of this expansion involved setting up of new ventures, a good proportion was realized through acquisition. The Birlas became expert corporate raiders before the term had even been coined. They took control of Century Spinning and Weaving Mill in Bombay, Sirpur Paper, Sirsilk and Hyderabad Asbestos in Hyderabad, Bally Jute, Rameshwara Jute, Soorah Jute and Air Conditioning Corporation in the Eastern region, and Shree Digvijaya Cotton in Suarashtra. It seemed as if no part of India was going to be left untouched. In such a list of successes, there are bound to be a few failures, and in this period it was the Birlas' attempt to acquire substantial equity in Ashok Leyland which was not realized.

Century Spinning facilities

It was also during this period that GD's greatest ambition was firmly frustrated. He had dreamed of emulating the Tatas by setting up his own integrated steel plant. In 1954 he registered a company named Durgapur Iron & Steel with an authorized capital of Rs 50 crore ($42 million). But the government's decision to retain all new steel plants in the public sector cut short the life of the new company. In 1958 the Birlas liquidated it. They did not appreciate it at the time, but they had had a narrow escape–steel has not been doing well for decades now.

To cope with the increased activity, many of the original investment and trading companies were reorganized. Several companies were amalgamated, many liquidated, and a phenomenally large number of new ones established– by 1958 the Birlas had 151 such investment and trading companies in operation.

Their expansion and diversification during this decade took several new directions. They took the first faltering steps into the international arena with the opening of a cotton mill in Ethiopia. Within India, the large mills were diversified: Century and Kesoram took up the manufacture of rayon, Birla Jute went into rayon, cement and chemicals, and Jiyajeerao Cotton also into chemicals.

G.D. Birla, Gandhi and the National Movement

The Birlas played an integral, if not clearly defined, role in the freedom movement. As the movement for national independence from the British gained momentum, GD's participation increased accordingly and gained crucial importance. Though he operated in the background, his intimacy with and deep knowledge of Gandhi's thought processes, combined with an ability to relate to British leaders, cast GD in the role of ambassador-at-large for India, mediating between Gandhi, the Congress Party and the British.

In a letter to Sir Samuel Moore (Lord Templeton), Secretary of State for India, dated March 14, 1932, GD described his own role as he saw it:

> *Evidently you are of a trustful nature and this increases my responsibility. I should, therefore, like you to know me as I really am. I need hardly say that I am a great admirer of Gandhi-ji. In fact, if I may say so, I am one of his pet children. I have liberally financed his khadder-producing and untouchability activities. I have never taken part in the civil disobedience movement. But I have been a very severe critic of the Government and so have never been popular with them.*

GD Birla boarding ship with M.K. Gandhi for London

GD's relationship with Gandhi lasted 32 years. As the Birla empire had grown, the extent of the Birla brothers' generous donations to the freedom movement reached seemingly limitless proportions. Naturally some detractors claimed that the donations were made in complete self-interest–with independence the Birlas could demand repayment in kind. Be that as it may, national movements are not won by courage alone and Gandhi used Birla as he wished. It was in the garden of Birla's house in Delhi that Gandhi was assassinated. GD had met Gandhi in Calcutta soon after the latter's arrival from South Africa in 1916. GD's nationalism had already been stirred. In the introduction of his book, *In the Shadow of the Mahatma*, GD analyzed the genesis of his patriotism:

> *When I was sixteen, I started an independent business of my own as a broker, and thus began my contact with Englishmen, who were my patrons and clients. During my association with them I began to see their superiority in business methods, their organising capacity and their many other virtues. But their racial arrogance could not be concealed. I was not allowed to use the lift to go up to their offices, nor their benches while waiting to see them. I smarted under these insults and this created within me a political interest which, from 1912 until today, I have fully maintained.[2]*

Impetuously GD threw himself into the nascent freedom movement which, in the 1910s, was going through a terrorist phase. Naturally he got into serious trouble and had to go underground for three months. He had no real taste for terrorism, however, and whatever traces remained were eradicated after he met Gandhi. This meeting was to radically change GD. Furthermore, the Birla family[3], which until now had never exhibited the slightest interest in politics, was now drawn willy-nilly onto centerstage.

The Birlas' involvement in the freedom movement was basically on three levels. GD, along with Purushottamdas Thakurdas, was the guiding force behind the creation of the Federation of Indian Chambers of Commerce (FICCI), a business association which soon emerged as the apex body for discussions between government and Indian big business. GD was an acknowledged and strident spokesman of the latter class and fought hard for the interests of nascent Indian capitalism. For him freedom from colonialism could only be possible if linked to economic independence, and he had a deep, almost religious commitment to industrial growth.

In 1920-21 he came out for fiscal autonomy which meant granting full protection for Indian industry. He adopted a strong stand on dithering British government currency policies regarding the value of the rupee. Along with several other businessmen he proposed a plan for the rapid industrialization of India. Under his constant prodding, Indian industrialists, wary of offending the British in power, were encouraged to come out openly in support of Gandhi or at least to secretly finance his cause.

On the second level was the Birla financing of the freedom movement itself. All the Birla brothers gave generously whenever they were called upon to do so, but GD's contributions outstripped all others.

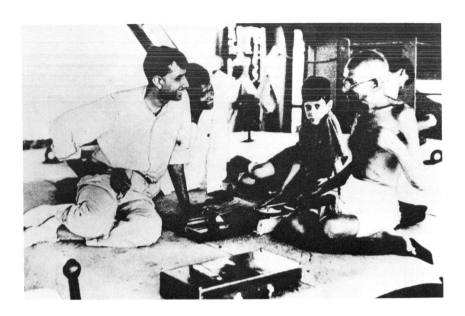

GD Birla with M.K. Gandhi at Wardha

"My thirst for money is simply unquenchable," wrote Gandhi to GD. He added that he did not want GD's contributions to the movement to become a source of friction among the brothers. GD replied that he could refuse him (Gandhi) nothing. The Birla support to Congress was viewed with great suspicion by the British. Lord Linlithgow (Viceroy of India from 1935-1943) in a "most secret and personal" communication to all Provincial Governors on November 2, 1942, wrote:

> I am anxious that every possible step should be taken to trace and bring home to those concerned the part played by 'Big Business' in the recent disturbances. It has always been known that Congress has depended for financial assistance on a number of wealthy capitalists and the D.I.B. has recently asked Central Intelligence officers to probe into the matter . . . may well have been fostered by the Birla Brothers with a view of their ulterior objects.

On the third level was GD's direct and active participation in Indian politics. After the end of his brief career in terrorist activities, in 1926 he became a member of the Central Legislative Assembly from the Benaras-Gorakhpur constituency on a ticket from the "Responsivist" Party led by Madan Mohan Malaviya and Lala Lajpat Rai. This too was a brief episode. Gandhi did not favor GD's standing for election. And Lajpat Rai wrote to GD:

> You must pardon me for saying that as a political leader . . . you would require a different kind of equipment, both mental and that of manners, from one which went to make you a successful businessman.

Increasingly GD became a mediator, "having to defend Englishmen before Bapu* and Bapu before Englishmen," as he himself put it. He now undertook visit after visit to England on his own to keep those in authority there well informed about the way in which Gandhi's mind ticked. He never claimed to act as an appointed agent on behalf of Gandhi and yet, having studied and understood his philosophy and his program, he took it upon himself to convey its implications to those who counted. GD often disagreed with Gandhi's policies, but as Rajendra Prasad (who was later to become President of India) described GD: "like a good soldier he obeyed the command of the master." GD did have some influence on Gandhi, however. As early as 1924, Gandhi wrote to GD that "God had given me mentors, and I regard you as one of them." Though not a decisive influence, GD's understanding of political events, both in India and England, were much appreciated by practically all Congress leaders. GD contributed in a small but crucial way toward the graceful manner in which the British and Indians ended an era of colonialism and imperialism.

Birlas and Politics after Independence

With Gandhi's death, the Birlas' direct participation in politics came to an end. Relations between the government and the Birlas became increasingly tense. The deterioration was partly due to Nehru's socialist inclinations and open castigation of business. For some time G.D. Birla adopted an uncritical attitude. "Because of their government's inexperience perhaps, they put forward policies which may not be quite helpful. But do not forget their objective and our [businessmen] objective . . . is to build up the country and if we build up the country, then, of course, everyone prospers.[4]

Though Nehru's early socialist aggressiveness later mellowed to some extent, G.D. Birla was one of the first to openly accept that businessmen in India would have to learn to live in a new environment, one in which the government would interfere and regulate to lengths which the British had not. As early as 1944, GD had advocated the need for planning. Along with Sir Purushottamdas Thakurdas, J.R.D. Tata, A.D. Shroff, Sir Ardeshir Dalal, Shri Ram, Kasturbhai Lalbhai and John Matthai, G.D. Birla had drawn up a blueprint, later known as the Bombay Plan, for the rapid economic growth of the country. The Plan called for the establishment of centralized planning, the imposition of rigorous controls, the development of heavy industry, and the introduction of radical agricultural reforms.

Thus both GD and his brother, B.M., stressed at the 27th annual meeting of FICCI in 1954 that "a businessman is not a businessman unless he can adjust himself to changing conditions" and that there was plenty of scope for them in the private sector.[5]

Later events disillusioned even GD. The constant threat of nationaliza-

---

* MK Gandhi was called "Bapu" or "father" by people close to him.

tion, the actual nationalization of some industries like coal mining and banking, the open contempt and disrespect of businessmen by vote-hungry politicians and the entry into the Congress Party of morally low-caliber politicians, did much to alienate and disgust him. Even so, GD continued to provide strong support to the Congress Party. He saw it as a bulwark against communism and was convinced that it was the only party capable of providing political stability. His unstinting support of what some believed to be an ethically decadent party often brought opprobrium on GD. Even members of his own family remonstrated him. But the failure of the Indian people to develop an effective and constructive alternative vindicated GD Birla's stand and highlighted his correct assessment of the realities of Indian politics.

In spite of their active and open support of the Congress Party, the Birlas have faced criticism and hostility from its members time and again. As one commentator put it:

Even as early as 1932, the then alien government instituted a politically motivated enquiry against the Birlas. The fault was that they befriended Mahatma Gandhi. This kind of enquiry continued off and on and developed into a habit which was inherited by the National Government after Independence. In almost every session of Parliament, the business activities of Birlas are raised in the Question Hour or during the No Confidence Motion moved by the Opposition against Government (whichever party is in power). From all counts, the Birlas have come out unscathed. [6]

The late 1960s were particularly bad. Immediately after the 1967

Birla Building, Calcutta

elections, business came under severe attack by the left wing opposition and a group of Young Turks within the Congress party. They wanted strong measures to curb the growing economic power of the top business houses through monopoly legislation and the nationalization of private sector banks to deprive them of control over credit for expansion (something which some say has not ended with nationalization). Singling out the Birlas as particularly guilty of corrupt practices, they demanded a complete government investigation of the activities of "Birla House."

Earlier the Monopolies Inquiry Commission had been set up to collect information on the activities of some 72 "large" business houses. This was followed by the Industrial Licensing Policy Inquiry Committee which came down heavily on the Birlas, accusing them of using the licensing system to corner licenses not only to grow at a disproportionate speed, but also to block the growth of other houses. Later the Sarkar Commission was appointed to inquire into the group's affairs. The commission was to give its report in a year, but dogged by law suits and non-cooperation, it dragged itself out for nine years before the government finally abolished it—without any report being submitted.

Intergroup Relations

The Birlas stress that there is no such thing as a Birla Group, that Birla companies are separate entities, each one managed as an independent company under a separate board, but each under the charge of a Birla family member. As GD's eldest son, Lakshminiwas Birla, explains:

> We are not a group in the sense that the public normally sees us. Each member of the family has his own companies in whose functioning the others do not interfere. There is no one in central authority, and at the end my father had direct responsibility of only a few companies that were especially dear to him. We have been running our own companies, and went to my father only when we felt the need for his advice.[7]

Keeping in mind that in 1983 the number of Birla companies were estimated at 175 with aggregate assets of Rs 2,840 crore ($2.4 billion), it is interesting to see how they control and manage their companies. Until its abolition in 1970, they had relied on the managing agency system. After-wards, most of the companies passed on to board management. Control was retained by the majority voting powers exercised by the sum total of the separate investments made by several companies of the group, none of them holding the controlling power as such. In a way the abolition of the managing agency system has helped the group to counter the charge of concentration of management powers by conveniently removing the only visible legal mark of inter-connection among many companies.[8]

In actual practice the companies in the group are managed by members of the family, each of whom controls what is a large group of companies in itself. Within each group again are sub-groups, each looked after by trusted

Birla family tree (six generations)

Birla family tree

subordinates, sometimes designated as presidents, but who are not necessarily members of the concerned boards. Thus an informal but direct chain of control and command runs from the top family group through trusted subordinates or relatives. The company boards are usually dummy bodies exercising only the shadow rather than the substance of control. There were, until recently, common departments for sub-groups of companies, a holdover from the managing agency days. There is also always a pooling of financial resources and management experience gathered in different companies. Finally, in recent years there is an unmistakable trend towards re-arrangement of companies among family members, partitioning the house into six groups of companies each under the control of a member of the extended family, but connected with other groups through no other nexus.

Technically the Birla Brothers split up in 1937. It was a private and relatively unpublicized event. As the freedom movement claimed more and more of GD's attention and dug more deeply into his wallet, unease set in among his brothers. Worried about the growth of their fledgling empire, they began to quarrel with GD. Gandhi, aware of the increasing tension in the family, begged GD not to send him so much money if it were at the expense of his brothers' affections. Realizing that a separation of assets would be in everyone's best interest, Birla Brothers quietly allocated the various companies among themselves. The whole operation was conducted in such a cordial atmosphere that even today no one knows which brothers managed which company. There were, however, three broad groups: that of GD, Rameshwardas in Bombay and Jugalkishore and B.M. working together in

Calcutta. All three branches continued to do very well, especially during the war years. But though they often helped each other out, rewards for growth went according to the original terms of the split. With the take-off during the 40s and 50s and as the second generation of Birlas entered management, business disparities emerged. Gradually GD's branch of the family became the strongest financially. The happy outcome of the 1937 split prompted GD to farm out his own companies among his three sons, Lakshminiwas, Krishna Kumar and Basant Kumar.

This has helped somewhat to eliminate internecine competitiveness though some competition is regarded as healthy. As G.D. Birla himself once put it: "Young people find it more difficult to work in harmony than those of my generation do and it is better for family relationships as well as the country that family members should compete rather than harbour resentments beneath a facade of cordiality."[9] There is no hard and fast rule about who should do what, but the family is generally careful not to tread on each other's toes, for the Birlas are still a joint family, at least in spirit.

But many Birla companies have often been engaged in fiercely competitive battles in the marketplace. Sudarshan Birla, LN's son, says his company, Universal Electrics, had once beaten a rival family firm, Electronic Construction and Equipment Company (in the BK-Aditya Birla group), in winning an order for electric motors after quoting at a price that left no room for profits. Sudarshan claims that this mutual competition is the basis of the Birla strength since each company has to stand on its own feet.

When GD died in 1983, there was widespread general interest in whether the Birla group would fragment into several smaller units. But the vacuum created by the founder's death was quickly filled. Within a fortnight of GD's death the family presented an image of rocklike stability to the world. In life, so in death, GD had painstakingly planned the transition by bringing the second generation into the forefront over the years. Potential zones of conflict had been scouted out in advance and defused by a shuffling around of the control of certain companies. Just a few weeks before he died, for · instance, Jiyajeerao Cotton Mills which had sales in 1982 of nearly $84 million was given to Sudarshan Birla to manage, partially evening what appeared to be a grossly unequal financial concentration in one group or the other. Such steps helped minimize possible wars of inheritance.

Despite this, it does not appear that all elements of hostility among family members have eased. Before the transfer of management of Jiyajeerao Cotton, Sudarshan had changed his status to that of a non-resident Indian by moving to Singapore and concentrating on expansion in southeast Asia. He no doubt felt that his room in Birla House was a little too small. Though Sudarshan is involved in the promotion of at least one new company in India, XPRO India, and manages several others, feelings of having been given the short end of the stick most likely persist. Aditya Birla somewhat reluctantly affirms that there is little cooperation between his most favored group and that of Sudarshan.

The Birla clan (ca. 1982)

Aside from the strong family tradition of appearing united to the world, the group is held together by more tangible forces. The intricate structure of cross-holdings of shares that bind various companies in the group is woven so finely that despite its best efforts even government commissions have never been able to pierce the veil that GD Birla and his brothers placed between the group's inner workings and the world. All that is known is that they control their fortress largely through companies such as Pilani Investments, Jiyajeerao Cotton and some investment companies, aside from a host of trusts. A longtime associate of GD, Durga Prasad Mandelia, says one reason for the crossholding structure is the fact that companies floating new ventures often had to turn to sister companies to raise the necessary finances. Thus, Century Spinning ($200 million), run by BK Birla, holds substantial shares in many other of the groups's companies, including Zuari Agro Chemicals ($97 million) managed by KK Birla. And Gwalior Rayon ($310 million) which is managed by Aditya Birla holds substantial shares in Mysore Cements ($33 million) run by Sudarshan Birla.

A Unique Management Culture

To keep the cogs of their ever-growing empire spinning in perpetual profitable motion, the Birlas evolved a unique management culture capable of adjusting to new situations and circumstances. Several business groups have tried to emulate this culture, developing similar systems with slight twists, but none has been as successful as the Birlas to any great extent.

The centerpiece of this culture is the "referral system", a method of recruiting management talent based on family background and shared cultural values. Thus, a Marwari, especially one hailing from within a small radius around Pilani, stands a better chance of obtaining a post in a Birla-run company than a non-Marwari. And the children of Birla executives have an automatic option to join the group. The casual onlooker is shocked at the extent of apparent nepotism prevalent in the group. Though influential references guarantee admission to the group, promotions are strictly on merit.

Once inside the fortress, the new recruit undergoes a rigorous practical training. Only those who measure up to certain seemingly inflexible standards will climb the ladder. The criteria are straightforward: results, loyalty, complete financial integrity and acceptance of the principle of accountability. Commenting on the system, Aditya Birla, GD's grandson, denies that there is a bias toward recruiting top management only from the Marwari community. "It is true, however, that the largest number is of Marwaris. It is natural . . . there is an affinity and I will never feel embarrassed or compromised if there are more Marwaris . . . Is there any group which does not have more people of its own community percentage-wise?"[10]

But Aditya admits that in recent years there have been certain changes in recruitment procedures. Whereas at one time they depended entirely on the "referral system" for management manpower, with a $2.5 billion expansion planned for the next few years, the Birlas have turned to advertising: "We now advertise very heavily–very heavily in fact. It is surprising the kind of budget we have for this purpose. We are expanding so fast that we cannot build up people to keep pace with our expansion."

Moreover, in common with other groups, it is the well-qualified young manager who is getting the plum post rather than the loyalist who has been with the group for several years. In some ways this is merely an extension of an old principle. Even with the older generation of Birla managers, one finds that all the top non-Marwari managers hold impressive technical qualifications. Today, through the exigencies of growth, this phenomenon is merely being applied at more levels.

There are other reasons for the declining importance of the "referral system." Marwaris seem less and less inclined to join the Birlas just because their fathers are Birla executives. They would rather set up their own businesses from the start and, since the Birlas are good paymasters, invariably the fathers have accumulated enough capital to help their sons into business. As one senior executive in Century Mills points out:

> *Working with the Birlas, one gets extensive experience which one can use to help set up one's children. Working in such a tough environment, I know the available opportunities. Besides, over the years, influential trade contacts are made which can be utilized very profitably. Further, my presence can get him into the organization, but he has to work his way up. He cannot automatically get my seat. And when they know that they can make better money in trade, they don't want to get rich the hard way.*

At top management levels there are also surprisingly few inhibitions regarding age. If a youngster proves the values of his ideas, his age is no bar to senior positions. Further, once a person's efficiency and loyalty are accepted, he is a member of the family. No one is allowed to retire. One senior executive said that every time he asked to be allowed to retire, he was told that they could hardly do a thing like that to him as it would be construed by outsiders as his having been caught in some financial irregularity. This approach also keeps the executive's valuable experience within the family. Senior Birla employees retire only on two counts–either they were charged with misappropriation or for following a "loose" life style.

Even upon reaching the top Birla executives continue to be motivated. GD Birla was convinced that certain inducements had to be continually offered to employees to ensure good performance. They were thus given a choice of money or fame–or a combination of both. Those opting for fame take a high profile in society circles. Those attracted more to wealth are given it in good measure. This is not all. The families of the senior executives are well-cared for. Very often, as hinted earlier, the Birlas have provided executives' progeny with the wherewithal to start their own businesses, frequently to meet a supply need of the Birla group itself. Employees themselves also become industrialists in their own right through the munificence of the Birlas. In fact, some former Birla executives head what can only be seen as satellite empires–the Saboos, Mandelias, Khaitans, Murarkas, Hadas and Kejriwals own large industrial enterprises of their own aside from their association with Birla concerns.

A Monopolistic Edge

Despite their strong management structure, it is frequently said of the Birlas that their success is largely due to the monopolistic position held by several of their key companies. Certainly it does not hurt their position. It is also said that they have usually avoided entering high risk or innovative fields. The emphasis has been on low risk, intermediate industries such as aluminium, paper, cement, capital machinery and fertilizers. They have not entered basic industries (reserved for the government sector for the most part, in any event), nor have they ventured onto the lists of the highly competitive light consumer goods market.

Aditya Birla reacted strongly to the criticism that the Birlas cannot market branded consumer goods:

> *I am in Gwalior Rayon suiting and Riviera suiting. The total sales of the two fabrics combined is about Rs 90 crore ($75 million) and growing by about 10 to 15 percent every year. Now this is completely consumer-oriented and I am selling a branded good. Rs 90 crore is not a small thing. We have enough exposure to direct marketing and, fortunately, we are doing extremely well. So we do have a certain amount of expertise and success in this field. It is not as if we are completely separated from the consumer goods markets.*

Hindustan Aluminium Company (Hindalco), Uttar Pradesh

While it is debatable that textiles in India can be called a branded product, the most important branded product manufactured by the Birlas, passenger cars, has a very poor reputation in the marketplace. Premier Auto's "Padmini" model (a Walchand group company) still has a waiting list while the Birla's "Ambassador," based on four decade-old British technology, is available for the asking—all this in a country where until recently there were only two options. This has been the situation since Indian independence. The Birlas have earned the dubious distinction of celebrating the single jubilee of a model.

But where the consumer might lose out, the shareholders win. Birla companies are among the most profitable in the country. While the Tatas have larger sales figures, the Birlas have the edge in terms of assets, profits and liquidity. A 1985 study by *Business Standard* of the average rate of equity dividend of the top 100 companies found no fewer than ten Birla companies among those listed as "the best paymasters," compared to only five Tata companies:

The Best Paymasters

Birla Companies		Tata Companies	
Rank	Name	Rank	Name
14	Century Enka	9	Tata Tea
45	Jayshree Tea	32	Indian Hotels
59	Kesoram	56	Tata Chemicals
66	Gwalior Rayon	63	Telco
67	Hindustan Motors	74	Tomco
68	Zuari Agro		
75	Orient Paper		
76	Indian Rayon		
87	Hyderabad Asbestos		
92	Texmaco		

Business Standard, January 15, 1985

This strong financial position can partly be explained by the tight management control exerted over the companies. But the Birlas move fast to shed units which do not make the grade profitwise. Equally important again, however, is the fact that in several fields the Birlas hold a monopoly. But as one Birla executive points out:

Great credit goes to the Birlas for identifying areas where the competition is either not there or shall not be there. I see nothing wrong in it. It is their sheer ingenuity that they thought of products or lines where the competition in the present or future or for some years to come would not be there or would be less.

But one man's genius may be mixed with a good grip on the industrial licensing system. One government report in 1967 undertaken by noted scholar R. K. Hazari indicted the Birlas especially for misusing the industrial licensing system to ensure that competition "shall not be there." Giving due credit to the Birlas for their determined push toward big growth and their willingness to sink huge amounts into industrial ventures, Hazari also noted some of the tactics used by the Birlas to become the foremost business group in the country. Large houses, among them the Birlas, would make multiple applications for a license to produce the same product under the names of various firms controlled by the group. One company would use one license at the stated capacity and the others, in the pockets of other companies in the group, would stall competition by not utilizing the licensed capacity. Frequently the companies applying for the license would not even have the resources for setting up the project. Hazari concluded:

> It is to some extent legitimate to infer that Birla enterprise, justifiable or not in terms of ultimate performance, does tend to pre-empt licensable capacity in many industries. . . Enterprise plus imaginative understanding of licensing formalities thus enables the Birlas to foreclose the market. Astute management turns this process into high and quick returns on investment, which earns foreclosure of economic resources generally, and helps magnify the halo round the House of Birla.

Growth After the 1960s

While the exhaustive investigations into the reasons for the growth of the Birla empire have never stopped the group in its tracks, the rapid growth the group enjoyed in the 1950s and 60s along with most Indian industry slowed in the 1970s, a generally bleak period for industrial growth. But the group began to expand once again in the 1980s when a lifting of controls ushered in a new era of industrial growth.

Though the 1970s saw a tightening of controls on big business in India, in one sense it was a period in which the inherent dynamism of the Birla group had a chance to show its stuff. While political elements whipped up the masses over the danger of economic concentration, the Birlas never did stop growing. If one door closed, they looked for an opening elsewhere. One of the untapped avenues of investment remaining to them in the 1970s was cement where the required investment was necessarily large and beyond the reach of many other business houses. The Birlas invested heavily in this field, becoming the largest cement producer after Associated Cement. Moreover, to prove that certain criticisms of their risk averse nature were untrue, they went into cement at a time when it was not a very paying proposition. But today it is these same cement ventures of the Birlas which are funding a large part of their expansion plans. With the partial decontrol of cement prices in February 1982, cement factories started filling the coffers of their owners.

Some other projects did not work out so well. Among the casualties was a $100 million pig iron plant in Bihar in collaboration with Kaiser Aluminum of the USA.

Timing has always been on the Birlas' side. Their profits have come in good time to exploit the exciting potential of the 1980s. As the government reopens doors to business, the Birlas are quick to apply for licenses to manufacture items as diverse as oil rigs, plastic sheets, sponge iron and fluorine, tires for their new models of passenger cars, and more cement.

Though a large part of the capital to establish these ventures is coming from internal resources, naturally the Birlas need to go to the marketplace as well. To prepare for market acceptance of their issues, there has been a spate of asset revaluations in Birla companies in recent years. Kesoram, Birla Jute, Birla Cotton, Jiyajeerao Cotton, Gwalior, Jayshree Tea, Century Enka, Hindustan Motors, Universal Electric and Orient Paper are among some of the well-known Birla companies which have recently revalued their assets. With enhanced images and low debt to equity ratios, the Birlas have been able to raise impressive amounts from the investing public through debentures as well as fixed deposits.

Many Birla companies also have a tax planning department to rival that of Reliance Textile. Birla companies have always been profitable and the astute Mawari collector's instincts have hoarded cash away from the tax collector to the maximum extent possible. One method is to undertake fresh investment only through existing companies rather than through the promotion of new companies. This enables the companies to take sizable tax deductions and attracts other concessions as well. One source of funding which the group has avoided has been the government-owned financial institutions. Loans made by these institutions carry the infamous convertibility clause (wherein the institutions can convert loans to equity) and also means that the board of the recipient company will have to make room for the nominees of the institution. The Birlas have preferred to retain complete control of their operations. Other groups acted similarly. Those who did not found themselves severely shaken by the events which followed an offshore, non-resident raid on two blue-chip Indian companies in late 1983.

The Swarj Paul affair, as it is known, revolved around the question of the influence of the financial institutions in the management of public limited companies. Family business groups, in order to expand more rapidly, had availed themselves of loans from the financial institions. Swarj Paul invested $13 million in Escorts, a Nanda-promoted company, and in DCM, a Shriram-promoted firm. With the then government in his corner, so it seemed to many, and with the Nanda and Shriram families holding less than a majority of the shares in their companies, Swarj Paul was aiming for takeover of these companies. With the support of the financial institutions, he might have done it. But Hari Nanda, chairman of Escorts, a tractor and farm equipment manufacturer, fought back to keep Paul out of his company. The matter was still in the courts in mid-1985. But the sensation which the case created made those groups who had held a tight rein over the shares of their companies feel very smug indeed.

Birla Companies in the Top 250 Companies in Private Sector

Bharat Commerce
Bihar Alloy Steels
Birla Jute & Industries
Central India Machinery
Century Enka
Century Spg & Mfg Co.
Electric Construction & Equipment
Gwalior Rayon Silk Mfg (Wvg) Co.
Hindalco
Hindustan Motors
Hukumchand Jute
Hyderabad Asbestos
Indian Rayon Corp.
Indian Steamship Co.
Jayshree Tea & Industries
Jiyajeerao Cotton Mills
Kesoram Industries & Cotton Mills
Mangalam Cement
Mysore Cement
National Engineering Industries
Orient Paper & Industries
Ratnakar Shipping Co.
Sirpur Paper
Sirsilk
Sutlej Cotton Mills
Texmaco
Tungabhadra Industries
Universal Cables
Zenith Steel Pipes & Industries
Zuari Agro Chemicals

The Basant Kumar/Aditya Birla Group

Most of the $2.5 billion expansion planned for the Birla conglomerate as a whole is being undertaken by the BK/Aditya Birla branch of the family, the largest and most endowed of the six parts of the Birla corporate conglomerate. The BK/Aditya group is most likely the largest single

Four generations of Birlas: GD seated with great grandson, Kumarmangalam. *Standing:* Basant Kumar, GD's son (r) and Aditya, GD's grandson.

employer in the private sector with over 125,000 employees working in their tea gardens, textile, pulp, staple fiber, rayon, cotton spinning, chemicals, engineering, power generation, insulator, aluminium, cement and spun pipe factories.

Domestic expansion took place under the careful and all-encompassing eyes of GD. His grandson, Aditya, despite his heir-apparent status, needed to find his own proving ground early in his own career. Aditya chose to concentrate on international corporate development. The group's first foray into international had come in the 1950s with the establishment of a textile mill in Ethiopia. While this project did not prove successful, Aditya's efforts were more so. He went on to set up no fewer than ten companies between 1965 and 1981 in Indonesia, Malaysia, the Philippines and Thailand with current aggregate sales of over $100 million.

One of its major achievements in the international sphere was the supply of a 9,850 ton-per-year semi-dull viscose staple fiber plant to the Republic of Korea. The $7 million plant was erected, installed and commissioned by Birla engineers and went into production in record time. Apart from the considerable acclaim that the export of this plant won in India, the satisfaction of the Koreans and the testimony of the Japanese Synthetic Textile Inspection Institution that the plant's output was equal to that of the Japanese plants added prestige to the Birla's international corporate image. Obviously Aditya was not satisfied merely to inherit a large empire. He had the industrial pioneer's blood as well. He says that what he has accomplished internationally "is just the beginning. In the future, we believe, you will hear more–much more–about our group's operations internationally."

Profiles of Foreign Joint Ventures Promoted by Aditya Birla

Indonesia

P.T. Elegant Textile Industry	1975	Textile yarn
P.T. Indo-Bharat Rayon	1981	Viscose staple

Malaysia

Pan-Century Edible Oil Sdn Bhd.	1977	Palm oil

Philippines

Indo-Phil Textile Mills	1975	Textiles
Indo-Phil Oil Mills	1978	Coconut oil

Thailand

Indo-Thai Synthetics Co.	1969	Synthetic yarns and fibers
Century Textiles Co.	1974	Textile processing
Thai Rayon Co.	1976	Viscose staple fiber, sodium sulphate, sulphuric acid
Thai Carbon Black	1978	Carbon black
Thai Polyphosphate	1978	Sodium tripolyphosphate

Within India the plans are even more ambitious. Besides two small plants to manufacture fiber boards and aluminium fluoride, the group is planning to establish a truck and car tire plant at a cost of nearly $85 million in collaboration with the Italian tire giant, Pirelli. Kesoram Industries & Cotton Mills will sponsor the project to be set up in Orissa. The Birlas' plans for the tire plant are meeting with stiff opposition from those already established in the industry. Faced with a tire glut over the past two years, the Modis and Goenkas, the tire industry leaders, are none too anxious to see another tire giant enter the field. R.P. Goenka said in an interview: "We do not mind newcomers. We welcome them . . . but their investment will be very heavy. It would not be a prudent judgment on their part."

The Birlas will continue their heavy involvement in cement as well by adding to their existing seven units. Moreover, in 1984 the group acquired a chemical unit from Rallis India Ltd. which produces sulphuric acid, superphosphate, hydrosulphite of soda and sodium silico fluoride. Despite its running battle with the government over price controls, since inception of the project, Hindustan Aluminium Company (Hindalco), a joint venture with Kaiser Aluminum of the USA, the aluminium concern is planning a Rs 100 crore ($83.3 million) expansion and modernization program over the next three years.

Principal Companies in B.K.–Aditya Birla Group

Name	Products
*Bharat Commerce & Industries	Yarn, cloth
Bharat General & Textile Industries	Spinning cotton
*Century Enka	Nylon & polyester filament yarn
*Century Spg & Mfg	Cloth, yarn, cement, tire cord, chemicals, engineering, paper, shipping
Eastern Spg Mills	Spinning cotton
Electronic Constructions & Equipments	Electrical engineering products
*Gwalior Rayon Silk Mfg (Wvg)	Viscose staple fiber, rayon grade pulp, paper
*Hindustan Aluminium Co.	Aluminium ingots, rolled products
Hindustan Cold Storage	Cold storage
Hindustan Gas & Industries	Files
Hindustan Heavy Chemicals	Chemicals
*Indian Rayon Corp.	Viscose filament, rayon yarn, cloth, insulators, cement
Jay Shree Chemicals & Fertilizers	Chemicals
Jay Shree Insulators	Insulators
*Jayshree Tea & Industries	Tea, plywood, superphosphate
*Kesoram Industries & Cotton Mills	Cement, viscose filament, rayon yarn
S. Lall & Co.	Ferro-alloys
Mangalam Cement	Cement
Mangalam Timber Products	Fiber boards
Midnapur Cotton Mills	Spinning cotton
Rajashree Cement (division of Indian Rayon)	Cement
Renusagal Power Co.	Power generation
Suarashtra Chemicals	Chemicals
Tanfac (Tamilnadu Flourine & Allied Chemicals)	Aluminium flouride
Woodcraft Products	Plywood

*Over $50 million in sales

There is no doubt that Aditya and his father, Basant Kumar, have inherited the bulk of the Birla empire, as the above list is only an indication. The father and son team make an interesting example of harmonious relationships. This may be so because of their scrupulous avoidance of interference in each other's companies which, in part, facilitates rapid growth and healthy bottom lines.

Indian Rayon will invest Rs 22 crore ($18 million) in a ceramics (vitreous sanitaryware, glazed tiles and tableware) facility if objections from the small-scale sector can be overcome. Gwalior Rayon, Aditya's flagship company, and one of two viscose staple fiber manufacturers in the country (the other being South India Viscose which has been closed for the past three years), began to face stiff competition from imports in 1984 when the government reduced the import duties. Despite the pressure on its profit margins, however, the company is poised for a Rs 200 crore ($167 million) investment program to include a new cement unit (Rs 45 crore), a bamboo plantation project (Rs 25 crore), a sponge iron plant (Rs 100 crore) and modernization of existing plants (Rs 16 crore). At the same time, Aditya wants to revive Ashok Paper Mills which has an installed capacity of 40,500 tons.

The flagship of BK's concerns, Century Spinning, often referred to as the barometer of the Bombay Stock Exchange, and one of the oldest companies in the group, is also one of the most up-to-date because of its continual diversification and modernization. Century Spinning plans a Rs 1,000 crore ($833 million) diversification over the next few years. Since 1951 when Century Spinning consisted of a simple cotton mill, it has expanded into rayon, tire cord, chemicals, engineering, paper and pulp, cement and shipping. During the same period of 33 years, the value of a Century share has multiplied over 33 times. Equity capital has increased from Rs 1.09 crore to Rs 16 crore in 1983. Reserves have moved from Rs 2 crore to Rs 206 crore and gross profit from Rs 1 crore to Rs 32 crore. Century promoted the highly profitable Century Enka Ltd. as well as three cement plants. The new fields identified for expansion are fertilizers and high wet module fibers. Three projects are planned for the manufacture of urea and nitrophosphate, liquid ammonia and diammonium phosphate. Additional cement units and pulp and paper mills are on the planning board. Century's remarkable record of growth and successful diversification as some of its activities enter a sunset period has earned it a unique position in the corporate sector. Rayon kept the cotton textile unit going in the 1950s, caustic soda and engineering kept the company moving in the 1970s and cement fueled the massive expansion planned for the 1980s. If the government were to allow commercially unviable units to close down, Century Spinning would gallop forward even faster.

Gangaprasad/Chandrakant Birla Group

1984 was the year of revolution in the Indian automobile industry. After 40 years of domination by the Birla group's Hindustan Motors and Premier Auto Ltd., the first Indo-Japanese joint venture started production of the Maruti-Suzuki car. A host of other collaborations between Indian and Japanese companies to produce cars, light commercial vehicles and motor-scooters and motorcycles were signed up in 1983-84. The age of the Ambassador,

Hindustan Motors' one and only model, are over. But the company has no intention of lying down and playing dead. With the end of the Birla monopoly of the Indian auto industry came the relaxation of government controls of the industrial sectors which Hindustan Motors could now enter. What the government had taken away with one hand, it had returned five-fold with the other.

While the first Maruti-Suzuki cars were coming off the assembly line in 1984, Hindustan Motors tied up with Caterpillar to manufacture a full range of earth-moving equipment. It joined forces with Isuzu Motor of Japan to introduce a new jeep as well as to update its diesel and petrol engine technology for both passenger and commercial vehicles. Simultaneously, Hindustan Motors unveiled its first new passenger model since the advent of the Ambassador. Despite certain initial engine design problems, the Contessa, based on a 1978 Vauxhall VX 6 model car, has been fairly well received. While the government also gave Hindustan Motors the green light to expand its capacity in both passenger and commercial vehicle production, operation of two new assembly plants began at Kanjari in Gujarat and Dhar in Madya Pradesh. Gangaprasad and Chandrakant Birla cannot be too unhappy at the loss of the auto monopoly.

Hindustan Motors was the brainchild of that "entrepreneur extraordinary," Brij Mohan Birla. Though BM's early industrial career was typically based in sugar, paper and insurance, by the mid-1930s he had begun exploring the possibility of setting up an automobile plant in India. With the onset of World War II, no progress could be made. After the war, BM enthusiastically returned to the project, goaded perhaps by competition with the Walchand group which was setting up Premier Auto at the same time. In his autobiography, BM related:

> *Mr. V. T. Krishnamachari, Dewan of Baroda, persuaded me to put up an assembly plant at Okha in 1942, and he was prepared to subscribe substantially to the capital of the company and also give a subsidy for supporting the automobile industry there.*
> *That is how the Hindustan Motors was registered in Baroda State. Mahatma Gandhi was kept informed of all the developments. But due to the Quit India Movement and the War, the project got delayed. After Gandhiji was released from prison in 1944, he called GD and me to Poona and gave his wholehearted blessings to expedite the project.*

The small beginnings that were made in 1942 at Okha developed into a formidable enterprise in Uttarapara, a few miles north of Calcutta. Anticipating demand, BM constructed a large assembly plant which was completed in 1950. At first, HM merely assembled imported components, but as India embarked on a program of self-sufficiency with the ban in 1953 of assembly activites of foreign car companies, HM began to indigenize fairly successfully. It was soon apparent though that HM could not control the quality of components supplied by ancillary companies. Such a shortcoming was compensated for somewhat by the excellent service and spare parts network which the group established throughout the country. Even today, anyone wanting to drive into India's heartland is advised to do so only in an Ambassador as it is the only one for which a mechanic and spare parts will be available within a few hours of any spot in the country.

Just as Aditya Birla looked at overseas expansion to prove himself in business, BM's son, Gangaprasad, found his entrepreneurial testing ground overseas as well, this time in Africa. Gangaprasad was responsible for establishing three major ventures in Nigeria and one in Kenya. The first Nigerian venture did not begin production until 1966, and then only months before the Biafran war ripped Nigeria apart. The joint venture for the manufacture of light engineering products was set up with Birla Brothers Pvt. Ltd., River State Government of Nigeria and the Nigerian Industrial Development Bank as partners. Though its production facilities suffered heavy damage during the war and had to be rebuilt, the project's eventual success prompted the Nigerian government to ask Gangaprasad's help in putting into operation an idle, but new paper plant. So in 1968, with the expertise he had gained in Orient Paper, GP managed to get the plant working. By 1974, Nigerian Paper Mill Ltd. initiated a substantial expansion program.

Principal Companies in Gangaprasad-Chandrakant Birla Group

Name

Name	Product
Airconditioning Corp.	Airconditioners
Birla Bros. Pvt. Ltd.	Investment company
*Hindustan Motors	Automobiles
Hukumchand Jute Mills	Jute, caustic soda
*Hyderabad Asbestos Cement	Asbestos products and sheets
MRVVN-Orient Plantations	Bamboo plantation
National Engineering Products	Rubber goods, bearings
*Orient Paper & Industries	Pulp, paper & board, caustic soda, cement, engineering
Sirpur Paper Mills	Pulp, paper, board
Sirsilk	Textiles
Taylor Instruments Co. (India)	Precision instruments

Overseas:
Nigeria Asbestos Industries
Nigeria Engineering Works
Nigerian Paper Mill
Pan African Paper Mills (E.A.) (Kenya)

---

*Over $50 million in sales

Gangaprasad's success in Nigeria encouraged him to expand his overseas activities. Panafrican Paper Mills (E.A.) Ltd. was promoted in late 1969 in Kenya as a joint venture between Orient Paper & Industries, the International Finance Corporation (World Bank) and the Government of Kenya, to produce paper and pulp. This was followed by a joint venture between Hyderabad Asbestos Cements Products Ltd. and the Government of Nigeria in 1978 to manufacture asbestos and cement products.

Gangaprasad's son, Chandrakant, for all his youth and lively interest in business, is inclined to take a low profile in public life. He prefers not to give interviews and has declined invitations to take an active part in the deliberations of chamber of commerce affairs. Chandrakant's attention is on the group's own expansion plans which include a new plantation to raise bamboo and wood required for the paper operations (MRVNN-Orient Plantations Ltd.), turnkey sale of its asbestos technology and a new cement unit. The Gangaprasad/Chandrakant Birla companies have always paid good dividends and continue to be popular on the Indian stock exchanges.

Standing: Basant Kumar (l), Gangaprasad.
Seated: Jugalkishore with Chandrakant as child

Ashok Vardan Birla Group

For all their conservatism which has survived in tact through the present day, the Birlas were once radical reformers. Their split with the orthodox Maheshwari caste (a sub-caste of the Marwaris) over Rameshwardas' remarriage to an "out of caste" lady very quickly engendered a larger debate over issues such as dowry, marriage and "westernization." Socially ostracized for several years, the Birlas ignored their pariah status and threw themselves wholeheartedly into reform movements. They fought for the abolition of purdah, education for women, the end of child marriages and reduction of wedding and funeral expenses. As they became more successful in business, however, opposition from the conservative wing of the community subsided. GD's experience as an outcast from his own community had greatly increased his sympathy for the depressed classes, however. He was all the more willing to support Gandhi's programs to uplift the lot of untouchables. Few industrialists at the time, apart from the Kirloskars, Bajajs and Sarabhais, showed anything more than antipathy to Gandhi's campaign.

But the bitter experience GD and his family suffered at the hands of the Maheshwari conservatives did not keep them from meting out an equally harsh punishment of ostracism to Gajanan when the latter fell in love with another woman. Gajanan Birla, Rameshwardas' son, was married with two children, Ashok and Asha, when he fell in love with Sumitra Grover and insisted on following her to Calcutta. His actions precipitated another split of the family's assets, the second, with Gajanan being given a few minor companies and some family property in Bombay. He was then cut off from the main branch of the family. Having displayed little interest in making money anyway, preferring to perfect his golf and tennis games, it was left to the next generation to try its hand at multiplying what few assets were left to the Gajanan group. Ashok Birla, Gajanan's son, has moved back toward the mainstream of the Birla family.

In 1977 when he inherited Zenith Steel Pipes & Industries in a swap with one of his uncles, it was producing only one product, steel tubes. Today it is the flagship of Ashok's group of companies with sales having increased from $31 million in 1977 to $86 million in 1983. Ashok set about diversifying Zenith's products immediately after taking over, going into paper and industrial chemicals. A half million-ton cement plant is set to come on stream under Zenith's flag in Andhra Pradesh in 1986.

The 1980s have seen a tremendous change in the Indian economy. Newly awakened ambitions for faster growth are pushing both entrepreneurs and government to explore fresh avenues for raising capital to fuel these ambitions. Despite the existence of stock and commodities markets in Bombay and Calcutta since the mid-1800s, it is only since 1980 that the stock markets have witnessed quantum leaps in the number of debenture and stock subscriptions being floated. Mutual funds and leasing also arrived on the financial scene in 1983/84.

Ashok Birla is taking part in this financial services' revolution by proposing to set up an offshore mutual fund facility in the Channel Islands in the form of a joint venture between his group and S.D. Warburg & Co. of the UK, one of the world's largest and oldest merchant banking organizations. The Birla-Mercury Fund is being established to attract resources from non-resident Indians (Indians living outside India). Such funds will then be channelled into profitable investments in India and elsewhere around the world. If finally approved by the Indian government, the Birla-Mercury Fund will mark a pioneering effort on the part of a private firm to tap international financial resources from an offshore, privately owned investment facility. With a growing resource gap threatening its ambitious growth plans, the Indian government may well permit such schemes to proliferate in order to increase its internal flows of portfolio-type investments—especially if it is Indian-controlled.

Ashok Birla

When Rajiv Gandhi assumed the prime ministership in late 1984, then won re-election quickly thereafter, his new broom started sweeping clean very quickly. An energetic group of younger politicians whose major preoccupation was the streamlining of a choked-up system replaced the old familiar faces of Delhi's backroom politics. Ashok Birla caught the headlines at the same time that news of the anti-red tape revolution was hitting the newstands. As president-elect of the Indian Merchants Chamber of Bombay, he was expected to assume the leadership role in early 1985. At the midnight hour, Birla withdrew his name from nomination and threw the 2000 member organization into the role of the headless horseman. He cited his displeasure over the undemocratic way in which the executive committee of the organization was handpicked by the old boys of the IMC. Birla wanted to modernize the IMC, he said, and felt he could do it better if the executive committee appointments were thrown open to a vote. His stance brought bouquets and brickbats. His opponents noted the grandstand-like nature of

---

Principal Companies in Ashok Birla's Group

Name	Products
Birla-Yamaha	Portable gensets
Dagger-Forst tools	High precision metal slitting saws
TransAsia Carpets	Man-made carpets
*Tungabhadra Industries	Vanaspati, refined and hardened oils
*Zenith Steel Pipes & Industries	Steel pipes, ingots, billets, sockets
Indian Tool Manufacturers**	Cutting tools
Oudh Sugar Mills	Sugar, alcohol, food processing

Overseas:

Edible Oil Products (Malaysia) BHD	Palm and other vegetable oils
Evertex Industries Inc. (Philippines)	Textiles
Imperial Industrial Chemicals Thailand Ltd.	Chemicals
Philagro Edible Oils (Philippines)	Solvent extraction
P.T. Daralon Textile Mfg. Corp. (Indonesia)	Textiles
P.T. Horizon Syntex (Indonesia)	Textiles
P.T. South Pacific Viscose Indonesia (in planning stage)	Plastics
Birla-Mercury Fund (in planning stage)	Mutual fund

Planning seven other ventures in Southeast Asia besides P.T. South Pacific Viscose.

---

*Over $50 million in sales
**Now merged with Zenith Steel Pipes

the last minute withdrawal while others welcomed his refreshing viewpoint. The controversy drew attention to the Ashok Birla group of companies as well, especially when Birla cited preoccupations with business expansion as an additional reason for declining the IMC presidency. With the favorable climate being created for business expansion by the Gandhi government, Ashok's excuse for bowing out made some sense.

For all the disadvantage which the 1946 split of assets may have caused the Gajanan Birla branch of the family, Ashok Birla has been busy rebuilding his group at home and abroad. In addition to Zenith Steel Tubes, a vanaspati manufacturing plant, Tungabhadra Industries, has a turnover of $60 million a year. A manmade carpet unit, TransAsia, was set up in 1979 and boasts one of the most beautiful advertising campaigns for carpets throughout the subcontinent. Assuming continuing power shortages in India, Birla set up a company in 1985 which will manufacture portable gensets. Assembly is already taking place and indigenization of all the components will be phased in over the next few years. Birla has. established seven overseas ventures in Southeast Asia for the most part and he plans at least seven more in the same region.

Ashok is well-versed on international monetary and political issues. He sees a need for countries like the USA to become more "introspective" and sensitive in its approach to other nations and he feels India should take a bolder approach to its development. He is a man who wants to follow his own star, "not be a sheep." Ashok is moving quickly to expand his operations on · a global scale. Because he did not grow up with the emotional buffers and financial clout of the GD Birla branch of the family, Ashok has been forced to think of himself as part of a larger, more egalitarian world. For this reason, if for no other, he is better prepared to meet the challenge of international competition which is fast arriving on India's doorstep.

Austere Behavior, A Comfortable Life Style

G.D. Birla often pondered the reasons for his attraction to Gandhi. He realized that "there was not much in common between us so far as our mode of life went. Gandhiji as a saintly person who had renounced all the comforts and luxuries of life . . . I, on the other hand, led a fairly comfortable life." But a 32 year-old relationship is bound to have an impact. Gandhi's austerity reinforced the Marwari's engrained thriftiness to create a lifestyle which GD not only followed himself, but which those in contact with him had to follow if they wanted the association to continue. His tenets were clear:

eat only vegetarian food, never drink alcoholic beverages or smoke, keep early hours, marry young, switch off lights when leaving the room, cultivate regular habits, go for a walk every day, keep in touch with the family, and above all, don't be extravagant.

These tenets, GD stressed, were to help you enjoy life. For example, the last

Principal Companies in K.K. Birla Group

Name	Products
*Central India Machinery Mfg.	Textile & cement plant machinery
Hindustan Times	Newspapers, publishing
India Steamship Co.	Shipping
Ratnakar Shipping	Shipping
Sutlej Cotton Mills	Synthetic & cotton yarns, cloth
*Texmaco	Wagons, textile machinery
Upper Ganges Sugar Mills	Sugar
*Zuari Agro Chemicals	Chemical fertilizers

Overseas:
HighSea Steamship Pvt. Ltd.	Shipping

* Over $50 million in sales

Principal Companies in M.P. Birla Group

Name	Products
Bihar Alloy Steels	Alloy, tool & special steels
*Birla Jute & Industries	Cement, jute
Indian Smelting	Steel
Universal Cables	Cables

* Over $50 million in sales

Principal Companies in L.N.–Sudarshan–Siddharta Birla Group

Name	Products
Shree Digvijay Woollen Mills	Textiles
India Plastics	Plastics
*Jiyajeerao Cotton Mills	Textiles, chemicals
Mysore Cement	Cement
Oriental Carpet Mfrs (India) Ltd.	Machine-made carpets
Universal Electric**	Electrical equipment
XPRO India	Plastic sheets and film

*Over $50 million in sales
**Merged with Shree Digvijay Woollen Mills in July 1983

tenet did not mean being miserly. He saw no harm in spending millions on temples or status symbols, but there should be some return.

GD's own strict adherence to these rules served him well. At the age of 89 he undertook the arduous pilgrimage to Kedarnar, the source of the sacred Hindu River Jumuna on a trek through the Himalayas. Few Indians have undertaken such a journey because of the rigors involved. GD insisted on walking the last 4,000 feet.

Departures from family tradition are significant only for their very innocuous nature: almost every Birla goes for an early morning constitutional, but Chandrakant is an enthusiastic rider while another Birla might enjoy a hard game of squash. Where Sudarshan prefers classical music, Sidharth, his son, prefers rock. There is, however, no lack of individual talents showing through various members of the group, despite their penchant for uniform behavior. L.N. Birla is a poet with fourteen books to his credit, including one on the folklore of Rajasthan. LN is also a horticulturist and one-time president of the Horticulture Society of India. B.K. Birla is an art collector and has a formidable collection which he has gifted to the Birla Academy of Art and Culture—a collection valued today at over nine million dollars. Quite a number in the clan have followed religious ways. Jugal Kishore devoted the latter half of his life almost exclusively to building temples and organizing charities. That interest is now shared by LN and GP who have also developed their strong interest in vocational training. A fervent Hindu, Gangaprasad has viewed with concern the conversion of Hindus to the Muslim religion to escape the chains of caste. He has promoted programs to help stem this growing phenomenon. GD himself took a great personal interest in developing the educational institutions created on the sands of Pilani.

Birla Haveli (Birla mansion), Pilani

Aerial view of Pilani with temples built by Birlas highlighted

The Birlas have built some of the most beautiful temples in India in recent years in addition to their special attention to building educational institutions in and around Pilani. Few have doubted their sensitivity to the general welfare of the country. But growth of a corporate empire such as theirs has caused some problems for society as well, especially in the environmental sphere. By no means alone, some Birla companies nevertheless have come under scrutiny for their lack of concern for the lethal after-effects of some of the industrial processes carried on in their plants. With a growing awareness on the part of the public for such issues, Indian industry has begun to install long overdue pollution-control devices in their plants.

In 1984, an executive of Zuari Agro Chemicals, located in Goa, issued a press statement stressing "that the company is aware of the need for preserving and protecting the environment. It shares public concern about the quality of the environment and ensures that its actions are in conformity with the policies and guidelines set by the government." Indeed, in August 1983, a government study carried out at Gwalior Rayon plants revealed that workers' exposure to various chemicals used in the plant were now well within established limits. As early as 1958, however, studies were made to assess the occupational health hazards of three Birla rayon plants. And in 1965, a labor group formed vigilance committees to publicize the effects of sulphur dioxide, sulphur trioxide and carbon disulphide on humans as well as on the environment. It is clear that citizens will continue to monitor closely the manner in which industrialists meet their environmental duties.

Zuari Agro Chemicals complex, Goa

The Contradictions Recede

It was once noted that GD Birla's pragmatism and morality often came into conflict, leaving unresolved contradictions. While throwing up factory after factory, schools and temples, environmental considerations were ignored, for example. Early on, the Birlas fought for women's rights, yet it is rare that a woman is seen in the ranks of the Birla companies. GD felt that if Indian capitalism were not allowed to flourish, a deadening hand of fascism would clutch the throat of his country in the form of communism. Yet true capitalism flourishes in a competitive atmosphere, and the Birlas' effective cornering of industrial licenses for decades helped keep the lid on true capitalism. GD detested his ostracism from the Maheshwari community, yet found little sympathy in his heart for Gajanan's need to follow his own destiny. Indeed some contradictions remained unresolved.

One thing is certain, however, GD accepted contradictions. He mixed his disciplines—politics, religion, business—if it would achieve freedom for India, bigger market shares for his clan or greater understanding and tolerance among peoples of different backgrounds. As a pioneer industrialist, naturally he was unafraid to act when the outcome was uncertain or to think big when politicians talked small. He was able to keep his family level-headed when their inheritance put them easily out of reach of their 750 million fellow Indians.

Out of the Rajasthan desert came a people with an iron flexibility. The Marwaris, a merchant class, were ever alert to opportunities to make a life out of sometimes unyielding environments. For centuries the men moved out of the desert, followed the trading routes, then returned. The Birlas never left Pilani though their empire now spreads around the world. GD died and his family quickly gathered in London, where cremation rites were performed. Then all returned to India with the ashes. In the end the word one hears most often in tandem with the name Birla is "Pilani."

Goenka

Automobile tires
Carbon black
Chemicals
Cigarettes
Cables
Pharmaceuticals
Rayon Yarn
Tea
Textiles
Power transmission towers

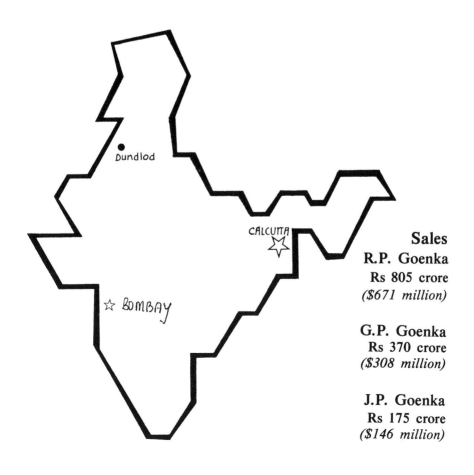

Dundlod

CALCUTTA

BOMBAY

Sales
R.P. Goenka
Rs 805 crore
($671 million)

G.P. Goenka
Rs 370 crore
($308 million)

J.P. Goenka
Rs 175 crore
($146 million)

Headquarters

R.P. Goenka:
Ceat Mahal
463, Dr. Annie Besant Road
Bombay, India 400 025

Dunlop House
Mirza Ghalib Street
Calcutta, India

G.P. Goenka:
Tobacco House
1 & 2, Old Courthouse Corner
Calcutta, India 700 001

J.P. Goenka:
Nirmal Building
241/242, Backbay Reclamation
Nariman Point
Bombay, India 400 021

Heads of Groups
R.P. Goenka
G.P. Goenka
J.P. Goenka

Sir Badridas Goenka (1883-1973) (l) and Keshav Prasad Goenka (1912-1983)

GOENKA

The British came to India to trade, tantallized by sensuous whiffs of eastern riches. Along with the French and Portuguese, they were keen to indulge their new tastes and earn fortunes in the process. The first English merchants to come to India were Fritz and Newberg in 1568. Though their efforts at trade were largely unsuccessful, by 1757[1] the economic penetration of the subcontinent was well under way, taking the form of tax levies, erection of factories and trading with domestic producers of the finest muslins, spices and crafted jewels.

In the early years, the British boasted few skills which could help them penetrate India's interior to enable them to buy directly from the skillful craftsmen in the tens of thousands of villages. Since British outposts were confined to the coast and to the larger cities for the most part, the Indians necessarily acted as middlemen. Calcutta soon emerged as a leading port as caravansarais of camels and horses, not to mention bullock carts, laden with all sorts of prized Indian manufactures, wound their way to this emerging metropolis.

With this development, several enterprising Indians hurried to Calcutta to offer themselves as brokers to the British firms. These men, called banians, on a commission basis, would arrange for the purchase of the desired products, the transport of the goods to Calcutta and storage there until the time of shipment to Europe. They were responsible not only for timely deliveries but for their quality and quantity as well. With the emergence of an import business, the activities of the banians increased. They became selling agents for British manufacturers. As trade between India and Britain expanded, so naturally did the scale of operations of these banian firms. Indian traders who perceived these trends early on were able to establish themselves quickly and earned substantial profits.

Among the earliest to establish such trading contacts with the British was Ramdutt Goenka[2] who left his home in Dundlod, Rajasthan to reach Calcutta around the turn of the nineteenth century. Along with his brothers and sons, Ramdutt managed to acquire several profitable brokerships with early British firms such as Kinsell and Ghose, Kettlewell and Bullen. He also linked up with the important Greek firm of Alexander Ralli which was the largest importer of cotton piecegoods and among the leading exporters of raw jute and hessians.

Having acquired these agencies, the operations of the earliest Goenka firm, Ramdutt Ramkissendas (so named after the founder and his son), expanded rapidly. By the turn of the twentieth century, the Goenkas were taking an active role in the jute and tea trades. It was the beginning of a rise which was to see two of the fourth generation Goenkas, Sir Hariram Goenka and Sir Badridas Goenka, knighted by the British. They also assumed positions in Calcutta's local government and later in the central legislature. They became prominent leaders of the Marwari community of Calcutta and hence held sway in business communities throughout India.

Sir Badridas Goenka

Sir Badridas Goenka in particular played an important role in public life and national politics. Born on July 29, 1883, Sir Badridas was the second son of Ramchandra Goenka. Though the Goenka family even today presents the image of a conservative, ultra-traditional Marwari family, Sir Badridas was the first Marwari to graduate from the university, Presidency College in Calcutta. Besides he was interested in physics and chemistry, a rare trait in an era when Marwari boys by the age of ten were sitting next to their elders in the family shop absorbing business techniques and strategies. After graduating from Presidency College in 1905, Badridas entered the family business.

Within a short period of time, Sir Badridas began to display his zest for public life. In 1910 he was elected secretary of the influential Marwari Association. (He became its president in 1928). Within a few years he came to dominate the association, along with Ramdev Chokhany, an influential Marwari banian like himself. Sir Badridas soon clashed with G. D. Birla, another leading Marwari which culminated in G.D.'s withdrawing from the association altogether in 1923.

The differences between the two men reflected the rifts in a society which had been tightly knit for centuries, but which was under pressure to change because of the industrial revolution taking place in India. The Marwari community, particularly in Calcutta, had become wealthy largely because of its symbiotic relationship with the British trading firms. Their whole business centered around foreign trade. Naturally the development of militant nationalism threatened them by its attack on the very source of their livelihood. There were, however, a few Marwaris who after World War I began to move away from trade and towards industry, thereby reducing their dependence on the British. The Birlas in Calcutta and the Singhanias in Kanpur were among the earliest to make this transition.

While social norms within the community were usually the bones of contention, in 1923 the rift took on a more intense political tone. In 1909 the British colonial government agreed to grant nominal powers of self-government to the Indians. Elections would be held on the principle of representation of special interests of minority communities. The Marwari Association eagerly took up this issue and began to lobby for separate Marwari representation. In 1923, under the Montagu-Chelmsford reforms, the Marwari community's request was accepted and a seat in the national legislature was reserved for them. Naturally this led to a struggle in the Marwari Association as to who would be their representative. G. D. Birla offered a nationalist candidate while the Goenka-Chokhany opposition favored a conservative one. The latter's success caused Birla to leave the association and in 1925 he set up a new organization. The Indian Chamber of Commerce of Calcutta was established for Marwari industrialists and eventually joined with other Indian commercial organizations to form the Federation of Indian Chambers of Commerce and Industry (FICCI).

Apart from his activities in the Marwari Association, Sir Badridas was on the boards of several government bodies such as the Bengal Council, the Calcutta Corporation and the Calcutta Improvement Trust. In 1930 he was invited to be a member of the Imperial Council which he declined because of a certain independent stance on his part, despite his close ties to the British. Such views did not prevent him from accepting several British honors: the title of Rai Bahadur in 1925, C.I.E. in 1928 and Knight Bachelor in 1934.

In the late 1920s, several banks collapsed all over India and the ensuing crisis compelled the government to set up the Indian Banking Inquiry Committee in 1928. As an eminent businessman of the time, Sir Badridas was invited to participate. A short while later, in 1930, he was elected a Director of the Imperial Bank of India and in 1933 he became the first Indian Chairman of this bank. In the same year a committee was formed of which Sir Badridas was a member. It was a committee set up to draft the constitution of the Reserve Bank of India. Sir Badridas later became its Founder Director. Re-appointed Chairman of the Imperial Bank in 1941, he continued in this position until 1955. With the formation of the State Bank of India, he was made its Founder President and held this post on and off from 1933 to 1957.

As the national freedom movement gathered momentum, the differences between the orthodox and reformist Marwaris narrowed. Moreover, Birla's Indian Chamber of Commerce was becoming an influential body while the Marwari Association was definitely on the decline. Sir Badridas now patched things up with Birla and joined the Indian Chamber of Commerce. By 1941, he had even become its president. The Marwaris drew closer together during the Bengal Famine of 1942. The Bengal Relief Committee produced remarkable results under Sir Badridas' leadership, all in spite of the then government's lack of cooperation. The high point of Sir Badridas' public career came a little later, however, when he was elected president of FICCI in 1945. But soon after his completion of the FICCI presidency, Sir Badridas retired from both business and voluntary associations.

Sir Badridas and son, KP

Despite his extremely active public life, Sir Badridas continued to keep a finger on the pulse of his business. Sometime during this period, the three Goenka brothers[3] managed to become banians to two important British managing agencies, Duncan Brothers and Octavius Steel, a development which was to have important consequences after independence. At this juncture, jute trading was the most important activity, though moneylending was an important and profitable sideline. Also during this period, the Goenkas went in for moneylending on the Western model by establishing the Hind Bank. Relations with Ralli and with Kettlewell and Bullen continued apace. Interestingly, the Goenkas did not follow the example of other enterprising Marwaris during this period by establishing themselves as industrialists. They were content to remain banians, growing along with the foreign firms with which they were connected.

The next impetus for growth came from the fifth generation of Goenkas represented by Isswari Prasad, Devi Prasad and Keshav Prasad. The successful streak of entrepreneurship which had manifested itself in Ramdutt Goenka in the 1830s continued along the line a century later. All three men showed considerable business ability, undiluted by birth into a privileged life style. They managed to steer their companies through the difficult pre- and post-independence era and in the 1950s embarked on a course of expansion and diversification at an escalating tempo.

The firms to which the Goenkas acted as banians were well-known. Duncan Brothers was an offshoot of a London-based firm, Walter Duncan and Goodricke Ltd. The Indian company in the 1950s had under its management several tea gardens and a jute mill, the Anglo Jute Mills Company Ltd. Octavius Steel also managed several tea gardens but was more diversified. It controlled a sugar mill (the Purnea Sugar Company), a colliery (the New Manbhoom Coal Company), and operated four electric supply companies.

Soon after independence, Octavius Steel decided to pull out of India and sold their interest to the Goenkas. Meanwhile the Goenkas had acquired a 25 percent interest in Duncan Brothers (with 70 percent being held by Walter Duncan and Goodricke) and they were eager to acquire full control of the company. As Keshav Prasad put it once, his only ambition was to own the company, serve as its chairman and bring it under total Indian operation. Fortune smiled on Keshav Prasad Goenka.

The 1950s were disastrous years for the tea business. International tea prices crashed and Duncan Brothers, with its large interests in quality teas, was badly hit. In 1951, Goenka lent funds to Duncan in return for a 25 percent equity interest and a place on the board. As the tea slump continued, the Goenkas kept on pumping money into the company. In 1957, KP was made the chairman and six years later, in 1963, he achieved his life's ambition: Duncan Brothers, with all its associate companies, was under total Goenka control. With the acquisition of Octavius Steel and Duncan Brothers, the Goenkas finally made the transition from banians to industrialists, albeit via acquisition rather than starting from scratch.

Duncan Building, Calcutta

The Rise of Keshav Prasad Goenka

The transition brought friction in its train. The group at this time was made up of five members of the family: Isswari Prasad, Jagmohan and Devi Prasad (Sir Hariram's three sons) and Keshav Prasad and Lukhi Prasad (Sir Badridas' two sons). The ambitions of KP and the rapid expansion of the Sir Badridas side of the family alarmed the Sir Hariram faction. They decided that a split was necessary before relations soured even further. Thus sometime between 1958 and 1960, the Goenka assets were divided, Octavius Steel going to Sir Hariram's branch and Duncan to KP and his brother.

On the face of it, KP's side got a bad deal. But luck was still with him. It was as if the split had released a spring. Between 1960 and 1962, KP promoted three companies in the automobile tire ancillary industry: Phillips Carbon Black (carbon black), Schrader-Scovill Duncan (tire valves), and National Standard Duncan (beadwires).

Even as construction work began on the plants, KP got full control of Duncan Brothers. A short period of consolidation followed. The thirteen odd tea companies managed by Duncan Brothers were merged to form a more cohesive unit, the Birpara Tea Company.[4] A losing unit of the Anglo India Jute Mill was separated from the main company. It was converted into Isaac Holden (India) Ltd. to manufacture wool tops and foreign technology was brought in to revive the unit.[5]

By 1966 KP was ready to expand further. He acquired a textile mill and an electric cable company, the Coorla Mills and Asian Cables, respectively, both in the same year. The location of both the companies in Bombay enabled KP to acquire a footing in the burgeoning commercial capital of independent India. Three more acquisitions followed in quick succession: minority interests in the Balmer Lawrie Group (1967 but sold in 1972), Jubilee Mills (1969) and Swan Mills (1971). Thus within a decade of separating from his cousins, KP had acquired substantial interests in tea, automobile tire ancillaries, jute, cotton textiles and electric cables.

The Goenkas entered the cable industry in 1966 when they bought the Asian Cables Corporation Ltd. Originally established in 1959 by a cotton trader, a Mr. Kotak, Asian Cables had not done well in spite of having access to some of the best technology in the field through its collaboration with Phelps Dodge of the USA and Enfield Cables in the UK. Consequently, at the insistence of the foreign collaborators, the Kotaks sold their interests in the company to a group that had more experience in running industrial ventures. Even after the takeover of Asian Cables by the Goenkas, the company did not do very well. But executives of the firm maintain that Asian Cables' performance was better than all of the other cable companies in India.

KP Goenka (r) with President Rajendra Prasad

Although KP pumped a lot of cash into the acquisition, the first three or four years were simply a fight for survival. The 1966 devaluation of the rupee hit Asian Cables hard. Foreign exchange liabilities on newly commissioned projects rose by 57.5 percent in terms of rupee repayments. Then a slump in the cable market ensued, lasting for three years. Orders for Asian Cables' products were scarcer than rain in Rajasthan in its early years as a Goenka company. To crush hope further, the government banned

Sir Badridas (top row, far left) with Queen Elizabeth and Prince Philip and Indian industrial delegation

the type of cables which Asian Cables manufactured. Not only was the plant obsolete with a stroke of the pen, but the company's rubber division was obsolete as well and it was closed.

Asian Cables was put under the charge of Madhukar Bakre, a Maharastrian who had joined the Goenkas in Calcutta in 1954. In April of 1966, Bakre moved back to his hometown of Bombay to reorganize the failing Asian Cables. Faced with problems of such immense magnitude, Bakre and his associates looked around for means of reviving the company. They organized seminars in the major cities to popularize their products and exhibit their quality while waiting for demand to pick up. To keep the equipment in use they manufactured polyethylene sheets and pipes. The only highspots in these lean years was Asian Cables' participation in its foreign collaborator's projects of establishing factories in Lebanon, Zambia and Venezuela.

From 1977 onward, things began to look up. Asian Cables put up a new plant to manufacture XLPE cables and in December 1978 it received a large order to supply this type of power cable to the new iron ore mines at Kudremukh, in Karnataka. The company was able to increase its dividend to 20 percent from an earlier low of eight percent.

Prospects for the cable industry are linked directly with the government's actions in the power sector over which it holds a monopoly. While the government permitted certain price increases for the industries supplying inputs to cable manufacturers, it did not permit the cable industry to pass along the increased costs by way of price increases for cables. Moreover, since demand for cables is governed by the government's ability to generate power, the industry is at the mercy of five year plans which are rarely met. Though the government promises in each plan to increase power generation, if performance were ever to match the plans' projections, the cable industry could attain nirvana. Facing reality, Asian Cables had to try to diversify into other lines such as tires, consumer products, communications and telecommunications.

Despite the setbacks with Asian Cables, the Goenkas were moving ahead on other acquisition fronts. Top management now included KP's three sons, Rama Prasad, Jagdish Prasad and Gouri Prasad. The three had expertly overseen the takeover of the B. N. Elias group in 1973, had promoted two more carbon black companies, Oriental Carbon and Gujerat Carbon in 1973 and 1974, and acquired Murphy India in 1974 as well. Except for the automobile tire ancillary companies set up in the 1960s making carbon black, beadwire and valves—where the Goenkas hold a monopoly in the market—most of the companies in the group were acquired. It was only in the early 1980s that they began establishing new units. But their acquistions continued as well.

Toward the end of 1973, focus was on acquisition of the B. N. Elias group, owned by an old Jewish family based in Calcutta. A jute mill, the Agarpara Company Ltd. and a cigarette manufacturing unit, the National Tobacco Company of India, were part of the Elias group which began as a

Sir Badridas with President S. Radhakrishnan

small managing agency in 1931. Converted to a public company in 1943, it did well right into the 1960s when militant labor in West Bengal upset the applecart. At National Tobacco Company labor became so troublesome that managers were physically attacked. The Elias family decided to get out of India and sold their interest at a bargain basement price to the wily Goenkas. The Eliases headed for England, leaving two very sick companies in the hands of KP and his sons.

It was to take five years before the Goenkas could turn the acquisition around. When National Tobacco was purchased, it was losing Rs 50 lakh ($416,000) a month. At its peak in the mid 1960s, it had a 20 percent market share, producing 1.2 billion cigarettes annually. When the Goenkas assumed control, production had more than halved, and the payroll was stuffed with unnecessary workers who had been hired in a last ditch effort to stave off the inevitable collapse in labor relations. Rama Prasad (RP) brought in professional management to get National Tobacco in shape. Praful Goradia, the new manager, started by trimming the number of employees. Then National Tobacco was merged with Birpara Tea to form Duncans Agro

KP in The Netherlands: "With flowers, a totally different person" (Mala Goenka)

Industries Ltd. (DAIL). The merger gave the tobacco operation access to the cash in Birpara's coffers which had built up during the mid 1970s tea boom. All together, it took Rs 8.8 crore ($7.3 million) to turn National Tobacco around. But the Goenkas' careful nurturing has pushed DAIL into the top one hundred companies in India's private sector. It became the flagship company of the group with assets of Rs 54 crore ($45 million) by 1980.

The Elias acquisition had made up in part for the abortive outcome of the Goenkas' purchase of the Balmer Lawrie group in 1967, a group with interests in engineering, containers, lubricants and tea trading. The Goenkas had hoped to gain complete control later on, but settled for the purchase of 22.6 percent of Balmer Lawrie's equity at the start. When the government nationalized the Balmer Lawrie group's holding company, Indo Burma Petroleum, in the early 1970s, the Goenkas were pressured into selling their shares to the government. The transfer took place in 1972. The next year the Elias proposition presented itself and the Goenkas were onto a new challenge.

Though KP himself gave a large measure of the credit for the group's promising growth to his sons, his own contribution was still significant, despite his now frequent thoughts of retirement. During several of the group's crucial years, KP had worked alone, with Sir Badridas having retired and Rama, his eldest son, still studying. A large measure of KP's success was due to his ability to delegate authority to his managers and his recognition of the importance of their contribution to his group's performance. This is a rare trait even today in Indian business which has been nurtured on the belief that only blood members can give the company the type of selfless loyalty that ensures growth.

To a certain degree, of course, KP was helped by his family background. The family history went back a long way. The century old association with foreigners made them aware of different business systems. Though KP, along with his cousins, retained an orthodox approach to life, he had few inhibitions about traveling abroad where he could pick up useful management ideas. In the new business environment, KP's willingness to accept such intrinsic changes allowed him to grow at a fast pace where others might have hesitated in favor of the seeming safety of following tradition. KP's adaptability to the latest changes in the wind was essential to his success and it is an adaptability which continues in his sons and grandsons.

Finally, KP's perfection of the art of the corporate takeover had also been passed on successfully to his sons. Their success has prompted numerous fitting tributes in the press, of which the following is perhaps one of the most accurate protrayals of their well-won spurs:

> The Goenkas have over the years perfected acquisition to such a fine art that seldom is a flutter heard when they move into any one company. This partly explains why this once-upon-a-time Calcutta-based house—now they are more or less based in Bombay—has become one of the fastest growing industrial groups in the country. In a rather restrained and tactful fashion—except for some aberrations like the aborted attempt to acquire Bombay Dyeing in 1973 and the infamous attempt to seize control of PAL (Premier Auto Ltd.) last year—the family has bought over interests in so many companies that the ·list reads like an Industries "Who's Who.[9]

KP, like his father, was able to see beyond his own group and took an active part in business associations. Generally he was a moderate and believed in keeping a low profile, but he could speak out boldly if occasion demanded it. One such occasion was in 1965 during his term as President of FICCI. Though the 1960s saw the Duncan group growing at a scorching pace, the period from 1963 to 1971 was a difficult one in Indian history. There was stress, strain and crisis in almost all spheres of Indian life. Economic development faltered under the impact of two major wars, two disastrous droughts, inflation and weak planning. As the government showed definite signs of leaning to the left, businessmen became concerned. At the 1965 FICCI annual meeting, Goenka struck out at the government and moved to table a handful of resolutions which criticized the government's policies so fiercely that the Prime Minister at the time, Lal Bahadur Shastri, joined G. D. Birla to intervene and caution Goenka to tone down his remarks.

KP moved more and more into the background as the group moved into the mid 1970s. For some time after KP's virtual retirement, the three brothers continued to work together. By 1979, however, KP began to suffer from bouts of depression brought on by the increasingly visible tensions among his three sons. The torment of another split in the family, similar to the one which KP suffered through in 1958, appeared inevitable. The successful expansion and profitability which the group had achieved by the late 1970s was not producing harmony, just as it had not in 1958. KP, always a man of action,

KP with Prime Minister Lal Bahadur Shastri (center) and industrialist S.L.Kirloskar

decided to draw up three lists, each with a set of companies from his group. He called in his youngest son, Gouri Prasad, showed him the three columns, and asked him to take his pick. The next choice was offered to the middle son, Jagdish Prasad, and the remainder was given to Rama Prasad, KP's eldest son, always considered KP's blue-eyed boy, not an insignificant source of friction between him and his brothers. Within twenty minutes or so, more than fifteen companies with an estimated combined asset base of Rs 145 crore ($121 million) changed hands.

Harsh Goenka, RP's son, recalls that his father came home and simply remarked, "This is what we've got." But at the same time, Harsh says, "we youngsters were about to join business. It was better to separate before there was infighting among the new generation which would have been quite probable. It was better to separate amicably now than bitterly ten years later."[7]

KP Goenka

The 1979 Split

Rama Prasad	**Jagdish Prasad**	**Gouri Prasad Goenka**
Phillips Carbon Black	Swan Mills	Duncans Agro Industries
Asian Cables	Anglo-India Jute	National Standard Duncan
Agarpara Jute	Duncan International	Gujerat Carbon
Murphy (India)	Oriental Carbon	
	Woolcombers of India	
	Schrader-Scovill Duncan	
	Petrosil	
	Aryodaya Ginning & Manufacturing	

Though all three brothers tried to present a satisfied image, it was clear that certain battle lines had been drawn. The Duncan Goenkas in 1979 had an aggregate sales turnover of Rs 360 crore ($300 million). It was felt that the split would impell the three new groups to expand because of the competitive factor which the split engendered. As RP pointed out: "When you have your own group, family restrictions are not there to slow down growth. Between 1971-79, we were not expanding in any fashion." Five years later, the Rs 360 crore figure has changed to Rs 1345 crore ($1.1 billion).

Since the split in the group's assets, relations between the three brothers and their families have regained a measure of cordiality, though the process has taken a couple of years. For some time there was tension, hostility and bitterness as one or another felt he had been given the short end of the stick. But a new spirit of competition emerged which, while painful for them and their friends, in the long run laid the basis for more equal and harmonious relationships. As they gradually realized that it was possible to interact on two distinct levels, that of family and business, the extended family gained deeper, more permanent foundations. Thus, for example, when RPG and GPG openly competed with each other to take over Bakelite Hylam in 1982, a year later RPG used his good offices to ensure that his younger brother acquired National Rayon Corporation and Herdillia in the teeth of other corporate wolves who might have had a better chance to gain control of the companies.

Harsh Goenka maintains that the split in the family businesses in 1979 was done in a cordial atmosphere. More important, however, today the three groups co-operate, trying not to enter competing industries and if proposals for new projects are more suitable for a brother's concern, it is passed on to him first. For instance, Gouri Prasad has a proposal in the auto ancillary industry, but first offered it to RPG's group since they were already in the business.

Gouri Prasad Goenka

INDIA'S INDUSTRIALISTS

Gouri Prasad Goenka

The companies in GP's fold were three: Duncans Agro Industries Ltd., National Standard Duncan and Gujerat Carbon Ltd. with a combined sales turnover of Rs 71.5 crore ($60 million) in 1979. By 1984, GP controlled nine companies with sales in excess of Rs 370 crore ($308 million). As the youngest son in the group, GP had always felt overshadowed by his two brothers. With his post-split success, he established his place in the impressive universe of Goenka success stories and, in the process, threw off past complexes.

While the increase in assets and turnover has been achieved principally through the acquisition of Herdillia Chemicals, National Rayon Corporation and Bakelite Hylam, the company that has seen truly remarkable growth is DAIL, the tea and cigarette concern. Since 1978, when GPG had taken over its management, DAIL has taken on some of the largest multinationals in India to seize a bigger market share in the cutthroat industries of tea and cigarettes. ITC, Brooke Bond and Lipton have felt the heavy breath of GPG as he ensured that his company adopted strategies which would upset century old traditions in the industries.

DAIL traces its origins to 1859 when its principal business was tea, though the number of gardens it controlled has fluctuated widely over the years. A merger between Birpara Tea which operated thirteen "rupee" tea gardens, and National Tobacco, which became part of the group in 1973, occurred in 1977. GPG was barely at the helm of DAIL when news of events on the London Stock Exchange shook Indian tea companies to their roots. Charles Fox, an astute Canadian, had picked up on some facts overlooked by both Indian and British businessmen for over three decades. At one stroke, owners were reduced to managers or less.

The genesis of the Indian tea crisis lay in the pattern of corporate growth in colonial India. Britishers, sent out to the Empire to atone for their misdeeds in their mother country, founded tea gardens in inaccessible areas of India. Their minds blown away by loneliness, these men gradually turned over the running of the gardens to Indian managers. With independence, the Indian managers became owners, or so they thought, until Charles Fox came on the scene.

Several of India's earliest companies were incorporated in England, with capital raised on the London money market. Known as "sterling" companies to differentiate them from "rupee" companies (i.e. those whose initial capital was raised within India), these companies continued to be quoted on the London Stock Exchange. Naturally prices of shares were abysmally low. Scenting out these facts in London, Fox bought up the shares of numerous "sterling" tea gardens for less than a song and announced that he was now the rightful owner of many of these Indian companies. Legally, he was correct.

The Goenkas were among those hard hit by the Fox coup. Between

November 1974 and July 1976 they had unsuspectingly bought no fewer than six "sterling" tea gardens in India. They controlled 17 such plantations altogether. Upon taking over the UK Walter Duncan Goodricke group, Charles Fox now claimed that the 17 gardens were his. The Goenkas, acquiescing reluctantly, saw their annual tea crop fall to 17 million kg. from 30 million. GPG began salvage operations. A boom in the tea industry in the mid 1970s combined with GPG's management savvy meant that DAIL, though diminished by Mr. Fox, nevertheless was flush with cash. GPG turned his back on the export market and jumped into the home market. With the slogan "from bush to cup in 40 days", an all-out effort was made to carve out a brand name in an arena already littered by the victims of the all-powerful multinationals. GPG wooed the discerning consumer by promising the best, freshest quality tea ever.

Realizing that profits were not merely in growing tea and selling in bulk, but in the complete product, DAIL moulded itself to become a producer, blender, packer and marketer of Duncan tea. From mini-auctions to tea bags, from tea chests to cardboard boxes, DAIL tried every marketing experiment to succeed where so many others could not.

GPG applied himself in similar manner to the cigarette and tobacco division. National Tobacco was still a losing entity when GPG came into the picture, though clearly the company had turned the corner. With two cigarette manufacturing units (at Agarpara and Bikkavom) having an installed capacity of 1.4 billion sticks, 1978 production was at 500 million sticks. GPG's first move was to replace existing management with personnel who knew the latest marketing techniques or had experience in other successful tobacco companies. He raided the Indian Institute of Management in Calcutta to recruit motivated people who seemed as keen as himself to prove themselves in a marketing oriented firm. From six brands of cigarettes, of which only one, "No. 10," was really known, DAIL promoted nineteen new brands in a wide price range. Carrying out elaborate market research, each brand was systematically positioned in the market. Production shot up from 500 million sticks to 1.2 billion in five years.

The dynamism which marked GPG's early years on his own continues today. In 1983, GPG hit the headlines when he overwhelmed his competition to tie up with Rothmans. For years, Indian manufacturers of premium brands struggled against the competition of smuggled international brands. By tieing up with Rothmans, GPG hoped to do better, following the philosophy "if you can't beat them, join them." At the same time, he had spiked his Indian competitors. The Modi's company, Godfrey Phillips (India) Ltd., had been trying for several years to combine forces with Rothmans. GPG's success in doing so was the firing shot in a race among major Indian companies to either revive old international connections, or enter into new ones. Though the success of this venture, as well as the launching of the tumeric based cigarette, "Smokette", is yet to be gauged, there is no denying that GPG is a man with several aces up his sleeve. DAIL will continue to forge ahead, trying to tie up with other international consumer brand leaders to continue its success to date.

Jagdish Prasad Goenka

Arvind, JP's son

J.P. Goenka Takes Over

KP's middle son, JPG, took over Duncan International, Swan Mills, Anglo India Jute Mills, Aryodaya Ginning Mills, Oriental Carbon Black, and several smaller units with an estimated combined sales turnover of Rs 70 crore ($58 million). By 1984, this figure has increased to Rs 163 crore ($136 million). JPG's relatively slow growth has been largely attributed to his heavy involvement in the sunset cotton textiles and jute industries. For over a decade now, the sixty units which make up the Bombay cotton textile industry have been going downhill, hit equally by government regulations, a politicized labor force, antiquated machinery and competition from the decentralized powerloom textile sector. Similarly, the jute industry has fared badly with the encroachment of the synthetic substitutes for jute. JPG has been hit hard by these factors. His four cotton textile mills (Swan, Jubilee, Coorla, Basanti) and his jute company, Anglo India Jute, perhaps the largest jute mill under any one corporate roof, have kept his growth in check.

JPG is not standing still, however. Though he has not undertaken dramatic takeover coups as RPG and GPG have, he has invested over Rs 11 crore ($9 million) in Swan Mills to modernize it and is promoting a. new company, Maharashtra Explosives. The Rs 7 crore ($5.8 million) company will produce 10,000 tons of slurry explosives per year. In JPG's stables also is Petrosil, a company wholly-owned by Gulf Oil of the USA until 1975 when the Goenkas bought a controlling interest. Petrosil sells the parent company's petrochemical technology in India. JPG is also looking at cement and plans various projects which call for a total investment of Rs 210 crore ($175 million).

The Goenkas have long been regarded as leading members of the Marwari aristocracy, an elite class which held sway over Calcutta for almost two centuries. Wealthy beyond reason, they still had to pay lip service to their British overlords, a fact much resented to this day by several prominent families. The Goenkas, while subscribing to very orthodox views· for their inner family mores, pursued an extraordinarily "enlightened" policy toward the foreigners. Mingling with them easily, accepting their titles, and gaining their confidence by lending them money, the Goenkas attained prominence in public affairs while simultaneously retaining their position as leaders of an Indian community.

This combination of wealth and status nurtured an appreciation for the arts and the Goenkas enthusiastically set about organizing recitals and building up art collections. JPG in particular has shown a steadfast desire to attain what he sets out to do in this sphere. His collection of Indian miniature paintings has developed into one of the finest such collections in India. The same dedication has been applied to race horses. Within ten years, he has become known as one of India's gutsiest punters and is a leading owner of race horses, some of whom have won major classics. These serious non-business interests notwithstanding, JP Goenka maintains his standing in the business community as well, though no doubt he is overshadowed by the exploits of Gouri and Rama.

Rama Prasad Goenka

Among the architectural landmarks of Bombay is a unique eight-tiered building in Worli. The front of the building slopes pyramid fashion to flatten out at the top. Its design enables office staff to have a view of tiny gardens on the balconies which cascade down the building, all in the midst of one of the world's largest urban centers. The building houses the offices of Ceat, India's third largest tire manufacturer (after Dunlop and Modi Rubber), and is the corporate headquarters of Harsh Vardhan Goenka, RP's eldest son.

The corporate headquarters of Sanjiv Goenka, RP's second son, is more traditional, but no less impressive. Built during the heyday of colonial enthusiasm, the office of Dunlop India Ltd. (which RP acquired in 1984) are a landmark on Calcutta's Mirza Ghalib Street. It seems somewhat extraordinary that Harsh and Sanjiv's father has no distinct headquarters for himself. But whether operating from the first class section of an airplane or from one of his five Indian residences, or even from a hotel room in any of the financial nerve centers of the world, it is apparent that the question posed by one of the brothers after the split, "ten years hence, which horse will win?", has been answered. RP was given the leftovers from KP's empire. But they have grown into a veritable feast of companies with a turnover of Rs 805 crore ($671 million) compared to the Rs 75 crore in 1979.

RPG was KP's heir apparent whose business instincts were honed to a fine edge over several decades of intense involvement in building the group's strength. RPG is the perfect poker player, an enigma operating behind a most cordial visage. Always his father's trusted lieutenant, RPG early on displayed his business acumen. Graduating from Calcutta University with only a Bachelor of Arts degree, he joined the family business at a delicate moment. KP was having differences with his cousins, Isswari Prasad, Jagmohan Prasad and Devi Prasad. KPG subsequently left the family firm of Ramdutt Ramkissendas as a result of the differences and, though still young and inexperienced, his son RPG helped KPG consolidate his holdings and expand. RPG organized the tea gardens more efficiently and helped set up a number of companies in the tire ancillary industry. RPG learned fast, but he came into his own only after 1977 when he successfully turned around National Tobacco Company.

Ceat Mahal, Bombay: RP's headquarters

The achievement of putting the old Elias company back on its feet brought RPG personal recognition. It also sowed the seeds of dissension between RPG and his two brothers. Jagdish and Gouri began to resent RPG's public image and, more crucial, his influence with their father. RPG's higher public profile, earned through participation as an office holder in many prominent industrial and commercial associations such as FICCI and the Indian Jute Mills Association, did nothing to quiet the discomfort his brothers felt with each added kudu heaped on RPG. It was obvious that a split in the group would be in the best interests of the health of each member of the group, not to mention the health of the companies as well. It was no secret that family feuds could have devastating effects on bottom lines.

RP and his wife Sushila with Prime Minister Indira Gandhi

RP's son, Harsh, pointed out in the aftermath of the split that "all three groups are doing well. They have grown much faster for having split than if they had remained together in business. Earlier, each brother had a veto power in joint family policy decisions. Some were aggressive and some conservative when looking for new activities. The veto power slowed down growth."[8] Another factor not mentioned by Harsh was that the split forced his father back into the forefront of business activity. The goad of competition resulting from the split stirred up some long dormant embers of ambition in RP. Once again through necessity he would experience the challenge of fast-paced corporate growth.

RP was given Phillips Carbon Black, Asian Cables, Murphy (India) and Agarpara Jute which had combined sales of Rs 75 crore ($62.5 million). It was not exactly an exciting clutch of companies with which to begin a second corporate life. By 1985, however, RP had added Wiltech India, Deccan Fibre Glass, Ceat Tyres of India, KEC International and Searle (India), Dunlop and Bayer, increasing his group's sales to Rs 800 crore ($671 million), outstripping both his younger brothers' performances by a healthy margin. The method in an old man's madness seemed to be shining through with the second coming of his eldest son.

RP disclaims:

> When we were together, the desire for business was not greater. But I was more careful. I think there is more adventurism in me now. I would have touched Pepsi [RP signed up with Pepsi in 1985 in a three-way deal which included Voltas, a Tata Company]. Dunlop I would not have touched. Also, when you are on your own, you can make faster decisions. The Bayer [The Ghia Group] people came to me . . . to sound me out, not to sell their company. I looked at the papers and signalled to Harsh. He nodded and I proposed an offer. I asked them to shake hands and, before they knew it, the deal was concluded. I don't know if they realized instantaneously that they had sold their company.

Harsh Goenka with KP, his grandfather

RP's razor sharp business instincts and large cash war chest make very compatible marriage partners. His business is buying and selling companies, more the former for the time being. The group promoted its carbon black companies from scratch, but they excel still at the corporate takeover, most friendly, some hostile. The latter rarely work, as in the case of their raid on Premier Auto, because Indian business families can still appeal to the general public's distaste for something that is forced on another.

RP's impressive growth in a little under five years came initially from his acquisition of Ceat Tyres. With sales of Rs 254 crore ($212 million) in 1983, Ceat was RP's flagship at one point. Acquired in 1981 for Rs 11.9 crore ($9.9 million) for which he received 11 percent of Ceat Tyres' equity, performance of the company under his stewardship has catapulted RP's group into the industrial sweepstakes of India and placed it among the top 50 companies in the private sector.

Originally a joint venture between Ceat of Turin, Italy, and the Tatas, Ceat Tyres of India Ltd. was incorporated on March 10, 1958. It was conceived almost casually with a chance meeting between two Italians and J. R. D. Tata at a social occasion in Delhi. Ceat was looking for an opening in India, preferably in their original field of specialization, cables. The enthusiastic Tata response insured that the project was realized, but not in cables. The joint venture would manufacture automobile tires and tubes instead.

The initial capital was a modest Rs 1.15 crore ($958,000). The Italian partner contributed 60 percent of this with a provision that it would be reduced to 50 percent after twelve and a half years. They also brought in the machinery and the technical know-how. The Tatas put up five percent of the capital and two members of the company's board were top Tata men, A. D. Shroff and P. A. Narielwala. Ceat built its factory on 124,000 square meters of land at Bhandup. It was among the first factories to come up in an area that was soon to become an important industrial satellite of Bombay. The original workforce consisted of 200 people. The first tire rolled out on February 22, 1960 and total production that year was 45,246 tires valued at Rs 1.37 crore ($1.14 million).

Under Italian management the company did extremely well, helped by the fact that the 1960s and 1970s spanned a period of shortages. Tires, especially truck tires, sold at a premium which sometimes went as high as 100 percent. With sales spiralling, investments increased from Rs 1.15 crore in 1958 to Rs 24 crore ($20 million) in 1978. The labor force grew from the initial 200 to over 3000.

In the late 1970s, problems loomed on the horizon, largely set in motion by regulations which required a divestment of the foreign owned majority positions in many companies in India. The regulations which caused IBM and Coca-Cola to leave India (insiders say politics and less than cordial relations between company management and government officials also played a part in their exits), started to hamper Ceat as well. By this time Ceat had acquired a 17 percent share of the commercial tire market and a 20 percent share of the passenger car tire market. Company expansion, however, was now limited by provisions of the Foreign Exchange Regulation Act (FERA) and the only way to grow was to Indianize the company by diluting its foreign equity percentage. For a few years, Ceat International (Switzerland) dallied over this decision, but finally acquiesced, influenced partly by the fact that its own holding company, Ceat Spa. Italy, was facing problems of its own.

Ceat had a ready buyer in RPG. Particularly at this time, RPG was interested in expanding the operations of his group. Further, he had some knowledge of the tires and tubes industry since one of his companies, Phillips Carbon Black, was a pioneer in the manufacture of carbon black, an essential raw material in the tire industry. Ceat was also attractive because of its cash resources. With a minimum outlay, one could obtain a company with over Rs 200 crore ($166 million) turnover, thereby outdistancing one's brothers in a single stride.

Ceat tire plant

Harsh Goenka

RP Goenka

Sanjiv Goenka

The acquisition proved satisfactory in other ways as well. It provided the financial muscle to revive Wiltech and Deccan Fibre Glass which had fallen on rocky paths. Ceat also sustained Asian Cables in a period of recession, and enabled RPG to acquire Searle (India) and KEC International. Though beset by oversupply in the industry and excise tax disputes endemic to the industry, Ceat continues to be one of the best run Indian companies in the private sector with an equally good reputation in the marketplace.

A Very Sophisticated Take-Over

RPG's next acquisition was not so easy. On December 11, 1983, a leading Bombay daily published a report:

> Last month, the changing of the guard in the Rs 54 crore Kamani Engineering Corporation (KEC) Limited was so courteous that to call it a 'take-over coup' would be unforgiveably indiscreet. With a few humourous asides in a board meeting on November 14, seven directors present out of a total of 11 quietly endorsed the IDBI directive elevating a private industrialist—RP Goenka—to the chairmanship of the managing committee for the first time since the financial institution-sponsored professional management took over in 1975. [9]

Though the report made the take-over look like a cakewalk, considerable maneuvering had been involved prior to the congenial November 14 meeting. With several prominent groups interested in the deal, RPG worked quietly and patiently before his final pounce.

Founded in 1945 by Ramji M. Kamani, KEC established the Kamani group's reputation as pioneers in the field of power transmission towers. Soon after independence, India embarked on an ambitious plan to spread the benefits of electricity throughout the country. KEC nobly rose to the demands made on it and executed its projects efficiently and in a timely manner. The original plant at Kurla in Maharashtra was augmented by a second unit at Jaipur in Rajasthan. By 1967, KEC was supplying three-fifths of India's demand for transmission towers.

Around this time, KEC came to be controlled by Poonamchand Kamani, eldest son of the founder. Under his direction, KEC began to aggressively market its products in the Middle East and North Africa. Between 1966 and 1972, KEC's sales increased three-fold. The character of the company also changed with a new and stronger emphasis on exports. By 1972, 80 percent of its turnover of nearly Rs 20 crore ($16.6 million) was earned through exports. KEC also became not only the biggest manufacturer of transmission towers in India, but the second biggest in the world, next in rank to SAE of Italy.

Though everything seemed well in the company, below the surface tensions were bubbling. The Kamani family was a large one with several

Power transmission tower built by KEC International

ambitious members. The death of Poonamchand released the battens on a family power struggle. With infighting and shifting alliances, there could be no long term direction for the company. All the Kamani companies began to show losses and KEC was no exception.

When KEC accounts for 1975 showed a record loss of Rs 442 lakh ($3.7 million), financial institutions began to worry. They had invested some Rs 23 crore ($19 million) in KEC and they pressed for professional management. At this point, Texmaco, a Birla concern, began to show interest. KEC shares had plunged from Rs 10 to Rs 3.50, and the prospects of turning the company around looked good. The Birla bid for control of the company was frustrated, however. It became ensnared in a noisy debate on corporate amalgamations. The Birlas backed away and the financial institutions stepped in. They appointed nominees to take over management control from the Kamanis. Under the new management, the company began to limp back toward profitability. It returned to the dividend list in 1976, reserves improved from Rs 62 lakh ($516,000) in 1972 to Rs 20 crore ($16.6 million) in 1982 and sales climbed from Rs 20 crore ($16.6 million) in 1972 to Rs 55 crore ($45.8 million) in 1982. It was a tribute to the professional managers appointed by the lenders.

All the while, a small percentage of KEC shares still remained with some members of the Kamani family. RP Goenka maneuvered very carefully to purchase these shares, making certain that he did not fall into the same pitfalls which had defeated the Birla's attempts to acquire KEC. The Kamani shareholding was negotiated and the approvals of the financial institutions sought before bidding in the court auction. The report of the cordial "changing of the guards" at KEC was possible because of RP's expert handling of a delicate takeover. While RPG was quietly stalking Kamani shares in KEC, his attention was on a new project as well.

The Sharp Edge of the Blade

With four major companies acquired in as many years, RP showed how thoroughly he had learned the art of takeover from his father. But RPG's expertise as a strategist par excellence really came into the limelight with his handling of Wiltech India, a company producing shaving blades. A rather humble fraction of his corporate empire, the company nonetheless provides insights into RPG's business style. While developed nations are shifting over to shaving systems, in India the razor blade continues to be a popular consumer product.

The earliest company to manufacture the razor blade in India was the Hind Razor and Blade Company Ltd.[10] which began production as late as 1948. Four other producers followed suit though the industry became profitable only after 1958 when the government was prevailed upon to restrict the import of blades into India. Within a very short time one of the five pioneer manufacturers, Harbanslal Malhotra and Sons, was able to carve out an 85 percent share of the market for Indian blades. His lock on the market continues today, in spite of the new competition and rapidly expanding market.

By the late 1970s, the government began to worry about the lack of effective competition in the blades industry. In particular, the Karnataka government initiated negotiations with Wilkinson Swords of England[11] to set up a new razor blade company in India. At the same time, the Karnataka government began to look around for a partner who would run the company. Around this time, Asian Cables was looking for new product lines to make up for the slack in the cable industry. RPG wanted Asian Cables to have a profitable sideline. Thus Karnataka Blades Pvt. Ltd. (later renamed Wiltech India Ltd.) was jointly promoted by Asian Cables and the Karnataka State

Industrial Investment and Development Corporation in technical collaboration with Wilkinson Swords. The Rs 11 crore ($9 million) plant located at
Belagola near the city of Mysore in Karnataka began commercial production
in April 1982.

The incorporation of Karnataka Blades was a signal for open warfare in
the blades industry. Even before Wiltech India had begun production, the
established manufacturers had lobbied against the licensing of another new
company. But in the face of the Karnataka government's determination, they
could achieve nothing and the Asian Cables-Wilkinson collaboration went
through.

In April 1982, however, Wiltech India begain to feel the effects of the
opposition. On the occasion of the formal inauguration of the manufacturing
plant (April 13), Wiltech had planned an advertising blitz with advertisements
in several major newspapers. Somehow these newspapers were persuaded to
drop the Wiltech ads. Further, the entire Wiltech campaign was torpedoed
when the competition launched an almost identical campaign with the probable
aim of confusing the consumer. Wiltech officials could not understand the
anxiety of the competition. At best, Wiltech's licensed capacity would permit it
to enjoy a 10 percent market share. Asian Cables' disingenuous appraisal of
the situation did not impress its rivals. The principal competitor had come in for
criticism time and again for apparently attempting to scotch anyone's entry into
the market. A Monopolies Inquiry Commission Report of 1964-65 had noted
the monopolistic share of the Malhotras in the razor blade industry. In 1977
when Sharpedge Ltd. in collaboration with Thabaud Gibb of France introduced
a successful brand called Erasmic Silk Edge, the Malhotras launched their
Esquire Sleek Edge which used a logo and color scheme similar to that of
Sharpedge. Earlier, Centron Industrial Alliance, which has been unprofitable
for the past decade, had suspected that the competition had tampered with their
products in northern India to put off buyers.

The Goenkas were not cowed by this formidable history of foiled attempts
to blunt the Malhotra's blade monopoly. As politically astute as the competition
in lobbying the halls of Parliament, the Goenkas pushed past them to use
their own considerable clout. A suit was brought against the Malhotras for
copyright infringement of Wiltech's advertising campaign. The Calcutta High
Court judge who heard the case observed:

> It also appeared that the plaintiff (Malhotra) in the past had substantial
> business in India without any effective competition. It appears that the
> plaintiff has been taking steps to shut out competition. In the instant case the
> plaintiff at each step dogged the footsteps of the defendant Wiltech and every
> move of the defendant either in selection of a name or in selection of a device
> or registration of a mark was immediately countered by a similar move by the
> plaintiff.

Moreover, in a surprise move, the government cracked down on Malhotra
stockists in Bangalore and three brands of razor blades were confiscated for
alleged violation of the Weights and Measures Act and the Packaged

Commodities Act. Having checkmated the competition, Wiltech India has asked for and received government permission to double its capacity. While its blades like "Savage" and "Wiltedge" have become popular, it remains to be seen whether the company can increase its market share in any significant way.

RPG's long-standing support for the Congress (I) Party and friendship with the late Prime Minister Indira Gandhi and her advisors, particularly R.K. Dhawan and Pranab Mukherjee, former Finance Minister, had perhaps given him a certain confidence that his corporate plans would not be stymied. He admits that one could expect at the most a marginal latitude from a favorable government, no more. His ability to come out on top consistently in his busi-maneuvers demonstrate his remarkable skills at making the most of even a "marginal latitude", indeed if one exists.

His dyed-in-the wool support has sometimes cost him dearly. His homes and offices were raided no fewer than 43 times during the Janata Party's tenure in office (1977-1979) and at least one major expansion scheme was thwarted. RP recalls somewhat whimsically, somewhat regretfully:

> *Actually I became quite friendly with the officer in charge of the operation. You cannot find incriminating papers every week. So he would ask me if he could watch cricket on my television set. But this was the time when I had one of my biggest business disappointments. We had negotiated to buy Assam Frontier. It was a very good deal for about 2.1 million pounds, 100 percent share and a net valuation of 75 pence per kg. Jokai Tea was sold last year for Rs 22 per kg. On 16 March, all the approvals were in hand, but we decided to remit the money a week later, after Lok Sabha elections. The government changed and the deal fell through.*

With a nose for business nuances, changing political equations do not mean much. RP's persistence and consistent success year after year discredits some press's view that politics rather than talent has made his garden grow. He has certainly left nothing to chance if he could help it. That is to his credit where business is concerned.

New Money — New Management Systems

In recent years, moreover, perhaps because of the entry into the RPG family business of RPG's two sons, Harsh and Sanjiv, the group is engaged in promoting several new companies and expanding old ones in diverse fields such as telecommunications, polyester fiber, agrochemicals and micro-processor based electric typewriters. The new style of growth which is emerging is also partially due to a change in fundamental management thinking. Though for instance KPG was one of the first industrialists to join hands with the government in promoting a company in what has come to be known as a "joint sector company," traditionally the Goenka's growth was always funded internally with close control maintained at all times. Large-scale borrowings from banks were virtually taboo. But as newer industrialists such as Dhirubhai

Ambani have sped up the corporate ladder by boldly throwing over traditional views toward borrowing, so too have groups like the Goenkas and the Bajajs found it necessary to fund growth from borrowing. Like KP, his sons have adapted to the times.

RPG remains free of the day to day hassles of decision-making and keeps his eye peeled for the new project which can be taken up with ever-ready expansion funds. Two years ago, Harsh Goenka related, the group started a relatively new management concept which greatly professionalized its operations. An executive committee of eight or nine people was formed which consisted of the chief executives of all their companies. RPG is the head of the committee. It meets each month and discusses basic group policy and individual company problems. But, by and large, the group is very professionalized.

Like a true pioneer, RP's soul is a restless one. The same indomitable spirit which forced a Mafatlal Gagalbhai into establishing a jute mill in Calcutta at the age of 57, a G.D. Birla to control Hindalco in his ninetieth year, a Walchand to fight for the control of Scindia when almost on his deathbed, compels RP, now in his late 50s, to found a new business empire all over again.

> *In January 1985 I called a meeting in Udaipur of all my top executives. I told them that in 1990 I would retire and that those who wanted to retire before me, fine. But those who were going to continue in the group should consider whether they would like to work under the chairmanship of Harsh who would take over in 1990. If they didn't want to work under him, they should say so now.*
>
> *Though I will retire from the group, I will not leave the business. I do not want to lean on my sons, or go to them for money, or be in a position where they can say, "Father, take this Rs 50,000." Rather, I will take one of the companies in the group, say one having sales of Rs 25 to 50 crore. I have not decided which one. I will manage it, and build a new group.*

On Business and Government in India

Harsh Goenka, a Calcutta University graduate with an MBA from CIE Geneva, likes to compare the relationships between business and government in countries around the world. In Japan, for instance, business gets a lot of support from government. "In India," Harsh says, "this is not so. There are, of course, some very good bureaucrats. But India follows the British system which is unfortunately a slow process. Decisions can be taken only after everyone has had a chance to consider and comment. On the practical level, however, there is a lot of interaction and there is an appreciation on the part of bureaucrats for the problems facing business.

"And while there is a formidable state-controlled industrial sector, there has not been a great deal of competition between private business and government companies, except perhaps in the field of semi-conductors. But there is again much cooperation. The Goenkas pioneered the joint sector company when they were the first to promote a venture with the Cochin Refinery in which they took a very small equity holding, but were given management control. The venture was in collaboration with Philips Petroleum. This was in the early 1960s. After that deal, Harsh relates, the concept of joint sector companies became very popular.

"In some cases, the private sector has no choice but to link up with a public sector entity," says Harsh. "For example, my group is undertaking a project in polyester fiber with Du Pont technology in collaboration with a state industrial development corporation. The central government had only given out two licenses in the field and both went to state corporations. So if the Goenkas wanted to promote a project in this arena, they had to link up with the state."

Nevertheless, these ventures are seen as potentially very profitable with the government providing a bulk of the financing and turning them over to the private joint venture partner perhaps after they become profitable. The public joint sector concept can also be an important tool to help turn around what is predominantly an unprofitable public sector which for the most part is engaged in the infrastructural core of the economy. If these companies are not run well, Harsh says, naturally the infrastructure is not good and this means that private enterprise or even national wealth for that matter declines and degenerates. By cooperating with large-scale infrastructural undertakings, the private sector, which has proven it can produce results, may finally enter fields which were closed to it through post-independence industrial policy."

On New Fields for Investment

Harsh Goenka feels that there are exciting investment opportunities in the fields of computers and offshore oil. All high technological fields are good. The RPG group is exploring these fields itself. He does not see why India cannot go in for fourth and fifth generation computer technology. It will be difficult, he points out, as experience in Ceat shows. Ceat imported some very sophisticated equipment with numerical control devices, but the workers could not cope with it at first. Worker training will need to be emphasized to teach the workers to handle the new technology. But there is no doubt in Harsh Goenka's mind that India needs to import the latest technology rather than intermediate or outdated technology. While his father concentrates on acquisitions, Harsh thinks about the sectors into which he would like to expand. RP sees great scope in basic products like pharmaceuticals and tires, while Harsh thinks about oil rigs and computers.

Like his father RP, Harsh Goenka loves business. His devotion to the task causes no internal conflicts for him, despite the fact that he works eleven and twelve hour days six days a week. At times, however, he has had to face the inquiries of his wife, Mala, over the dinner table and afterwards about how to figure variable costing and other such things. Serving for a time as executive director of the Goenka's venture with Lovable Bras, Mala Goenka, encouraged by her father-in-law, RP, to enter business, did not hesitate to pick Harsh's brain when she had the chance. This is perhaps where a certain feeling of conflict set in on Harsh. Two business tycoons sharing the same pillow, so to speak, might be a little too much even for the consummate business family named Goenka. Harsh admits to looking forward to relaxing when he gets home. He does not, he says, bring the office home with him. Even a Goenka draws the line somewhere.

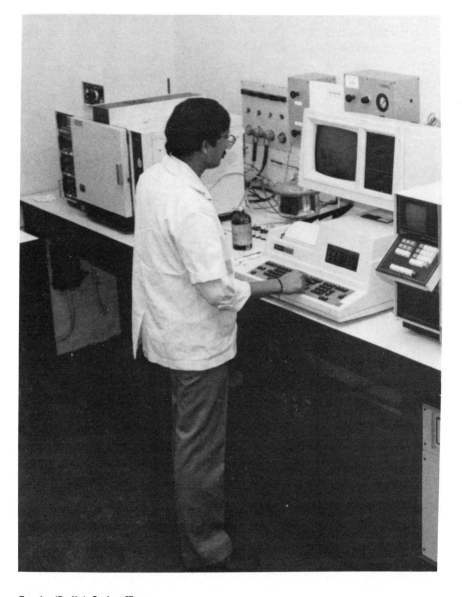

Searle (India) Ltd. offices

GOENKA

Principal Companies in RP Goenka Group

Name	Products
Ceat Tyres of India Ltd.	Automobile tires and tubes
Dunlop India Ltd.	Automobile tires and tubes
KEC International Ltd.	Power transmission towers
Phillips Carbon Black Ltd.	Carbon black
Asian Cables	Power cables
Murphy India Ltd.	Radios, electronics
Searle (India) Ltd.	Pharmaceuticals, agro-chemicals
Bayer (India) Ltd.	Pharmaceuticals, rubber products
Wiltech India Ltd.	Blades, shaving systems

Principal Companies in GP Goenka Group

Name	Products
Duncans Agro Industries	Tea, cigarettes
National Rayon Corporation	Rayon yarn, caustic soda, tire cord, sulfuric acid
Herdillia Chemical Ltd.	Heavy organic chemicals
Bakelite Hylam	Laminates
Gujerat Carbon Ltd.	Carbon black

Principal Companies in JP Goenka Group

Name	Products
Swan Mills	Cotton textiles
Anglo-India Jute Mills Company	Jute articles
Duncan International Ltd.	
Oriental Carbon Ltd.	Carbon black
Aryodaya Ginning & Manufacturing	Cotton cloth

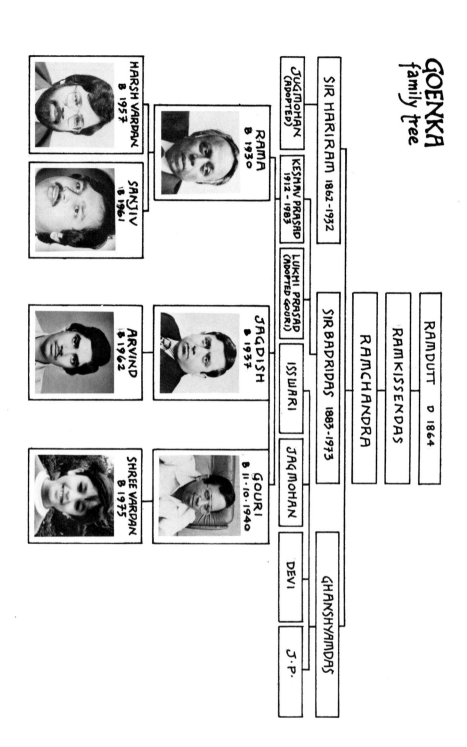

GOENKA
family tree

RAMDUTT D 1864

RAMKISSENDAS

RAMCHANDRA

SIR HARIRAM 1862-1932

SIR BADRIDAS 1883-1973

GHANSHYAMDAS

JUGMOHAN (ADOPTED)

KESHAV PRASAD 1912-1983

LUKHI PRASAD (ADOPTED GOURI)

ISSWARI

JAGMOHAN

DEVI

J.P.

RAMA B 1930

JAGDISH B 1937

GOURI B 11-10-1940

HARSH VARDAN B 1957

SANJIV B 1961

ARVIND B 1962

SHREE VARDAN B 1975

Kirloskar

Diesel engines, high horsepower
Electrical engineering equipment
Machine Tools
Pumps
Tractors
Iron castings
Bearings
Switchgears
Compressors
Consulting/computer services

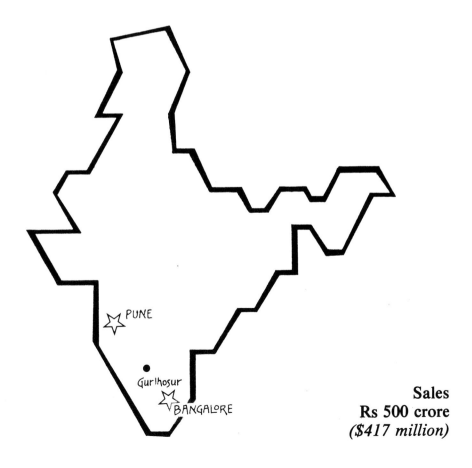

Sales
Rs 500 crore
($417 million)

Headquarters

Kirloskar Cummins Ltd.
Kothrud
Pune, India   411 029

Kirloskar Brothers Ltd.
Laxmanrao Kirloskar Road
Pune, India 411 003

Head of Group
Shantanu L. Kirloskar

Laxmanrao K. Kirloskar (1869-1956)

KIRLOSKAR

When I went to various developed and developing countries to locate markets and potential collaborators, I had the advantage of my experience in manufacturing and of a certain clarity of objectives. I take a long view in business, holding that while short-term gains might bring more benefits for the immediate future, policies framed upon a long view lay a strong foundation for continuous gains for years to come. Experience had taught me to learn and endure during long years of preparation, gestation and trial in establishing manufacturing enterprises. For all this I accounted myself fortunate.[1]

S.L. Kirloskar

Mahatma Gandhi once rejected a spinning wheel designed and manufactured by Ganesh Kale and Laxmanrao Kirloskar because he said it looked too much like a machine. The two engineers had entered their state-of-the-art charkha in the All-India Spinners Association contest in 1933 in solidarity with the homespun cloth movement advocated by India's nationalist leaders. The Association had recommended the Kirloskar-Kale charkha to receive the 100,000 rupees prize, but Gandhi balked because of the machine-like qualities of the invention. He felt the illiterate villager would be put off by such qualities. The Kirloskar team decided to pay a visit to

> Question to S.L. Kirloskar:
> *Why can't everyone do what you've done?*
> Response:
> *Why can't everyone sing?*
> *Business depends on the right two persons getting together—it's not budgets or government policies which make the deals.*
> *We've had 70 collaborations or more and only two or three have gone sour— and those over different philosophies.*
> *One has to get a fair price in a deal, but then not bicker or waffle once a deal is made.*
>
> S.L. Kirloskar

Gandhi at his ashram in Wardha to discuss the Mahatma's objection to their otherwise award winning entry.

The Kirloskar team was met at the train station of Wardha by Jamnalal Bajaj, a close friend and supporter of Gandhi and a businessman in his own right. They proceeded to Gandhi's ashram to see Gandhi's reaction firsthand.

Shantanu Kirloskar, then 30, recalls:

> ...Some men I saw working with a stone grinding-wheel to produce flour and some others sweeping the Ashram premises with brooms. In the whole Ashram the only furniture consisted of small "Chatais" or straw mats.
> The philosophy behind this austere pattern of living was obvious and already well known: rely on your own labour, do away with machines and the dependence on foreign goods which accompanies them. No flour mill: use the stone grinding wheel. No furniture: use chatais. And yet in that world of extreme austerity, my eye was caught by a well fitted with a kerosene engine and a pump! What had become of the traditional wooden wheel and bucket tied to the end of a rope, for drawing water? I felt I was looking at something suspiciously suggestive of a double standard in the atmosphere of this 'machine-free' Ashram.[2]

From production of India's first home-made plough in 1904 to the sophisticated numerically controlled machine tool factories fashioning modern diesel engines, the annual sales of the Kirloskar group of companies surpassed the Rs 500 crore ($416 million) mark in 1984. Laxmanrao Kirloskar, founder of the group, had slowly and painstakingly built one of India's first modern engineering conglomerates. His sons and grandsons honored him by multiplying the fruits of his labor many times over.

Laxmanrao Kashinath Kirloskar

Born on June 20, 1869 at Gurlhosur, Dhawar District, now in

Karnataka State, in a poor Maharashtrian Karhade Brahmin family, Laxmanrao was one of five children and the youngest of three boys. Their father, Kashinath Vasudevrao, a government land surveyor, lost his wife when Laxmanrao was only three. Kashinath gave up his job to look after his five children and those of his brother as well. He later secured a job as a clerk in a private firm at Dharwar for eight rupees a month. The salary could barely

Laxmanrao and Radhabhai, 1914

support his family, yet somehow Kashinath managed to provide the boys with education. His eldest son, Ramuanna, born in 1857, passed the matriculation examination and got a job as a teacher. The middle son, Vasudevrao, studied at Grant Medical College in Bombay and started a practice in Sholapur. Gangadharrao, Kashinath's nephew, also qualified as a doctor and settled down in Hyderabad.

Only Laxmanrao was a problem. Bored with standard schoolboy subjects, his failure to master the three R's must be laid at the door of his devotion to two hobbies. The first was to take apart any mechanical object he came across and reason out why and how it worked. The second was to paint. He would draw or paint anything he could put his hands on (his son Shantanu would also take up painting and drawing). When he was 15, Laxmanrao informed his father that he wanted to give up school, go to Bombay and join the Jamshedji Jeejibhoy School of Arts to study painting. The outraged Kashinath refused to consent. He warned his youngest son that no painter could earn enough to maintain himself and a family. The warning passed over Laxmanrao's head. He appealed to his elder brother, Ramuanna, who intervened and persuaded the father to let the boy go to Bombay, promising to send the money himself to maintain Laxmanrao there. With great reluctance Kashinath gave his permission and in 1885 Laxmanrao found himself in the fast-growing metropolis of Bombay.

His first disappointment came when he learned he was color-blind. He had to give up his painting career, but he soon took up mechanical drawing with similar passion at the J. J. School. Conscious of the financial burden that his family was bearing to allow him to follow his dreams, Laxmanrao looked for a job immediately after completing his courses. He had impressed the British principal of the prestigious Victoria Jubilee Technical Institute in Bombay, despite his young age, and he was promptly appointed an assistant teacher in mechanical drawing on a salary of Rs 45 a month.

Laxmanrao worked as a teacher for about ten years. While teaching at the Institute, between and after his lectures, he used to putter around the Institute's workshop. In a short time, he became familiar with the inner workings of all kinds of machines, gaining valuable experience for his future. He also earned the opprobrium of colleagues who did not like his "ungentlemanly" habit of "soiling his hands and getting his clothes dirty." Laxmanrao, however, could now install and repair machines and thus earn additional income. The money was all the more useful when he married Radhabai and settled into family life.

From Buttons to Bicycles

Laxmanrao was ambitious and constantly explored opportunties to start his own business. He made two unsuccessful attempts before Kirloskar Brothers came into existence. The first was to make shirt buttons which at the time were only imported into India, and the second attempt was to make paper containers for ointment used by medical practitioners. The returns were not encouraging enough to continue the ventures.

One day Laxmanrao caught sight of a Parsi gentleman riding majestically on a new two-wheeled contraption to the awe of bystanders. He inquired as to the nature of the object and when he was told it was a bicycle, he decided to learn the art of bicycling, as well as the mechanics of the machine itself. At the same time, he wrote an enthusiastic letter to Ramuanna in Belgaum suggesting that they introduce the new invention there. Stimulated by the letter, Ramuanna made enquiries and sent back word that the rich men living in and around Belgaum were eager for the product. Soon a flourishing business emerged.

Laxmanrao bought bicycles in Bombay and forwarded them to Belgaum where Ramuanna sold them, serviced them and even taught the new buyers how to ride them. As the business grew, letterheads in the name of "Kirloskar Brothers" were printed and the brothers secured a dealership from Belgaum from the British bicycle manufacturer. With increasing sales they even brought out a catalogue. Meanwhile events in Bombay were far less promising. Laxmanrao was passed over for promotion at the Institute in favor of an Anglo-Indian. He immediately resigned his post and joined his brother in Belgaum. But by the time he arrived in Belgaum in 1897, sales were already declining. They looked around for other products to sell to Belgaum's wealthier citizens and decided on windmills. They secured an agency from Samson Windmills of the USA. The windmills sold well for a year, then came the idea to manufacture steel furniture on a very small scale. Soon the opportunity to manufacture for a much larger market than the better-off citizens of Belgaum presented itself to the two Kirloskars.

While in Bombay teaching at the Victoria Jubilee Technical Institute, Laxmanrao had begun subscribing to Western technical journals such as the *American Machinist* and *Scientific American* as well as to mail-order catalogues. Ramuanna had meticulously filed and indexed these magazines, a habit which proved invaluable when the brothers embarked upon their manufacturing activities. Laxmanrao noticed an illustration of a fodder-cutter in one of the magazines and he immediately sensed its possibilities in an agricultural country like India. He ordered one, tested it and then made one of his own. He advertised in newspapers, describing the implement in language which any literate farmer could understand. Sales of the Kirloskar fodder-cutters were slow at first, but gradually picked up. The brothers began to perceive the potential market for agricultural machinery.

The success of the first product encouraged them to make an iron plough. With little formal education, but with rich practical experience, Laxmanrao overcame the technical difficulties in setting up an iron foundry and workshop next to the bicycle shop. Unfortunately the six ploughs made by Kirloskar Brothers did not sell. Some unfinished business saved the day. Several years earlier the Kirloskars had been commissioned to erect an assembly hall next to a temple in Aundh. The Raja of Aundh had advanced 17,000 rupees to the brothers for the work, but the work had to be halted because of the estate dispute which followed the Raja's death. At a great loss to Kirloskar, he returned to Belgaum, vowing to manufacture his own products from then on. Reliance on third parties for work was too risky for Laxmanrao.

After the ploughs had been manufactured, but remained unsold, the late Raja's estate was settled and the Kirloskars were asked to complete the assembly hall which they did at a handsome profit. When Laxmanrao again returned to Belgaum, his luck continued when a prosperous farmer walked into the foundry one day and bought the six two-year old ploughs. He promised to report back to the engineers about the quality of their work. When he advised the Kirloskars that British-made ploughs had longer-wearing tips, the Kirloskars quickly researched the problem in Ramuanna's files to find a process for hardening the plough tips. A chilling process was identified and the new ploughs were as good as the British implements. True to his word, the farmer spread the good news about Kirloskar ploughs and sales increased to nearly 400 units over the next two years.

The Founding of Kirloskarwadi

Laxmanrao took the natural next step for an entrepreneur. He went to the bank to borrow for expansion of his business. The Belgaum branch of the Bombay Bank Corporation advised him that he did not have sufficient collateral. Since no suitable guarantor could be found, the Kirloskars were out of luck. Almost impossible to keep any news a secret in the village-like atmosphere of many Indian towns, news spread that they had been turned down by the bank, making it difficult for Laxmanrao to secure even day-to-day credit now. A local Marwari moneylender who admired the Kirloskars came to the rescue. He dropped in the foundry one day and offered a low interest loan to the brothers, telling them to repay it when they could. Then, just as the expansion plans were being drawn up, the Municipality of Belgaum gave notice to Kirloskar that a new town plan called for a suburb to be built on the site of the Kirloskar foundry. It was 1909. Ramuanna was well over 50 and Laxmanrao 40. What had been built up during twelve years of struggle was to be wiped out in one stroke and with negligible compensation.

A Masonic meeting was taking place in Belgaum around this time and an old friend of Laxmanrao from Bombay days, Balasaheb Pant Patinidhi, son of the late Raja of Aundh, and now Raja of Aundh himself, came for the meeting. Along with him was Jacob Bapuji, his chief administrator, who also knew the Kirloskars and liked them. Kirloskar could hardly keep the news of his imminent eviction from his old friend. When the Raja of Aundh heard the story, he immediately offered both land and money to the Kirloskars if they came to his state. Laxmanrao was overwhelmed, but politely put off accepting the Raja's offer until he could confer with his brother that evening. The offer was accepted, a point on the map of Aundh chosen for the new factory site, and a request of 10,000 rupees to get started was met by the Raja. Laxmanrao's noble friend did not let on that he had to go out and borrow the sum from a moneylender at six percent. The Raja absorbed the interest cost himself.

The 32-acre piece of wasteland near the railway station in the princely

Kirloskarwadi before development

state of Aundh in southern Maharashtra was soon the site of Kirloskarwadi (Kirloskarville). Out of the harsh, cactus strewn land poked up huts, a small factory, and eventually paved roads, wells, electric power for his factory and houses. It all took time. In the beginning, two families of Kirloskars and 25 workers reached the site of the future Kirloskarwadi on March 10, 1910. All the baggage, machines and materials had to be carried into the interior on human heads and backs as bullock-carts were too few. Within days huts were built. The factory shed received priority for as Laxmanrao explained to his workers, "Unless we produce and sell, we will have no money to build our houses and dig wells for our drinking water."[3]

As production began, problems only seemed to multiply. Trained hands were simply not available. Raw and mostly illiterate peasants had to be patiently trained to perform work of precision and high quality which was as natural to the Kirloskar business philosophy as air was to living creatures. The onset of World War I meant a sharp contraction of imports—iron, steel, machine tools, guages, paints, oils—all essential inputs for the manufacture of Kirloskar products.

As the war continued, Papa ran short of so many needed materials that he was forced to hunt for substitutes. He replaced the imported green paint, used for painting Kirloskar ploughs, by the ancient process of mixing red ochre with linseed oil. When he could not get coke and coal for the foundry, he sent teams of men and women along the railway track to pick up chunks of coal dropped from the steam locomotives, and mixed these with charcoal to heat the cupola. When even dropped chunks of coal were no longer available he used charcoal and firewood; yet during the last two years of war the supply of even these fell short. Papa therefore bought a block of forest near Koyna, so that he could get a regular supply of firewood and charcoal.

With such serious shortages, low production, high costs and poor sales, Papa became desperate to find some fresh sources of money. His attempts to make wooden wheels for bullock carts and to manufacture nuts and bolts, both failed and these failures aggravated his financial difficulties.[4]

The brothers could not give up. Their hard work and faith in themselves paid off. Though always short of funds, demand for their products was fairly steady. In 1912, Ramuanna left Kirloskarwadi to teach the Raja's wife English. Soon nine Kirloskar boys of school age joined Ramuanna and his wife in Aundh to attend school as Kirloskarwadi did not yet have adequate learning facilities. By 1920, with a growing family and the demands of a growing business, more funds had to be found. The Kirloskars decided to invite the public to join their enterprise by converting their operations into a public limited concern. Laxmanrao sold his interest in the private Kirloskar Brothers to the new Kirloskar Brothers Ltd. for which he received shares in the new company. As was common business practice at the time, a managing agency was established to run the company, in this case, Kirloskar Sons & Company, with Laxmanrao, Shantanu, Shankarbhau, Shambuanna and Anantrao Phalnikar as partners. A not so common feature of managing agencies was adopted by the Kirloskars, however. The managing agents decided not to take any part of the profit until the company was able to pay a nine percent dividend to the shareholders in Kirloskar Bros. Ltd.

Laxmanrao with brothers and sisters (1915) (left to right, counterclockwise): Ramuanna, Durgatai, Batuakka Jambhekar, Laxmanrao, and Dr. Vasudevrao

With the cash raised from the public issue of shares, Kirloskar Bros. purchased new machines to make new products. Riding ploughs, cane-crushers, groundnut-shellers and more began to blanket the countryside. By 1924, 40,000 ploughs a year were being sold. Six hundred employees worked in Kirloskarwadi now. As news of the success of the township circulated, officials of the Bombay Presidency from which the Kirloskars had been unceremoniously uprooted in 1906 regretted aloud that the Municipality of Belgaum had been so shortsighted.

The boom of the 1920s ran headlong into the shadow of the Great Depression which gradually enveloped India and in its wake millions of small enterprises like Kirloskar Brothers. As demand rose and dipped, the management struggled to keep the workers employed by cutting back one day on the work week. Indigenous materials were experimented with to substitute for costly imports, marketing techniques were honed to a fine degree. Amid all this, the second generation of Kirloskars, notably Shantanu Laxmanrao, the founder's eldest son, was absorbing the difficult lessons of resource management with the sole objective of survival.

Laxmanrao's Son in America

In January of 1922 Shantanu Kirloskar, along with his cousin four years his senior, Madhav, traveled to America to study at the Massachusetts Institute of Technology (MIT). Shantanu was to study mechanical

Shantanu L. Kirloskar at MIT as a young military cadet

Madhav Kirloskar

engineering and Madhav, already a graduate in physics and chemistry from Bombay University, was going to study electrical engineering. Laxmanrao was dreaming of manufacturing electric motors and diesel engines. Madhav could take up this project upon his return to Kirloskarwadi. The two cousins were so happy to be studying together in the preppy atmosphere of Boston where they made friends easily. But the bliss was to end tragically when Madhav was diagnosed as having tuberculosis. Madhav never saw India again as he was too sick to be sent home. While Shantanu's younger brother, Ravindra, would study electrical engineering, the loss of their brilliant cousin could not be made up.

Shantanu continued his studies at MIT and, after four years, bid a sad farewell to his good American friends to return to Kirloskarwadi. While in the USA he had spent time in American plants absorbing the latest technologies. Shantanu's psyche was as up to date as the machines he was seeing in these factories. There was no doubt in his mind that Kirloskar Brothers would try to produce some of the latest machines. He could not help but notice when he returned how far his country and his own company had to travel to get where the Western nations were at that time. Always sure of himself, as his father had been, unafraid of modern notions and unsympathetic to hide-bound traditions, Shantanu arrived in Bombay in 1926 ready and willing to join his father's business of making machines and the machines which make machines.

In 1928, just two years after his son came home, Laxmanrao was already nearly 60 and was devoting more and more time to social welfare activities and agricultural experiments. He began to delegate to his younger team which now consisted of Shantanu and his three brothers and their cousins, Shambhurao, Jambhekar, Nana Gurjar, Anantrao Phalnikar and Shankarbhau. Laxmanrao had trained his team well, fully accepting the value of education, especially technical training. Ravindra studied electrical engineering and Rajaram, Shantanu's other brother, while disliking schoolbooks as much as his father had, had a sixth sense when it came to machines. Laxmanrao refrained from forcing formal education on Rajaram and encouraged him to gain practical experience instead. Appreciative of highly qualified engineers and managers, the Kirloskars always were on the lookout for talented people who might not necessarily have graduated. In fact, they made it a policy in their group to seek out engineers who failed, fully expecting to uncover a genius or two for whom degrees were not of paramount interest. Laxmanrao noticed that Prabhakar had an eye for farms, gardens and animals, and accordingly sent him to Cornell University in the USA to acquire a degree in agriculture and animal husbandry.

Laxmanrao Kirloskar had always been a man of few words. He was most at home with his workers, his machines and his family. His artist's eye, though color-blind, carefully studied the nature of things and people and he did his best to create an atmosphere in which the potential in any situation could be realized. He trusted those around him to refrain from disturbing the delicate mixture of chemicals and thought which allowed him to create a modern world which could free men from age old oppression. Once something is accomplished, however, life must go on. When the second generation of Kirloskars gradually assumed more responsibility and new managers were taken on, Laxmanrao's importance to the organization appeared to lessen. One day a new recruit brashly challenged Laxmanrao on some matter. The offense was too much and Laxmanrao left his home at Kirloskarwadi. He moved to Bangalore where one of his sons was and then shifted to another son's home. Nothing could convince him to step foot back in the town he had sweat blood to build. (Many years later, at the insistence of a workers' delegation which made a personal appeal to him to return home for an anniversary celebration, Laxmanrao returned to a happy homecoming in Kirloskarwadi.)

Shantanu assumed more and more of the leadership of the group during the 1930s and 40s. A gifted engineer, he was a shrewd businessman and a good administrator. He combined within himself the old and the new: working alongside his father, he had learned to appreciate the thought processes of the Indian farmer, their chief customer. His exposure to American business practices broadened his vision, enabling him to conceptualize, sustain and direct the rapid growth which the group undertook during and after World War II. His "post graduate" degree was earned when in 1930 he designed and sold a new sugarcane mill. But Laxmanrao's dream of manufacturing diesel engines and electric motors which he had in the early 1920s was put off because of the onset of the Great Depression.

Kirloskar oil engine supplying to a Kirloskar sugarcane crusher, 1939

Several honors had by now come Laxmanrao Kirloskar's way. He was invited in 1929 to inaugurate the Dharwar Industrial Exhibition as a successful Indian industrialist. It was in Dharwar that Laxmanrao was a low-paid clerk trying to put his struggling sons through school. Then in an industrial exhibition in Kolhapur just a month later, Kirloskar products won four gold medals for their excellent quality. The "Kamal" sugar-cane crusher which Shantanu had redesigned extracted 77 percent juice out of the sugarcane, higher than any other crusher. As demand slackened for their products due to a depressed agricultural scene, Shantanu looked around for work to utilize idle capacity. It was back to the salaried, middle class consumer who now found himself with higher disposable income due to the depressed prices for food. The Kirloskars started making furniture for homes and hospitals. Furniture manufacturing at one point reached one third of their total output. Shantanu and Laxmanrao continued to improve their agricultural machines in part to keep their workers busy. They succeeded in developing an 8 and 16 h.p. diesel engine and a water pump for irrigation. Shantanu was philosophical about the Depression years:

> The years of the Great Depression were, in a sense, a period of preparation for a better future, particularly since we concentrated on developmental work. We suffered financially, but less, I believe, than other entrepreneurs. Papa, a veteran fighter against bad market conditions, had covered himself by making such standard products as ploughs, pumps, crushers, shellers and oil engines. From each opportunity that we were able to grasp, we reaped rich benefits. I had the inestimable advantages of building on the foundation, strong and wide, which Papa had erected with his practical wisdom and farsighted business view. [5]

Shantanu returned to America in early 1934 to catch up on developments in machinery and business. His wife Yamutai found it difficult to refrain from criticizing the barbaric Americans for eating meat and carrying on together in public. Kissing and holding hands in public is still not done in India today. Fifty years ago it must have been quite an eye-opener for the young Brahmin wife. A tour of Europe followed and by June of 1934 Shantanu was back in harness.

The Kirloskars were asked in 1937 by a mutual friend who was importing machinery and machine tools if they could duplicate a Japanese lathe which the friend's firm was importing. Shantanu found it to be of inferior quality and designed his own which became quite popular. They received orders for more and more of their new machine tool products. They realized too that the demand would continue in the face of Hitler's move to engage the world in a costly war. Toward the end of the 1930s it was obvious that the group would have to establish separate operations for the machine tools business as it was encroaching on the company's main production. Years earlier the Maharaja of Mysore had offered the Kirloskars a place to set up a factory in his state. Now that they were ready and in need of a new factory site, they took up the offer. Mysore Kirloskar Ltd., India's first and largest machine tools factory in the private sector, was born. Rajaram Kirloskar

Ravindra, Yamutai and Shantanu on European tour

was given responsibility for the new enterprise. One hundred acres at Harihar on the south bank of the River Tungabhadra were selected. It took only eleven months to get production started. By December 1941, seven lathes were ready for market. It was just in time. The Kirloskars would experience what most of Indian industry experienced during World War II—high demand for indigenously-manufactured products and high profits.

Shantanu resisted the temptation to turn their factories into total war machines even though the British government pressed them to do so. He realized it would take time to retool after the war ended when demand for industrial goods promised to continue. He did not want the Kirloskars out of circulation with respect to the products they had been producing for forty years now. They took a middle road, producing for the war effort, obtaining valuable raw materials in the process, all the while continuing production of their traditional products. As the war waged, negotiations were started with two British manufacturers, Brush Electrical Engineering Company (electric motors) and British Oil Engines Export Ltd. (diesel engines) for the manufacture of their products in India. The companies were already represented in India by Parry & Company of Madras. The Kirloskars had chosen Parry to act as sole distributor of its products in India as well. So while the initial contacts with the British firms were made through Parry, it was soon clear that Shantanu Kirloskar would have to get to London to complete the negotiations. It was almost impossible to get a flight on any plane going to London. But SL pressed forward with the awareness that to gain the

Kirloskar Brothers' Board of Directors, 1945

Kirloskar Sons' Partners, 1938

advantage of time in business can ensure success. He appealed to a friend and fellow industrialist, Lala Shri Ram, to intervene with the authorities in Delhi to get him two bookings to London.

SLK and his cousin, Nana Gurjar, a lawyer, were on the plane in 1945 and arrived in London during a blackout. They hitched a ride to their hotel on any army vehicle. As negotiations began, VE Day was declared. It was not long before plans were afoot in England to "inspect" the enemy's industrial developments during the war. During one of the negotiating sessions, SLK overheard the British executive make plans to go to Germany to lay claim to interesting technologies. He advised SLK to get in on the action. When SLK returned to India, he convinced the authorities to sponsor a similar delegation from India. The outcome was that SLK spent four months travelling throughout Germany in the Allied uniform which won him entrance to any factory he wished to inspect. He writes in his autobiography:

For four months, through the bitter winter cold of which we Indians had been carefully warned, I visited many factories which manufactured agricultural machines, pumps, machine-tools, diesel engines, small tools and several other products of interest to me. Factories turning out these products were spread all the way from Hamburg in the North-West to Radolfzel in the South and Munich in the South-East.

Whenever I wanted to visit any factory, there was no question of making a previous appointment. It was only necessary to go to the door, ask for the Manager, tell him "I am so and so and I want to see your factory; give me a technical man to show me around" and it was done. I found the interpreters with me could hardly translate the technical conversation, so with by broken German and pictures on paper, I managed sufficiently to get the idea of what was going on. Being also given the authority to ask for any drawings or equipment that I thought would be useful to India, I commandeered from one machine-tool factory three lathes and one shaping machine as models for us to follow in India with their detailed drawings. (Our Mysore Kirloskar at Harihar later started their gear head lathes line from these drawings).[6]

SLK made a few lasting business connections, one which was to result in a German engineer coming to India to spend a decade with SLK in Kirloskar Oil Engines Ltd. Another German industrialist, Fred Schule, whose factory was totally destroyed during the war, struck up a friendship with SLK on the latter's post-war journey throughout Germany. When Schule wanted to sell his company twenty years later, he turned to SL Kirloskar as the preferred buyer.

SLK was anxious to get started on the two new companies which would be set up to make oil engines and electric motors based on the British collaborations. While the Kirloskar group had been manufacturing diesel engines and some electric motors, it felt the need to leap ahead by seeking the latest technology on the market. SLK was again thinking of timing which he knew was a "crucial factor" in business. Upon his return to India from Germany, therefore, SLK and his brothers and cousins worked to get Kirloskars Oil Engines Ltd. and Kirloskar Electric Company off the ground. Kirloskar Oil Engines Ltd. (KOEL) was SLK's responsibility. Kirloskar Electric Company (KEC) would be put together by SLK's younger brother, Ravi, who had returned from the USA in 1942 after taking his degree in electrical engineering from a polytechnic institute. Nana Gurjar joined Ravindra Kirloskar in Bangalore.

SLK chose Pune as the site for the KOEL operation. It had better climate than Bombay and there were many experienced engineers in the military town which doubled as a summer resort. Materials and workshops were also available, but Kirloskar ran into delays in trying to procure the necessary land for the project. Finally the land was purchased and in 1949 the first 5 h.p. Kirloskar-Petter AV1 engines were coming off the line. By 1951, KOEL had declared its first dividend, but SLK related that "the work was hard and for almost the first twenty years there was no fun in either office or factory."[7]

It was difficult enough to get a factory up and running after the war. Then the market for diesel engines was badly disrupted in the early 1950s when the Planning Commission overestimated their demand and allowed imports to a degree which swamped the local market. In fact, demand was low and both importers and domestic producers were stuck. The government agreed to help some of the companies through the bad times its planning had wrought, and KOEL got a Rs 400,000 loan to tide it over. Kirloskar and his colleagues in the industry also formed an association of Indian Diesel Engine Manufacturers to lobby for measures which would eliminate the glut.

The crisis prompted SLK and his associates at KOEL to take a very close look at their operations to see where they could improve. They noted that Parry & Company which had initially served them well as a marketer of Kirloskar products in India was no longer doing an adequate marketing job. They terminated the relationship and, based on their own experience, established a network of dealers and subdealers over the entire country. Lala Shri Ram who was serving as chairman of KOEL also suggested that KOEL get its collaboration agreement with British Oil Engines Export Ltd. amended to allow KOEL to export its engines. In 1954, such an amendment was negotiated. KOEL agreed to drop the famous Petters name from its engine on its export products in exchange for permitting the British company to sell its own engines in India. The British firm thought it would wipe KOEL out of its own market given its well-established name. But a government ban on import of engines and Kirloskar's own penetration of the Indian market with its home-made product made the swap favorable for KOEL only. The British executive who had negotiated the amendment was totally out of touch with the Indian market and the interest of the former colony in patronizing its own country's products.

SLK and his team were following in Laxmanrao's footsteps. Every threat to survival had to be met with new answers. It was the entrepreneur's job to find those answers before it was too late. So in the wake of the Planning Commission disaster came KOEL's determination to take control of its own marketing operation in India and to venture into exports. While their exported products had to be sold at a loss for some time to enable them to break into the international scene, when domestic demand slackened, the exports to more than 14 countries helped tide them over.

The success of Shantanu's engine project turned out to be a landmark in the growth of the Indian diesel engine industry. Until KOEL was born, there were only two other companies in India making diesel engines, Cooper Engineering Company (later amalgamated with Walchand Industries), established in 1932 in Maharashtra and Orient-Engineering Works Ltd. started in the Punjab in the early 1930s. KOEL was the third company and its success encouraged other entrepreneurs to enter the field. By 1960, 23 companies were producing 43,215 diesel engines of all types. By 1982 there were 34 large and medium-scale manufacturers and 800 small-scale manufacturers producing 176,000 engines a year in a wide range of horse powers and for all types of applications: marine, automotive and stationary.

Executives of Kirloskar Oil Engines Ltd. (left to right): C.S. Kirloskar, S.L. Kirloskar, Arun Kirloskar

By attracting the latest technology from abroad, SLK assured that India would have relatively inexpensive small vertical diesel engines for farm irrigation which farmers could move about from farm to farm and well to well. In its continual search for ways to make its engines more efficient and reliable, KOEL developed a wide range of engines from 1.7 h.p. to 3600 h.p. Not only establishing itself domestically as a leading diesel engine manufacturer, KOEL ranks among the top five manufacturers in the world.

The Korean War also helped stimulate a new division at KOEL. The import of bearings was cut off due to war demand abroad pushing KOEL to try to manufacture its own supply. KOEL gradually began supplying others in India who were finding it difficult to obtain bearings. The Bearings Division of KOEL soon began experimenting with substitute materials and tried bronze and white metal in place of steel. By 1960 KOEL had established itself as the largest diesel engine factory in Asia (excluding Japan) with the highest export earnings. But SLK had only just begun.

SLK had in the 1950s taken a trip to Russia with a business delegation and had found most of the factories below standard. In 1957 he became involved in India's export promotion by taking on the chairmanship of the Engineering Export Promotion Council. As head of the Council, SLK made important recommendations to the government for the establishment of an export credit guaranty scheme which other country's governments offered

Kirloskar Cummins' 6 cylinder, 302 hp (225 kw) NT855 engine

their exporters. Soon the Export Credit Insurance Corporation was set up. During that same year, SLK travelled to the USA again on a trade and investment mission led by industrialist G. D. Birla. On this trip, Kirloskar renewed acquaintance with his room-mate from MIT days, Bob Huthsteiner, now President of Cummins Engines. The reunion eventually led to a new joint venture between Cummins and KOEL, but only five years later did the actual incorporation of Kirloskar Cummins Ltd. take place.

The Cummins' president had sent an office worker to the airport to meet Kirloskar, but the young man had not approached the Indian industrialist as planned. Just as Kirloskar was getting ready to leave the airport to make his way to the club where he would stay overnight, the Cummins' representative hestitatingly came forward and asked SLK if he were Mr. Kirloskar. SLK asked him what the reason was for the delay in meeting him. The answer was that SLK looked much younger than Mr. Bob Huthsteiner and the Cummins' representative could not believe that they had both been in school together at MIT. When Kirloskar met with Bob the next day, he was in for quite a shock as Huthsteiner had gone completely white-haired and seemed much older than SLK looked or felt himself. They were both 54 years old at the time.

Regardless of how the busy intervening years had settled on the two old friends, discussion began in earnest about the possibilities of doing some business together. Kirloskar would come up against Cummins' interest in having majority control of any joint venture to produce internal combustion engines. Cummins wanted nothing less than 75 percent equity. Since the Kirloskars had never been in a minority position in any of their firms, preferring to work on a technology transfer, rather than equity, basis, there was little point in continuing the talks at the time. But two years later, a team from Cummins visited India and a 50/50 joint venture proposal was worked out. The public offering of shares in the new joint venture was oversubscribed by 200 times. Start-up operations were difficult, but it was Chandrakant, SLK's elder son, who was to cut his industrial teeth on the Kirloskar Cummins joint venture.

Kirloskar Cummins' executives (left to right): Arun Kirloskar, C.S. Kirloskar, S.L. Kirloskar, and A.K. Mulye

The new joint venture plant which would manufacture engines in the 60 to 1600 h.p. range went up on 100 acres of land at Kothrud on the outskirts of Pune. Delays in deliveries of key raw materials and high interest costs, among other things, threatened the project. The initial strategic planning undertaken so painstakingly by Chanda Kirloskar and his business school whiz kids broke up on the rocks of reality. SLK watched from the sidelines as the faces became longer, the tempers shorter and hope for success disappeared. At one point, Cummins got edgy after the plant went up but projections were not being met. SLK went to America to calm the partner's fears, but found them skeptical about the future of the deal. The Americans even suggested that Kirloskar sell out its interest in the venture to Rolls Royce, a larger, more experienced company. In turn, SLK offered to buy Cummins out. The offer took them by surprise and Cummins ended up throwing its support behind its Indian partner. But SLK was successful in convincing them to withdraw their representatives from the project to let the Kirloskars run the show. Amidst all the external factors which threatened the new venture, Cummins' people in India had perhaps inadvertently gotten in the local partner's way. The various moves to save the joint venture worked. The faith they showed in each other resulted in Kirloskar Cummins Ltd. (KCL) being named the most profitable company in the private sector by the *Economic Times* in 1982. KCL had the highest return on total capital employed at 43.9 percent. It had been done with a concentration on continually modernizing plant and equipment and boosting worker productivity.

KCL is the only engineering firm in Asia whose production processes and engines have been certified by the American Bureau of Shipping and Lloyd's of London. With one of the best after-sales service networks in the country (no dealer is more than 100 kilometers from a KCL engine), 33 quality circles within the manufacturing units, no credit policy for direct sales, and a profitable 30-60 day credit financing policy for its suppliers, KCL built up strong reserves with which to continue modernization of its operations. Productivity was so high that KCL had not added any employees since 1974, but production more than doubled in the ensuing decade.

KCL took a critical decision in 1971 to get out of the manufacture of completed gensets. This was in the face of a high projected increase in demand for gensets. Realizing it could not get a lock on both the genset and engine market, KCL decided to go after a bigger share of the diesel engine market, providing 17 types of engines for genset applications. It would help spur the growth of genset manufacturers, all the time creating a demand for its own engines. The strategy worked and KCL increased its market share for engines from 30 percent in 1972 to 76 percent today.

The Kirloskar Cummins success story is well known both in India and America. It has been a true joint venture in the sense that while Cummins USA continues to give KCL access to its latest engine technology, Kirloskar Cummins in India performs R&D for the American firm and shares in the technology it has developed on its own. KCL is the only company in the world, for example, to manufacture gas powered engines which it then exports to the US and also sells to the Oil and Natural Gas Commission and Oil India Ltd. The demand was not great enough to justify their being manufactured in the USA, so KCL undertook the project in India. From its initial use of simple lathes, KCL's introduction of numerically controlled machines has dramatically reduced its inventory requirements and the time needed to manufacture a wide variety of engines.

As power shortages became the norm, sales of Kirloskar engines soared in the late 1970s and early 1980s. From sales of just Rs 35 crore ($29.2 million) in 1978, KCL moved over the Rs 100 crore ($83 million) in 1982. Export sales continued to increase. By 1980 KCL was applying to the government for a license to manufacture 15,000 trucks in collaboration with Hungarian Railway Carriage and Machine Works. Along the way, it had steadily increased its capacity and had received approval to arrange a collaboration with Holst Engineering Company of the UK for the manufacture of turbochargers. The jumpy start-up which KCL experienced was eventually fine-tuned to a profitable purr. But as in all the Kirloskar ventures, the market ups and downs put them under constant pressure to produce higher and higher quality goods at more controllable costs.

KOEL'S Expansion Keeps Pace as KCL Takes Off

KOEL found itself in the early 1960s in need of more manufacturing space and consequently set up factories in Madras in the south and Faridabad in the northern state of Haryana. In 1959 KOEL had acquired a small foundry, Shivaji Works Ltd., to cater to KOEL's growing requirements for castings. The 1970s were marked by steady growth domestically and solid growth in exports. An export office was opened in the UK (earlier offices had been opened in Rotterdam, Bangkok and Sydney, Australia) and sales had reached $10 million by 1980. The company's products reach 70 countries in six continents.

In 1974 the company developed a new series of medium horse power, light weight, high speed diesel engines from its own R&D department. A four cylinder model, the first of the series, was developed and taken up for regular production. Two more models followed in 1975. Expansion of its bearing manufacturing activities from six million to 12 million pieces per annum was also undertaken. A new plant at Ahmednagar to manufacture metal powder and bimetal strips, the raw materials of bearings, was completed in 1978. KOEL continued to look for new technology in the diesel engine field and by 1983 was implementing a project to manufacture engines in the 500 to 3550 h.p. range in collaboration with SEMT Pielstick of France. KOEL obtained technical design expertise from AVL Gesellschaft of Austria to help implement the Pielstick diesel engine project. Sales moved up quickly at KOEL in the early 1980s to $75 million in 1983.

Kirloskar Electric & Ravi Kirloskar of Bangalore

There were just four of us then, Mr. N.W. Gurjar, Mr. Ravi Kirloskar, Mr. Marathe and me. We shared all the work there was. I remember Mr. Kirloskar would often go out to collect the mail from the 11th Cross Malleswaram Post Office. And if Marathe or I were busy, he would cycle off to the railway station with a thermos slung across his shoulder and bring back tea for all of us. [8]

Kirloskar Electric's first secretary, Laxminarayan Rao, recalls the beginning days of a successful enterprise to manufacture electric motors. As early as 1939, a senior engineer of the group, N.K. Joshi, had built a satisfactory 5 h.p. electric motor. Ravindra Kirloskar, SL's youngest brother, had also started making electric motors at Kirloskarwadi after his return from the USA in 1942. When SL Kirloskar and Nana Gurjar negotiated the technology collaboration with Brush Electrical Engineering of the UK

Kirloskar Electric's early days (left to right): Ravi, Laxmanrao, and N.K. Joshi

toward the end of the war, the group had already some experience with the technology. As Kirloskar Oil Engines was being sculpted by SLK in Pune, Ravi, Nana Gurjar, N.K. Joshi and Rao broke ground for Kirloskar Electric Company (KEC) in Bangalore in 1946.

KEC began with the manufacture of AC motors and gradually expanded its product line to include geared motors, AC generators, transformers, DC motors, welding products, control equipment, induction heaters, tube welders, thyristor control units, and other process equipment and instrumentation. Sales had reached Rs 91 crore ($73 million) by 1984 from just Rs 20 crore ($17 million) ten years earlier. KEC was the first Indian company to meet the demand for electric motors after the war when more and more companies were switching from coal to electricity.

Laxmanrao Kirloskar had sent Gurjar, an expert in company law and finance, to Bangalore to help Ravi, still a young man, get KEC started. Gurjar was involved with the management of several of the group's companies simultaneously, but it was he and Ravi, working very well together, who ensured the successful implementation of the corporate plan. Land was purchased from the Mysore Development Authority whose official was startled at the team's request for 25 acres. Rao recalled that the official asked what they wanted with so much land. Ravi replied: "You are thinking of today. I am thinking 20, 30 years ahead."

When Kirloskar Cummins was set up in 1962 the personnel recruitment policies were quite formal from the outset. Only new, inexperienced people would be hired to be moulded after hiring into the image and likeness of the Kirloskar man. This approach, according to executives, minimizes labor-management disputes, ensures high productivity and product quality. Upon the establishment of KEC, sixteen years earlier, the recruiting was not so scientific, but the results were perhaps as effective. As one of the first engineers to be hired by Ravi tells it:

> Recruitment in those early days was an unorthodox affair. I met him when I was a student in the engineering college. He'd come to test some motors there. He told my Professor, Mr. Thacker, that he wanted to hire a good engineer. I had the habit of working late in the lab and the peon called me to the office. When I was introduced, Mr. Kirloskar said, 'Well, young man, would you like to work for Kirloskar Electric?' Within a fortnight I had joined them.[9]

Ravi would also move to hire someone if he saw some unusual talent or ambition displayed just in passing. Even when KEC had grown larger and recruitment had to be more formalized, Ravi would continue to practice his unerring instinct for recruiting the right person for the right position.

A quieter, more humble person than his older brother, SLK, Ravi had the same restless, inquisitive mind. No new breakthroughs in his field of expertise got by him. As in all the Kirloskar companies, there was a constant upgrading of the plant and equipment. Ravi's reading of all the latest journals, his overseas travels and his constant observations formed the bases for his ideas—which were always being passed on to his executives. KEC also tracked the government's Five Year Plans as closely as possible. Every company had to do the same.

A major diversification took place in 1953 when KEC began to manufacture transformers. A modern foundry was set up the same year to meet casting requirements. When KEC began manufacturing alternators in 1958, it was amid a period of a comfortable power supply which would not last. At first used in mobile power units for defense, when the energy crisis hit in the 1970s, KEC became the biggest supplier of alternators in the country. In 1964, Ravi Kirloskar recognized the opportunity which the invention of the thyristor drive held for DC motors. KEC had begun three years earlier to manufacture DC motors on an experimental basis. With the new invention on the market, KEC signed an agreement with Thorn EMI Automation Ltd. and eventually controlled a large share of the DC motor market in the small and medium range. To protect the infant industry's development, Ravi and Gurjar had as early as 1948 started the Indian Electrical Manufacturers' Association, a few years before SLK was prompted to establish the Indian Diesel Engine Manufacturers Association to lobby against a flood of imports.

It was only in 1970 that Ravi became managing director of KEC, having served from the outset as deputy managing director. He became chairman in 1976. The 1970s were a period of steady growth in sales, but after 1979 sales took off. A bouyant economy had sent sales from Rs 46 crore ($38 million) in 1979 to Rs 72 crore ($60 million) the next year. As sales increased, however, so did costs, making it difficult for KEC to maintain the record peak of profits it had hit between 1979 and 1981. When executives presented Ravi with their operating plan for 1982 on the basis of the great leap forward in sales in the preceding year, Kirloskar hesitated to endorse their production and purchase plans. An executive recalls:

> *He did not produce facts or figures to back him up. But he was a very observant man and he was able to use the past to analyse and interpret the future. Along the way his mind had read the signs portending a worldwide economic recession.*

When the executives projected a Rs 100 crore turnover, Ravi said: "I think you'll be lucky if you touch 80." Sales that year touched only Rs 74.5 crore ($62 million) and profitability declined. In 1982-83, sales increased to Rs 84 crore and in 1984, Rs 91 crore. Ravi Kirloskar's sixth sense was working well.

Ravi Kirloskar, N.W. Gurjar, Mrs. Gurjar and Indutai Kirloskar (l. to r.)

While purchasing the latest technology from around the world, KEC never stopped developing its own R&D as Ravi was well aware of the dangers of total dependence on foreign expertise. For example, with power shortages being the norm after the advent of OPEC, Kirloskar initiated some alternate energy projects, joining with firms like Bajaj Tempo and Amco Batteries to build an electric car prototype. He also persuaded the Karnataka Electricity Board to try out the concept of mini-hydel power plants. He was hopeful that such joint public-private efforts could help accelerate the availability of power without which his country could not move forward in a big way.

Ravi Kirloskar with KEC workers

Toward the latter part of the 1970s, after he had become chairman of KEC, Ravi restructured the management system which boiled down to a broader delegation of powers. This left him freer to think new thoughts. The list of new ideas he left his company upon his death was long enough to keep them busy for ten years, one executive said, and to provide employment for 10,000 people.

KEC went international in 1971 and set up its first joint venture, Indo Malaysia Engineering Company, and one in Kenya to manufacture electric motors, alternators, pumps and diesel engines. Later a trading company was started in Malaysia. Today KEC exports to over 20 countries.

Ravi Kirloskar founded the Indian Association for Quality and Reliability in 1972. Within seven years, there were 2000 members and seven branches. It is no secret that the Kirloskars have emulated the famous quality circles of the Japanese. To reinforce this approach to quality consciousness, Kirloskar sent teams of his managers to Japan to visit plants and quality control associations. These have now become part of a regular routine. Trained on the shop floor of Kirloskar Brothers, Ravi Kirloskar was a frequent visitor to his "shops" throughout his life, checking on the precision and discipline of his team, and looking for new ideas and the people to realize them. He apparently came up with simple solutions to knotty problems quite frequently. The numbers that he ran through his head before finding the solution were no doubt a little more complicated.

Around 1979-80, KEC set up a new production unit in Mysore to produce industrial heating equipment in collaboration with Electroheating

(London) Ltd. and industrial measuring instruments in collaboration with Alfred Herbert Ltd. of the UK. Expansion of the Mysore unit continued with new collaborations being negotiated continuously.

Ravi Kirloskar died in November 1982. Though the Pune-Kirloskars were more in the limelight nationally, the Bangalore-Kirloskars were no less important to the group or the nation. Just as the Birlas have been known to help their executives get set up in their own businesses after a time with the firm, Ravi Kirloskar did the same. One employee noted: "My father was a government servant. I work for KEC. My sons, thanks to Mr. Kirloskar, are independent entrepreneurs."

An amateur photographer, trained singer, and a sportsman, Ravi Kirloskar's true passion was golf. He succeeded in having golf included in the Asian Games which took place in New Delhi in 1982 and selected the Indian team which walked off with two gold and one silver medal. He was a member of the South Asia [Golf] Addicts Society. A friend reminisces:

> *I remember an incident about golf and Ravi Kirloskar. He promoted the game any way he could. He once gave a brand new golf set to one of his customer-friends, but with a proviso: He said, 'I'll give you this set if you give your old one to the caddy.'*

Kirloskar Brothers Is Not Forgotten

Ravi Kirloskar—the golf addict

The first Kirloskar public company, Kirloskar Brothers Ltd., promoted in 1903, has not been left in the shadows of the flashier concerns promoted by Kirloskars since the 1940s. Sales had reached a respectable Rs 62 crore ($52 million) by 1983. Constant diversification of KBL's product line has kept it a vibrant and important factor in the agricultural market as well as in the export sphere. KBL was the first manufacturer of pumps in India. After Laxmanrao's first plough was manufactured back in 1903, a plethora of products followed after the 1920s: centrifugal pumps, diesel engines, lathes, electric motors and compressors. Each of these products gave rise to the establishment of separate Kirloskar ventures eventually.

In the field of fluid handling and control, Kirloskar Brothers leads the way, manufacturing a variety of pumps and valves for industrial and agricultural application. The firm has undertaken turnkey projects for pumping plants in thermal and atomic power stations, off-shore oil platforms, water supply, sewage and effluent disposal schemes. KBL produces hermetically sealed compressors and numerically controlled machine tools. As with most of the other Kirloskar companies, KBL is an international company, with manufacturing and trading ventures in Africa, the USA and UK. Its products reach more than 60 countries.

With the wide variety of products produced by KBL, a drop in demand for one product is not devastating to the firm's performance. As in many companies, development of a healthy export market tides the company over a domestic slump at times. But just as the other Kirloskar companies have to pay special attention to rising costs of inputs, so KBL suffered somewhat in the mid-1970s and after from lower profit margins. This situation corrected itself for the period 1979-1981, but picked up again thereafter. From its principal location at Kirloskarwadi, KBL expanded its facilities to include one at Karad in the Satara district of Maharashtra and at Dewas in Madya Pradesh. In 1982 and 1983, KBL issued both convertible and non-convertible debentures to augment its long-term funding needs for working capital for the next few years. Unlike many Indian groups which promote new companies to make new products, leaving older companies to die on the vine, the Kirloskar companies stay modern through promotion of new products in already established companies for the most part. In the case of Kirloskar Tractors, however, difficulties led the group to merge it with a healthier unit within the group.

Kirloskar Tractors—A Troublesome Diversification

Promoted by Kirloskar Brothers and Kirloskar Oil Engines in 1970, Kirloskar Tractors has not had an easy row to hoe. In 1970 the Kirloskars entered into a technical collaboration with Klocknew Humboldt Dentz AG of West Germany to assemble and manufacture a D 4006 K tractor at its main manufacturing plant at Nasik Road. By 1972 all government clearances had been received. Production commenced in 1974, but sales remained minimal (below 1000 units against a licensed capacity of 10,000 and an installed capacity of 3600 units) through the late 1970s due to lack of adequate financing from the banks. When the situation changed for the better in 1979, sales nearly doubled to Rs 5.5 crore ($4.6 million) and previous years' losses were reduced. In that year, 1979, KTL also achieved 96 percent indigenization. By 1981 sales had climbed to Rs 17 crore ($14 million), but plummetted the next year due to serious labor troubles and recessionary trends in the tractor industry. Such conditions forced KTL to lay off 50 percent of its work-force. By this time, KTL had introduced higher horse power tractors of 100 h.p. and the collaboration with Klockner Humboldt had ended. The major advantage of the Dentz product was its air-cooled engine which, compared to water-cooled engines, was nearly maintenance free, according to SL Kirloskar. He explained: "An air-cooled engine lasts longer and cuts out the expense of radiator, water pumps, hosepipes, and cylinder water-jackets."

Kirloskar Tractors' plant

The Kirloskar tractor nonetheless had trouble getting a profitable piece of the action. There were already giants in the field, Escorts Ltd., the Nanda-Ford joint venture in Faridabad, Haryana State, and Mahindra & Mahindra also produced a popular tractor. Not only that, but the government, in an apparent election year mood, had granted an Indian importer a license to import 3000 tractors at the same time that the Kirloskars were getting ready to bring in the same amount from their collaborator in Germany. The importer had been given the import license based on his representation that he too would be manufacturing tractors soon thereafter. But the tractors were imported from a firm which had gone out of the business recently and was no longer in a position to supply spare parts or new components. The 3000 tractors were sold and the importer returned his manufacturing license to the government a few years later, unused. The Kirloskar tractor project seemed jinxed.

Then the Punjab government imported some East German tractors which turned out to be defective. Farmers throughout the six states in which the tractors were sold were up in arms because the product was useless. All this stalled the viable entry of the Kirloskar product into the Indian market.

In 1982 the Kirloskars decided to merge Kirloskar Tractors with Kirloskar Pneumatic, a profitable company established in 1958 to manufacture compressors for air conditioning units and hand tools. Broom and Wade of the UK were the technology suppliers. Larger compressors, refrigeration and air conditioning plants, torque converters and marine reverse reduction gear-boxes were added under technical collaboration with many foreign firms. SL Kirloskar explained:

> *I did not . . . sign any collaborations and contracts on the basis of preference for some particular countries . . . I took whatever was useful and saleable and could be made at reasonable cost.*

Kirloskar Pneumatic became a division of Kirloskar Tractors. Its sales overshadowed those of Kirloskar Tractors and its successful development of indigenous technologies and a steady demand for its products made it profitable. It was in a good position to use the tax write-offs which came with the merger. Initially, there was talk that Kirloskar Tractors would be merged with Kirloskar Oil Engines or Kirloskar Cummins. The American partner reportedly was not too keen on the idea that KTL be joined to their joint venture. The Tractor/Pneumatic marriage was more of an even match than the other two would have been and has been proceeding smoothly.

Kirloskar Systems Ltd.

A Swedish collaboration, Kirloskar ASEA Ltd., was formed in 1962 (name was changed to Kirloskar Systems Ltd. in 1977 when the collaboration ended) to manufacture motor control gears, switch gears and other electrical and mechanical equipment. It is one of the smallest concerns in the Kirloskar group of companies, but it is also a company whose managing director, Jayant Gurjar, wishes to take into the high tech revolutionary era which is sweeping the world. Originally promoted by Kirloskar Electric (directors and employees received shares), Mysore Kirloskar Ltd. (the first and now one of the largest producers of machine tools established in 1941) and Allmanna Svenska Elektriska Aktiebolaget (ASEA), Kirloskar Systems is on the lookout for computer-related projects. Gurjar is the son of Nana Gurjar whose legal and financial wizardry provided the basis for the successful proliferation of foreign collaborations (more than

70) which have kept the Kirloskars at the cutting edge of technology. It was SL Kirloskar and Nana Gurjar who negotiated the first two collaborations in England at the end of World War II.

Kirloskar Systems executives: Jayant Gurjar, Managing Director (right), and C.S. Kirloskar, Chairman

Consulting and Computers

The Kirloskars also set up a consulting firm and computer systems firm as a natural outgrowth of their turnkey project work and their utilization of a large computer system purchased by KEC for in-house needs. With excess capacity to offer outside users, Kirloskar Computer Systems entered the capital market in 1982 with a public issue to fund an idea of Ravi Kirloskar. When he floated the venture, Ravi commented: "These days, just about one out of every five computer professionals [in the world] is an Indian. As such, software should be no problem at all for us." There is no foreign collaboration tied to Kirloskar Computer Services Ltd. which was initially promoted by Kirloskar Electric and Kirloskar Systems, managed by Jayant Gurjar.

The Kirloskar Corporate Culture

D.V. Tikekar, Managing Director of Kirloskar Consultants, told a journalist once:

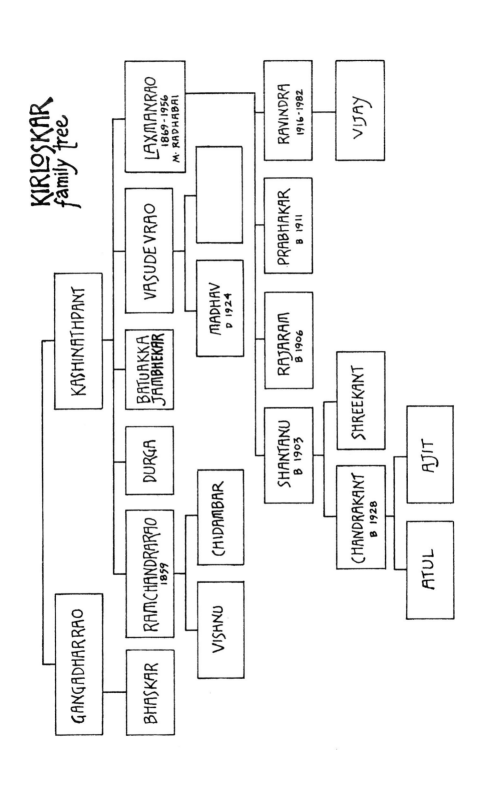

KIRLOSKAR family tree

SL Kirloskar believes that centralized planning which is bad for the economy is equally bad for the Kirloskar group. Thus the companies in the Kirloskar group are wholly independent of each other with perhaps the only link being Mr. Kirloskar himself . . . he leaves his chief executives free to manage their companies as they think best . . . except for certain basic policies which all in the group are supposed to follow.[10]

What are these basic policies or currents that link the Kirloskar companies? Conservative values. Honesty and hard work. Delegation of authority, but also respect for the boss, SLK, is a must. Human development. The Kirloskars have a nose for talent as most successful industrialists do. A concentration on profitability, but not at the expense of quality. Perpetual technological innovation is the key to profitability, quality and productivity. (SLK knows, in any event, how to strike a profitable deal from the start of the negotiations.) An openness to other cultures. If SLK sent a team abroad for training, he made sure the members of the team would be willing to adapt to the new culture, make friends and learn the language. A natural genius for machine-making carried down from the founder and solidified by the best formal education. They were the first to produce their goods in India by and large and reaped the benefit of the absence of initial competition. Pioneers in agricultural machinery, avoiding the traditional route to Indian industrial success via textiles and sugar.

The Kirloskars stuck with what they knew in the way of products and customers. Growing up in a rural area, they understood the mind of the farmer, the cornerstone of their empire. Their after-sales service system is an integral part of their corporate philosophy. The farmer, unlike the mobile urban dweller, does not move on. In agricultural markets, you rarely sell twice in the same place if the initial product was faulty. They have not relied on close relationships with governments to ensure their success. More often than not, they were critical of policies which restrained their natural ability to grow. Just like farmers. Independent, hard-working, no-nonsense. Close to the earth.

Principal Companies in Kirloskar Group

Company	Products
Kirloskar Cummins Ltd.	High horsepower diesel engines
Kirloskar Electric Co. Ltd.	Electrical engineering equipment
Kirloskar Oil Engines Ltd.	Diesel engines
Kirloskar Brothers Ltd.	Pumps and valves
Mysore Kirloskar Ltd.	Machine tools

Kirloskar Tractors Ltd.	Compressed air and gas equipment, refrigeration and air conditioning tractors
Shivaji Works Ltd.	Grey iron castings
Kirloskar Systems Ltd.	Motor starters and control gears, medium voltage switchboards
Kirloskar Consultants Ltd.	Management consultancy
G.G. Dandekar Machine Works Ltd.	
Dixit Printing Press	
Kirloskar Automation Ltd.	CNC turning machines
Wardhaman Automotive Electricals Ltd.	Automotive electricals

Overseas Ventures

Indo-Malaysia Engineering Co. BHD (Malaysia)	Electric motors and AC generators
Kirloskar (Malaysia) SDN BHD (Malaysia)	Assembly of coupled parts
F.H. Schule Gmbh (Hamburg, West Germany)	Diesel engines, grain processing plants
Hydodyne Ltd. (Mauritius)	Manufacture and marketing of pumps and valves
S.P.P. Inc. (U.S.A.)	Marketing of pumps
S.P.P. International Ltd. (U.K.)	Marketing of pumps
Kirloskar Kenya Ltd. (Nairobi, Kenya)	Marketing of Kirloskar products in Kenya

Mafatlal

Cotton textiles
Petrochemicals
Caustic Soda
Dyes
Building Materials

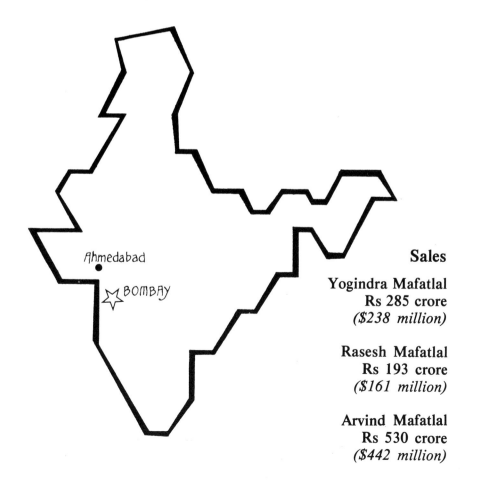

Sales

Yogindra Mafatlal
Rs 285 crore
($238 million)

Rasesh Mafatlal
Rs 193 crore
($161 million)

Arvind Mafatlal
Rs 530 crore
($442 million)

Headquarters
Mafatlal House
Backbay Reclamation
Bombay, India 400 020

Heads of Groups
Arvind Mafatlal
Yogindra Mafatlal
Rasesh Mafatlal

Mafatlal Gagalbhai (1873-1944)

MAFATLAL

Forty-five miles from Ahmedabad, near the industrial complex of Nadiad, is an ancient shrine. Projecting a listless image for most of the month, the picture changes dramatically on the days of the full moon, when a mela held nearby draws people from the surrounding countryside. Among the hawkers who vie with the priests to make the faithful part with their money is a young boy of thirteen. Nervously spreading out his small bundle of fabrics on a mat, he listens attentively to his father's sales patter. The year is 1886 and the boy's name, Mafatlal. Watching the scene, few could have imagined that the boy was to become one of India's shrewdest industrialists and the founder of the third largest industrial empire with sales of Rs 1005 crore ($838 million) producing cotton textiles, chemicals, jute, dyestuffs, caustic soda and building materials, and ready to expand into any area which promises growth.

Mafatlal's success was due as much to the changing business environment as to his entrepreneurship. The latter part of the nineteenth century was an era of transition and upheaval for India. Fundamental changes manifested themselves not only in colonial conurbations like Calcutta, Bombay and Madras, but also in smaller centers. Ahmedabad, a city established in 1411, was no exception. Its inhabitants watched with astonishment tempered with concern and hope as one capitalist after another tried to propell the city into the forefront of India's industrial movement.

Situated in the heart of India's cotton growing tract and with a long tradition of spinning and weaving, it was only natural that Ahmedabad's participation in the industrial revolution would be in the form of modern textile mills. The development spurred by pioneers like Ranchhodlal Chotalal and Kasturbhai Lalbhai caught on fast and by the turn of the twentieth century 25 mills had been erected. These mills in turn opened up new avenues for all types of local business people. One of those able to seize the opportunity to move ahead, rising above traditional caste occupations, was Mafatlal.

An Ambitious Ahmedabadi

Born June 22, 1873, son of Gagalbhai, a master weaver and petty merchant of Ahmedabad dealing in gold lace, Mafatlal entered business when he was barely thirteen. He had already been married six years. Business meant scouring the neighboring countryside for buyers of the bundles of textile goods which hung from the shoulders of Mafatlal and his father. Some years later Mafatlal and his father were able to establish their own small shop where they sold fabrics woven by themselves as well as those manufactured by the new mills.

After his father died, Mafatlal continued to peddle goods from village to village, all the while keeping a close eye on their shop. In these early days it seemed highly unlikely that he would be able to break away from his social heritage. His father was a Kanbi, an agricultural caste positioned fairly low in society. His ancestors had lived for generations in Ahmedabad without making their fortune, and there was no reason to believe that things would change appreciably. Neither properous nor educated, Gagalbhai had left his family in much the same condition as he had found it on his birth. Thus Mafatlal had barely acquired any formal knowledge. He had only his ingenuity upon which to rise above his circumstances.

Mafatlal was nonetheless ambitious to the core. During the course of his hawking, he cultivated wealthy, reliable and progressive-minded merchants and dealers, winning their trust and confidence. The contacts proved invaluable when he embarked on the industrialist's path, for not only did they finance him, but at interest rates far below industry norms.

Besides trading in fabrics, Mafatlal took up a job as a millhand in one of the new textile mills. He weighed cotton bales and kept an accounting of them. The new job gave him direct access to the workings of large-scale industry. He absorbed the experiences quickly and soon was ready to place his foot on the first rung of industrial prominence. By the time he died, Mafatlal was one of India's largest cotton textiles magnates, owned a jute mill and had substantial interests in insurance, shipping and sugar. But more important— along with his sons and grandsons—he had established nothing less than an institution. Even though he attained his success in the pre-licensing era when taxation was minimal, few fortunes could be said to have been made without some wheeling and dealing. As a family, the Mafatlals came to have a remarkable record in Indian business, distinguishing themselves by their scrupulous business practices.

The millhand job introduced Mafatlal to Chandulal Acharatlal Mahadevia, a fellow Kanbi, and an Englishman, Arthur Gordon Shorrock. The former was a master weaver like Mafatlal's father, and the latter, the manager of a mill near Ahmedabad which enjoyed close connections with British machinery manufacturers in England. The friendship between the three in due course of time became the basis of a partnership, Mafatlal Chandulal & Co., which in 1905 took over the management of a small defunct mill. They renamed it The Shorrock Spg & Mfg Co.

Before they could assume control of the mill, however, they needed funds. Though experienced in the cotton textile trade, neither of the three partners had sufficient capital to launch themselves as millowners. To solve the problem they evolved an innovative scheme which met with instant success. Until as late as 1967, most business concerns in India were run by managing agencies which pocketed large chunks of the profits of the managed companies, in addition to making money through commissions for supplying the units under their management with raw materials, energy and other commodities. Knowing full well that few would invest in a venture promoted by unknown and impoverished entrepreneurs, the three promoters promised anyone who bought shares in the mill a corresponding share in the managing agency. This ploy assured investors that they would get some return on their investment. Thus Mafatlal and his friends easily mustered the required funds to acquire their first mill. Equally shrewd was their method of retaining control of the managing agency. They issued 100 "promoter" shares with a face value of Rs 1000. But they were bought by "promoters" for only Rs 25. Mafatlal managed to buy an unspecified, but obviously substantial, number of these shares, paving the way for his eventual unchallenged control of the managing agency.

The timing of the takeover could not have been more perfect. The British government had just committed a faux pax by partitioning Bengal. The resultant outcry among Indians provided a platform for the fledgling nationalist Congress Party of India from which to launch their opposition to British rule. Starting their attack for independence by first demanding economic freedom, the Congress Party urged Indians to buy "swadeshi" (or Indian-made) goods. Units like the Shorrock Mills, despite having an Englishman at the helm, rode the wave of general prosperity which the new political situation ushered in.

Profits poured in for other reasons as well. Shorrock, using his connections, had bought new machinery for the mill on highly advantageous terms. Mafatlal's trading connections ensured that with the right product mix, dealers would lift their stock willingly. And he concentrated on producing goods of coarse and medium quality which were in great demand. The mill did extremely well, so much so that when in 1912 a mill in the neighboring town of Nadiad came up for auction, the three partners acquired it and named it the New Shorrock Mills.

The new acquisition was a calculated gamble. Mafatlal himself was not in favor of bidding for the mill, being somewhat awed by the steep bids of other competitors. But the general manager of the Shorrock, one Gordhandas H. Patel "literally egged the Sheth into clinching the deal at the auction," recalls an old associate of the family. Taking help from the same people who had helped finance the acquisition of his first mill, Mafatlal got down to putting the New Shorrock into working order. Gordhandas proved to be astute as well as persuasive. The reorganized mill soon became a profitable addition to the group's activities.

Because of India's colonial status during the important formative years of its industrialization, international political events have frequently played a crucial role in that process. Thus World War I became a key factor in the Mafatlal success saga. With its insatiable demand for goods of all types, the

Mafatlal House, Backbay Reclamation, Bombay

war ushered in an era of prosperity for India. Furthermore, the German blockade of Britain resulted in halting, if only temporarily, competition from European goods which enabled India to develop a tiny industrial base for the first time. The war also opened the eyes of the British who now came to feel that an industrialized India would be of better use to it than merely an agricultural one supplying raw materials.

For Mafatlal and many others in business, these events meant large orders, and even larger profits. Consequently between 1912 and 1919, the scope of his business activities expanded exponentially. Though the partnership with Mahadevia and Shorrock still continued for a while longer, Mafatlal began to increase his individual activities. In 1916 he bought the Jaffer Ali Mill, founded by a nawab of Surat in 1885, and renamed it the Surat Cotton Spg & Wvg Mills. Mafatlal's trading activities had never ceased, and these also saw a substantial increase. Trading profits in fact remained of paramount importance well into the 1930s after which his industrial interests gained an edge.

Pransukhlal Mafatlal, Gagalbhai's eldest son

In 1920 he set up the first limited company bearing his own name: Mafatlal Gagalbhai & Co. It was an investment company looking after the financial requirements principally of his own group, but it catered to other industrial enterprises as well. Meanwhile he set up Pransukhlal & Company (named after his eldest son) which, among other things, provided insurance for his mills. Mafatlal also opened a series of shops in Bombay, Calcutta, Bangalore, and Amritsar which operated as selling agents for his mills' products.

By the end of World War I, Mafatlal was an important Ahmedabad businessman whose three mills probably brought in a combined profit of Rs 12 lakh ($1 million). But Bombay was the real business center and Mafatlal hankered to carve out a position for himself there. During the war the three partners had operated a Bombay mill (The Islam Mill) on a lease basis. Though the mill was returned to its owner after the expiration of the lease, Mafatlal's involvement in its management exposed him to the dynamic business environment of Bombay. Thus when a small Bombay mill, The China Mill, founded by a Parsi family in 1887, came up for sale in 1921, Mafatlal bought it through the New Shorrock Mill, and renamed it the New China Mill.

Post-War Expansion

The years after the war were boom years. Everyone was making money. Mafatlal began to expand and diversify. He took steps towards both backward and forward integration. He established cotton gins in Gujarat which could supply his mills with clean cotton and took over in 1918 an existing textile processing plant which he renamed The Indian Bleaching, Dyeing and Printing Works.

Mafatlal dabbled in ventures beyond the cotton textile industry during the 1920s and 30s. Generally his participation was financial, not managerial, and was prompted by a recollection of days when he himself was in need of funds. Mafatlal never forgot that his success had been made possible because of well-wishers who had helped him both with money and advice. With a strong net worth position behind him, he extended similar help to numerous associates. Thus the group came to have equity participation, but little management involvement, in several diverse industries.

The Gujarati, however, was somewhat like a canny Scotsman. There was a streak of practicality within Mafatlal which prevented aid from becoming charity. The tradition started by Mafatlal of providing venture capital to other groups was continued by his descendants. His dabbling in various ventures as minority partner sometimes brought unexpected rewards. On at least three occasions the original promoters were not able to manage the concerns they had floated, resulting in the units coming within the control of the Mafatlals, who then proceeded to turn them around most profitably. This has been the case with Surat Cotton Spg & Wvg Mills (1916), Maharani Shri Mahalsabai Mills (which became a part of the group in 1951), and Indian Dyestuff Industries (1957). It is quite possible that in the near future the Mafatlals will feel compelled to take over the Cellulose products group in which it holds a significant equity interest.

During the war years Mafatlal made contact with the family firm of C. Parikh & Co. It was to lead to a long and fruitful association. Some members of the Parikh family emigrated to Uganda in Africa. With financial support from Mafatlal, they began to establish cotton gins there. Within a remarkably short period they became a name to be reckoned with as 40 ginneries were under their control. Meanwhile in India, Mafatlal established the Bombay Uganda Company in 1920 to market cotton from these African gins. By 1938, however, the Parikhs felt that they had done enough in Africa and returned to India. Mafatlal again came to their aid by helping finance their promotion of Jaybharat Mills, Jaybharat Insurance and Jupiter Mills.

When the post-war depression finally arrived in India (which it did in 1923), Mafatlal was relatively well placed to weather it, in part because of the many investments he had made in so many different industries. In any case, Ahmedabad mills with their emphasis on domestic sales (rather than exports to China and the Far East), a wider product mix, and stronger management structure, were better able to withstand vagaries in the business climate than Bombay mills. As an ex-millhand, Mafatlal knew inside-out the most economical ways of operating a mill, and he applied the Ahmedabad formula to his Bombay mills.

The upshot of all this was that during the difficult period of the late 1920s and 1930s when many well-established mills were in trouble, he acquired several important assets quite cheaply. He bought the Standard Mills from the Tatas, large chunks of valuable real estate in Bombay, and a jute mill in Calcutta. These acquisitions, particularly of a Tata company, finally brought him status and reputation in cosmopolitan Bombay.

By now Mafatlal had come a long way. Persistent efforts at self-improvement had paid off. Dressed in suave Western clothes, Mafatlal presented a vastly changed personality from his early Ahmedabad days. Dedicated application to a mastery of the English language, frequent trips to European countries and minute attention to social niceties helped Mafatlal entrench himself and his family in Bombay society. This position was bolstered by the construction in 1937 of a swank mansion in the poshest of Bombay's residential localities.

The real measure of his strong financial position, however, can be guaged from the fact that in the midst of the depression years he promoted one of his flagship companies, Mafatlal Fine Spg & Mfg Co. Promoted in 1930, it indicated that the busy industrialist was moving in new directions. Until now most of his mills produced coarse, or at the most, some medium quality textiles. Mafatlal was convinced that Indian mills were now capable of producing better quality textiles. The Indian cotton textile industry was now almost seventy years old, and though suppressed through frequent discrimination by the colonial government in favor of Lancashire mills, the Indian mills had built up considerable experience and a stronger base from which to take risks. Moreover, the new nationalistic movement strengthened demand for domestically produced goods, rewarding those who tried to compete with imported goods. In his new mill built on 69 acres of land at Navsari in Gujarat, Mafatlal thus installed machines capable of spinning and weaving counts higher than the 20s and 40s which were until then the industry norms.

True to Mafatlal's expectations, the mill was a success. Flush with

Navinchandra Mafatlal

funds, Mafatlal embarked on further expansion and diversification of his burgeoning empire. Though over 57 by now, his dynamism remained undiminished. In the face of stiff opposition from his sons, he promoted a jute mill in Calcutta. His grandson, Rasesh Mafatlal, recalls:

> *There was a lot of dissension within the family. They did not understand why my grandfather wanted to go to Calcutta when the going was so good in Bombay, nor why he wanted to get into a new business when the existing one was doing so well. Grandfather got quite annoyed and he retorted, 'All right. If you don't agree, you don't agree. I will go to Calcutta. I came penniless and I can go back penniless, but I want to prove to all of you that I am worthy enough to start a new mill in a different corner of this country.' He stayed almost three years in Calcutta. He put up this jute mill, started it, made it into a highly profitable concern and then told the boys to take it over.*[1]

Jute was not the only new industry in which the group embarked in the 1930s. In 1930 sugar had become a very profitable proposition under the government's new sugar policy. Several Indian business houses, Mafatlal's included, jumped onto the sugar bandwagon. In partnership with V. S. Apte and Nihalchand Lalluchand, Mafatlal established the Phaltan Sugar Works. Though he held 40 percent of the equity in Phaltan Sugar, Mafatlal remained outside direct management of the company. Similarly he invested heavily in Maharashtra Sugar (holding almost 20 percent of its equity), but again did not participate in running the company. On the one occasion when he strayed from this policy of taking equity positions without management responsibility, Mafatlal burned his fingers quite badly.

The success of his jute and sugar ventures encouraged Mafatlal to be more ambitious, and to diversify even more. Shipping was the new area he identified and he promoted Ratnagar Steam Navigation Company in partnership with Scindia Steam owned by the Walchand group. But this time management control was with Mafatlal. Ratnagar Steam was a humble operation—it had only one steamer, the S.S. Ratnagiri, which it plied along the Konkan coast. It immediately drew the wrath of the Bombay Steam Navigation Company who felt that this area of coastal shipping was its special preserve. As was the usual international protective device among shipping companies in this era, Bombay Steam initiated a ruthless rate war. All too soon Mafatlal was drowning in uncharted waters. The competition between the two companies began to assume the hues of a conflict between nationalism and imperialism. Bombay Steam was then controlled by Killick Nixon, an English managing agency house having a few prominent Indians like Sir Chunilal Mehta and Sir Purushottamdas Thakurdas on its board as sops to Indian nationalistic fervor.

Gateway of India, Bombay

With little experience in this line of business sufficient to wage battle with Bombay Steam, the Mafatlals turned to Walchand Hirachand. A few years earlier Scindia had baled out another company, the Indian Co-operative Navigation & Trading Company, which had dashed against Bombay Steam and would have splintered but for Walchand Hirachand. Walchand threw himself enthusiasically into the fray, his financial participation in Ratnagar Steam through Scindia serving as the technical basis for his more than willing participation in the fight. He launched his first attack during his presidential speech at a Scindia meeting on November 18, 1937:

> *The wiping out of any Indian shipping venture or its absorption by non-Indians has always been and will always be a serious menace to the development of an Indian merchant navy. It is therefore enlightened self-interest – if not true service – to stand by an Indian shipping concern and prevent it from falling under the axe of the outsiders. It is these broad considerations which have guided hitherto the policy of the Scindia Company in its relation to the other Indian shipping companies on the coast and I am sure you will agree that it is the only sound policy which can give true National shipping the strength it needs to live and grow in spite of the deadly onslaughts of powerful outsiders and without even the semblance of support from the government of the country.*

The British were not slow to return the stinging verbiage. At a session of the Central Legislature, the then Commerce Secretary to the Government of India, Hugh Dow, gave vent to the opposition's position:

> *In this rate war, you have one Indian company less powerful than the other, and a powerful company coming to its assistance, taking the smaller Indian company under its protection rather in the way perhaps that Herr Hitler has taken Czechoslovakia under his protection.*

Soon newspaper readers were being regaled by claims and counter-claims as both Scindia and Bombay Steam embarked on publicity blitzes to bolster their respective defenses. The Konkan rate war rose to fever pitch and ended only on December 20, 1939 when Walchand manipulated a takeover of Bombay Steam.

The episode proved to be too much for Mafatlal, however. He willingly allowed Ratnagar Steam to be merged with Scindia, though the family retained a tiny stake in Scindia's equity as late as 1958. Even after surrendering his interest in the firm, relations between the two groups continued to be cordial and it is only since the 1980s that there has been no member of the Mafatlal family on the Scindia board.

A Period of Consolidation

The floating of Ratnagar Steam Company was Mafatlal's last new venture. He was getting old now and he had his three sons to look after the

Mafatlal Gagalbhai in later years

empire he had built from scratch. Though he never fully retired—his business instincts were far too finely honed to allow that—Mafatlal increasingly mellowed, allowing the reins of business to slip into the capable hands of his eldest son, Pransukhlal.

Like his father before him, Pransukhlal received his business grounding in Gujarat. Proving his capabilities quite early, he was soon rewarded by being given control of all the Gujarat operations of the group. Naturally this entailed extensive travelling between Ahmedabad, Nadiad, Navsari and Bombay. During one of his frequent train trips, Pransukhlal suffered a fatal heart attack, dying on the train. The year was 1938. It was a crushing blow for Mafatlal, and he never fully recovered from it. It prevented him from taking joy in the rapid advances made by the group in the next few years.

In 1939, while World War II ushered in so much destruction, for Indian industry again there were limitless business opportunities. With demand for cloth spiralling upwards, the Mafatlal group's six mills (Shorrock, New Shorrock, Surat Cotton, New China, Standard, and Mafatlal Fine) worked frenetically. The group found little satisfaction in business prospects, however, for Pransukhlal's death was followed in 1944 by that of the founder, Mafatlal himself. Barely a few months later, the youngest brother, Bhagubhai, who had shown signs of mental imbalance, committed suicide. Leadership now devolved on Navinchandra who had little help since his own three sons (Arvind, Yogindra, Rasesh) and Bhagubhai's son, Hemant, were still just raw recruits to the business. Only Arvind had had some business experience, having joined the management team in 1941 when he was 18.

Bhagubhai Mafatlal, tragic son

It was soon apparent that Navinchandra had all his father's business acumen combined with a dash of entrepreneurial spirit all his own. Under his direction the Mafatlal group invested heavily in further expansion of their cotton textile interests to become the third largest millowner in India. This was achieved in a relatively short span of time, for Navinchandra died in 1955, barely eleven years after assuming the chairmanship of the group.

Talking about this period of the group's history, Rasesh Mafatlal describes the duration of his father's guardianship as a period of high profits and consolidation:

> The eleven year period of stewardship under my father was a real period of consolidation. My grandfather was basically an expansionist. My father left the companies in much better shape, completely modernized. And he left a lot of cash in the companies. That's why I call it a period of consolidation. We were not rated as a No. 1 group even in textiles in the days of my grandfather. We had extensive business, but only a reputation for honesty. But under my father's stewardship we probably became the No. 1 textile group in India: from the point of view of quality and high levels of profitability. This we could do.[2]

In 1949 Navinchandra bought two large mills. The pre-independence years saw several European groups disinvesting in India. Hit hard by the swadeshi movement in the 1930s and 40s, these business houses felt that there was no place for them in an independent India. Among those who pulled out were three Jewish firms, all members of the same family, the Sassoons. They had come to Bombay as refugees in 1832 in the wake of the Jewish exodus from Turkey. Penniless, but with international business contacts nurtured over centuries, the founder of the group, David Sassoon, established foundations in the one country which had sheltered them. They became Anglophiles and tried to set themselves up, with some success, as members of the English nobility, with country estates and townhouses, dancing attendance on the English Royal Family. By the 1920s only one Sassoon, Sir Victor, had any personal interest left in India, though they had considerable assets in the form of property, buildings, docks, and cotton mills. With political upheavals, increasing taxation, higher productivity costs, and constant strikes, even Sir Victor gave up. He began to dispose of the Sassoon assets.

Navinchandra bought two of the Sassoon group's mills: Sassoon Spg & Wvg and New Union. At one stroke, the Mafatlal's position among millowners shot up from seventh place to third. The acquisitions were dicey business propositions, however. Established in 1874 and 1888 respectively, the mills were by and large antiques, although New Union had some good looms and spindles which had been put in in 1928 when the original Union Mill had burned down.

The year 1949 was not a particularly good period for the textile industry. Navinchandra's purchase of the Sassoon mills might have raised a few skeptical eyebrows. The only favorable aspect of the deal lay in the fact that

Navinchandra Mafatlal

being now under the complete control of an Indian group, at least the mill
would no longer face boycotts from suppliers, dealers and consumers. But
shortages of raw materials, labor unrest, and uncertainties about the new
government's textile policies continued and made millowners an anxious
class. Navinchandra nonetheless retained his boundless, if perhaps mis-
placed, faith in the textile industry. The Sassoon mills were bought for the
proverbial song. In 1951 he took over yet another cotton mill, the Maharani
Shri Mahalsabai Mill which his father had been supporting for several years.
Refusing further financial aid to the mill at Dewas in Madhya Pradesh,
Navinchandra proceeded to add it to his expanding business empire which
drew the group deeper and deeper into the world of cotton textiles.

In 1947, Navinchandra had set up one of the largest textile machinery manufacturing concerns in India, the National Machinery Manufacturers Ltd. Renamed Mafatlal Engineering Industries Ltd. (MEIL) in 1980, the company's products made in collaboration with leading international firms like Platts of the UK and Ruti of Switzerland, quickly gained acceptability. Sales were helped by protective tariffs promulgated by a government bent on showing the world that India could be self-sufficient. Thus in its jubilee year, MEIL could proudly boast that "more than 25% of the installed spindleage in India were manufactured and supplied by MEIL. Similarly more than 25% of the installed automatic looms were also manufactured and supplied by MEIL."*

In 1954 the group indirectly entered the textile dyes industry by participating in the venture capital of Indian Dyestuff Industries Ltd., promoted by Anandlal Sheth. Though the dye industry was overwhelmingly dominated by Europeans, Anandlal Sheth was emboldened to enter this field in light of the encouraging policies of the new nationalist government which wanted an indigenous base for this industry. Consumers of the product, like the Mafatlals, also supported the idea. But Sheth was inexperienced in business and could not cope with Indian Dyestuff's teething troubles and stiff competition from established foreign firms. The Mafatlals generously supported him with financing for three years, but in 1957 finally took over management of the unit themselves.

The Mafatlal group's involvement in the textile industry now had a truly catholic aspect: from cleaning the cotton to spinning it, weaving it, printing and retailing the cloth, to making the machines to do this, and the dyes to process the cloth. The only non-textile related growth of the group during Navinchandra's tenure came in 1943 when he acquired the Mysore Commercial Union (renamed Mysore Plywood), a building materials firm.

A Push Toward Petrochemicals

With Navinchandra's acquisition of the Maharani Shri Mahalsabai Mill, the Mafatlal interest in cotton textiles reached a saturation point. Though they spent money on continuous modernization with its natural corollary of enhanced capacity, no new mills were erected nor old ones acquired after Navinchandra's death. He was an excellent manager with the cotton industry in his blood. Though his mills earned handsome profits and enjoyed the confidence of the investing public, it is nevertheless apparent that Navinchandra's faith in the future of cotton textiles pulled down the group's ranking in the corporate sweepstakes. As the group's position among millowners rose, their corporate ranking correspondingly fell, hitting an all

---

*Other important textile machinery manufacturers; Texmaco, Central India Machinery Manufacturing Co. (Birla); Machinery Manufacturers Corp. (Mahindra); Laxmi Machine Works, Textool (Laxmi Group); SLM-Maneklal; Star Industries; Suessen Textiles.

time low in the mid 1960s. Then the picture changed dramatically. In less than another decade (1958-1965) the Mafatlal group moved from 15th rank among other corporate groups to third place, overtaken only by the Tatas and Birlas. Their praiseworthy place notwithstanding, the group made a modest third with assets in 1965 of Rs 46 crore ($38 million) compared to the Tata assets of Rs 418 crore ($348 million) and Rs 293 crore ($244 million) for the Birla group.

It was the third generation of Mafatlals, represented by Arvind, Yogindra, Rasesh and Hemant, supported by Laxmanbhai D. Vasa, a relative, which had pushed the group to third place. Arvind had become the head of the group on his father's death in 1955. As the first among equals, Arvind came to the position well experienced despite his young age. He was only 33 years old. With funds garnered during the prosperous years of World War II, and with youth's impatience to make a mark on the world, the third generation of Mafatlals took the critical step of diversification away from textiles. They moved into chemicals and petrochemicals.

The group had begun actively to survey the chemical field only after the acquisition of Indian Dyestuff Industries (IDI) in 1957. Within two years Mafatlal management had resuscitated a faltering company and made it into a highly profitable concern. Success was reflected in the upward movement of IDI's share prices. When the Mafatlals bought IDI, the Rs 100 face value shares were trading for Rs 90. Two years later the same shares had appreciated to Rs 150 and were moving towards Rs 200. In 1960 when the company issued equity right shares (in the ration of 9:1) to support an expansion program, the share market reacted with a phenomenal rise in the share price to Rs 1800 per share (in 1984 the value of a Rs 100 share was Rs 256).

The heady experience of IDI's meteoric recovery at the hands of the Mafatlal group encouraged it to expand in the chemicals industry. It was a short, logical step into petrochemicals too. Soon they had a blueprint ambitious enough for *Time* magazine to file a report. The Asian edition dated May 10, 1963 carried a feature on the Mafatlals, describing Arvind Mafatlal as the canny chairman of a $61.9 million family-controlled business.

> *Mafatlal's jute plant and ten textile mills employ 25,000 Indians, produce 4% of India's cloth, and specialize in the low-cost cottons that make up the traditional dress of most Indians. Dissatisfied with too much dependence on textiles, Mafatlal recently linked up with West Germany's Farbwerke Hoechst to build a $21 million nine-plant petrochemical complex that will be India's largest.*

Shell International Chemical Company was involved in the project and two new companies were established in quick succession, National Organic Chemical Industries Ltd. (NOCIL) and Polyolefins Industries Ltd. (PIL), with Shell holding one third of the equity in NOCIL and Hoechst one third of PIL. By 1968 a modern, integrated chemical complex of 14 plants located on

Arvind Mafatlal at NOCIL facilities

a 290-acre site at Thane had been commissioned, manufacturing a variety of plastics and chemicals such as ethylene, propylene, butadiene, and benzene, along with their derivatives.

Naturally such a sharp escalation in their operations necessitated an overhaul of management patterns within the group. Until now the Mafatlals had pursued a typically "sheth" type of management where all decisions emanated from the top ("sheth" literally means "the boss"). While the system worked in the textile industry which had been nurtured on this diet, it could not work in the technologically sophisticated chemical industry. It was no longer realistic for one or all members of the Mafatlal family to give day to day instructions on minute details such as the daily loom program. Some decentralization and professionalism had to be introduced. A further impetus for change came in the form of the government's move in the 1960s to abolish the managing agency system. Until now all group companies had been maintained under the overall control of Mafatlal Gagalbhai & Sons, a managing agency, and Mafatlal Gagalbhai & Co. Pvt. Ltd., an investment company. The Mafatlals realized that they could not hope to solve these new problems of management and they called in a professor from the Indian Institute of Management in Calcutta.

The result was a completely revamped management hierarchy with strict lines of authority defined from the four Mafatlals down to the most junior executive. The companies were also restructured in keeping with the new government regulations and new holding companies established to retain control. A number of mergers took place around this time, New China Mills became a part of Standard Mills, as did the Maharani Shri Mahalsabai Mills, and New Union Mills was merged into Sassoon Spg. & Wvg.

For the first time, also, there were decentralized operations and working managers did not have to report everything to each brother. To keep some coordination alive, however, Mafatlal Services Pvt. Ltd. was created in 1967 which would manage the group's family shareholdings, provide general economic and statistical reporting important to all companies in the group and provide a pool of management personnel for the group as well.

For a decade it appeared that the new management system was working well. While Arvind Mafatlal was in overall charge of the group, his brothers were managing specific operations. Yogindra became director-in-charge of the two dyestuff companies besides being responsible for cotton purchasing for the group. Rasesh became director-in-charge of the jute mill and one of the cotton mills, besides looking after the marketing of the group's fabrics. The Bhagubhai branch of the family continued to have a low profile as Bhagubhai's son, Hemant, as his father had before him, died at an early age, leaving behind a 13-year old boy whom Arvind immediately took under his wing. Laxmanbhai Vasa was in charge of the other two mills as well as the plywood company.

Under the new system, considerable duplication and friction was eliminated. The streamlined system went right to the bottom line. Sales shot up from Rs 43 crore ($36 million) in 1964 to Rs 476 crore ($397 million) in 1978. Despite its impressive growth, by the late 1970s all was not well within the group. Though the group managed to retain its leading position in India's corporate rankings, it was clear they would soon be overtaken unless they could come up with new projects. But increasing friction among the three brothers seemed to preclude this. Associates of the group were heard to whisper a small ditty to each other: "Raseshbhai proposes, Arvindbhai opposes and Yogindrabhai disposes." Soon the rift was out in the open.

On March 9, 1979 *The Financial Express* predicted an imminent split within the ranks of the Mafatlal top management. The front-page story was a bolt from the blue for bankers, stockbrokers and even the group's own executives. From a low profile, the Mafatlals became the target of widespread speculation and interest.

There were a few who remained unruffled by the news. Operating from that hotbed of gossip, the Mulji Jheta market, some textile dealers and merchants, showing remarkable prescience, claimed they had known that the group would split almost three years earlier. They buttressed their view by pointing to the intrinsic changes which had taken place in the cloth distribution system of the Mafatal group of mills over a three year period.

Mafatlal Gagalbhai, starting life as a cloth trader, had established a wide network of dealers for his mills' cloth. Navinchandra continued the policies set by his father. As the number of Mafatal mills increased, a truly national system of merchants, wholesaler and semi-wholesalers emerged. They were tied to the group as a whole, but not to any particular mill within the group. Handpicked by the Mafatlal marketing department, they were trusted traders who repaid loyalty with loyalty. Around 1976-77, however, the scenario changed. As one trader said: "The sheths started dividing up the wholesalers and merchants and allocated them to individual mills. So now we can only buy from a particular mill, and we are bound to it." From this the traders rightly concluded that a division was on its way.

Unused to such publicity, the three Mafatlal brothers shied away from public statements. While Arvind insisted that the division was an internal affair, the others either refused to comment at all or murmured innocuous remarks about the need to separate so as to remain outside the restrictive monopoly dragnet, a statement which fooled no one.

If the brothers were reticent, their friends and associates were not. Everyone had his or her own pet theories for the split. Some pointed to the vast differences in the personalities of the three brothers. All three had cotton in their bones but there the similarity ended. Rasesh, with a flair for finance, wanted to steer the group onto a much faster track than the others wished. Yogindra, conservative and cautious, was quite happy to let events carry the group along. And Arvind, who had been chairman of the group since he was 33 years old, was slowly being weaned away from the tension-filled board room to India's poor villages by his guru, Ranchhordas Maharaj. The latter came to wield enormous influence on Arvind and he gradually withdrew from active participation in business, throwing himself into the role of the Indian capitalist's conscience.

Nature abhors a vacuum and Yogindra, as the next in seniority, moved in to fill the gap in the group's leadership caused by Arvind's withdrawal. With his low-key approach, however, it was but natural that clashes with younger brother, Rasesh, would become routine.

The potentially explosive situation became even more so when Arvind's sons, Padmanabh and Rishikesh, joined the top management. In the 1965 reorganization, each of the four Mafatlals (Arvind, Yogindra, Rasesh, Hemant) had been given an operating unit and a distinct function. After Hemant's death, Mafatlal Fine had come under the overall charge of Arvind in trust for Mihir, Hemant's son. The entry of Padmanabh and Rishikesh now threatened the delicate balance. Some Mafatlal managers have tried to explain the split as a reaction to Arvind's attempts at carving a position for Padmanabh in Standard Mills, a unit under the direct supervision of Rasesh.

As news of the split spread, conjectures about its cause became almost libellous. Within a relatively short span of time the mode of division was apparent, if not the motives. According to a tacit agreement probably made a generation ago, the three Mafatlal assets were equally divided—one half going to Navinchandra's three sons, and the second half going to Mihir, the only grandson of Bhagubhai.

This was in keeping with Hindu joint family customs whose communistic nature compells an equal division of assets along familial lines, irrespective of the rights of the earner of these assets. Thus, even though the group's growth was largely engineered by Arvind (as both his brothers readily admit even after years of strained relations), Arvind, Yogindra and Rasesh each got merely 17 percent of the Mafatlal cake. The equation changed, however, by the action of Mihir. Brought up by Arvind who played the role of a surrogate father, Mihir threw in his lot with Arvind, so since 1979 in effect there are only three distinct groups.

The 1979 Mafatlal Split

The Classic Group	The Sungrace Group	The Stanrose Group
(Arvid & Mihir)	(Yogindra)	(Rasesh)
Mafatlal Fine Spg. & Mfg. Co. Ltd.	IDI	Standard Mills Co. Ltd.
Mafatlal Industries Ltd.	Hoechst Dyes & Chemicals Ltd.	Surat Cotton Spg. & Wvg. Mills Pvt. Ltd.
National Machinery Manufacturers Ltd.	Mihir Textiles	Mafatlal Apparels
National Organic Chemical Industries Ltd. (NOCIL)	Mysore Plywoods	
Polyolefins Industries Ltd. (PIL)	Pransukhlal & Co. Pvt. Ltd.	

The years following the split were particularly traumatic. In the midst of healing wounds caused by the Solomon-like split of the family's business, the companies faced a deteriorating industrial climate. The unprecedented Bombay textile workers strike in 1982, which was to last 18 months, led by the fiery and militant trade union leader, Datta Samant, came on the heels of the worldwide recession. Initially several millowners had secretly welcomed the strike as stocks of unsold fabrics and frequent power cuts had already eaten into the profits of the mills. But as months went by without any dialogue between management and labor, red ink began to splash across the balance sheets of heretofore healthy mills. The Mafatlal companies did not escape, despite their strong foundations which were reinforced by the 1965 reorganization. Their very heavy involvement in cotton textiles naturally proved a disaster. All three groups registered poor results as a result of the prolonged strike.

MAFATLAL
family tree

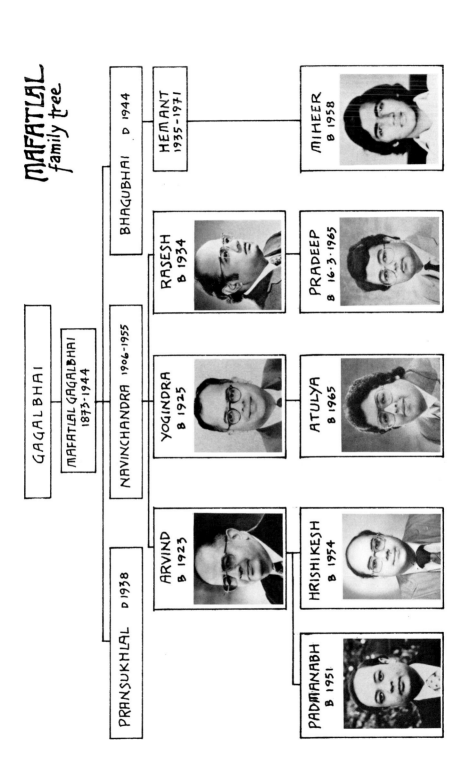

GAGALBHAI

MAFATLAL GAGALBHAI
1873–1944

PRANSUKHLAL D 1938

NAVINCHANDRA 1906–1955

BHAGUBHAI D 1944

ARVIND B 1923

YOGINDRA B 1925

RASESH B 1934

HEMANT 1935–1971

PADMANABH B 1951

HRISHIKESH B 1954

ATULYA B 1965

PRADEEP B 16·3·1965

MIHEER B 1958

There was nothing to be done except to tighten up administration and cut costs wherever possible. Some mills began to lower the price of cloth. Mafatlal mills followed suit for some of their fabrics, but as each mill caved in one by one, they were forced to cut prices across the board. Though the workers gradually returned to work, the damage had been done. The mills have not returned to their former health even after two years.

Arvind and Mihir Mafatlal

Other equally distasteful measures had to be taken, including drastically reducing the sponsorship of sportsmen. The Mafatlal group as a whole had, over the years, earned laurels for the high performance of its sportsmen at local and national meets. For years they had one of the best cricket teams in the country with ace cricketers and one of the top five football clubs. It was a hard decision to take, especially as the Mafatlals gained tremendous advertising mileage from sports reporters. It was basically Arvind's decision since most of the sportsmen were employed in Mafatlal Fine Spg. & Wvg. Since the 1979 split Mafatlal Fine had been part of the Classic Group headed by Arvind. But as one of his executives pointed out: "So bad has been the performance of the company last year (1983) on account of the prolonged textile strike that, for the first time in 51 years, we could not pay a dividend to our shareholders this year." Nor were other group companies faring much better. MEIL's Kalwe plant, just next door to the shut-down Mukand Iron & Steel (see chapter on Bajaj), faced a similar lock-out for 13 months as a result of labor problems. Production started up again only in January 1983. Though the company's Baroda unit worked satisfactorily, naturally the results for 1981-1983 were poor.

Meanwhile Mafatlal Industries also suffered setbacks. The sale, however, of its Pune-based dye and chemical unit (formerly known as Sahyadri Dyestuffs & Chemicals Ltd.) to Deepak Nitrite Ltd. (part of the upcoming business house of C.K. Mehta) cushioned losses. Further, imports of cheap chemicals put pressure on profit margins in PIL. The silver lining proved to be NOCIL where gross profits shot up from Rs 4.83 crore in 1982 to Rs 10.32 crore in 1983.

As the textile crisis receded, the Arvind-Mihir group began to consolidate. With a pick-up in demand, cotton textile mills decided to modernize and The Classic Group risked expanding their textile machinery activities by promoting Padmatex Engineering. Offering the latest in draw and speed frames, the new company's prospects are reputedly good.

Of the three Mafatlal groups, the Arvind-Mihir group is the weakest, managerially speaking. Top management consists of Arvind (who has semi-retired from business), his two sons Padmanabh and Rishikesh, and nephew, Mihir. Internal differences have strained relations between Arvind, Padmanabh and Mihir, leaving the brunt of management responsibilities of looking after 67 percent of the Mafatlal empire on the young shoulders of

Rishikesh. Padmanabh's health is also weak, and stress is inadvisable. Disinclined to involve himself in a volatile situation which might easily get out of hand, Mihir immerses himself in computers. No doubt a highly seasoned and intensely loyal management cadre built up over decades help to keep the Mafatlal group running smoothly, but several executives privately worry that the internal tensions prevent growth.

Arvind Mafatlal with sons Padmanabh (l) and Rishikesh (r)

Arvind & Mihir Mafatlal Group (The Classic Group)

Company	Products
*Mafatlal Fine Spg. & Mfg. Co. Ltd.	Textiles
*Mafatlal Industries Ltd.	Textiles, chemicals
*National Organic Chemical Industries Ltd. (NOCIL) –Thane –Ratnagiri, Maharashtra	Agrochemicals, petrochemicals
*Polyolefins Industries Ltd. (PIL)	Polyethylene, rubber chemicals
Mafatlal Engineering Industries Ltd.	Textile machinery
Padmatex Engineering Ltd.	Textile machinery
M.G. Consultancy Services Ltd.	Computer consultancy
Mafatlal Engineering Exports Ltd.	Trading, export & import
Overseas ventures: Mafatlal Ltd. U.K.	Import & export of cotton goods, chemicals
Polyolefines Pipe Sdn. Bhd. Malaysia	Steel pipes

* Sales over $50 million

Rasesh Mafatlal

At the time of the split, Rasesh had three companies with combined sales of Rs 81 crore ($66 million). By 1984 this figure had reached Rs 189 crore ($156 million) even though the number of companies remained static.

In common with the other two Mafatlal groups, Rasesh's group had a baptism by fire. Some of the oldest mills were in the Stanrose fold: Surat Cotton was established in 1861, the Prabhadevi unit of Standard Mills was the Sassoon unit set up in 1892 while the Sewree unit was the original China Mill established in 1892. The Dewas unit was relatively a youngster, having come up in 1939. Admittedly new machinery had been installed, yet combined with the Bombay textile strike and overwhelming competition from the powerloom sector, these mills began to look suspiciously like white elephants.

The chemicals division of Standard Mills, one of India's largest producers of caustic soda and its derivatives, hardly looked promising either, as demand from cotton mills, the chief consumers, declined and a sharp price war among caustic soda manufacturers ensued to entice whatever demand there was. But as the textile strike fizzled out and demand for cloth picked up, the horizon began to clear. A commendable feature of the group at this time was that while the borrowings of other Bombay mills shot up to impossibly high levels, the balance sheets of the Standard Mills for the difficult 18-month period 1982-83 showed a relatively conservative debt equity ratio of 1.94:1.00.

Rasesh has often been described as "the flamboyant Mafatlal." But the term is more relative than absolute. It is true, however, that he is more accessible than his brothers. Alone among his generation, he has some inclination toward public life. This is reflected in his acceptance of membership to the FICCI executive committee. For almost 20 years the Mafatlals had kept away from the federation — since 1962, in fact, when along with the Tatas they walked out of FICCI in protest over the refusal of the association's leadership to take a positive stand on the Dalmia-Jain scandal.

Rasesh Mafatlal Group (The Stanrose Group)

Company	Products
*Standard Mills Co. Ltd.	Textiles, caustic soda
Surat Cotton Spg & Wvg Mills Pvt. Ltd.	Textiles
Mafatlal Apparel Mfg. Co. Ltd.	Readymade garments, textile trading
Sandeep Holdings Ltd.	Investment activities
Overseas Ventures: Mafatlal Ag. Zurich, Switzerland	Trading

* Sales over $50 million

A government committee appointed to investigate the affairs of the Dalmia-Jain group published highly damaging conclusions of financial

irregularities and stock manipulations. The report was published in the same
year that Shriyans Prasad Jain, one of the leading figures in the Dalmia-Jain
group, was president of FICCI. The Mafatlals and Tatas felt that Jain should
resign immediately, but other FICCI heavyweights maintained that a hasty
resignation would damage the prestige of the federation. The Mafatlals and
Tatas strongly disagreed and consequently resigned, considerably weakening
the association. With the disintegration of the Mafatlal group into three
factions, independent views could now be maintained, and Rasesh joined
the federation in 1982.

Rasesh echoes his brother, Yogindra, when he expresses a desire to
expand and diversify in directions other than textiles. While the mills have
repaid the investments made in them many times over, with the powerloom
sector becoming increasingly more competitive Rasesh sees little future in
large composite mills. Diversification into the fields of pharmaceuticals and
fine chemicals are under active consideration.

Differences with his brothers have not soured Rasesh's feelings for his
family. The limited cooperation with Yogindra at the top has not upset what
is a remarkably close cooperation at junior levels. The younger generation
looks to him for help and advice. It was to Rasesh that nephew, Padmanabh,
turned when the latter had differences with his father, Arvind.

Yogindra Mafatlal

Extremely reticent and fiercely protective of their personal lives, the
Mafatlals rarely give interviews or participate in public activities. Perhaps
the most reclusive member is Yogindra Mafatlal, head of the Sungrace group
which, after the 1979 split, comprised five companies with an aggregate sales
turnover of $93 million. Yogindra's studiously low-key approach cannot
mask the fact that his group has taken impressive strides in the last five years,
more than doubling its turnover to $237 million. The performance is all the
more impressive considering the handicaps Yogindra faced in 1979.

Although Yogindra was not a millowner, he was badly hit by the
Bombay textile strike since both his major companies, IDI and Mafatlal Dyes
& Chemicals (formerly known as Hoechst Dyes & Chemicals), were major
suppliers of textile dyes. Reorganization and consolidation was made all the
more difficult because of a major shake-up in Hoechst Dyes & Chemicals
(HDC) which saw its sales tumble from $76 million to $25 million. At the
same time Hoechst Ag of West Germany which held a one-third interest in
HDC decided to pull out of India, forcing Yogindra to buy out their shares in
a period of financial strain.

Several factors were responsible for HDC's shake-up. HDC had been
jointly promoted by Hoechst Ag and the Mafatlals mainly to market PIL's
products. With both companies doing well, HDC expanded and went public
in 1973. Its shares were well received by the public as there was a steady rise

in earnings, dividends and bonus share issues. HDC gradually began to expand and diversify, setting up a small manufacturing unit at Mulund, Bombay, to produce synthetic resin dispersions in addition to undertaking the marketing of various plastics and chemicals manufactured by other companies. Still over 60 percent of its business was directly linked to PIL, Arvind's company. This link was severed in 1979. At this point Hoechst Ag, with its own substantial investment in Arvind Mafatlal's firms, NOCIL and PIL, decided to withdraw from HDC, sparking off immediate rumors that Yogindra would not be able to buy up their shares. The takeover wolves licked their chops. Yogindra squelched the rumor when he officially changed the name of the company from Hoechst Dyes & Chemicals to Mafatlal Dyes & Chemicals. Even so, it was a sadly diminished company. The silver jubilee was celebrated on a somber note. Speaking to shareholders at the annual general meeting, Yogindra tried to inject a note of enthusiasm and hope:

Your company will, however, continue to manufacture and sell synthetic resin dispersions, the turnover of which increased by about 15% during the year under review. Efforts continue to be made to increase further the production and sales of these dispersions. Your Company will also continue to market other products and to act as an indenting agent for polyester stable fibre. Your Directors are pleased to inform you that the company has already taken up marketing of dyestuffs and pigments manufactured by Indian Dyestuff-Industries Ltd. Barring unforeseen circumstances, your Directors expect to achieve an aggregate ex-stock turnover of Rs 30 crores during 1984.

The tide was still to turn for Yogindra. News trickled in that Mafatlal Plywoods (formerly Mysore Plywoods) was on strike. The strike lasted for seven months. Matters were not helped by Yogindra's acquistion of a small cotton textile mill in Ahmedabad. Associates explained this apparently inexplicable action by pointing out that Yogindra has been deprived of any textile manufacturing activity by the terms of the split. This was felt to be a very real deprivation by one whose family had been in cotton textiles for well over a century. It was also felt that only by being a millowner could a certain status in society be achieved. While this mode of thinking may have prevailed in 1979, there appears to be no trace of it in 1985. Talking about future growth, Yogindra Mafatlal sees little future in large, integrated cotton mills, or in dyestuffs. "I want to diversify into consumer articles if I can. Anything really, if it's profitable . . . I want to keep moving . . . If I stop, I cannot keep level. That does not mean that I have to force my pace. Just that one should always look at proposals of growth. Move one step forward at a time."

By 1984 it was clear that the Sungrace group was out of the woods. Yogindra was after all a descendant of Mafatlal Gagalbhai and Navinchandra. Careful husbandry of his companies' resources paid dividends and soon he was in the black, if only marginally.

In June of 1984 Yogindra hit the headlines again when he purchased the SG Chemicals & Dyes unit at Ranoli (Gujarat) from Ambalal Sarabhai Enterprises for $14 million. Describing the plant established by the renowned scientist, Vikram Sarabhai, as a well-laid out garden returned to nature, Yogindra saw distinct possibilities in the acquisition. His company, IDI, was a major consumer of the unit's products. It was a step in backward integration—so backward into chemicals that there were opportunities to move out of the world of textiles and into the sunrise plastics industries.

A retiring man by nature, and extremely religious (one is greeted by a "Jai Shri Krishna" rather than the more prosaic and westernized "Hello"), Yogindra attributes his success to his wife, Madhuri: "I am what I am because of my wife, who is even more publicity-shy than I am. Though she prefers to remain incognito, 98% of my person is my wife." Atulya, their son, is equally willing to endorse this view, remarking that she is the backbone of the family, one who soothes, cajoles, scolds and brings out the best in their family. Young and ambitious, Atulya would like to see the Sungrace group move onto a fast track, "but not at a pace where one would get out of breath," he says with a caution worthy of his ancestors.

Yogindra Maftlal Group (The Sungrace Group)

Company	Products
*Indian Dyestuff Industries Ltd.	Vat dyestuffs
*Mafatlal Dyes & Chemicals Ltd.	Synthetic resins, markets dyestuffs
Mihir Textiles Ltd.	Textiles
Matulya Mills Ltd.	Textiles
Mafatlal Plywood Industries Ltd.	Plywoods, block boards, doors
M. Pransukhlal & Co. Pvt. Ltd.	Holding company, export house

Overseas Operations:

Company	Products
Matangi Dyestuff Industries Ltd. Bangkok, Thailand	Dyestuffs
Indian Dyestuff Industries Ltd. Baltimore, U.S.A.	Trading
Megara Ag. Zurich, Switzerland	Trading
Milee Corp Pte. Ltd. Singapore	Trading

---

* Sales over $50 million

Mahindra

Jeeps
Tractors
Alloy and specialty steel
Electronic equipment
Engines
Elevators
Textile machinery
Material handling equipment

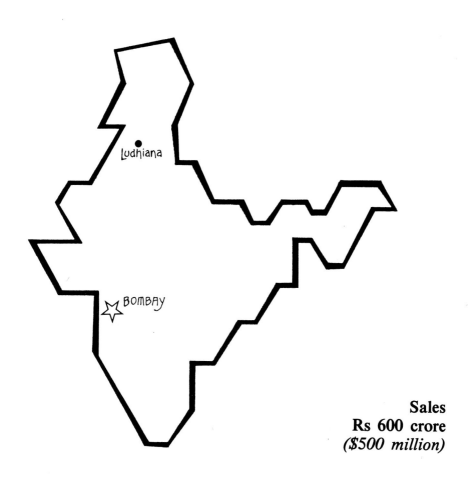

Sales
Rs 600 crore
($500 million)

Headquarters
Gateway Building
Apollo Bunder
Bombay, India 400 039

Head of Group
Keshub Mahindra

K.C. Mahindra (1890-1963)

J.C. Mahindra (1894-1950)

MAHINDRA

If one wants to drive from the Khyber Pass down the full length of India to Kanyakumari, the probability is that one cannot do it unless one uses the ubiquitous four-wheel drive known as the "Jeep." While India is one of the oldest civilizations in the world, besides being one of the most densely populated, there are few good roads running through the length and breadth of the country, apart from the Grand Trunk Roads built soon after the 1857 Mutiny which were built to facilitate the movement of troops from one trouble spot to another. Paucity of funds have been the main reason for this lacuna in the infrastructure of the country. Besides, the railways had already proved efficient and were filling the void somewhat. So a government hard-pressed to allocate limited resources to unlimited necessities, postponed road construction activity to an indefinite future date.

The potential in this situation was perceived simultaneously by three men: K.C. Mahindra, his brother, J.C. Mahindra, and Ghulam Mohammad who teamed up in 1945 to set up a private limited company under the name of Mahindra and Mohammad to import steel and jeeps.

The initiative for founding the company reportedly came from KC Mahindra. KC was a senior executive and junior partner in Martin Burn, one of the oldest British agency houses in India with interests in construction, railways, collieries, docks, mines, tea, timber, power, cement, iron and steel and refractories.

Khatri Soods by caste, the Mahindras trace their roots to a small village in Ludhiana, Punjab. KC's father, Bishen, was a landowner with fairly extensive properties, a large portion of which was lost to Pakistan in the partitioning of British India. Bishen died young, but his capable wife — illiterate, uneducated — brought up their two sons, KC and JC, and looked after their inheritance as best she could. Her uneducated status apparently bothered her, for she determined that her boys should get the best education possible. KC was sent to Cambridge and JC to Oxford. It was an unusual step — few Indians visited Britain, let alone stayed there. Moreover, a Western-style education was expensive for an Indian family. Naturally Oxford and Cambridge were even more expensive.

Even though KC and JC knew that they would never starve, they were fully conscious of the necessity of adding to the family coffers. Accordingly, after completing their education, KC took a job with Martin Burn and JC with the Tatas.

KC was fortunate in obtaining a post almost immediately. He had worked with Martin Burn in England for a year. It was a training period for induction into the group's activities. It was always clear that KC would return to work for them in India.

His apprenticeship over, KC was sent to Calcutta to be private secretary to Sir Rajendra Mookerjee. A Bengali Brahmin who was westernized to a remarkable degree, Sir Rajendra had come in as a partner in Martin Burn just before World War I. The Martins (holding 40 percent of the equity), the Mookerjees (37 percent) and the Banerjees (17 percent) constituted the three controlling families in Martin Burn which grew from inception in 1871 to become one of the four largest business houses of India in the 1960s.

Among the myriad interests of the group was railways. Introduced in India during the last quarter of the nineteenth century, India gradually opened up through massive railway construction projects. With limited funds and in keeping with world trends, the British had thrown open this field to private enterprise. Martin Burn had been quick to enter the fray, but problems emerged even faster. As the war-induced boom tapered off, there was an all-round financial squeeze.

At one point during this frenetic time, Martin Burn hosted a party. The guests included some privy councillors from England, who, so the partners of Martin Burn hoped, might help them out of their financial bind. After a while Sir Rajendra stood up and dramatically announced: "Here's a young man who could find a solution that you could not, and I am making him a junior partner of Martin Burn." The young man in question was Kailash Chandra Mahindra.

KC's forte was finance, but his brother JC excelled as a technocrat. After completing his Oxford course, JC returned to India where he soon found himself a niche in the booming Tata organization. At this time, the Tatas were busy fulfilling J. N. Tata's vision of an iron and steel industry for India. Finally established in 1909, after much controversy, Tata Iron & Steel became India's first integrated steel plant, and JC was soon involved in this path-breaking venture, rising in its hierarchy to become a sales executive.

The Mahindra Family Moves Toward Independence

By the late 1930s, both brothers became disillusioned with the groups for which they were working. Personal differences with Sir Biren Mookerjee who succeeded his father, Sir Rajendra, caused KC to take up an offer from the government to go to the USA on the Lend-Lease Program as an excuse to break his connections with Martin Burn. JC also broke with the Tatas and joined the government to become India's first iron and steel controller.

Settled in Washington as a member of the procurement mission, buying supplies for India, KC made valuable contacts. These encouraged him to give in to an itch to be his own master. He called Keshub, his son, who had just completed his course at the University of Pennsylvania (Wharton), JC and his son, Harish, who had just graduated from Harvard, to Washington, to chalk up a plan which would enable them to go back to India to start their own company.

It was an era of reconstruction. The Mahindras bought a company in Chicago, Venn-Severin Ltd., which made large diesel engines. They planned to transport the whole plant, lock, stock, and barrel, to India. The viability of the project depended on large government orders, but at the last minute, the Indian government backed out, leaving the Mahindras with a virtually useless plant on their hands.

Back again in McLean, a Washington suburb, in KC's house *Deep Water,* a family conclave took place to consider the options open to them. A buyer from Mexico had materialized for their white elephant, and once again horizons looked promising. Keshub disagreed. He had been offered a job in Brazil and was all set to go. JC immediately vetoed the idea. The family would stick together and return to India. They would surely find something to do.

Picking up B.R. Sule, a classmate of Harish from his Boston days who had joined them a year earlier in Venn-Severin, the Mahindras left the "land of opportunity" in August 1947. Though they had not made their fortune there, the five men had gained valuable experience, made some influential contacts and retained memories of good times.

Keshub recalls: "So we came back to India. We avoided going to Calcutta as it would have embarrassed our friends (associates in Martin Burn), and we settled in Bombay. This was in the 1940s. We had a Moslem friend, Ghulam Mohammad, and we had these ideas of Hindu-Moslem unity. So we entered into a partnership with him." On October 2, 1945 Mahindra and Mohammad was founded, with a sizable portion of the required capital being put in by the Ranas of Nepal.

Within two years of Mahindra & Mohammad's existence, however, a cataclysm of epic proportions engulfed the country, leading to the creation of a new Moslem state, Pakistan. Its founder, Mohammed Ali Jinnah, needed every capable Moslem available. At the time of partition, Pakistan's life and destiny lay in the hands of 386 men: the 69 members of the Constituent Assembly, 157 bureaucrats, and 160 army officers. All previous thoughts of Hindu-Moslem unity forgotten, Ghulam Mohammad left India to become Pakistan's Governor-General from 1951 to 1955.

Bereft of their partner, but saddled with numerous company seals proclaiming M&M, KC and JC were faced with the question of renaming the company. Pondering over this vexing problem, KC and JC simply changed Mohammad to Mahindra. Very little stationery had to be thrown out.

Luckily Ghulam Mohammad's financial participation in M&M had never been very large, and the company survived the traumatic post-independence years with bearable strains. In 1945 the principal business of the company was the import of steel and jeeps, though it also promoted and acted as managing agents of Machinery Manufacturers Corporation (MMC). Incorporated in 1946 at Bombay, the object of MMC was to manufacture textile machinery.

The Indian Jeep Industry Is Born

The profits, however, really came from their import of jeeps since the Mahindras were the only ones to do so. These were bought from Willys Overland Co. Ltd. (now a part of American Motors), a company with whom KC had made contact during his Washington days. Within a couple of years the Mahindras were working on the feasibility of assembling these jeeps in India. In October of 1947 the first batch of 75 jeeps in CKD condition were imported from Willys Overland Export Corporation. It was an overwhelming success and on June 3, 1949, M&M leased 11,071 square yards at Mazagaon (Bombay) from the British India Steam Navigation Co. Ltd. to build its first jeep assembly plant.

M&M had obtained rights from Willys to manufacture a jeep with a petrol driven engine. A sturdy model with few pretensions, the vehicle was somewhat euphemistically named the "Hurricane." In spite of its short-comings, it was popular as it was suited to Indian conditions.

These years saw the birth of the automobile industry in India. The Walchands were setting up Premier Automobile Ltd. and the Birlas Hindustan Motors. The Tatas and Ashok Leyland were busy with heavy commercial vehicles. Before independence India's automobile production was virtually nil. Between 1948-50, India produced a total of 9,267 cars. Most of these, such as the Mahindra jeep, were, in effect, mere assemblies, but the figures showed India's determination to progress towards an automobile industry of her own. Despite a vocal lobby which maintained that

M&M's Mazagaon jeep plant

in a resource starved nation, cars were a dispensable luxury, India's industrial groups pushed forward.

For M&M the mid-1950's were a period of hectic growth. Describing the events, B.R. Sule, Managing Director of M&M, said:

> *As the Indian Government began to formulate its automobile policy, they stressed that companies would have to indigenize. Hindustan Motors, Premier Automobiles, we and some others said we would. Ford and others refused and pulled out of India. If we had known what was going to be involved, I don't think we would have agreed. We just didn't know what we were talking about. And we didn't get much help from the Americans. The plans they proposed were so expensive—they were based on much bigger volumes. We had a good set of engineers, but we were operating on a shoestring budget. The Americans simply left us alone to cope with our market as best we could.*

The first steps toward independent manufacturing were taken in 1954. On November 1, the government approved a scheme for the "progressive manufacture" of 2500 jeeps per year. Willys agreed to collaborate. To raise finances for the project, M&M went public on June 15, 1955. Part of the fresh funds went towards acquiring an automative plant at Bhandup, and in January of 1956, the phased manufacturing program for jeep vehicles commenced.

The process of indigenization in the case of M&M's first venture as approved by the government involved the setting up of their own manufacturing capacity for some of the critical components and assemblies (approximately 40 percent) while the rest of the components were to be manufactured by ancillary units. It was to the credit of M&M that within a decade the indigenous content of their jeep was 65 percent and by 1965 the level had risen to 80 percent. Production also increased in the same period. Planning became easier. While in 1954 they were producing slightly over a thousand jeeps, in 1967 they were rolling out 6761 units. Surprisingly, but perhaps understandably considering their partners were an American firm, the M&M jeep was a left-hand drive in a country which drove on the right. In 1967 this anomaly was corrected and necessary changes in design and manufacture were developed by M&M to produce a right-hand drive wheel. This seemingly trivial detail brought home the fact that M&M had come of age.

In the first fifteen years of its existence M&M did extremely well, moving up to the top ranks of Indian business houses. For a group formed only after World War II, competing with business houses which in some cases had been established in 1850, this was no small achievement. The "good" fortune was partly the result of a regional tragedy which came within months of the establishment of the venture. One of the first acts of India and Pakistan on gaining freedom from colonial rule was to embark on a war with each other, over Kashmir. "The government needed a lot of jeeps, and this was our first real break. They took a lot of stock from us," recalls Sule. Gradually, M&M became the nucleus of an ambitious industrial group.

With the help of a minority participation on the part of the Tata group, the Mahindras took over Turner Haore in 1948 (now Mahindra Spicer), a well-known trading company in Bombay dealing in engineering goods. In 1953 they promoted an elevator company with Otis Elevator of the USA (now a subsidiary of United Technologies) which soon emerged as one of their most profitable sister concerns. (Today, in fact, this company has a waiting list of five years for its product, demands and gets advances two years before delivery.) Around the same time, the group rather surprisingly acquired an advertising agency and went into publishing by buying up an engineering trade journal. Its absolute monopoly in the import and manufacture of jeeps continued and as the group's financial position strengthened, they sped up their transition from a trading and assembly firm to manufacturing on a ever larger scale.

1958 saw the group really take off as it entered into collaboration with a number of foreign concerns for the manufacture of various engineering products. On November 1, 1958, Mahindra Owen was established to take over and expand the already existing trailer manufacturing activity of M&M. A few months later Mahindra Sintered Products was formed for the manufacture of a wide range of self-lubricating bearings. In 1962 the Mahindras went into the manufacture of tractors in collaboration with International Harvester of the USA to set up the International Tractor Company of India. In 1963 they went into the manufacture of alloy steel in a new company, Mahindra Ugine Steel Company. That same year MMC

M&M jeep ad:
"We must go on and ahead without waiting for a road to be built."

expanded its range of textile machinery. A couple of years later the group entered the field of hydraulic pumps and valves and other oil hydraulic equipment. Around the same time, M&M introduced a small truck with a payload of one ton. By 1967 they were producing over 1250 such trucks. It was also around this time that they bought 65 acres of land at Kandivili, a sprawling suburb of Bombay, on which the Mahindras have continuously built to form one of India's large industrial complexes.

Throughout this expansion-cum-diversification program, the major thrust was undoubtedly in steel. Mahindras were able to tie up with Société Ugine of France to promote Mahindra Ugine Steel Company (MUSCO) which reached sales of $43 million. MUSCO, the second largest company in the Mahindra group, is one of the principal manufacturers of alloy steel in India with a capacity of 75,000 tons. The company symbolized the realization of a dream: JC, a steel man for most of his life, had always wanted a steel company of his own. Although MUSCO was established only after his death, his son, Harish Mahindra, is currently chairman of the company.

JC, one of the original founders of the group, had died in 1950 of a heart attack. Though deprived of an able administrator with broad engineering experience at a critical stage of growth, M&M continued to expand and diversify at a satisfying rate. This is said to have been a function of the professional approach to management practiced by KC, the second founder. MUSCO was the last company of the Mahindra group to be promoted in his lifetime. A dynamic man, always forward-looking, KC still evokes glowing tributes. His son, Keshub, who currently heads the group, merely follows in his father's footsteps when he openly delights in the knowledge that the group

M&M executives at jeep plant: Harish (far left), Keshub (fourth from left), I. Chatterji, B.R. Sule. W. Panee (second from right) and Atanjit Singh (far right).

can get along without him or any other Mahindra. The shareholders' interests are safeguarded.

Many have talked about KC's generous nature. The way in which the company went public in 1955 is often cited as proof that KC always put the interests of the companies before his own. Corporate growth, rather than the narrower interest of ownership share held by family members, always prevailed with KC. While most business groups in India have private holding companies which retain a certain percent of the stock of the companies in their groups, thereby justifying their predominant role in management, the Mahindras do not have any such holding companies.* They hold a mere two percent of the equity of M&M yet retain management control on the strength of the approval and confidence of financial institutions (who together hold 43.39 percent of M&M's equity) and their foreign collaborators (who hold 14.97 percent).

A Crisis Leads to Positive Change

In business the easy part is to set up a company. The tricky part lies in making money. The late 1960s and early 1970s saw the Mahindras in a bind. Though difficult to clearly identify tangible causes for their troubles, some issues did stand out. Their rapid expansion had spread funds too thinly, so that any crunch would leave little room for manoeuvering. And problems came pouring in. Rising raw material costs and scarce credit began to eat up profit margins. At the same time the government introduced controls on the price of the final product.

If this squeeze on profit margins was not enough, the tractor division showed alarming signs of going into a recession. Tractor sales depend largely on the availability of government credit to farmers to enable them to buy the tractors. With the general credit crisis in the country during the first two years of the 1970s, naturally this line of credit too was affected. Moreover, just a few years earlier, several new groups and old ones, too, such as the Kirloskars, had entered the tractor field and for some years there was surplus capacity.

The Mahindras were not well equipped to handle competition. Being pioneers with a reputation for technological competence, they had still not had to meet hard competition in the first 25 years of their existence. To compound their woes, the oil crisis of 1974-75 hit them as it did the entire automobile industry. The Mahindras were, if anything, worse hit because their engine was the heaviest petrol engine in the market. Suddenly the roof caved in stunning the Mahindra management into a total reassessment of its operations.

The campaign to survive the crisis was basically three-pronged. The

* In 1983/84 this aspect of the Indian business scene had been the center of a storm of controversy, kindled by the British industrialist of Indian origin, Swarj Paul.

R&D and Engineering Departments at M&M started looking at both the short-term and long-term solutions to the fuel problem. The short-term measures were planned and implemented by mid-1974. A fuel efficient and economy-oriented carburetor was developed along with a changed axle ratio which gave 15 to 20 percent better mileage. The long-term solution involved the major switch from petrol to diesel engines. For the truck they chose the Simpson engine, but for the jeep they were able to use their own engine. The tractor was already diesel-based and its engine fitted the jeep, if not to perfectly desirable levels, at least to acceptable ones. They killed two birds with one stone, helping the jeep and tractor companies simultaneously. While satisfactorily outfitting the jeep with the tractor's diesel engine, the tractor company, which was short on funds, got a needed shot in the arm as well.

The advertising section's contribution to Operation Survival was its all-India "Maxi-Miler" campaign. Existing vehicles were given a free check-up and engine tuning as well as free fitment of a carburetor-modification-kit for fuel economy. Free-wheeling flanges were also made available at low prices for use when the vehicle was not used in four-wheel drive. This campaign was also aimed to reduce fuel consumption by 10 to 15 percent on existing vehicles. More than anything it convinced customers that the company cared. M&M also now made a push to broaden its market. Until now, almost 75 percent of jeep sales were to the army, the government, and quasi-government bodies. M&M now made a strong push to get into the corporate market. Government sales after the campaign came down to 65 percent. The Mahindra group thus retained, even marginally expanded, its market share during this crisis.

The role of management in all these fundamental changes was naturally important. The fact that management reacted positively and prevented M&M from going under speaks a great deal for both its technical and managerial capability, two characteristics on which both the founder brothers had placed great stress. Professionalism has been the hallmark of the group — it could not have been otherwise given the background of the founders. Problems which could have meant the end of M&M were solved by principal operating executives who were well-qualified professional managers. The point was well taken by both Keshub and Harish Mahindra – the principles of autonomy and delegation were now scrupulously adhered to and a strict budgetary system was enforced as well.

These pillars of good management notwithstanding, several companies in the Mahindra group have not done too well of late. The biggest headaches for the management are to be found in MUSCO where bad planning, poor timing, recessionary trends, and government intervention have combined to ruin a company. In 1981 MUSCO stepped up its alloy steel manufacturing capacity from 24,000 to 75,000 tons per year. The timing could not have been worse. In April of 1981 the government announced the liberalisation of imports for alloy and special steels.

Explaining to shareholders the causes for MUSCO's poor performance,

M&M's top management: B.R. Sule, Managing Director (seated on left) and Keshub Mahindra (seated on right) with other executives.

Harish Mahindra denounced government policies at the company's 20th annual general meeting:

Operations of your company were not affected by any factors such as lack of adequate power, non-availability of raw materials, breakdowns to plant and equipment or production bottlenecks etc. As mentioned in the Director's Report, two major macro-economic factors were responsible for the reverses in the Company's fortunes; firstly the government announced the liberalisation of the Imports for Alloy & Special Steels in April 1981 and the impact of this policy was felt throughout last year. Import liberalisation had resulted in virtual dumping of Alloy & Special Steel from industrially advanced countries where the capacity utilisation in Special Steel Plants is at a distressingly low level.

The second factor which exacerbated the situation for your Company was the deepening recessionary trend in the economy as a whole and, particularly in industries like automobile, forging, tractor, ball bearing, etc. which are major consuming sectors of the economy for Alloy & Special Steel. Factors described above combined to create a situation of intense competition amongst indigenous producers who, despite escalations in various important inputs like power, furnace oil, graphite electrodes, ferro alloys, etc. were obliged to reduce the selling price to an extent that margins for most grades of Alloy & Special Steel were totally eroded.

Harish Mahindra, Chairman
Mahindra Ugine Steel Company

For the Mahindras, it was a case of history repeating itself. Earlier the losses in their tractor division had forced the merger of The International Tractor Company of India with the more financially sound M&M. In the 1960s, tractors were a tempting proposition, and the M&M team felt that it was a good market to enter. They managed to interest Voltas (a Tata company) and International Harvester (USA) in the project, and each put in 17 percent of the equity of the new company. At first the company did well, but suddenly the government allowed the import of tractors. All tractor companies in India—and several had come up to meet the demand from the

Indian farmers — reported losses. Voltas pulled out, and in order to survive, ITCI was merged with M&M in 1977.

Though at first sight it appeared that the merger favored ITCI, M&M also benefitted: under Section 72A of the Income Tax Act, the accumulated losses of ITCI and unabsorbed depreciation could yield Rs 3.5 crore ($2.9 million) in tax benefits to M&M. Besides, the pooling of resources, especially manpower, has helped in strengthening the base of the combined company. Today top management is sanguine about M&M's tractor division. "Tractors are a bright spot," says Sule, "I think farmers are also optimistic about the future."

M&M headquarters: Gateway Building
Apollo Bunder, Bombay

A Thorny Path

Being the only manufacturers of a versatile and essential form of transport until now with the government as their chief consumer, questions are naturally asked time and again about the Mahindra's relationship with the government. Keshub Mahindra has learned over the years to parry such questions diplomatically:

> No company can operate without liaison work with the government. We do not avoid contact with the government. But there is a distinction between government and politics. We have tried to keep away from politics . . . I feel that if you want to play politics, play it big, but it is a dangerous game.

Some journalists, and even political opposition parties, claim that they know an election is just around the corner when the prices of jeeps shoot up in the black market. Even the prices of second-hand jeeps tend to spiral upward. There is some inkling of truth in the observation. Sule explains:

> Our jeeps are very sturdy, and during election time there is a very heavy demand for them. From the very beginning we made our position very clear with the government. The government is a very large buyer of our jeeps, nonetheless election jeeps are given priority even over government orders. These 'election jeeps,' we made clear, are to be made available to all parties, not only to the party in power. We also made it clear that we would only sell jeeps outright, not hire or lease them, whatever the pressure.

These policies have been well vindicated, especially in 1977 when a non-Congress Party government was in power for a brief period. Sule recalls: "The Janata Government wanted to pick on the Congress Party. They wanted to find any fault they could, and they came to check us out. We were raided. For two days they sifted through everything, but they could not find anything."

Keshub Mahindra, Chairman   B.R. Sule, Managing Director

Joint Ventures

The Mahindras had the desire, knowledge, ability and experience to set up pioneering projects, but like Walchand, they did not have sufficient capital. Partners were essential if dreams were to be translated into reality, and the Mahindras showed considerable resourcefulness in finding backers for their projects. Some, like the Ranas of Nepal, were rather surprising choices. Others like the Tatas were more obvious. Most of the Mahindra companies have been set up in collaboration with foreign companies and generally the collaborators have a financial stake in the new venture. The need of the two brothers over the years developed into a corporate philosophy. As Keshub Mahindra explains:

If I buy technology, it must come with financial participation so that the collaborator has a continuing interest in updating technology and I have access to the latest development.

KC and JC's resourcefulness in successfully putting together collaboration packages is all the more remarkable if one considers the environment in which they operated. The world was barely recovering from the second world war. Business was beginning to think in terms of peacetime demands. In India, these were the years also immediately following independence. A few years earlier, British capital had been steadily fleeing the country, and those assets which could not be taken out of the country, were being sold to Indian owners. The Indian government, inexperienced, its hands full solving the refugee problems, could not hope to tackle business and economic questions for some time. With the world watching to see if Indians could make a nation for themselves, it is truly surprising that any Indian company could get foreign companies to invest in India.

In some ways the desire of the Mahindras for foreign collaborators was equally surprising. India had won independence on the strength of Mahatma Gandhi's call for "Swadeshi." The Mafatlals and Walchands for over a decade after independence kept away from external financial collaborations. The Birlas entered into foreign collaboration only when they had to, and only in a few select enterprises. In fact, partnerships with foreign investors and collaborators were practically confined to the Tata and Mahindra groups in the early post independence years.

Nonetheless the stake of the foreign parties in companies of the Mahindra group is relatively small. In 1960, of the total share of capital of Mahindra companies, foreign companies held only 4.5 percent. In M&M today, American Motors holds 8 percent of the equity, while International Harvester has 6 percent. Effective management always remained with the Mahindras, with the exception of Otis Elevator (India) Ltd. where, out of the 2,520,000 equity shares issued, 1,411,200 shares or 56 percent – and hence majority participation – are held by the parent company, Otis Elevator in the USA.

Foreign Collaborations of Mahindra Group

Mahindra Company	Year	Foreign Collaborator	Country
Mahindra & Mahindra	1945	American Motors	USA
	1962	International Harvester	USA
		G.C. Elliot Brothers	UK
		Comp Industrial Ltd	UK
		Automobiles Peugeot	France
MUSCO	1963	Ugine Aciers	France
Dr Beck & Co (India) Ltd.		Dr. Beck GmbH (BASF Group)	W. Ger.
Machinery Manufacturers Corporation	1964	Whitin International	USA
	1963	Carding Specialists (Halifax) Ltd.	UK
		Crosrol Varga	UK
		Fratelli Marzolli	Italy
		CPU Computers	UK
		Data Recording,	UK
		BASF	W. Ger.
Otis Elevator Co (India) Ltd.	1953	Otis Elevator	USA
Mahindra Spicer Ltd.		Dana Corporation	USA
Vickers Sperry of India Ltd.	1965	Sperry Rand	USA
Mahindra Owen Ltd.	1958	Rubery Owen	UK
Mahindra Sintered Products Ltd.	1959	Birfield Ltd	UK
		GKN Powder Metals Ltd	UK
Roplas (India) Ltd.		Rubery Owen	UK

A Merger Miscarries

The Mahindras have frequently been criticized for their conservative approach to business. Tacitly acknowledging this, B.R. Sule replies: "We have to work within certain parameters, by keeping in mind what our business is. If we expand, it should be within our business . . . we are constantly consolidating and updating . . . but that does not mean that we are not looking at other projects."

A major attempt to diversify was made in 1983, but failed for lack of government sanction. M&M proposed a merger with Indian Aluminium Company. If it had come off, it would have been the biggest merger in Indian corporate history. At the time, Indal was the 22nd largest company in the private sector and M&M was the 29th. If they had combined their turnover and assets, the new company would have become the third largest corporate giant in India after Tata Iron & Steel and Tata Engineering & Locomotive.

Keshub Mahindra proposed the merger. He was the common chairman of the two companies (he is also chairman of Union Carbide India and Remington Rand). The merger made sense from Keshub's point of view (some Indal people today are not unhappy that the merger did not occur) for several reasons. Indal needed money to get itself out of a vicious cycle of poor performance. M&M had the cash. Indal's parent company abroad, Alcan Aluminum, was engaged in major research in the use of aluminum in automobiles, work that M&M with its jeeps, tractors, trailers and light commercial vehicles could profitably put to use. Finally, the new company would have greater financial strength merely because of its size. Expansion in many areas could have been possible.

Indal had been one of the pioneers of the aluminum industry in India. Established in 1939, the company grew rapidly until the 1970s when disruptions in power supplies—almost a raw material in the aluminum industry—made the manufacture of aluminum quite unviable. In an unbelievably short span of time, the company saw profits slip away. It needed cheap power, but unlike Hindustan Aluminium, a Birla-Kaiser aluminum joint venture, it did not have the finances to set up its own captive power supply.

It was at this point that Keshub saw a way out, using the merger technique (which the Mahindras had used successfully several times in the past: ITCI, Bank of Baroda, Union Bank, Mahindra Spicer). There were problems, however. Though Indal's shares moved up on the country's stock exchanges soon after the merger's announcement, not all the shareholders were happy with the allotment scheme. As drawn up, the scheme offered Indal shareholders four shares in the new company for every nine shares they already held. Since Indal had a larger asset base than M&M, Indal's shareholders argued that the share ratio was unfair to them. Company spokesmen, however, justified the scheme by pointing to current market prices of the two companies' shares which in 1982 stood at Rs 24 for Indal and Rs 60 for M&M.

The role placed in this drama by the multinational, Alcan Aluminum, was also viewed with suspicion. It was felt by some that the merger would give Alcan, who had just bought the British parent company of another Indian company dealing in aluminum, India Foils, a much broader base of operations in India without any additional investment. Though this seemed a far-fetched phobia since Alcan already held 50 percent of Indal's equity and, by virtue of the merger would hold 28 percent of the new company's equity, such rumors helped sour the talks.

The government ended the controversy by declaring the merger not expedient or in the public interest. The chapter was closed. Reacting to the government's decision, Keshub Mahindra expressed great disappointment and said though he did not agree with the decision, there was no other option to be considered. In all probability, this merger was too avant-garde for the Indian business scene at the time which was not used to Western-style mergers. The involvement of a large foreign multinational and an Indian corporate giant fed the flames of anti-monopoly fears as well and doomed the daring proposal of Keshub Mahindra. The government ruling was seen by some as a reflection on Keshub's business acumen and was an apparent loss of personal prestige. Were such a move to be made again today, however, in the interests of efficiency and innovation, it might well be approved.

M&M's Export Drive

An accusation often levelled at Indian industry is that it has been pampered by a protective government, and that given laissez-faire conditions, it would collapse like a pack of cards. While this may be true of some industries, it is certainly not true of all. As with most generalizations, the statement has flaws. The Mahindra group notably has managed to keep India's flag flying in this respect with their export of jeeps to nations all over the world. Several multinationals such as American Motors, Nissan and Toyota manufacture more sophisticated jeeps. But the Mahindra jeep, perfected over the rugged Indian terrain, has found international acceptance because of its ruggedness and versatility.

In recent years, Iran has emerged as the most important market for Mahindra jeeps. The genesis of the group's involvement in Iran highlights the important role politics plays and how it can make a mockery of the best business planning.

Sule explained:

> American Motors, in the days when the Shah was in power and American influence in Iran was very strong, set up a jeep plant there. When the new government came in, they nationalized the company and took over the plant. It was a massive project: mainly assembly, but making bodies also. We came in to supply the spares, dies and even batteries. Our connection with American Motors made us ideal partners. Our products were compatible and others couldn't match this.

Fighting for a Principle

In 1979 Keshub Mahindra took up a fight on behalf of Indian managers.

Salaries of managing directors and other whole-time directors of public limited companies are fixed according to scales drawn up by the government. In 1978 a zealously egalitarian administration reduced the upper limits of the scales creating a curious anomaly. Senior executives lower down on the corporate ladder earned more than executives who were directors of the corporation. Mahindra, still indignant about the affair, recalled:

> *I had a salary, starting from 1964. According to our law, every five years my contract has to be approved by the government. One year they just cut my salary by half. This was in 1979. I did not feel that this was correct. I went to my lawyer and raised the fundamental issue in the courts . . . and I won. But I was alone. No other industrialist came to my support.*

Other industrialists thought perhaps that the fight was academic. Between 1964 and 1975 Keshub had been earning a salary of Rs 120,000 a year, plus perks (but no commission). But the government, in approving his reappointment, now fixed his salary at Rs 60,000, perks at Rs 60,000, and commission at Rs 12,000. The M&M board protested. They pointed out that three senior executives who were being promoted as directors to the board were faced with the prospect of cuts in their salary if they accepted the directorships. As in Keshub's case, the net cut was not very much, but it was the principle of the matter which prompted the board to protest. While they

Gateway Building, Front View

had been getting Rs 77,000 plus perks as executives, as directors government decreed they would get Rs 60,000 salary, Rs 12,000 commission plus perks. The government remained adamant. Keshub Mahindra resigned from the Board in October 1979. At the same time, the three executives (S.K. Roy, R.K. Pitamber and B. DeSouza), Keshub and M&M moved in the Delhi High Court that the government had acted arbitrarily. While upholding the government's right to fix remunerations, the court agreed that the government's action had been high-handed and quashed the order by which the remuneration of the petitioners had been fixed. Alone or not, Keshub Mahindra had taken on a fight for principle and received some modicum of justice.

Keshub and Harish Mahindra (l. to r.)

The Bhopal Tragedy Hits M&M

Union Carbide Corporation has a 50-year long history of operation in

India with 14 factories throughout the country. The 1984 Bhopal disaster put the Mahindra group on the line because its chairman, Keshub Mahindra, also serves as chairman of the American multinational's Indian company. Both Keshub Mahindra and Warren Anderson, chairman of Union Carbide in the USA, were placed under house arrest in Bhopal when they visited the Bhopal plant shortly after the disastrous gas leak occurred in December of 1984. The office of chairman of multinational companies in India is often held by a prominent Indian industrial leader with ventures of his own to look after. This is the case with Union Carbide. There is little doubt that the Bhopal tragedy will affect the head of the Mahindra group for years to come.

Principal Companies in Mahindra Group

Company	Products
Mahindra & Mahindra Ltd.	Jeeps, tractors, electronic components, trading in steel, export of machine tools
Mahindra Ugine Steel Co. Ltd.	Alloy & Special steels
Dr. Beck & Co. (India) Ltd.	Synthetic chemicals, electricals, insulation, varnishes
Machinery Manufacturers Corporation Ltd.	Textile machinery, industrial haulage equipment, data processing equipment
Otis Elevator Co. (India) Ltd.	Elevators
Mahindra Spicer Ltd. (formerly Turner Hoare Co., Ltd)	Ash handling plants, centrifuges, clutch plates, trading, printing
Vickers Sperry of India Ltd.	Fluid powered equipment
Mahindra Owen Ltd.	Trailers
Mahindra Sintered Products Ltd.	Base powders, sintered bushes/ bearings
Roplas (India) Ltd.	Fiberglass reinforced plastics
Indian National Diesel Engine Co.	Diesel engines

M&M's Plan for the Future

Since the fast growth of the 1960s, the pace at both M&M and Mahindra Ugine Steel has slowed somewhat. Ranked among the top twenty groups in the private sector in 1977, M&M had moved closer to thirtieth place by 1983. M&M's top management, Keshub Mahindra and B.R. Sule, both say that growth has been "moderate" and it is due in part to the group's conservative philosophy. The Mahindra group does not like to borrow heavily and they believe in growth by promotion of new companies rather than by acquisition. The abortive merger with Indian Aluminium might have succeeded in shaking M&M out of its slow growth syndrome and placed it on a faster road to growth.

Nonetheless, the Mahindra management had seen the need to move ahead in the early 1980s. A massive modernization and expansion project at its plants in Kandivili in Bombay and at Nasik and Igatpuri in Maharashtra is under way. The $65 million expansion envisages changes in both the automotive and tractor divisions. The existing M&M diesel engine will be replaced by a Peugeot XDP 4.9 diesel engine. The automotive division's capacity will now be 25,000 units while the tractor division's will rise to 15,000 units. With the government permitting much more competition in the automotive sector, M&M's modernization and expansion plan is coming just in time to help keep the group ahead of, or at least even with, new entrants in the field or competitors already busy with expansion plans of their own. Competition will no doubt serve as an efficient fuel for further growth at M&M. While other groups still hestitate to lose too much control by taking on additional public shareholders, and may thereby stunt their growth, M&M long ago took the Indian public into their confidence to build what is a true "all-India" industrial empire. The Tatas had acted similarly in order to finance what were massive projects for the times for any private entrepreneur to undertake. The Mahindras and the Tatas have shown that large industrial projects can be promoted in the private sectors in cooperation with an enthusiastic public. The results have kept the shareholders coming back for more.

Modi

Automobile tires
Cigarettes
Synthetic fibers
Textiles
Cement
Reprographic equipment
Agro-chemicals
Alcohol
Vanaspati
Steel
Welding electrodes

Patiala

MODINAGAR

Sales
Rs 850 crore
($708 million)

Headquarters
Modinagar (U.P.) India 201 204

Head of Group
Kedar Nath Modi

Gujar Mal Modi (1902-1976)

MODI

Gujar Mal Modi, founder of the Modi group of industries, was caught up in the spirit of the times. The breezes were blowing in the direction of freedom and economic independence when Gujar Mal broke away from his family's successful trading concerns to found a sugar mill in 1933. The move represented a leap into industry from trading as well as a shift from his home area of Patiala in the Punjab to a small town near New Delhi in Uttar Pradesh. For the young man completely preoccupied with doing business, the British-ruled state of Uttar Pradesh was a welcome change from what he found to be the rather arbitrary reign of the Maharaja of Patiala. A license which had been granted to the Modis for a textile unit in Patiala had been revoked at the last minute, quashing Gujar Mal's hopes for setting up an industry in his home state. This one event gave Gujar Mal the impetus to move to what he saw as a more hospitable environment in which to realize his industrial ambitions. He could also escape the unrelenting gaze of a dis-approving father.

Gujar Mal's dream of setting up factories was clouded by the fact that he had no surviving children from his first marriage, much less the all important son. He eventually remarried and had five sons and six daughters.

Gujar Mal's step-brother, Kedar Nath Modi, joined him in the early years of World War II. Together they established some of the money-spinning enterprises which benefitted from the wartime economy. Kedar Nath was to have three sons, contemporaries of Gujar Mal's five sons. All eight Modi boys were well-educated. They were trainined under the sometimes ruthless eye of Gujar Mal and calmer hand of Kedar Nath to do one thing—business.

The growth of the Modi group in its first 40 years is the story of two brothers—Gujar Mal and Kedar Nath Modi. The continued expansion of the group will be the story of eight sons whose individual personalities and ambitions sometimes strain the image of a tight-knit Hindu joint family. In order to keep their place in a rapidly expanding industrial community, the second generation of Modis, some say, will have to continue to pool the resources required to give life to ever larger industrial projects. But the outcome of the Modi group under eight dynamic sons will not change the story of the founding of an industrial conglomerate by a man called Gujar Mal Modi and it's coming of age under Kedar Nath.

From Trading to Small-Scale Industry

By the end of the eighteenth century, colonialism had destroyed local industries and transformed India into a supplier of raw materials to the mother country. Thus the stage was set for the rise of the Indian trading class who acted as middlemen to the Western newcomers. A century later, but within a few years of its development, these same Westerners introduced modern industry to India. But whereas the industrial revolution in the West was heralded by the artisan class, the Indian industrialist had to come from the trading class as the talented artisans of the subcontinent were by then extinct for all intents and purposes.

With the capital accumulated from trading activities, some Indian businessmen, especially the Bombay-based business houses, entered into partnership with Western entrepreneurs to establish modern large-scale industry. Indian entrepreneurs also ventured into small-scale, trade-related industries such as cotton ginning, flour milling and oil pressing. But these were seasonal activities at best and trading at this stage remained the most profitable business. It was in operating these small factories, however, that their owners acquired a certain confidence in industrial management and the experience encouraged them to enter the more attractive and lucrative arena of larger-scale industry.

The growth of the Modi group from 1857 to 1933 follows the second pattern quite closely. The name 'Modi' in Hindi signifies a person who supplies grains and provisions, and the Modi family for well over half a century supplied the troops—both Indian and British—of Patiala, a city in southern Punjab. Their reputation for promptness and efficiency enabled them to set up a network of branches in Patiala State, mostly selling foodstuffs. Up until 1894 they were only traders, but that year they bought a flour mill to which they had been supplying wheat. Though trading continued

Patiala Flour Mills

to be their paramount interest until 1928, they acquired an old cotton mill that year to which an oil pressing division was added. But the Modi's first real foray into industry came in 1933 when, along with several other Indian business groups, they realized the potential of the sugar industry in the wake of changes in government policy.

From 1928, Gujar Mal Modi had been dreaming of setting up factories of his own. Until 1933, however, he had been frustrated in his ambitions for the most part by his conservative father. Multanimal resisted the family's transition from trade to industry by refusing to advance any funds towards his son's proposed sugar mill. It was not only that the father felt the scheme would fritter away the family fortune, but Multanimal also worried about losing the valuable services of Gujar Mal in the traditional family trading concerns. His fears were well-founded as his business did suffer later on in his son's absence.

Gujar Mal was Multanimal Modi's second child and his first son. His second wife died shortly after Gujar Mal's birth, then his third wife died as well early in the marriage. It was only when Multanimal married his fourth wife that the boy, then just two and a half, was to have the motherly affection which every child needs. Gujar Mal's education was cut short by happenstance and Multanimal did not hesitate to enlist the young man's services in the family business. He was just 17.

He acquired knowledge of practical aspects of business management and the intricacies of the trade. He worked very hard, spent long hours of his leisure in reading books on commerce, architecture, engineering and marketing. What he missed by not going in for formal college education, he more than made up by the practical training and the dedicated application he brought to bear on his chosen subjects. The father encouraged him in his studies and provided him with opportunities to gain practical experience.[1]

Modi family home in Patiala (with long balcony)

Gujar Mal proved his worth early on. He designed a new accounting system for the business, ultimately helping to ensure his father's obstinacy in letting Gujar Mal spread his industrial wings. Even in the face of strong parental disapproval though, the strong-willed Gujar Mal moved ahead with his plans. Begumabad, a village roughly 50 miles from New Delhi, was selected as the site for Gujar Mal's sugar factory. In the center of rich canefields and near a major railway line, there were also some formidable drawbacks. The area was infested with dangerous wildlife, not to mention hardened dacoits who did not welcome intrusion from any outsiders. But the vision of a sugar mill rising out of the open fields across which Gujar Mal stared was enough to keep Gujar Mal's eyes fixed on his goal. His eldest son, Krishan Kumar (KK), said his father's strongest trait was his ability to look straight ahead, his full attention always focussed on his goals. Nothing diverted him.[2]

GM had convinced some established businessmen in Delhi to back his industrial plans and once he had selected the site for his mill, he set about raising the remainder of the capital needed for the first Modi industrial venture. Production began in September 1933 when a spate of new sugar mills were coming up in the area as well. Some initial technical setbacks forced GM to look outside India for qualified personnel since what limited local talent existed had been drawn off by his competitors. The higher salaries and living accommodations demanded by the two European experts GM called in would further trim the already threatened profit margins. But Gujar Mal did not spare anything to get his factory on track. The foreign experts did not work out, the problems were not solved, morale declined among the workers, and then discipline fell apart. GM fired the foreign managers, moved to the factory site himself and within a short time, conditions in the factory showed a marked improvement. Gujar Mal's move saved the operation from further losses and while sugar mills in the neighboring areas continued to show losses, Modi Sugar Mills turned profitable.

But his troubles were not over. For a couple years more it seemed Multanimal's prophecy would come true. The Modi sugar unit continued to suffer from lack of skilled workers and from farmer resistance in supplying sugarcane when gur fetched higher prices. Then a frost blighted the crop, threatening the sugar industry in general. At least GM was not alone. By the end of the 1930s, however, the industry had stabilized and profits rather than losses were the norm.

Shortly before he had set off for New Delhi in search of his new life, GM's personal life had not been free from deep disappointment. His first wife was unable to bear healthy children and in sixteen years, they lost ten children. The businessman took to meditating and visiting holy Hindu places to seek solace. His dilemma ended when he finally acceded to his father's suggestion that a second marriage be arranged. Gujar Mal married Dayawati Lal of Uttar Pradesh. Eleven children were born to GM and his new wife, five of whom were sons.

The Budding Industrialist

Gujar Mal's happier personal life coincided with the turnaround of his factory in the now budding industrial township of Begumabad. The profits started to flow in the late 1930s and they came at an opportune time. With World War II looming, those with sufficient funds and enterprise could capitalize on war demands. GM lost no time in establishing several small factories to meet the expanding needs of the local market. Among the earliest of these war-stimulated ventures was a vanaspati (vegetable oil) factory. He had been toying with the idea for this project since 1928, but at that time could not obtain official permission to establish the unit in Patiala. KK Modi reminisced about his father's early attempts to establish his industrial roots:

> *My father's earlier efforts to set up a vanaspati factory were not wasted. He learned from the experience and when the time came to establish the unit, the lessons were put to good use. Later, he used to stress to us the importance of learning the lessons of failure.[3]*

1939 was a better year for promoting a vanaspati factory in any event and GM was able to get into production before the war slowed down the import of capital machinery into India. The unit proved to be a gold mine and the Modi brand 'Katogem' became sufficiently popular throughout north India to cause alarm to the British multinational company, Lever's, which had introduced the product to India. Lever's offered to buy out the assets of Modi Vanaspati Manufacturing Company at twice the amount the Modis had invested. When GM refused the offer, a price war ensued. After a year of cut-throat competition, the two companies decided to co-exist peacefully.

Rooftop view of Modi Industries, ca. 1940, Modinagar

The vanaspati operation spawned several ancillary companies. A washing soap factory was set up in 1940 to utilize the waste sludge from the vanaspati factory. A few months later Modi Tin Factory came up to fulfill the demand of the vanaspati unit for tin containers. The success of the washing soap venture encouraged the group to try making toilet soap. And the need of the vanaspati unit for pure cottonseed and groundnut oils set the stage for Modi Oil Mills.

The war also encouraged the expansion of the Modi's traditional metier of supplying provisions to the armed forces. Thus in rapid succession were established Modi Food Products to process dehydrated vegetables and Modi Supplies Corporation to process dry fruits into cakes and tablets. The success of their food-processing units—all catering to military needs—led the Modis to set up a biscuit factory and confectionery plant as well. The vegetable dehydration project presented GM with a technological challenge. But GM always met hurdles head on.

"In 1945 the industrial colony founded by Gujar Mal Modi was officially named Modinagar."[4]

When the year 1945 saw the winding up of companies such as Modi Food Products and Modi Supplies Corporation as the war ended, the group continued to do well. The British government was anxious to show its appreciation to Gujar Mal for services rendered on behalf of the war effort. In one of the more ostentatious shows of acclaim, GM was taken on an imposing procession through the main streets of Meerut, seated atop a splendidly decorated elephant and accompanied by the British District Magistrate. As the procession wound its way through the streets of the city, coins were showered on Rai Bahadur Gujar Mal, a title he had been given in 1942. A knighthood was next and the British were looking for ways to confer this grand honor on GM. In preparation, Begumabad was renamed "Modinagar" to give sufficient stature to the industrialist to help justify the gesture.

But such exhibitions in a country wracked by the final struggles for independence could hardly be tolerated, much less helpful to GM's future prospects in a free India. As the British bureaucracy gave way to Indian rule, therefore, GM's lifestyle underwent the necessary metamorphosis. Encouraged by the popular Chief Minister of the state of Uttar Pradesh, Govind Ballabh Pant, GM changed his style of dress from the expensive attire of traditional churidars and achken studded with gold buttons to plain cloth and Gandhian white cap. But the turbulent years leading up to independence did not slow GM's plans for industrial growth. On the contrary, he made good use of his war profits and in quick succession set up factories to manufacture paints and varnishes, hosiery, tents and lanterns. He built schools and houses for his workers and their families and gradually expanded Modinagar. It was also during this time that the first large-scale Modi industrial enterprise was established. Conceived as early as 1946, Modi Spinning & Weaving Mills was realized only in 1949 after several setbacks.

There was local resistance to the site selection and tribals in the area, already dissatisfied over the government decision to permit acquisition of land for the plant, were egged on by a few radicals to resist the Modi textile project. Resentment spread rapidly to include landlords and farmers. A mob formed to stop production at various Modi factories in Modinagar. As work at the plants ground to a halt, smaller mobs began to roam the streets of the town. Ugly riots followed. GM sought help from the state authorities to protect life and property in Modinagar, but it was more than a week before order was restored. In order to ensure permanent peace, GM had to accede to a selection of a new site for his plant.

Additional difficulties arose when delays occurred in the delivery of machinery ordered from England for the mill. The resultant escalating costs and disrupted schedules sent the value of shares in Modi Spinning & Weaving Mills to almost half their face value. Only GM's intervention to buy up the shares being sold kept the price up. But GM quickly dispatched his younger brother, Kedar Nath (KN), to England to look into the cause for the delays. KN had entered the business with GM during the war. He had quickly gained GM's hard-won confidence so much so that the 26 year-old was now sent off on his first mission abroad. The trip was an eye-opener for the young man on his own in an alien culture for the first time. It also taught a few lessons to those who had to deal with him. GM's biographer relates the story of what KN faced in 1948 in London:

> *In England he was greatly disappointed by the lack of sympathy shown towards Indian business interests by the Indian ambassador there. Mr. Kedar Nath Modi issued a press statement saying that the Modis had come to the conclusion that conditions in the British industries in England were deteriorating and since they had not been able to get all the textile machinery for which orders had been placed as far as two years back, they were now obliged to place their orders in America. This statement was refuted by the Minister for Trade in the British Government who insinuated that Modi belonged to an average class of Indian businessmen and may not be in a position to pay for the machinery. Mr. Kedar Nath Modi thereupon issued a rejoinder. He declared that he was prepared to show 'letters of credit' and other documents to prove that the Modis were in position to pay for the machinery*

*worth 10 million rupees. The Indian ambassador initiated enquiries . . . he
was sorry for the apathetic attitude adopted by him towards Mr. Modi. The
British Government . . . expressed its inability to secure the machinery . . . Mr.
Modi left for America and secured the necessary machinery there.[5]*

KN ordered the machinery from a firm in Rhode Island in the USA. He
had taken a large risk in purchasing American technology when no one in
India was familiar with its workings nor its reliability. The successful
outcome of his risk-taking not only saved Modi Spinning from being still-born,
but set the stage for a major diversification of Indian industry away from
British textile technology. The Modis were the fastest to learn from this
lesson. Their future foreign collaborations were to be with well-known
industrial names throughout the world.

In the midst of the problems of getting Modi Spinning off the ground,
GM had to face a tax assessment enquiry. Many industrialists had earned
hefty profits during the war and the government now set up an enquiry board
to go into the question of possible tax evasion. As one who had undertaken
considerable expansion during the war, GM was one of those chosen as a
subject of the enquiry. GM resisted the advice of his financial advisers to
drop the plans for Modi Spinning in the face of the enquiry, believing that
maintaining one's public image was all important to an industrialist, more so
than losing money as a result of a tax assessment. With KN's successful visit
to America to order the new machinery for the plant and GM's persistance in
the face of the tax enquiry, the textile mill was inaugurated on June 29, 1949.
Modi Spinning was more than amply to fulfill the ambitions of its promoters
since the profits from this plant provided the basis for the group's expansion

Modi Spinning and Weaving Mills

in the 1960s particularly. New units were added to produce better quality textiles and increased capacity. Even larger profits resulted and each new project seemed more ambitious than the last. Toward the latter part of the 1970s, however, the newer industrial ambitions of the second generation of Modis were to overshadow Modi Spinning's earlier pioneer status in the group. Added to unfavorable market conditions for textiles and growing labor problems, Modi Spinning eventually ran into major difficulties.

But the news of the strong performance of Modi Spinning in its maiden years was overshadowed by another personal setback. In 1951 GM had to face charges of colluding with railway officials to embezzle railway consignments in the confusing days of 1947. Even though GM succeeded in vindicating himself and the case was later dropped, the incident served to isolate GM from the mainstream of public life for some time. Moreover, in 1952, frost destroyed the sugarcane crop and prices of groundnut oil halved. The business downturn forced the Modis to sell a large plot of land near Delhi which they had bought to establish new vanaspati and textile units. An oxygen plant was sold as well to weather the slump. The only bright spot in these otherwise troubled years was the visit of Prime Minister Nehru for the second time to Modinagar in July of 1952. Avowed socialist Nehru meeting avowed capitalist Modi produced an interesting dilemma for the local Congress Party leaders who did not wish their Prime Minister's image tarnished by hobnobbing with an industrialist. In the end, two successful Indian citizens met in a quiet setting away from the public eye to talk freely between themselves about their respective views on life, business and politics.

By 1954 things were looking up for GM personally and for Modi Industries as well. Previous losses were wiped out, a new oxygen plant was set up and a tubewell company acquired. GM was elected to the executive committee of FICCI, an important step toward becoming its president, an ambition which he realized in 1968. Plans were also made for the establishment of a silk factory, a second unit for Modi Spinning and an acetylene gas factory. Apart from hitting a bad patch in 1958 when labor unrest erupted at Modi Spinning and competition forced the closure of the toilet soap factory, luck was on their side. His biographer wrote: "The year 1963 marks the beginning of a period of pre-eminence in the life of Mr. Modi. [. . .] He had established himself as a great industrialist with a large vision and a dynamic outlook."[6]

The group's turnover was by then approximately Rs 12 crores ($10 million). Though he had established himself as an industrialist, his largest earnings still came from flour milling which involved large cash transactions and equally large returns. A substantial part of these profits were reinvested in industrial activities. Still, by 1960 the Modis had only two projects with any pretentions of size and scale, Modi Spinning & Weaving and Modi Sugar. The first step into a bigger industrial league came with the establishment of a polyester filament yarn and nylon plant, Modipon Ltd., in Modinagar in 1967.

GM Modi with Prime Minister Nehru

GM Passes The Baton

Though GM lived to see the success of Modipon and other major under-takings by his group, by 1965 his health had begun to deteriorate. He delegated increasing responsibility to his brother, KN, and his son, KK, who had by now entered the ranks of top management. In any event, GM was more and more caught up in his social and public life.

Modipon's promotion was in the hands of KN, KK and a cousin, Suresh. The project came to fruition by a chance meeting between some American executives from the firm of Rohm & Haas and the Modis in West Germany in the early 1960s. Faced with the need to buy foreign technology, but within the Indian government's restrictions which included no payback of foreign loans before ten years, the Modis first travelled to a rupee currency country to search for appropriate nylon technology. East Germany, their first stop, did not offer any possibilities. The technology was out of date and the East

Germans did not offer any hope that they could oblige the Indian businessmen. The Modi executives proceeded to West Germany to meet with Lurgi's executives to discuss the deal. When the Lurgi executives related that only two of them could come to dinner because some Americans were also in town to buy equipment, the Modis, always generous hosts, invited the Americans to dinner as well. As it happened, the Modis and the executives from the Philadelphia firm of Rohm & Haas had been in correspondence about the nylon project, but the Indian firm had hesitated to travel all the way to America to work out a deal on the almost impossible terms set by the Indian government. The Modis had written to a firm named Scranton Fibers in Pennsylvania in the USA which had just been acquired by Rohm & Haas. The American executives, formerly of Scranton, remembered the Modi's correspondence and pursued the deal at the dinner in Germany. They urged the Modis to continue on to the USA to negotiate a deal with Rohm & Haas.

The Modis arrived in Philadelphia and, with the help of a friendly and astute Rohm & Haas executive, Don Murphy, came to an agreement within the bounds of the terms set by the foreign-exchange short Indian government. While the American firm entered into discussions, it was clear that they would not budge when the nature of the ten year loan requirement was put on the table. KK Modi relates that it was a meeting which Don Murphy arranged with Mrs. Haas, the widow of the founder, that saved the day. As the Modis were about to depart Philadelphia empty-handed, Don Murphy had Mrs. Haas invite them to tea in her home. As strict Hindus, they did not drink. After the meeting, Murphy explained the dilemma to Mrs. Haas who held 60 percent of the Rohm & Haas stock. Many years later, the Modis learned that Mrs. Haas had placed a phone call to her son, Otto, in the company and advised him to sign a deal with the Modis and to include a ten year, no-recourse, "best efforts to repay" loan. Even Indian government officials doubted the source of the funds when informed that the Modis had met the terms of the license they had issued. A few checks through official channels confirmed Mrs. Haas' generosity and risk-taking spirit.

When KN and KK arrived home to Modinagar, they met a stern-faced Gujar Mal. The thought of a large loan possibly remaining unpaid upon his death, placing his next life and those of his successors on a lower rung of the caste system, was too much for GM. A guru was consulted to rescue the exuberant returnees from Philadelphia. There was a reasonable end when GM was advised that breaking an agreement would be as damaging to his next life as leaving a loan unpaid. The American executives travelled to India to conclude the negotiations. GM again hesitated as Rohm & Haas wanted the new plant to be located in Modinagar, but it wanted to retain control. The mighty Gujar Mal could not see himself dwarfed in the town he had built by a large American corporation whose chiefs would control the new facility. He recommended that the plant go up in Bombay, well away from Modinagar. Modipon Ltd. was set up in Modinagar with the Modis retaining equity and management control. The Rs 2 crore asset base of the new joint venture was supplemented by the Rohm & Haas loan and a local currency Cooley loan as well. The plant was profitable in its first year of operation.

The project's timing was fortuitous for it was pushed through just before a difficult period of foreign exchange availability. Textile units had slowly changed over to synthetic blends. When the foreign exchange squeeze came in the late 1960s, mills had to buy their synthetic fibers from indigenous sources. Modipon enjoyed a virtual monopoly. The company has expanded far beyond its original capacity and has gone into related industries as well.

K.N. Modi   Madan Lal Modi

Vinay Modi and Modi Rubber's Birth

Until the late 1940s growth in the group had come from fairly related activities. From wheat trading the Modis entered flour milling. Sugar manufacturing led to a distillery, while vanaspati led to soaps, tin containers and oil pressing. Modi Spinning was the first break from this pattern and its success enabled the group to enter the joint venture with Rohm & Haas. The Modipon success in turn helped the group promote Modi Rubber Ltd., more difficult and more ambitious than the previous endeavors. Since the late 1970s Modi Rubber has been the flagship of the group. Set up to produce automobile tires and tubes, Modi Rubber had a long gestation period.

In the 1960s, GM had worked on a bicycle tire project which never materialized. Later on the group examined a tractor project which also did not pan out. Recalls Vinay Modi, Vice-Chairman and Managing Director of Modi Rubber, and GM's second son: "By a quirk of fate, the person my father had corresponded with (for the bicycle tire project), a Mr. Damson of Firestone in the USA, wrote back to me inquiring, why didn't I think about car tires instead."[7]

Though still lukewarm about such a project, the Modis had by now acquired some knowledge about the tire market and went ahead to apply to the government for a letter of intent to manufacture tires and tubes. Around the same time, the state government of Uttar Pradesh asked the Modis if they were interested in setting up a tire plant in the state. Earlier the Birla group had expressed interest in setting up such a plant, going so far as to obtain a letter of intent. But they had merely set up a bicycle tire unit in Allahabad. Worried that some other state would snap up the idea, the state government was anxious to find a willing entrepreneur.

A market study commissioned by the Modis revealed that there was a 150 percent premium on the prices of automobile tires in 1968. The project was too tempting and the Modis decided to move forward with responsibility given to Vinay Modi, then 25 years old, to pursue the project. What Modi Spinning did for KN's reputation and Modipon for KK, Modi Rubber was to do for Vinay. With little formal business background except that gathered by osmosis, and limited experience, Vinay's entry into industry was to be a baptism by fire.

It took Vinay two years to tie up a technical collaboration agreement for the project. In this case, the leading West German firm of Continental Gummi-Werke was chosen. Established in 1971, another four years would pass before Modi Rubber's commercial production could begin. And this was only the beginning of years of struggle to establish a foothold in a market dominated by foreign-named firms producing at much lower costs than the new Indian plant. The plan was to produce high profit-yielding truck tires, but a cost overrun of 60 percent squelched hopes of early returns. In the first two years of operation, losses exceeded the paid-up capital of Rs 8 crore ($6.6 million).

Modi Rubber headquarters, Modinagar

Modi Rubber, Modipuram

The oil crisis of 1973 hit all petroleum-based industries hard. The Modis' tire project was no exception and the dramatic rise in costs of inputs put the already high cost product beyond the reach of what the market would bear. Along with an unyielding market resistance to the high price of a Modi tire was the fact that the Modis had not yet joined the cartel of tire manufacturers. Bhupendra Modi, Vinay's younger brother, and Managing Director of Modi Rubber, recalled that tires were stacked up all over the plant and the surrounding area. The crises facing the birth of a healthy Modi Rubber were no different though from those which GM had faced time and again. It seems that it was never to be easy for the Modis to break into a new industry. They were faced with make or break decisions. They decided on a fire sale to clear the stocks, generate some cash, lift worker morale which had hit rock bottom, and they hoped to find favor with the truckers who had as yet resisted the Modi tires. The move proved successful and Modi Rubber was finally launched—without the Modis having had to join the foreign-dominated cartel. The government of U.P. also pitched in with a large order.

Keeping its head above water soon was not enough. A new strategy had to be found to set the company on a steady road to profitability. Vinay Modi took to the halls of government in New Delhi to lobby for a rebate on excise duties, claiming that as a new company competing against multinationals producing from fully depreciated plants, survival would depend on tax concessions for local industry. The government agreed and in 1976, the Modis received tax concessions in the neighborhood of Rs 20 crore ($16.6 million). The favorable treatment obtained by the Modis for their new plant would be sought in the future by other Indian firms. Only the Modis would

Vinay K. Modi   Bhupendra K. Modi

not benefit because of the unfavorable cut-off dates applied to the future rulings. For the time being, however, the excise concessions, better sales, higher production and some technical innovation began to pay dividends and by 1979 Modi Rubber was making substantial profits. GM did not live to see Modi Rubber turn around.

Toward the later years of his life. GM concentrated more on social welfare activities. He had also mellowed considerably. Early on, he had set aside all those who could not keep up with his breathless pace. His two step-brothers, Harmukh Rai and Madan Lal, KN's brothers, were two such victims. Having helped in the establishment of the sugar mill, and associated with the traditional businesses of the group such as flour milling and cotton ginning, the brothers nevertheless were relegated to the role of silent partners. GM's attitude toward his workers on the other hand could be exemplary. He established an industrial township with relatively high standards of living. Low rents, schooling facilities, recreation grounds, health clinics, temples, all existed to make the Modi employee's life as comfortable as possible. Generous with his time as well as his funds, legitimate requests for assistance from any of his extended family in Modinagar did not fall on deaf ears.

But GM's was a complex personality with paradoxes not uncommon to pioneers in any walk of life. He was an orthodox Hindu, deeply religious, living according to the tenets of his faith. He fasted regularly, visited temples and places of pilgrimage often. But his tradition-bound life did not preclude him from acting with passionate impatience if occasion demanded it—usually in the interest of growth. Hot-tempered, but believing in the value of hard work, his ascent to industrial eminence was achieved by a gift for decision-making which he always followed with quick action. He never hesitated to act.

The town he established as the home of Modi Rubber was a reflection of his generous spirit and appreciation for a pleasant environment. Modipuram, located slightly beyond Modinagar as the helicopter flies, boasts

Top: KK, Mahendra, Manmohan, Vinay, Satish, Sudarshan, Suresh
Middle: KN, GM, Multanimal, Rukmini, Harmukh Rai, Madanlal
Bottom: Mahesh, Yogindra, Devendra, Sudhir, Raakesh, Bhupendra

award-winning architecturally-designed buildings with the latest in modern furnishings. The Modis' penchant for good design and pleasing environments was shared with their workers as schools and hospitals in the new towns which sprang up continued to win awards for design.

After GM's death in 1976 at the age of 74, the leadership of the group devolved upon KN, his younger brother by his father's fourth wife. The group's annual turnover had moved from Rs 12 crore in the early 1960s to Rs 204 crore ($170 million). Under KN's direction, the Modi companies went from strength to strength. Educated in Patiala, KN entered business while still in his teens. He was the perfect foil for his older, hard-driving brother. As ambitious as GM and equally shrewd, KN was not as overtly aggressive. He learned fast and this is what helped him gain GM's confidence.

KN was also responsible for maintaining effective relations with government officials. He followed government policies closely and at one point in the 1950s when socialist winds were blowing strongly, KN thought it wise to establish smaller-scale industries in keeping with a growing dislike on the part of politicians for bigness, monopoly and other Western ills. But GM was not swayed from his plans for bigger and bigger projects. He could not change his natural bent for growth any more than the government could change its political philosophy. Somehow they would co-exist. Thus KN went along, sticking closely to GM in all business decisions, but adding his own more subtle personality to GM's larger-than-life presence. It was a winning combination, one which KN did not resent despite the fact that he lived for the most part in GM's shadow for almost 30 years. Even in a paternalistic Hindu joint family, it could not have been easy for someone of KN's caliber, possessing his own pride and ambition, to take a back seat to the mighty GM.

KN Leads Group Into Diversification

Just as GM was responsible for taking the group into industry from trading, KN has steered the group away from being just a large north Indian business house to one with a national character. His willingness to share the limelight with his eight "sons", GM's five and his own three, is partly responsible for the takeoff in growth which the group experienced from 1979 to 1983. Whereas there was never a question but that all family members would bow to GM's wishes, KN gave the Modi sons a freer hand. Their personal lives changed. They moved out of Modinagar where they had been expected to arrive at the plant very early each day (even after an all-night bridge party), and built homes in New Delhi and Bombay. Held on a tight leash by GM, they began to enjoy their wealth and new found freedom.

Had the Modis spent lavishly on themselves out of the sight of friends and officials, many people might not have wondered aloud how the group dared consume so conspicuously under the eyes of a society still officially espousing Gandhian austerity. But their open-handed personalities soon burst upon the social and business scenes of New Delhi, Bombay, London, New York and beyond. They soon became, if not the largest industrial group, one of the most talked about. But beyond their open-door policy and an ever-widening circle of friends and associates was not simply the Modi quest for friendship and social status, but an unrelenting search for new ideas and people to help realize them.

Since the 1970s the Modi group has grown in a host of unrelated industries, reflecting the interests and strengths of the second generation. From tires to cigarettes, carpets to copier machines, pharmaceuticals to soybeans, cement to sponge iron, the Modis have, as one journalist put it, "stepped on the industrial levers in an aggressive push for the best technologies and greener fields of opportunity." Along the way their diversification plans threw fear into the hearts of larger, more established groups who saw market shares being sawed in half if the Modis were allowed to enter even half the markets their ambitious plans encompassed.

Despite their growing confidence as a leading industrial force in their own right, the Modis maintain an abiding faith in the value of foreign joint venture partners. The early success of Modipon with Rohm & Haas encouraged the Modis to continue the practice of seeking the most well-known technology leaders in the world as joint venture partners. To the Modis, enlisting the participation of internationally recognized companies as partners is sound business practice for a variety of reasons. The Modis

K.N. Modi with Prime Minister Indira Gandhi

believe, as do other leading industrialists, that "Indians have a love affair with international brand names and technology." Any product manufactured under license or in partnership with well-known names such as Xerox, Courtaulds, S.C. Johnson, Rohm & Haas, Continental Gummi-Werke and Hospital Corporation of America—some of the Modi partners—is felt to be assured of consumer patronage, stockholder subscription and financial institution support.

Though the emphasis in the group has always been on promotion and erection of new plants, this pattern changed somewhat in recent years with the acquisition of Bombay Tyres from Firestone Tire & Rubber Company of the USA, Godfrey Phillips (India) Ltd., a Philip Morris affiliate, and Indofil Chemicals, now a joint venture between the Modis and Rohm & Haas. These acquisitions contributed significantly to the group's assets and turnover.

The Modis were lured into acquiring Firestone of India by the desire to expand. Handicapped in expanding production in Modipuram by licensing regulations, the Modis sought to extend their interests in the tire industry through acquisition. They found a ready seller in Firestone Tire and Rubber.

Firestone had come to Calcutta in 1930 and established a private limited company there with their tire plant located in Bombay. For 30 years they did well, but mounting competition from firms such as Modi Rubber, an increasingly difficult worldwide economy and Indian government pressures on multinationals to divest to minority positions finally convinced Firestone

Mrs. Dayawati Modi (wife of GM Modi), with her son, B.K. Modi

to pull out rather than divest partially or modernize their equipment to compete with better quality products. In 1979 negotiations began with the Modis. The decision by the government to allow the Modis to buy a controlling percentage in Firestone disturbed some fellow industrialists, but the deal was consummated in December of 1981.

Firestone had performed miserably from the early 1970s. Production plummetted from 800,000 tires in 1975 to 500,000 in 1981. Profits fell and workers' earnings suffered accordingly. With an uncertain future hanging over their heads, labor became increasingly restive and the plant was struck in early 1981. During that time an American director of the company was assaulted by the workers.

When the Modis finally assumed control of the company (renamed Bombay Tyres International Ltd. since a settlement could not be reached over the use of the brand name), the company's operations were crippled. With the acquisition, however, the Modis's share of the tire market on the basis of licensed capacity reached 35 percent. But it was going to take a lot to revive Bombay Tyres. Its outdated plant and machinery were worthy of a museum. But Vinay and Bhupendra Modi set about the task of modernizing the Firestone plant, improving productivity, cancelling holidays and doubling and tripling shifts. The employees who were worried about their fate under a local owner were pleasantly surprised that there were more opportunities for promotion under the new managers. Some executives who were advised to leave the company by well-meaning American managers later regretted their decision.

Godfrey Phillips (India) Ltd. (renamed Hindustan Marketing Ltd. in 1983) was originally established in 1936 by Godrey Phillips Ltd. of London. The Indian company which manufactured cigarettes did well and just before independence, in October of 1946, it was converted into a public limited company. The Indian company came under new management in 1968 when Philip Morris International Financial Corporation acquired Godfrey Phillips of the UK and through it, Godfrey Phillips of India. The company's activities expanded in India, but the 1974 Foreign Exchange Regulation Act clipped its expansion plans somewhat. By 1979, the same year negotiations began between the Modis and Firestone, Philip Morris International Financial Corporation and other foreign shareholders decided to offer just over 200,000 shares of the company to the Indian public to reduce the foreign shareholding to the desired norm of 40 percent. The "Indianization" of the company was completed when the Modis bought 15 percent of the offering, and with it, managing control of what is now a Rs 133 crore-plus ($110 million) operation.

The acquisition of a major share of the cigarette company took the group into the consumer product field, an area it saw as having vast potential. The Modis initially saw the affiliation with Philip Morris as an access to that firm's soft drink, 7-Up, which could possibly fill the vacuum left by the exit of Coca-Cola in 1978. They decided instead to concentrate on making the cigarette business, their mainstay, more profitable. Under Modi management, marketing budgets were increased and new brands introduced. Production was stepped up and higher efficiency norms set. Profits climbed to previously unrealized levels. With success, however, came the inevitable headaches. Rising costs of inputs stimulated all the cigarette companies to jump into the marketing game with renewed energy simply to survive.

Vazir Sultan Tobacco, another Indian company, launched their remarkably successful *Charms* brand which quickly cut into their competitors' market shares, and Duncans Agro Industries Ltd., a GP Goenka company, walked off with the collaboration with Rothmans which the Modis had also been hoping to obtain. (The Modis eventually launched Chesterfield cigarettes in Bombay in the early part of 1985, putting the heat back on the Goenkas.) All things considered, the Modis were right. The cigarette industry turned out to be one of the toughest marketing grounds the Modis could have chosen for their launch into consumer goods.

The acquisition of the Indian company which became Indofil Chemicals Ltd. (now being merged with Modipon) was a luckier choice for the Modis. Purchased in collaboration with Rohm & Haas from another Indian firm, Amar Dye Chem, in 1976, the Modis gained management control in 1980. Sales of Rs 16 crore in 1983 yielded a Rs 2.2 crore ($1.8 million) profit. A manufacturer of pesticides, fungicides, herbicides, special tanning agents and fat liquors, Indofil is slated for very healthy growth and is a favorite in the Modi stables. It was so named because the headquarters of Rohm & Haas was Philadelphia and it was an Indian-based company, thus Indofil.

In the early 1970s, when Bhupendra Modi was studying at the University of Southern California, he wrote to the Xerox Corporation. He invited them to tie up with the Modis in India. Bhupendra's letter was the beginning of an eleven year off-again, on-again relationship which culminated in the formation of a joint venture, Modi-Xerox Ltd., in 1984 to produce Xerox products for the Indian market. The road was one of the longest yet which any Modi had travelled to bring a world-renowned name to India's doorstep. GM's fourth son, known as BK, proved the Modi mettle.

Xerox was flexible enough to consider entering the Indian market via the export door. In 1981 the Indian government, with a view to boosting exports, decided to encourage entrepreneurs to set up units whose total production would be exported. Tax concessions were offered and the Modis were quick to perceive the potential in the new policy. They registered two such export units, Modi Carpets, promoted by Satish Kumar, GM's third son, and later Indian Reprographic Systems Ltd. While the Indian government had rejected a 1979 proposal from the Modis to form a 50-50 joint venture with Xerox's UK subsidiary, Rank Xerox, the Modis saw the export program as a way to get started with Xerox in India.

For the Modi group, a successful export collaboration would mean not only profits, but higher export figures which would in turn ensure a relaxation of import regulations for the group as a whole. The export sales to Eastern Europe and Russia also beckoned the two partners to form their venture quickly once the government gave the green signal by way of special concessions. Indian Reprographic Systems was incorporated with the Modis holding 60 percent and the balance held by Rank Xerox. All components would be imported, assembled at the plant in the Thane industrial belt outside Bombay, and re-exported at a minimum 30 percent value added on the imported price. Even before it turned out its first Xerox plain copier, the joint venture had firm orders for five years for copiers valued at between Rs 30,000 ($2500) to Rs 100,000 each ($8,330).

Now that Xerox was in India, the partners did not lose any time in setting up a much more ambitious domestic operation. There was a host of industries in which large groups could expand in a similar fashion without too much red tape. Modi-Xerox Ltd. was formed. On a 137-acre plot in Rampur in the state of Uttar Pradesh, with an investment of Rs 30 crore ($25 million), · the project introduced its first copiers in March 1985. The new plant is one of the most sophisticated Xerox operations in the world. Bhupendra Modi remarked at the press conference announcing the project: "That Xerox should choose India to be the first developing country to set up a full scale manufacturing plant is bound to restore confidence in investing in India that was shaken with the exit of IBM." From their first joint venture with Rohm & Haas, and even farther back to KN's first trip to America in 1948 to buy textile equipment for Modi Spinning, the Modis continued to be a pioneer in attracting some of the world's best companies to India's shores.

Modi logos

In his early years of building up his companies, GM's talent and ambitions far outstripped the resources and infrastructure required to build a large empire. But he persisted until the profitable war years contributed the fuel for his industrial visions. His base was established before independence, however, in an industrial landscape where rules were few. His successors, equally hard-driving and motivated, operate in an altogether more complex environment of regulation, planning and licensed production. To cope with these and to maintain their breakneck growth, the Modis embarked on an aggressive tax planning scheme. The easiest way to minimize tax liability in India is to promote new projects which carry with them a host of investment tax credits, holidays and concessions. The Modis also lobbied in the halls of government for tax breaks and obtained them. But this year's tax break may disappear with next year's budget proposal. Growth fueled by cash generated from a reduction in taxes is vulnerable to changes in tax laws or court rulings on disputed tax matters.

A 1983 Supreme Court decision relating to the bases on which excise tax is figured hit the Modis particularly hard. Some 14,000 companies throughout India who had been withholding excise tax payments to the government pending resolution of the case were affected. In the May 1983 decision, the Court struck down Bombay Tyres' contention that post manufacturing expenses like packaging and marketing are costs of production and therefore should not attract excise assessment. Excise taxes are part of the price of an item, collected by the manufacturer to be remitted to the government. The court decision reportedly could yield billions for the government if the disputed taxes could be collected.

The Modis were among the worst hit with interests in no fewer than seven out of the top 20 revenue yielding product categories: cigarettes, man-made yarn, tires and tubes, iron and steel, cement, sugar, synthetic fibers, cotton fabrics and cotton yarns. Rivals were quick to suggest that many of the ambitious expansion plans of the affected groups could stall because of the ruling. But the skirmish of claims and counter-claims has only begun.

The Modis went on the offensive. The tire industry was doing badly, at least those companies who were no longer enjoying the tax break the Modis had pioneered for new tire companies in the 1970s. KN, the chairman, at the thirteenth annual general meeting of Modi Rubber held in April 1984 fired a salvo at the government calling for a uniform approach to the meting out of tax rebates for the industry. KN explained the issue to the shareholders:

During the last five to six years, the Government of India had issued industrial licenses for substantial expansion of the capacity of tyre units. As the cost of expansion has gone up considerably due to substantial increase in cost of plant and machinery, import duty etc., the new tyre units have been representing to the Government for granting excise duty relief for additional capacity created by them by way of implementing substantial expansion licenses. The Government also felt the need for partially compensating the incidence of the high project cost for expansion of tyre units and announced an excise duty relief scheme in April, 1984 by which excise duty relief is available to the extent of 30% of the value of capital investment. However, under this scheme, the relief has been granted to only such of the new tyre units which had commenced production after April 1976.

Your company which is a new unit set up in November, 1974 though given the Excise Relief on its initial cost was deprived of the relief on the huge capital cost incurred on its balancing/expansion scheme. The Government is required to extend the relief to this new unit also which has spent a huge amount in implementing the licence granted to it by the Government. Otherwise, this will cause serious discrimination as between the new tyre units and will also result in unfair competition and distortion in market conditions.

What KN did not emphasize was that the Modis had been the leading proponent of the rebate scheme and that they had reaped considerable benefit from it to get their plant on a profitable footing. Other newer tire units were just taking a leaf out of the Modi book. But the world market situation for tires was reflected in India as well.

1983 had seen a combination of circumstances that drove the worldwide demand for tires to almost half of what it had been in 1982. Small companies around the world closed their doors and large producers had to consolidate their operations. Even in the face of the worldwide crisis, the Government of India continued to license more capacity in the tire industry to prevent monopoly. From mid-1983 costs skyrocketed while prices could not keep pace because of government intervention. When relief came in the form of government approval of price increases, the bigger companies, including Modi Rubber, became locked in a price war. Lower demand exacerbated the industry's troubles. Demand in 1983 was for 10 million tires against an industry capacity of 12 million. Even the demand projected by 1990 could be met by the 12 companies which already existed.

Appeal to the government for excise rebates was a necessity in order to keep afloat. And as if the failure to obtain the needed rebate on tire excise and the negative 1983 post manufacturing excise ruling were not enough for the Modi group to withstand, Modinagar's largest employer, Modi Spinning & Weaving Mills, ran into serious trouble in 1984. Accumulated losses and a history of labor troubles dating back several years led the group to seek relief from the state to minimize the impact on the economy and workers in Modinagar. There is no doubt that the Modis' movement into more sophisticated and higher technology industries and the generally poor health of the textile sector had left Modi Spinning to languish.

From just over Rs 200 crores ($166 million) of sales at the time of GM's death in 1976 to near Rs 1,000 crores ($833 million) in 1983, it was inevitable that an adjustment period would come for the Modi group. Their growth and development as a family and a business group could provide a classic case study for business students. A Hindu joint family and a corporate group with nine members possessing powerful ambitions, yet differing approaches to business, but with natural vision and a certain charisma—they have provided plenty of material for journalists over the years.

The team spirit KN has tried to foster among his sons and GM's five was exactly the opposite approach of that of GM. KN talks in terms of his

Mahendra Modi

Yogendra Modi

Devendra Modi

"cabinet," consensus and equality. Ironically, KN's more democratic personality has permitted some of the second generation Modis to follow in GM's footsteps; by their actions they espouse a survival of the fittest philosophy. GM had ruled with an iron hand, pushing his sons hard. Satish and Vinay recalled once that they had fled home several times because of the pressure. The resentment was transformed into an aggressiveness in business which few would dare to match. What has this meant for KN's sons, quieter in nature, but no less ambitious? KN points out that each Modi company has one of his sons, and one of GM's at the helm. But GM's sons have the edge in the 1980s. Without GM around to dictate, scrutinize, intimidate, Krishan, Vinay, Satish, Bhupendra and Umesh have had to fend for themselves. KN's sons, Mahendra, Yogesh and Devendra, follow a subtler path. KN's youngest son, Devendra, a Ph.D. in management from Lucknow University, did his dissertation on the impact of personality on an organization. He is acutely aware of the differences between his father's style of business and that of GM.

Whereas GM's sons generally announce their projects when they are in the planning stages—to mark out the terrain in a country of limited resources—KN's son, Devendra, for example, prefers to negotiate quietly, lining up necessary support before the general public is aware of his plans. Since each of the Modis has an equal share in the business, however, a consensus on future paths to growth will have to include all of them. KN's philosophy is realistic in this sense. His attempts to keep the family together are seconded by GM's eldest son, KK, who points out that the group has some very ambitious projects involving huge investments. Only by pooling their combined resources can these projects materialize. Thus, KK says, there is no question of splits in the family.

There is a $45 million soybean processing project promoted by KK and Mahendra Modi in collaboration with A.E. Staley of the USA. A $130 million cellulose fiber joint venture with Courtaulds of the UK is being promoted by Satish Modi and Vinay has promoted an $80 million cement plant with Blue Circle Industries of the UK. In the meantime, Umesh, GM's youngest son, is busy getting a pharmaceutical project off the ground in collaboration with Sterling International of New York. Devendra is negotiating a Rs 100 crore ($86 million) project with a North American firm and working to get the new Modi-Xerox venture on stream with his cousin, Bhupendra. A break-up of the group's assets would inevitably threaten their new projects, more so than any tax assessment.

Satish Modi

Umesh Modi

Partial relief appeared in the form of a renewed Soviet shopping spree for consumer goods in India in late 1984 following a severe downturn in that demand in 1983. KK Modi projected Rs 100 crores ($83 million) in sales to the USSR of Xerox copiers, cigarettes, toiletries, carpets and other consumer goods produced by Modi plants. The sheen taken off the Modis' high-flying growth of the late 1970s and early 1980s by adverse tax rulings and over-expansion would be partially restored by increased sales to the Eastern Bloc

Modipon Ltd., Corporate Headquarters

countries which has been an important, if sporadic, export market for every type of Indian consumer product from silk to soap.

As the Modi group grew into an empire of 25,000 employees, GM's paternalistic approach to the welfare of his family of workers which kept crises from striking at the roots of growth would need updating. The transition to so-called professionalization of the owner's attitude toward management and workers is under way. The inevitable splits and strains among family members serving in the same company have led to tension among the professional managers themselves, causing a backlash of unhappiness and frustration on the part of some managers. It was not altogether helpful therefore when KN was quoted in an interview as saying that professional managers could never be involved to the same extent in the performance of the companies that they manage because they do not have a vital stake in the enterprises they help run. But family-dominated businesses the world over have made the transition. Bhupendra Modi may have started the group down the right path with his plans to promote a new hospital outside New Delhi.

Modi Temple, Modinagar

Most Indians who are well-off travel abroad for medical treatment. It was when GM once travelled to Boston for eye treatment and was not treated very well that he decided to build an eye hospital in Modinagar. A new hospital project in collaboration with Hospital Corporation of America's UK subsidiary came on the drawing board in the early 1980s. It was to be located outside New Delhi. Bhupendra began circling the globe on the trail of the Indian medical diaspora, offering Indian physicians an opportunity to return to India as shareholders, managers and practitioners in the new hospital. Many were attracted to the proposition because of the ownership feature. Stock options have long been part of the Western executive's perquisites. The Modis were introducing the concept into their group to make the hospital project viable. The move by BK coincided with the Indian government's interest in attracting home investments of non-resident Indians with disposable income and an interest in their homeland. The Modis were quick to put the policy into practice for their project. The same concept could be applied to any number of their other ambitious investment plans.

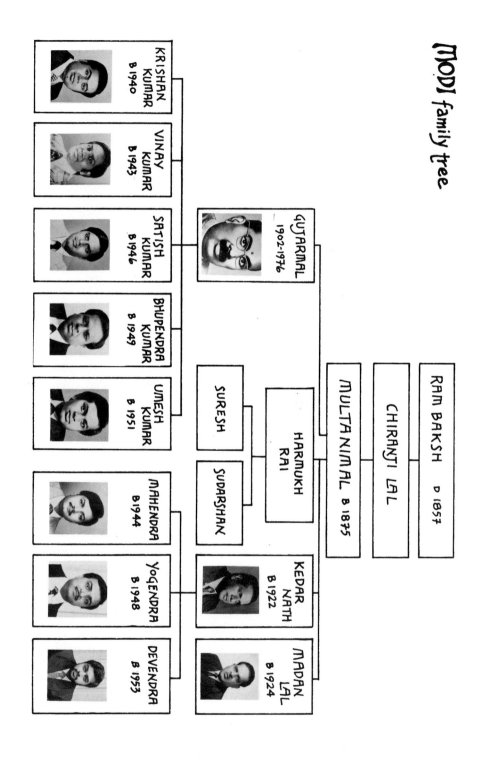

MODI family tree

KRISHAN KUMAR B 1940
VINAY KUMAR B 1943
SATISH KUMAR B 1946
BHUPENDRA KUMAR B 1949
UMESH KUMAR B 1951

GUJARMAL 1902-1976

SURESH
SUDARSHAN

MAHENDRA B 1944
YOGENDRA B 1948
DEVENDRA B 1953

HARMUKH RAI

KEDAR NATH B 1922
MADAN LAL B 1924

MULTANIMAL B 1875

CHIRANJI LAL

RAM BAKSH   D 1857

GM Modi (from oil painting)

Failure was not a word in GM's dictionary. Setbacks, personal or in business, were only stepping stones to reaching one's ultimate goals. His deep faith in his gods and confidence in his abilities always carried GM through any crisis. It was difficult for his sons to develop similar strengths of character because GM was always there to tell them what to do. His omnipresence sent the message that failure would not be tolerated. Such pressure created a barely perceptible fault line of diffidence in the personalities of his five sons – a softening feature in otherwise seethingly competitive natures. Voracious in pursuing GM's dreams of industrial success, caring little for public or private opinion, they know instinctively that in business, history will recall the results, not the struggles, risks, ruthlessness or vision which were necessary to create them.

KN likes to say that he owes everything he is to GM. Contemplating the events affecting the group's activities in 1984, he even wished aloud that GM were around today. Three young boys, ranging in age from five to seven, enter the room where the founder's spirit is being recalled. KN's grandsons are anxious to pull him away from business talk. He has obviously promised to spend some time with them. They wait politely for a minute or two and then succeed in pulling on his arms and pantlegs, leading him down the hallway toward some unknown destination. Business may not be on the minds of the third generation of Modis as yet, but the singlemindedness with which they have captured the chairman of the Modi group and led him off should convince KN that the future of the group appears to be in capable hands.

Principal Modi Companies

Name	Product
Modi Industries	Sugar, vanaspati, oils, gases, paints, soaps, cosmetics, spirits, steel, welding, electrodes
Modi Spg & Wvg Mills	Textiles, threads
Modipon	Synthetic yarns and fibers
Modi Rubber	Automobile tires and tubes
Bombay Tyres International	Automobile tires and tubes
Godfrey Phillips India	Cigarettes
Modi-Xerox	Copiers
Modi Cement	Cement

KK Modi, GM's eldest son

Oberoi

Five-star hotels
Inflight catering service
Travel agencies
Trading

Sales
Rs 120 crore
($100 million)

Headquarters
Oberoi Maidens
7, Sham Nath Marg
Delhi, India   110 054

Head of Group
M.S. Oberoi

Mohan Singh Oberoi

OBEROI

I was born on August 15, 1900 in a small village, Bhaun in district Jhelum which now forms a part of Pakistan. The story of my life has been, in many ways, a dramatic one—full of difficulties and hardships, in earlier days and later a spectacular rise to the position I now hold. But this was not achieved without incessant toil and a daily fight against tremendous odds. Yet it was a challenge to prove myself. When I look back to those days, as I sometimes do, in moments of leisure, I am thankful that I was able to accept this challenge and make good. These reflections also make me feel humble for I realise it was with God's help that I achieved what the world calls "success".[1]

M. S. Oberoi is India's first and foremost hotelier, beginning as a clerk in the early 1920s in a British-owned hotel and quickly moving into management and then ownership. Chairman today of an international hotel chain which owns or manages more than 30 luxury hotels worldwide, Oberoi expanded his business along the way to include a travel agency, inflight catering service, a hotel management school and an export house. Oberoi's son-in-law, Gautam Khanna, and a director of East India Hotels, predicts that eventually the food-related activities of the group will be expanded to contribute about half of the group's revenues. For the moment and for the last

55 years or so, however, the business of M. S. Oberoi has been first class hotels. Even though the management of his empire is still highly personalized because of the founder's presence at the helm, MS asserts that it is not the founder or his family, nor a board of directors, which makes or breaks a business. It is the system which management establishes which ensures the success and profitability of any enterprise. He might have added that sticking to what you know best and remaining true to one's standards of excellence may also make the difference between success and failure.

The pervading ambience of Oberoi hotels reflects MS's philosophy that you cannot succeed if you have tension around you, if you are a worrier, if you do not have a clear and peaceful mind. In his hotels, MS says, his prime objective is to keep the hustle and bustle away from the hotel guest. As you may notice, he says simply, his hotel lobbies are not cluttered with too many chairs and sofas, and moreover they are placed unobtrusively throughout the spacious lobby areas to minimize noise and confusion. The bars and restaurants are quiet. This is achieved by planning for a variety of restaurants and bars throughout the hotel complexes to assure a dispersion of guests and visitors. The higher tariffs keep away the crowds. And since profits in Oberoi hotels come from keeping the room occupancies high, not the food and beverage side, MS is not concerned if the restaurants and coffee shops in his hotel are not filled around the clock. Peace and quite comfort, the latest amenities for the well-heeled tourist and the business executive, are MS Oberoi's gifts to the world of travel. He has not wanted for critical acclaim and the love of his loyal employees and friends.

> *I am no longer young in years, but my spirit is the same; My determination to work and to succeed in whatever I undertake. I still rise at 5 a.m. and work for 16-hours a day, when necessary. I live simply, not multiplying my wants but remembering always to count my blessings. My farm is my refuge and gives me solace. It is a big venture and I enjoy the communion with nature. My roses are a special pride but the farm gives me the opportunity to experiment with ideas in improving my orchards, grain, the different breeds of poultry and dairy.*[2]

Oberoi's 90-acre farm on the outskirts of New Delhi is even more important to him since his son Tikki's death in 1983 at the age of 59. It is an event which MS says was the greatest blow in his life, one he found almost impossible to accept. On the farm which gives him so much solace, dogs as big as calves roam, 50,000 chickens are raised, deer play and the owner knows the age of each tree. His living quarters resemble a modest suite of hotel rooms and are part of a structure which used to serve as farm sheds. MS lived in his hotels for the better part of his rise to success. He saw no reason to live differently on his farm. But well-manicured green lawns as far as the eye can see, flowers, trees of all shapes and sizes, fifteen-foot bird cages, all recreate the resort-like atmosphere which India's elite enjoyed during their summer holidays in Simla when MS observed their comings and goings as a jobless newlywed.

M.S. Oberoi at center (in white turban), ca. 1914

The Early Days of Mohan Singh Oberoi

MS was raised by his mother. His father, Attar Singh Oberoi, a small-town contractor, died of influenza which had broken out in Peshawar where he had gone in search of work. MS's mother, Bhagwanti, took her six month-old baby home to Bhaun after her husband's death as her in-laws now considered her presence inauspicious. Fortunately, Bhagwanti's family did not share such suspicions. She was welcomed home by her father and soon became indispensable to the household. She gained the respect of the local Bhaun community in her own right and eventually assumed some of her father's responsibilities as a town leader. When the family's wealth came to be split, Bhagwanti received a quarter share, an unusual event in her country even eight decades later.

MS was the center of his mother's world. She determined early on that her son would have a chance to succeed in life. The love and attention Bhagwanti shared with MS throughout her life provided MS with a winning self-confidence. At the same time, she was rewarded with a son for whom hard work was not a problem. MS was sent off to school in Rawalpindi, his first experience with the big city. Bhaun, his hometown, numbered about ten to fifteen thousand people. He attended a progressive school, the Dayanand-Anglo-Vedic School, for two years. At 15, he moved on to the commercial and cultural center of Lahore to continue his studies at the Dayanand-Anglo-Vedic School there. Until now MS and his mother had not had any disagreements. But when MS arrived in Lahore, he did not take long to look up his father's family who had turned him and his mother out fifteen years earlier.

Sentiments had changed and MS's uncle welcomed him warmly, offered him a place to stay and even a job managing the family's shoe business after school. Bhagwanti's initial anger eventually subsided and her son enjoyed his new-found family's company. The job in the shoe factory gave MS his first taste of business and he knew, despite the fact that the company soon folded, that he wanted to continue doing business. Money ran out and he had to return home. Finding work was to be as difficult for MS as it had been for his father, it seemed. He travelled to Amritsar for a short time on the invitation of a friend and took a course in shorthand and typing. But he still lacked any identifiable skills with which to begin his adult life.

In 1920, MS wrote, "penniless, jobless and almost friendless," his marriage was arranged with the daughter of Ushnak Rai, the girl next door to the Oberois in Bhaun. It was only a short while after his marriage to Ishran Devi that the young couple fled Bhaun at the insistence of his mother to avoid being stricken by the plague which had broken out there. Around the same time, MS had seen an ad in a local newspaper for a junior clerk's position in a government office. He went to Simla to take the exam for the position, and failed. But Simla was the summer seat of the British-ruled India and held some fascination for MS. "There were many walks where one could be alone with one's thoughts," wrote MS.

MS with wife, Ishran Devi, and first son, Tikki

With little else to do but observe the goings-on of his surroundings, MS made a science of it. He studied every aspect of the well-dressed crowd which paraded by on the mall at Simla. He noticed that high-ranking military and government officials especially frequented a hotel called the Cecil. He quickly learned through inquiry who was in charge of the hotel and one day, with nothing to lose, MS approached D. W. Groves, the manager, to request a job. At first told that there was no position available, MS's persistence and quick description of his school certificates and stenography skills turned the mind of the sympathetic manager. Oberoi was even bold enough to request living quarters for his new wife and baby. It seemed that nothing would be refused him that day.

The year was 1922. The Cecil Hotel was part of the Associated Hotels of India founded by an Italian by the name of John Faletti. The new clerk from Bhaun soon proved himself invaluable, always looking to take on extra assignments, offering suggestions for improvement of various services, and earning additional money. When a new manager took over the Cecil, MS was invited to move into the chief clerk's position. Ernest and Gertrude Clarke, the new managers, found in the young clerk all they could hope for. When in 1924, Clarke decided to go into the hotel business himself, he invited MS to join him. But the one year contract Clarke had obtained to run the Delhi Club soon ran out, and he looked around for another hotel. He found it in Simla which MS had been reluctant to leave in the first place. But the Rs 100 salary Clarke had offered him was too good to pass up. Now they were back.

Front view, the Cecil Hotel, Simla (formerly the Falettis Hotel)

Side view,
the Cecil, Simla

The Carlton Hotel was in liquidation in Simla. Clarke leased it and reopened it as the Clarkes Hotel. By now the chief clerk has become an assistant manager. The changes he suggested in the operation of the resort hotel were revolutionary to the business. MS introduced the concept of professional service to the hotel after observing that the confusion caused by each guest using his own servant to fetch and carry was resulting in inefficiencies which were costing the managers profits. His attention was always on the specific details of the business at hand. If there were deliveries of food and fuel being made, he would stop the delivery men to check the quantity and quality. Inevitably he found discrepancies and quickly corrected the situation. His big break came in the early 1930s, less than a decade after his first clerkship at the Cecil.

The Clarkes were homesick and decided to return to England for a year. The decision was made easier because MS would be the one to take charge of the hotel in their absence. Close contact would be maintained about the operations of the Clarkes Hotel by long distance. When the year had passed and the Clarkes returned, they found the hotel more profitable than when they were managing it. They rewarded their Indian manager by offering him a one-third share in the business at a price of Rs 10,000 ($833). MS called on his mother and friends of the family to help him raise the money. It was the first of many times his family and friends would come through when similar opportunities arose in the future. The future was never far off for MS. Another sum of money had to be found a little later on when the Clarkes wanted to buy out the freehold in their Simla hotel from the bank which held it. MS had to come up with his share of the purchase price. That hurdle overcome, when the Clarkes decided to sell out and return home for good, MS was offered the hotel at a reasonable price. This time it was his wife's jewelry which had to be pawned and another appeal to his previous benefactors. MS wrote:

> *He made me an offer saying he would prefer someone who could maintain the tradition and efficiency of the hotel to run it. Acceptance meant that I would have to mortgage my few assets and my wife's jewellery in order to raise the necessary funds. However, I did not hesitate long. The opportunity seemed almost a Godsend as we Indians are a superstitious people. I took over the proprietorship of Clarke's Hotel with the help of a kind uncle who had stood by me in the past. I was now established in the hotel business.*[3]

By the mid-1930s, MS and his wife had five children, two sons, T.R.S. (Tikki), P.R.S. (Biki), and three daughters, Raj Rani, Swaraj and Prem. He was now a hotelier in a country not yet his own. He was moving very quickly in a business which was traditionally operated by the British and Swiss. Yet there seemed nothing to stop him from doing what he knew best—catering to the needs of the wealthier classes where the possibilities for improving the service and aesthetics of hoteliering went hand in hand with increased profitability. He had no problem reaching beyond his own small-town upbringing to imagine what it was that would make even the most particular guest happy. He had

learned through constant observation, experience and the native brightness
which had gotten him over the initial periods of uncertainty about wine lists and
exotic entrées. His only challenge was to grow. That chance came again just
before the start of World War II, a boom time for most of Indian industry. MS
caught a notice in the paper that the Grand Hotel in Calcutta was going into
liquidation and a friend suggested a partnership be formed to take it over. MS
was interested. He recollected:

> *It is a strange coincidence that nearly every turn in my life has been
> associated with an epidemic of some sort. In 1933 there had been a cholera
> epidemic of vast proportions in Calcutta. The Grand Hotel had been closed
> ever since, as more than a hundred foreign guests had died. People were
> afraid to visit Calcutta. I happened to see the advertisement placed by the
> liquidators and immediately decided to take over the hotel if I could get it on
> a low leasehold. The price asked was 10,000 rupees rent a month plus
> compensation for the goodwill. In return, I demanded compensation for the
> ill-will generated by the hotel. The rent was then dropped to 7,000 rupees a
> month. I agreed to this figure.[4]*

Oberoi Grand Hotel, Calcutta

Even four decades later, MS insists that war-time was the most crucial period for his group. After the lease was signed in 1938 to take over operation of the 500-room hotel, it took a strong stomach and a lot of elbow grease to renovate a plague-ridden hotel that had not been open for five years. When MS and his associates finally succeeded in bringing back the grand old hotel, MS had to head off a British government plan to requisition the hotel to house troops. He approached the Army command and signed an agreement to provide accommodations for 400 to 500 troops at a fixed price per soldier. Soon the numbers grew to 2,000. His agreement with the Army was to "provide a bed to sleep, a chair to sit and meals."[5] He set up a self-service restaurant so the troops could help themselves and he could cut down on waiters. There was plenty of food on the market, MS says—meat, poultry, fish—but the difficulty during the war was in obtaining adequate supplies of spirits. So Oberoi went public with an open letter to appropriate parties throughout the subcontinent inviting them to sell their liquor to Oberoi Hotels at whatever price they wanted to set. Even after providing 2,000 meals a day and 20,000 drinks, Oberoi's Grand Hotel made a profit of five rupees per head per day.

To manage the Grand Hotel, MS had invited the man who had given him his original job in Simla, D.W. Groves, to come to Calcutta. The offer was accepted. Eventually, MS bought out his three partners in the Grand and also bought the hotel itself for about Rs 60 lakhs ($500,000). The wheel of fortune was turning full circle. Oberoi gave it a final ironic twist in 1943 when he arrived at the annual meeting of the Associated Hotels of India Ltd. with enough shares to wrest control from Spencer & Company, the British firm which controlled it.[6] The Cecil Hotel in Simla was one of eight hotels owned by the Associated Hotels in India. MS now owned his original employer. MS had been quietly buying up shares in Associated Hotels and then borrowing against those shares to increase his holdings until the dramatic takeover coup in 1943. With his latest acquisition, he gained control of a chain of eight small hotels throughout north India: Flashmans in Rawalpindi, Deans in Peshawar, Faletti's in Lahore, the Cecil in Muree, Maidens and Imperial in Delhi and the Cecil and Corstophons in Simla. The Oberoi group now numbered 10 hotels.

MS did not stop. Three more hotels were acquired in quick succession, in Darjeeling, Chandigarh and Kashmir. But soon just buying what other people had already built was not satisfying enough. The urge to build his own hotels now dominated MS. His ambitions coincided exactly with those of his countrymen who by now were ready to assume control of their own country from the war-weary, economically depressed mother country. With independence came the terrifying partition of India, however, and those with property in the new countries of Pakistan or a diminished India lost whatever they had if they did not live in the place where the property was. Oberoi lost control over four of his ten hotels which were in Rawalpindi, Peshawar, Lahore and Muree. While ownership still was his, no profits were able to be repatriated. And in 1965, after one of three wars with Pakistan, all the hotels were declared enemy property and were lost. But MS did not linger over the loss. He chose a site in Orissa to build his first hotel, at Gopal-on-Sea. The Orissa Oberoi had a modest 20 rooms, but it was a great success and encouraged MS to think about far more ambitious projects.

After the war, the Oberoi group moved into the travel business. MS's son, Tikki, opened Mercury Travels and it became the sole agent for Himalayan Aviation which operated air service between Delhi, Calcutta, Bombay and Madras. Mercury's operations took a nosedive after independence when aviation became the government's business. MS turned to his new son-in-law, Gautam Khanna, to get Mercury on its feet. Gautam had married MS' daughter, Swaraj. Without the Himalayan Aviation agency, some new line would have to built up. Khanna began his stewardship by firing what he felt were many less than competent employees. He also began to travel around the world to promote India in international travel circles. Khanna turned Mercury around and it is now the second largest and most successful travel agency in India. Oberoi was the first chain to establish its own travel agency. Eventually, Gautam was asked by MS to take charge of the Grand Hotel in Calcutta and his connection with the principal part of the Oberoi business began. He went on to become one of the leading experts in the country on tourism and travel in addition to his increasing executive responsibilities with East India Hotels.

Khanna was born in Bihar in 1924 and educated at the prestigious Doon School. At the Government College of Lahore he was an English honors major. Shelley was his favorite author. His father had been an official in the East Indian Railways and died when Gautam was quite young. Upon leaving college in 1944 at the age of 20, Gautam joined the railways himself and managed their catering service for eastern India. When he met Swaraj at a ball in Simla in the late 1940s, Khanna had little idea of what business her father was involved in. It was an auspicious match from MS's viewpoint. Gautam would prove invaluable to the growth of the chain, not to mention the important role he would come to play in promoting India in worldwide travel circles.

Gautam Khanna, Director, East India Hotels Ltd.

M.S. Oberoi with daughters, Prem (l.) and Swaraj (r.), in Austria, 1953

Then in the early 1950s, Tikki Oberoi became involved in promoting a housing development project in Assam. The Indo-U.S. Investment Company was set up to build housing colonies along the new Assam railway line which was being built at the time. When Tikki lost interest, MS moved to Assam to oversee the completion of the project. He was rewarded with a hand-operated trolley car of his own when he arrived in Assam. Mail from Calcutta would be delivered to him daily and he ran his empire for awhile from the site of the housing colony. In the early 1950s, he had also taken his first trip to Europe with his family to see the European hotel industry first-hand. MS could not have helped but focus on the fact that his country could not boast any hotels in the European five-star category, except for the Taj Mahal in Bombay built at the turn of the century by another pioneer, J. N. Tata.[7] So MS's thinking naturally turned more and more toward building higher class hotels on a large scale which would offer the new breed of international traveler all the comforts of similar hotels in the well-patronized capitals of the world. Toward the mid-1950s, therefore, the idea of building a five-star hotel in New Delhi began to make sense.

The First Five Star Hotel in Delhi

Such a project would cost several million dollars, a formidable hurdle in itself for the still fledgling group. Financing was non-existent for what seemed MS's pipedream, a luxury hotel in a country which espoused an official philosophy of socialism. Besides, what monies there were for building a new nation had to be channeled into large infrastructural projects such as iron and steel plants. The Oberois looked around for funds. The US government accumulated billions in local currency in the early 1960s from sales of grain to India as well as many other countries. The funds had to be used in India and a loan fund was established to lend to joint ventures between American and Indian companies. Nearly every Indo-American joint venture which sprang up in the 1960s had borrowed from the so-called Cooley fund. The Oberois had to find an American collaborator in order to avail themselves of the Cooley funds. Pan Am's Intercontinental Hotel Corporation was approached as they had already some connection with each other through the travel business.

It was 1965, ten years after the initial concept had been born, before the Oberoi Inter-Continential Hotel opened in New Delhi. It had stood as a shell for five years while funds were sought to complete it. The day of its inauguration, war broke out with Pakistan and the guests who had come to help the Oberois celebrate the long-awaited moment fled to the basement air raid shelters. It seemed that MS's business karma was not only tied to plagues, but to wars as well. The inauspicious beginning did not continue, however. It was not long before MS's vision proved itself. MS related that before the event could take place, there were years of work and what seemed innumerable difficulties. The reward for his labor came through the fact that the Inter-Continental Hotel has become one of the most prestigious establishments in India. Located amid several historic monuments, linked to a golf course, and just ten minutes away from downtown New Delhi, the Oberoi Inter-Continental is one of eight Oberoi hotels listed in Rene Leclerc's 300 Best Hotels in the World, a hotel guide published by Harper and Queen.

To visitors from India's former motherland, the Oberoi Inter-Continental was almost an eighth wonder of the world as S. L. Kirloskar noted in his autobiography. Kirloskar, a leading Indian industralist in the engineering sector, had invited a group of British equipment manufacturers to India as late as 1974 to see his factories. He writes:

> *Most of the couples who landed at Delhi at 10 am on 24 February after a night flight by Air India, were visiting our country for the first time. The customs men at Delhi Airport were quick and efficient which pleased our guests. They were then taken to Delhi's Oberoi Intercontinental Hotel by air-conditioned coaches. Both the air-conditioned coaches and the 5-star hotel were a surprise to some of the party, one of whom frankly admitted, 'we thought of India as the Taj Mahal, sadhus, snakes, monkeys . . . and with a bit of luck, tigers.'*[8]

The importance of hotels of international caliber, even in a newly

Oberoi Inter-Continental, New Delhi

industrializing country, was apparent from the remarks of Mr. Kirloskar's British guests. In 1983, when the Oberoi Inter-Continental in New Delhi played host to heads of state, kings and princes, at the Seventh Non-Aligned Conference, the list of products specially imported for the guests conjured up visions of the old days of Indo-Roman trade. Except that instead of exporting all its riches in exchange for gold, India imported delicacies from the four corners of the world: orchids from Singapore, Egyptian cooks from Cairo, caviar from Russia, lamb from Australia, French champagne, Jamaican rum. But, most importantly, the hospitality was compliments of the Indian management of the Oberoi group. The Conference further proved the obvious need for first class hotels to win friends by providing them with maximum comfort. MS's vision was becoming self-evident.

By the early 1960s, MS was convinced he had shaken off "the star of ill luck." He ecstatically wrote: "Horizons had widened. I began to feel the world was my oyster—that I could succeed in anything I attempted." His hotels did well and public honors began to come his way. The British had made him a Rai Bahadur for his assistance in housing the troops at his Grand Hotel in Calcutta during the war. But more democratic recognition came in 1955 when he was elected president of the Federation of Hotels & Restaurant Associations of India. Five years later he was made President of Honour for Life of the Federation.

By the early 1960s, with the New Delhi project on its way to completion, MS had turned his attention to politics. In 1962, he was elected to the Rajya Sabha (Upper House) and in 1967 he won a seat in the Lok Sabha (Lower House) by a wide margin. He joined politics to broaden his understanding of his environment. As an industrialist before and after independence, MS perhaps felt that rather than be at the mercy of new policies and regulations, why not get behind the wheel and help draft some of the rules of the game. He also shared a healthy sense of patriotism and nationalism. One day in Parliament, MS drew a portrait of his first meeting with one of the leaders of the freedom movement:

> . . . *Pandit Nehru came to stay at the Cecil, which was his usual place of residence when he came to Simla. He was then leader of the newly formed Swaraj Party, but known throughout the country for having renounced a princely law practice to participate in the Freedom Movement with Mahatma Gandhi. Panditji had an important report which needed to be typed speedily and with care. I sat up all night to complete the report and when I delivered it to him the next morning, he took out a hundred rupee note and handed it to me with a word of thanks. I am an emotional person and had received little kindness in my short life. This gesture of Panditji's brought tears in my eyes and I quickly left the room. I could not have guessed then that I had met the father of the future Prime Minister of India and that I myself would be one day a Member of Parliament during his leadership. One hundred rupees, which the wealthy throw away, was for me a fortune and made a big difference in my salary. So high was the purchasing power of the rupee that I was able to buy a wristwatch for my wife, clothes for our baby and a much needed raincoat for myself.*[9]

Gautam Khanna also became involved in politics at this time. President of the Swatantra Party in Delhi in the 1960s (on the opposite side of the fence from MS), Gautam Khanna himself almost stood for election from the state of Rajasthan. The Maharani of Jaipur had offered him a constituency. But Gautam felt differently about the mixing of politics and business. He admits he was not a "masses" man, he could not understand or communicate with the new style of politicians which had come up in the 1960s. As President of Swatantra in Delhi, Gautam recalled that it seemed everyone just wanted a job. His old style view of what politics was supposed to be did not coincide with the new quid pro quo politics of modern India. So he stuck to business and left the political limelight to MS.

Oberoi Goes International

MS's experience in Parliament, his travels on official missions, and the success of his first large project, the Inter-Continental in New Delhi, served to stretch his vision to encompass the opportunities for growth outside India. In 1969, on a vacation to Nepal, MS and his family noticed the potential of the Soaltee Hotel in Kathmandu which had been running at a loss since its inception. The Oberois signed a management contract with the owners of

Soaltee Oberoi, Kathmandu, Nepal

the Soaltee and transformed it into a successful venture. With 300 rooms and the only casino "within 3000 miles of Kathmandu", the Oberoi Soaltee soon became the largest hotel in Nepal.

Oberoi's international expansion came at a time when growth by private industrialists in India was discouraged by a government which was trying more and more to adapt its policies to the explicit socialist policies of the Congress Party. Although Oberoi executives would never say, and MS himself was always a member of the ruling Congress Party, the move abroad was dictated by domestic constraints which included lack of financing for the hotel industry. Steel plants, engineering conglomerates, transport, these were the sectors sopping up the available funds for development. Wherever in the world there was financing, a good location and a need for the now experienced Oberoi chain to plan, construct and operate luxury hotels – these dictated the group's expansion, says Gautam Khanna.

After Kathmandu and the Soaltee Hotel came the Oberoi Imperial in Singapore in 1971. The group's activities in Singapore expanded to include management of several restaurants in its international airport. By 1972, Gautam Khanna had spotted some opportunities in Egypt. An agreement was signed with the Egyptian government to form a joint venture management company to refurbish and manage the Mena House Hotel situated beside the Pyramids of Giza. The peace talks between Presidents Anwar Sadat and

Oberoi family: *standing:* Gautam Khanna (son-in-law), sons Tikki, Biki, J.C. Kapur (eldest son-in-law); *seated:* Mr. and Mrs. Oberoi with daughters Swaraj (l.), and to right, Raj Rani (eldest daughter), and to far right, Prem (youngest daughter); *seated on rug:* the grandchildren, Vijai Kapur, Ashoka Khanna, Rajni Kapur, and Ajai Kapur

Mena House Oberoi, Cairo

Aswan Oberoi, Elephantine Island, Aswan, River Nile

Jimmy Carter leading up to the Camp David Accords were held at the Mena House Oberoi. Another project in Egypt came in 1975 with the opening of the Aswan Oberoi, situated on Elephantine Island in the Nile, and featuring both villas and hotel rooms. Two more sites were chosen in Egypt for Oberoi hotels in 1983 in Luxor and Fayoum. The Oberoi Auberge at Fayoum is an exclusive residential country club located on an oasis on the large salt water Lake Qarun. An hour's drive from Cairo, the Auberge was originally constructed as a rest house for the monarchy. An Egyptian architect, Amr el Alfi, an expert in restoration of historic buildings, was given charge of the Auberge's renovation. Riding stables, a marina and sailing and water sports facilities are part of the redesigned Auberge. A center for duck shooting in North Africa in the winter months, the Qarun Lake location promises to be everything a five-star luxury hotel should be.

The Luxor hotel, the Karnak Oberoi, scheduled for completion in late 1984, was designed as a luxury tourist village by Australian architect Peter Muller. Located near the 60-acre Karnak complex of temples built by the Pharaohs over a span of 2000 years, the Karnak Oberoi features a casino and an open air amphitheatre for performances of folk dance and cultural events.

In establishing a hotel, MS says, site is the first thing you look for. Then study the market, get good architects, good interior designers, engineers, well-trained staff, persons who know their job. On the average, the Oberois always have five to six new hotel projects on their drawing board a year. Always open to new proposals, MS feels that it is not an achievement to sit tight. One must always look forward, looking back only to assess what has been accomplished, not what opportunities one has missed.

Identifying the Middle East and Southeast Asia as the two most accessible markets for expansion, MS moved quickly to position his company for further growth. His son Biki, and son-in-law, Gautam Khanna, have taken over the globetrotting by and large to scout new projects, and Gautam Khanna's son, Ashok, is overseeing corporate development in Bombay. Ashok has charge of the expansion of the 700 room Oberoi Towers in Bombay where a new 300 room hotel is under construction next to the Oberoi Towers.

Despite the brisk rate at which the group's international activities were adding up in the 1970s, the Oberoi Towers in Bombay was conceived with characteristic vision by MS. The success of New Delhi's first international hotel, the Inter-Continental, prompted Oberoi to try his luck in India's gateway city. Compared to the Delhi project which cost four and a half crores, the Bombay Oberoi would cost Rs 30 crore ($25 million). Again, the Oberois would look for an American partner in order to take advantage of US Cooley loan funding. This time it was the Sheraton group which joined Oberois. The Oberoi Sheraton opened in 1973, but touched off a series of troubles for the group.

The high rate of interest on the loans taken to build the Bombay Oberoi wiped out profits in the early years. The group's ambitious expansion plans abroad strained its cash resources as well, and by mid-1970, the East India Hotels (incorporated in 1938 in Calcutta when MS took over the Grand Hotel) defaulted on its deposit holders.* Then the marketing tie-up with the Sheraton came undone in 1979 when Sheraton apparently hiked up the price for the franchise and Oberoi balked. Sheraton then went off with the ITC group to share marketing and reservations services. The market analysts speculated that the Oberoi's worldwide booking network would be considerably weakened. But the Oberois simply stepped up their own efforts to fill the impressive 37 floor complex which sweeps along Bombay's Marine Drive, overlooking the Arabian Sea. And in 1984, the Oberois announced an arrangement with Mandarin International Hotels to launch a reciprocal

---

*Indian companies are permitted to accept deposits from the general public.

reservations system through their satellite offices in the Asian region, further supplementing their marketing efforts.

In trying to recoup its initial heavy cash outlays, the group was eager to show full capacity at the new Bombay high rise hotel. It took on an image of a playground for international jet setters and brought to mind the manner in which MS had publicized the opening of the Grand Hotel in Calcutta in the late 1930s. Finding it hard to attract local patronage because of its former plague-imaged days, MS had invited a noted Calcutta citizen, a bon vivant who owned a string of movie theatres, to move into the Grand Hotel. This helped publicize the opening and set aside fears that the hotel was unsafe. Not quite so desperate in the mid-1970s when cash was scarce, the group no doubt did little to discourage any publicity which would bring in the business. It was also the first hotel to employ female staff which added to its already fast reputation. As the hotel became an established part of the city, however, and the number of visitors to India's business and film mecca increased, the clientele of the Oberoi Towers evened out, or so the local citizens felt as they got used to its looming presence on Nariman Point.

Oberoi Towers, Bombay

Lanka Oberoi, Colombo,
Sri Lanka

Hotel Babylon Oberoi,
     Baghdad, Iraq

The hotel got into the headlines again in the early 1980s when a 300 room expansion to the Oberoi Towers was announced. Local citizens' groups such as the Save Bombay Committee and the Bombay Environment Action Group lobbied for a park to be placed on the site of the expansion instead, claiming that the specifications of the new expansion violated local building codes. Only after intensive discussions in Bombay with the local development authorities and in Delhi with the central government were the Oberois permitted to go forward with the expansion.

By the early 1980s, the group had recovered from its financial crisis of the mid-1970s. Sales of the publicly-traded East India Hotels Ltd. (which owns and operates the Indian properties of the group as well as Mercury Travels, the inflight catering service and export activities) had increased 170 percent between 1977 and 1984 to Rs 50 crore ($36 million). (The Oberois' private company, Oberoi Hotels [India] Pvt. Ltd. holds a 40 percent interest in East India Hotels.) Another privately held company, Oberoi International (Pvt.) Ltd. carries on the group's international activities and holds the shares in the foreign joint ventures. The privately held company earns management fees as well as technical service fees for undertaking the design, construction or renovation of their overseas hotels. Their management contracts are usually for 25 years.

Even though sales data are not available on the privately held Oberoi companies, estimates put the group's total annual turnover well over Rs 120 crore ($100 million) as of 1984 and profits at a healthy 10 percent plus of annual turnover.

Overseas Expansion Continues

MS realized early on that expansion in itself did not ensure success. He commented in his autobiography: "Fortunately, I also realized that it was not good enough to keep launching out on new ventures if old ones were allowed to suffer. Too often efficiency and high standards once established are taken for granted. This is a great mistake and my constant aim has been to preserve the reputation of my hotels at the highest possible level." His two-pronged approach to growth has achieved its founder's aims.

The group's overseas expansion continued with hotels in Sri Lanka, Saudi Arabia, Indonesia and Australia keeping it occupied through the late 1970s. The Lanka Oberoi operated in partnership with the Sri Lankan government is the largest hotel on the island nation. The business center designed for the Lanka Oberoi won international acclaim and is being duplicated by the group in its other hotels around the world. Opened in 1975, the Lanka Oberoi was expanded in 1983 with a new 200 room wing. With all the traditional amenities of the Oberoi chain, the Sri Lankan property also boasts a playground, a mini deer park and an aviary on its grounds. Another hotel in Sri Lanka, at Kandy, the Queens Hotel, came under Oberoi management in 1981. Management of two hotels in Baghdad, Iraq followed in 1983 in cooperation with the Iraqi government.

About the time that the Lanka Oberoi was opening and the Bombay high-rise hotel was going up, the Oberois linked up with the large Saudi Arabian construction and oil development firm of Tamini and Fouad to develop the Saudi hotel business and ancillary activities. It was in the days when Saudi Arabia's fortunes were rising with every upward movement of oil prices. The joint venture established the Dammam hotel in 1977 and added another hotel, the Dammam Oberoi, in 1981. The Dammam Oberoi is situated on a seaside promenade and houses the largest convention and conference facilities in Saudi Arabia. The Indo-Saudi joint venture company also manages a bakery, hospital catering service and supermarket in Saudi Arabia. Then Australia and Indonesia beckoned the group in the late 1970s. MS's flare for site selection held.

The Oberoi/Saudi joint venture undertook the refurbishment of an historic 94 year-old hotel in Melbourne, Australia, by the name of The Windsor. The old building faces Parliament House and overlooks 78 acres of public gardens and parks. A political and cultural mecca in Melbourne, MS had spotted it during an official fact-finding trip he had taken for the Indian government. The Oberoi joint venture company won the bid from the Melbourne government to renovate the historic landmark. A public outcry quickly ensued, allegedly fanned by the hotel's former managers who had lost the $5 million bid to restore the landmark. Newspaper ads suggested that the city of Melbourne would become full of curry smells if the Oberois were allowed to operate The Windsor. Detractors claimed the Indian chain was out to turn the hotel into a "flashy money-spinner" and distributed "Save Our Heritage" leaflets. The Oberois responded with an ad campaign of their own reassuring local citizens that the group intended to return the old landmark to her original grandeur. The Melbourne government had been confident all along that the Oberois were the right party to reclaim The Windsor. MS's initial enthusiasm and belief in the success of a renovated Windsor had pleased the government officials. No one else had previously offered to renovate the hotel according to Gautam Khanna, who had originally been unethusiastic about the Australian expansion. Just prior to signing on to restore the Windsor, the Oberois had taken on the management of the Adelaide in early 1980, a structure housing South Australia's largest convention center. Continued expansion in the Australian market is contemplated, according to Gautam Khanna.

The recovery of profitability in the 1980s has allowed the Oberois' East India Hotels to go back to the market to raise funds for expansion and renovation. The $7.5 million renovation of the New Delhi Inter-Continental which was being completed in late 1984 is part of an overall Rs 80 crore ($67 million) expansion contemplated by the group for the 1983-1988 period. And for the first time since the opening of the Bombay Oberoi Towers in the mid-1970s, the Oberois are expanding in a big way in India.

In 1978, India received 750,000 tourists. By 1986, 2.5 million visitors are expected and optimism runs high that India will be as important a point on any Asian tour as Thailand or Singapore is today. The hotel industry in India, as elsewhere, is one of the largest employers in the country. Directly or indirectly, the industry employs about 3.5 million people and is a key foreign exchange earner. Along with road transport, hotels and restaurants are two of the largest creators of employment in the country. With growth in tourism in India on the upswing, the Oberois feel that the environment within India is for once favorable enough to justify establishment of more five-star hotels there. Biki Oberoi says: "A year ago if someone had asked me about expansion in India, I would have been less than enthusiastic. But with the changes coming for business, I am very bullish on India." Hotels under construction or planned for Bhubaneswar, Bangalore, Hyderabad, Agra, and Jaipur represent a vote of confidence in the country's future by men who know their business. MS Oberoi also feels that there is a great scope for three-star hotels in India and says that he has yet to see a three-star hotel in India that is well managed. For the moment, however, the group intends to stick to five-stars, catering to the business executive or foreign traveler seeking high quality personal service and the most modern amenities. MS believes that deluxe hotels are the last to feel an economic crunch in recessionary times. The one change which is contemplated is in the average size of his hotels. They will in the future tend to range in the 300-350 room capacity so that the renowned personal courtesies of the Oberoi Hotel chain are not sacrificed.

Dammam Hotel,
Saudi Arabia

Oberoi Adelaide, Adelaide, Australia

The Windsor, Melbourne, Australia

Oberoi Palace,
Srinigar, India

Hotel Jass Oberoi,
Khujuraho, India

Oberoi Bagmalo Beach, Goa, India

P.R.S. (Biki) Oberoi, Deputy Chairman (younger son of M.S. Oberoi)

In the early 1960s, faced with a need to train their employees in the fine art of hoteliering, the Oberois hoped to import technical personnel to assist in this training. But a tight foreign exchange situation forced them to create such a training nucleus within India itself and thus the now internationally acclaimed Oberoi School of Hotel Management was born in New Delhi. Established under the direction of Biki Oberoi, Deputy Chairman of the group, who attended hotel school in Lausanne, Switzerland, the school offers an intensive two year course in all aspects of hotel management. Allan Fernandes, Oberoi's Vice President for Marketing, says that more than 8,000 applications a year are received for the hotel school's 22 slots. While Oberois will be at the helm of the chain for the foreseeable future graduates of the management school fill senior positions throughout the international chain. Nationals from the countries where Oberoi hotels are located are brought to New Delhi and trained in the Oberoi school as well. MS says that manpower training is the most important part of the business. The waiter in a restaurant, for example, must be trained to watch the customer's face at all times and anticipate his needs.

When it comes to detail, Fernandes says there is no one like MS. The founder has a knack for vetting contracts and noticing the tiniest inconsistencies. He is also the one to take a risk which a more conservative management might eschew. Despite MS's life-long dedication to cutting unnecessary expenditures in his operations, he is not a man who is penny-wise and pound foolish. His penchant for risk-taking includes paying an apparently higher price to win a contract than seems wise at the time. He has not lost out over the medium or long term. While the monopoly his five-star hotel in New Delhi enjoyed in the 1960s and 70s disappeared with increasing competion from other chains (by the early 1980s, Delhi had no fewer than seven or eight five-star hotels up or under construction), the Oberoi reputation for providing high class, understated comfort to his guests has bestowed an exclusivity upon it which even Delhi's own elite are quick to admit.

A few Oberoi projects did not work out and the Oberois were unsentimental about backing away when it was apparent success in particular projects was to be elusive. In 1972, Oberoi invested in a brewery in Punjab with the government. But the state government insisted on interfering in Oberoi's management, making it difficult to make a go of the project. Then pro-hibition was introduced under the government of Morarji Desai, 1977-79, and brewery owners were going out of business in large numbers. It was also a time when another Indian corporate giant, Vittal Mallya, went around buying up all the floundering breweries, thus consolidating his monopoly of the beer and beverage business. The Oberois sold out to Mallya who had started making his fortune by trading on the Calcutta stock exchange. Mallya had been a classmate of Gautam Khanna at Doon School. A mathematician, son of a doctor in the old Indian National Service, Mallya was known for his brilliance in detecting a company ripe for takeover from a mere glance at its balance sheet.

The Oberois encountered more trouble with the Punjab government when a hotel they were managing in Chandigarh under contract with the government of Punjab which owned the hotel ended without notice. One night, Khanna related, the Punjab police just arrived and announced they were taking over the hotel. The disagreement and subsequent loss for the Oberois of management fees is under negotiation. A much bigger dent in their acquisition plans came in 1980, however. In collaboration with their Saudi partner, the Oberois moved into the New York hotel scene with the purchase of the New York landmark, the Barbizon Hotel for Women, located in New York's tonier Upper East Side. Some of the tenants proved difficult to lure from their hotel apartments except for what the Oberois considered unjustifiable compensation. The entanglement promised to expand into another public relations battle which prompted the Oberois to pull out of the deal. They sold off the hotel at a small profit and are actively searching for a replacement hotel property in New York. But there is no doubt that their selection of the Barbizon Hotel was on target as a hot hotel property.

Lobby of Lanka Oberoi Hotel, Colombo, Sri Lanka

The Second Generation

MS's empire is passing into the able hands of his children and his children's children. The first to employ women in his hotel in professional positions, not to mention as clerks, MS also encouraged his daughters to enter business. The memory of his mother as a young widow forced to take on the responsibilities of his upbringing had perhaps given MS a more enlightened attitude toward the potential roles women could play in society. Regardless, his daughters manage the book shops and beauty parlors in the Oberoi hotels. No doubt the Oberoi boys were slated for the high powered management roles, but MS had pioneered women's participation in business to a greater extent than the vast majority of his colleagues in business.

MS with Biki

MS's first son, Tilak, or Tikki, was good at finance, but with his death in early 1984, Prithvi, or Biki, assumed full command along with MS. His style naturally contrasts with his father's already well-analyzed character. Quicker than MS to take a liking to someone and support him regardless of the merits of any particular case at hand, Biki has that certain spark of leadership needed to push a company to perform well. In contrast to a son who led the life of an heir to a successful business tycoon, MS is more moderate in his initial reactions to people, slower to form hard and fast opinions, but once convinced of someone's worth, able to stand by him or her with great friendship. This quality alone has probably produced the fierce loyalty among employees and friends which MS commands. The father is still rooted in his quieter beginnings in Bhaun and Simla where hard work and imagination, together with luck, propelled him into the life of a successful business legend.

Bali Oberoi, Bali, Indonesia

Oberoi Imperial, Singapore

Oberoi Mount Everest, Darjeeling, India

The sons remembered that their father was always busy, but that he provided well for them. Biki says that he and MS agree on everything for the most part. MS says that Biki takes his advice sometimes. While the formula for success has obviously been transferred from father to son, the enthusiasm and discipline required to sustain the success created by MS is no less than that which was present at the creation.

Joining the business full-time in 1960, Biki Oberoi says he never considered a life outside the world of hotels. "I grew up in hotels. They are my life," he states. He reflects his father when he says that every new project takes patience and hard work. He is relaxed, self-confident and displays a lively interest in what other people think and how they react to his own opinions. The observation someone made that Biki works hard and plays hard sits very lightly on the deputy chairman's shoulders.

His plans for the business include a reorganization of some of the bigger

Oberoi Maidens, Delhi: Corporate headquarters for East India Hotels Ltd.

restaurants in his hotels. "The days of the big restaurant are over. We plan to turn the Taj Restaurant at the Inter-Continental into a small, 100-seat French restaurant. We will redesign others as well," he promises. He is excited about the new 300-room extension adjacent to the Oberoi Towers in Bombay and about the facelift which the Grand Hotel in Calcutta will be getting soon which will enable guests to keep from being swept away on the sidewalk outside the hotel during the monsoons. The rooms at the Grand have already been completely renovated, just in time to help the Oberoi group meet the new competition coming up compliments of the Taj group. For decades, the Grand has been the only hotel of international caliber in Calcutta and local citizens felt that the Oberoi chain took full advantage of the situation.

Enthusiastic about the potential for domestic growth, Biki nonetheless intends to continue the group's overseas expansion. A new agreement was concluded in early 1985 with the Iraqi government to manage a third hotel in Mosul. A representative of the People's Republic of China visited the Oberois early in 1985 to invite them to consider the hotel business in China. And, according to Biki, the group is still keen to find a replacement property in New York.

Biki Oberoi believes that you have to develop people as well as build attractive physical structures. "One has to care for one's employees. Monetary reward alone does not produce results in itself in the long term. The Oberoi group's strength is in its people. I know 80 percent of my people—at all levels." When Oberoi travels abroad, he appreciates being recognized and cared for in a personal fashion as well. When he goes to New York, for example, he prefers to stay in the Carlyle, a family-run hotel, owned by Peter Sharp whose mother owned a chain of hotels. The same people have worked at the Carlyle for years. The doorman knows him and a suite is always available for him, regardless of the brevity of notice. These are qualities which even some of the Oberoi hotels in major cities of the world are finding it difficult to duplicate because of their sheer size and high rate of occupancies. This is one reason why executives in the group say it will make an effort to concentrate on 300 to 350-room hotels for the most part. But the Oberois may already have passed the point of no return on this matter. The profitability of the Oberoi Towers in Bombay would encourage anyone to try and duplicate it again and again. Furthermore, once you have grown beyond a certain point, it may not be wise to change a successful course. MS Oberoi's projects were usually more ambitious as time went on. Thus it is more likely that the group will stick to the larger, five-star variety of hotels, rather than opt for the development of smaller, exclusive establishments.

MS Oberoi with industrialist Keshub Mahindra and Mrs. Mahindra

In 1981 MS was admitted to the American Society of Travel Agents' Hall of Fame, joining such pioneers as Charles Lindbergh, the Wright Brothers and Neil Armstrong. He went on to be named "Man of the World" in 1983 by the Hotels & Restaurants International. The international recognition which his efforts have attracted are for a man who stuck to his business of professional hoteliering. If you know your business, MS says, there is no question of losing money. Small details are important, too, MS says in an interview on a warm October afternoon sitting among the trees and green expanse of his Delhi farm. For instance, nowhere in my hotels around the world will you find a paper napkin. He knows if one person complains, you lose 10 clients; if one person compliments you, you gain 10 customers. One reason why MS answers his mail the day it is received is not only because of the legendary efficiency of founding fathers, but for the ripple effect one satisfied customer has on his bottom line.

Oberoi service being offered

MS Oberoi writes:

My hotels continue to expand. Some people refer to them as my Empire. A hotel is a small nation in itself, and a chain does perhaps merit the name of Empire. The empire is not an imperialistic one, but rather based on the idea of rendering service.[10]

Tata

Steel
Trucks, buses, heavy equipment
Power generation and transmission
Chemicals
Soaps, detergents, cosmetics
Tea
Hotels
Engineering goods
Exporting
Consulting
Computers

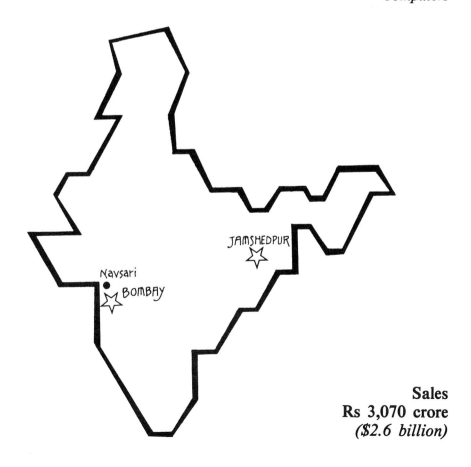

Sales
Rs 3,070 crore
($2.6 billion)

Headquarters
Tata Sons Ltd.
Bombay House
24, Homi Mody Street
Bombay, India   400 023

Chairman, Tata Sons
J.R.D. Tata

Jamsetji N. Tata (1839-1904)

TATA

There were people alternately excited and dismayed . . . by the rapid progress of science, the technological revolution, the speed at which men and ideas could move around the world.

Between 1875 and 1900 nearly five million square miles were added to the Empire, to make a total of some thirteen million square miles with 320 million people . . . the concept of an empire so much bigger than the Mother Country and yet obedient to her appealed to the familial mind of the Victorians. The Empire provided the image of unity which was being vainly sought in society at home.[1]

Having made a substantial fortune from trading and the textile industry, he could have rested on his laurels . . . Instead, he saw that under the exploitation of colonial rule his country was being by-passed by the industrial revolution which was rapidly transforming Europe and America.

Confronting him was an Empire whose motivation was economic gain. Jamsetji's projects had no patrons. They needed long periods of gestation and involved considerable risk. In no other colonial nation—and there were almost a 100—was such industrial endeavour undertaken by the subject of a ruling power.[2]

Had Jamsetji Tata taken a strictly materialistic approach to his industrial dreams, private industry in India might well have died with the end of colonialism so intertwined were political and economic domination in the minds of Indians. As it happily occurred, India's first large-scale, modern industrialist was intelligent and progressive as well as ambitious and clever. He could not act the part of the penniless Scotsman laying claim to large chunks of rich natural resources in America's heartland with little love for the land from which he did not spring. Jamsetji's family had emigrated to India in the twelfth century from Persia and came from a long line of Zoroastrian priests. The Tata men acted as advisers to the local government leaders, but otherwise led a humble, ascetic existence. One could expect that whatever activities a Tata would take up in life, therefore, would reflect certain lofty traditions handed down from a well-chronicled past.

Nusserwanji Tata Tries His Hand at Business

Jamsetji Tata's father, Nusserwanji, was the first in his long line to choose a new line of work. While still a young boy in Navsari where the Tatas were based, he saved his money and learned some basic business skills from a local country banker. Fortunately his father moved to Bombay and Nusserwanji accompanied him. It was a time of political upheaval in Gujarat and many Gujeratis had fled to the calmer atmosphere of British-governed Bombay. The opportunities for doing business were naturally greater and Nusserwanji was apprenticed to a Hindu merchant in the port city. He learned the business of weights and measures and where to source the best and cheapest commodities which he then would resell. Having built up a solid base in business, Jamsetji's father built a comfortable home and began to travel the world. Nusserwanji Tata was one of the first foreigners to visit Japan after Admiral Perry's shots were fired into Tokyo Harbor and the Japanese grudgingly realized that their days of isolation had ended. Around 1852, Nusserewanji called his son Jamsetji to Bombay. The boy was about 13 and the father was 30. Nusserwanji had been married at the age of five and his only son was born when he was 17. Jamsetji had only been given training in the scriptures in Navsari. As his father was now fairly well established, he could see that his son was given a more formal education than he himself had been privileged to obtain.

In 1854 Jamsetji started formal studies at Elphinstone Institute in Bombay and at 16 he was admitted to Elphinstone College. It was his exposure to literature and history, the humanities, which was pivotal to his development as an industrialist. His natural affinity for books and his capacity to absorb new ideas and modern technologies were the genesis of his industrial dreams. Jamsetji's intellectual bent of mind, fused with his father's love of travel and growing business acumen, equipped the future industrialist with the assets for worldly success. It would be difficult for any part of the industrial revolution which was sweeping the West to escape his notice.

As a student, Jamsetji was so much of a grind that his fellow students hardly noticed him in their midst. He was so studious that even a cyclone whirling around him in the attic of his home which served as his study could

Nusserwanji Tata

not disturb him. A story is told that Nusserwanji became so concerned about the ferocity of one monsoon cyclone that he rushed to the attic to get Jamsetji's nose out of his books and clear of the house. The boy escaped apparently just as the roof of the house was blown off.

At the age of 20 Jamsetji entered his father's firm of Nusserwanji and Kaliandas which was then a general contractor. The partners operated without a written contract and Nusserwanji, who kept the books, always passed on what was owing without exception. The cotton and opium markets were reaping huge profits for their traders and the Tatas developed links with China. Jamsetji set up a branch of the firm in Hong Kong to deal in these commodities and before long he was opening a second branch at Shanghai. When the American Civil War cut off American cotton shipments to England, the Indian cotton merchants made a killing. The Tatas were no exception. One of Tata's partners, Premchand Roychand, started speculating in real estate and set up a bank holding company, Asiatic Banking Corporation, to help leverage his money. Things were going so well that Jamsetji was dispatched to London to open a branch for cotton trading and to conduct business for the new bank. By the time Jamsetji reached London, however, the market in cotton had crashed and so had the shares of Asiatic Banking Corporation. Tata kept a stiff upper lip with the firm's British creditors and dealt with the crisis in such a straightforward fashion that the British bankers appointed him his own liquidator with a monthly stipend. Jamsetji had nonetheless learned a few lessons about speculation and the necessity for caution in business.

While in England Jamsetji used some of his spare time to learn the cotton manufacturing business as best he could. He became a frequent visitor to the Lancashire mills. Back at home, his father was not as ruined as Premchand, but he still had to sell his house and personal property to pay off his debts. By the time Jamsetji returned to Bombay, he had grown confident of his ability to survive the most embarrassing of crises. He was also ready to think of manufacturing as he had learned a few things during his stay in the Mother Country. It took him and Nusserwanji about three years to recover the family finances lost in the wild days of India's cotton crash.

Another's misfortune is easily the making of someone else's fortune and the Tatas' break came in 1867-68 when, along with several other merchants, they won a contract to supply a year's worth of provisions to the Indian troops who had been assembled by General Robert Napier in Bombay to march on Abyssinia to rescue thirty captured British subjects. The astute Nusserwanji made a few substitutes in the provisions which he felt more suitable to desert combat (and as it happened the materials were less expensive that what was called for). He reaped a comfortable profit and decided it was time to retire. Jamsetji was nearing the time when he would be on his own. Though Nusserwanji became quite ill, he recovered and began to travel to the East again, to China and Japan, and to his home in Navsari to drop off all the treasures he had picked up on his travels. He even did a little business while in China, re-opening a trading firm in partnership with two relatives who had continued to operate in Hong Kong. With some additional capital from Nusserwanji, the firm was expanded and for a number of years more the Tatas of Bombay kept their hand in the export-import business. But Jamsetji was thinking about setting up industry at home and felt that the Hong Kong business was too far away to keep an adequate eye on and both father and son withdrew their shares in the mid 1870s. Now Nusserwanji retired for good.

Acquisition of a Mill—An Industrialist in the Wings

In 1869, Jamsetji had purchased a defunct oil pressing mill at Chinchpoogly in partnership with several acquaintances. They turned it into a cotton mill, renamed it the Alexandra Mill in honor of the Princess of Wales and, after two years, sold it off after it turned a profit. Jamsetji had been placed in sole charge of the mill and had thereby obtained his first experience in manufacturing. Since it was successful and profitable, naturally he was encouraged to look for new opportunities. Before he decided on the exact nature of his next step, Jamsetji set out on a long roundabout journey to England where he was going to check up on the latest textile technology. His trip would take him through Egypt, Russia and the Middle East. It lasted nine months and the journal which Jamsetji kept showed him as much interested in every aspect of life around him as in business matters. It also hinted a fine descriptive style which his avid book-reading had obviously influenced. Nine months later, in 1974, Jamsetji returned to Bombay to look for the site of his first textile plant. Two sons had been born to him and his wife, Heerabai, Dorab in 1859 and Ratan in 1871.

Jamsetji set out to locate his mill near a raw material source, a profitable market and an area with good power and water supplies. His first selection in northern Madya Pradesh was fed by natural hydro-electric power and met his other criteria as well, but it was also sitting on the site of a holy shrine. Government permission could not be obtained and he looked elsewhere. Tata checked out the area around Nagpur in the Central Provinces. Again, it met most of his tests. There was a good market for the mill's spinning products as Nagpur was in the center of a large handloom industry. Transportation, power and raw materials were also plentiful. But when he wanted support for his scheme, local bankers were skeptical when the businessman decided to reclaim ten acres of swampland. Jamsetji moved ahead and Central India Spinning, Weaving and Manufacturing Company Ltd. was incorporated in 1874 with 3000 shares of Rs 500 each. It was the first joint stock company floated in that part of India. Most Tata ventures in the future would use the local stockmarkets as each project was more ambitious than the last.

By the time the mill was ready to be inaugurated on January 1, 1877, it was to have a new name, Empress, in honor of Queen Victoria's having been crowned Empress of India the same day. Though Jamsetji had taken on two key managers, Bezonji Dadabhai Mehta, an administrative expert, and James Brooksby, an Englishman with good technical background, the mill

The Empress Mill, Nagpur (Central India Spg., Wvg. & Mfg. Co. Ltd.)

got off to a rocky start. Tata had not purchased the best machinery for his mill, but got what he thought he could get by with, given his capital resources. Before long he was back in Europe buying better machinery as the share prices of Empress Mills started to fall following the startup problems. At any rate, a fire in the loomshed had destroyed some weaving equipment and he had to replace that as well. By 1881, four years later, Empress Mills was turning a profit and dividends were declared. Tata had stuck close to the mill's operations so that he could catch problems before they occurred. New technology was spotted by Brooksby while on home leave in England and it was adopted by Empress, enabling them to double the mill's efficiency.

Lack of Skilled Labor Leads to Progressive Solutions

The survival of the first mill depended as much on its ability to attract, train and retain workers. It was not easy as there was no industrial ethos yet established in Nagpur and workers came and went depending on their personal habits and family problems. Before the West had heard of worker welfare schemes, provident funds and healthy factories, Jamsetji Tata had put together a package of incentives to hang at his factory gate. It was not an altruistic decision as he was desperate to train a hard-working corps of people to turn out his product. He devised a system by which he offered training to the workers in many areas of the plant. After a probationary period, he offered to employ them for the rest of their lives in a position which the training had found suitable for them. From the promotion of his first mill, Tata companies always had something better to offer the worker and development of human resources ranked equal to, if not higher than, technological innovation.

Feeling confident, Jamsetji took a bigger risk without the enthusiastic advice of his managers. He bought one of the largest, but oldest, mills in India, the Dharamsi Mill at Kurla outside Bombay. He purchased it for less than one sixth of its original cost and he could have made money immediately by reselling it. Tata had it in mind to produce cloths of finer quality than the Empress was manufacturing in order to meet the demand for more home-made goods which was the basis of the growing "swadeshi" movement. He transferred the old mill's assets to a new company he had formed, The Svadeshi Mills. Again, Tata did not go all out to refurbish the mills with the latest equipment. Labor problems, bad equipment and a dismal reputation to boot in the market combined to challenge the wisdom of Jamsetji's decision.

The problems lingered and the credit of Tata and Sons, the managing agency, was threatened. Tata had to break open a trust he had established for his family and free the capital to keep his credit in good standing. He dispatched all his experts from Empress Mills to save Svadeshi Mills. He adopted all the workers' programs in Kurla that he had introduced in Empress Mills and gradually they got control of the tiger. The crisis shook Jamsetji quite badly and he suffered some seizures and faintness thereafter.

Tata also called back his son, Dorabji, to Bombay to help in the crisis.

Jamsetji Tata as successful businessman

Dorabji was quite happy settling himself in the French colony of Pondicherry where he had been sent to set up a guinea cloth mill. Worried about Svadeshi's future and possibly losing his son to the charms of the south, Jamsetji left no room for argument. Dorabji returned and took control of the Svadeshi mill and pushed for production of the finest yarns. Soon a balance was regained and the Bombay Tatas even started up their trade with China again.

Land Reclamation and Better Housing in Bombay

By 1890 Jamsetji was well on his way to becoming the biggest landowner in Bombay. He started going into debt to buy up land all over the city which he came to know well as he moved his family to a different locale every three years or so. Suddenly he reversed himself and started paying off the debt and accumulating large deposits which he lent out on a short-term basis, multiplying his fortune thereby. He picked up another textile mill, The Advance Mills in Ahmedabad, when bankruptcy led to a default on the mortgage Jamsetji had on the mill. He began renovation of the mill immediately and it proved to be a better business deal than Svadeshi. But "building became one of Jamsetji's chief hobbies" and he bought lands on islands and built the first apartments for working Englishmen, the Gymkhana Chambers. As it was in England, the housing situation in Bombay in the middle of the nineteenth century was dismal at best. Raymond Chapman in *The Victorian Debate* relates:

> *Housing was a major social problem, and one which the Victorians never fully solved. The slums of London and the new industrial centres were appalling throughout the century. At the other end of society, the nobility spent their time between the country manors . . . those who were as rich but of less ancient lineage built vast edifices in a mixture of styles and with a maximum of exterior ornamentation . . . even in areas that were far from being slums, speculators would crowd in as many houses as possible within a plot of land, neither they nor their customers caring a great deal about light and fresh air.[3]*

Frank Harris relates in his book on Jamsetji Tata:

> *In 1860, the central part of Bombay, though picturesque, was far from convenient. Narrow gates hampered the traffic which passed in and out of the congested streets. The Fort, which is now covered with modern buildings, was then an undeveloped tract surrounded by low ramparts. The residential quarter was little but a plague spot, for a population exceeding half a million souls was crowded into mean and insanitary dwellings . . . At the close of the nineteenth century the city was furnished with convenient flats, large hotels, a handsome station, and public buildings worthy of the capital of Western India.[4]*

Tata did his best to bring about the changes which were so noticeable by the end of the nineteenth century. In addition to building apartments for middle class workers, offices and homes for himself, Tata conceived the idea of a luxury hotel to be located in front of the Gateway of India which would welcome the growing number of foreign visitors in need of European type lodgings. It was for this reason that Tata had started accumulating funds. He bought the lease of a large piece of land at Apollo Bunder. The Taj Mahal Hotel is still India's most renowned five-star hotel as much for its location as for its history, gracious space and comfortable facilities. Travelling was in Jamsetji's blood. He appreciated the finest things in life and he wanted his guests to share in this appreciation. Though he did not intend it at the time, the Tata group would go on to become an international hotel chain with additional hotels in India as well as in Europe and America. Tata left much of the actual development of his large-scale enterprises in the hands of Dorabji who did not disappoint him though they differed over matters of taste in furnishings.

The Taj Mahal Hotel, Bombay

Travels in India

Jamsetji was not only the best-travelled Indian of his time and a collector of objets d'art and flora and fauna from the four corners of the world, but he travelled his own country extensively. He was constantly comparing the conditions in India with those in other places of the world to determine what could be successfully tried at home. He started a silkworm farm in Mysore based on Japanese techniques. He was the first to electrify his home and to equip it with the latest in European plumbing. The flats he built in Bombay shared the same comforts and the hotel project which he was dreaming up would be similarly outfitted. At all times throughout his travels and while at home, Jamsetji took great pains to spell out in exacting details his ideas on design, furnishings, finance and any other matter which touched on his schemes.

He had done the same with an idea of establishing an Indian shipping company to offer lower freight rates between India and the Far East. The British Peninsular and Oriental had a monopoly and because of the high rates charged was cutting into the profits of the Indian merchants and making the goods more expensive vis a vis growing competition from East and West. Tata moved to charter two vessels during a trip to London and started sending orders to Bombay to his firm about searching for Indian clients for his ships. He had travelled to Japan to arrange a collaboration with a shipping line there, the Nippon Ysen Kaisha line. But the P & O line cut its rates to nothing to undermine Jamsetji's efforts. Indian exporters would not

The Rambagh Palace Hotel, Jaipur, a later acquisition

The Tata Iron & Steel Company (TISCO)

patronize the Tata Lines and the scheme ended sadly for Jamsetji. It was one of his few defeats. But he was not alone in this defeat. Several other Indian industrialists would try their hand at shipping. While Walchand Hirachand had a bit better luck, the fights which took place between the domestic and foreign lines were fierce enough to shake up the Indians badly.

Iron and Steel: Jamsetji Tata Dusts Off An Old Scheme

American engineers, Indian capital, a Bengali geologist, two Maharajahs, sympathetic British government officials, one industrial genius and a devoted son, financial and marketing brains attached to the industrial genius' firm, seven or more years' worth of surveys and studies, tens of thousands of miles of travel by Indians and foreigners alike, meetings between Jamsetji Tata and American steel barons, visits to Pittsburgh and Cleveland, USA, add up to TISCO, the Tata Iron and Steel Company, known as India's first modern, large-scale industrial endeavor.

Jamsetji Tata
Lord George Hamilton
Burjorji Padshah
P.N. Bose
Ritter von Schwarz
General R. H. Mahon
Shapurji Saklatvala
Dorabji Tata
Julian Kennedy
Axel Sahlin
The Maharajah of Mayurbhanj
C.P. Perin
C. M. Weld
The Maharajah Scindia of Gwalior
8000 Indian shareholders

Any large industrial project anywhere in the world has always involved large numbers of people, great capital resources and enthusiasm to realize sometimes impossible dreams. Looking at the story of TISCO, what were the extraordinary hurdles which India and the Tatas had to overcome to bring about a successful venture? First, as a colonized country, the approval of the home government was needed for all projects which would involve some expenditures on infrastructure or exploitation of natural resources. For large projects, it was not wise to rely on the right messages getting back to the capital from the local representatives. One had to have entré in London to present a case successfully. As a frequent visitor and well-known industrialist already, Tata had good contacts in London and they encouraged him to move forward.

Next, there were gaps in information about the extent of India's natural resources and their location in the country. Thus, much more time had to be spent looking for adequate supplies of ore and coal without benefit of accurate information. If one had the time and funds to persevere, however, the rewards could be commensurate with the risks taken. Technology was also a major hurdle as it did not exist on home soil. Tata's travels and friendships with industrial leaders in the West gave him access to the knowledge he needed to set up an iron and steel plant. Coal had to be sent off shore to determine its cokeability. Ore had to be tested in foreign laboratories to determine its grade. With Tata's determination and his resources, while everything took time, he moved forward as usual.

Tata had conceived of putting up a modern steel plant as early as 1882 when he read a report by a German expert on the prospects of iron-working in the Central Provinces of India. The report had sparked his entrepreneurial imagination and he made some preliminary surveys in the Central Provinces because the government there knew him quite well as the owner of Empress Mills. But he could not get the required commitment from the government for control of a rail line and he shelved the project. In 1899, two things happened. The government liberalized the laws relating to mine prospecting and development and a new report was published authored by a Major in the British Army, R. H. Mahon. Mahon brought his readers up to date on the trends in the iron and steel industry and proclaimed that it was now time someone thought of getting India involved in this industry. Mahon's report pointed out that the rich coal-fields of Bengal were sufficient to provide a large-scale iron and steel mill with plenty of coal for blast furnaces. Tata took out the notebooks of clippings he had been accumulating since the idea first came to him in the mid 1880s. He started once again to survey the resources of the Central Provinces.

Tata travelled to America, met with all the steel barons, leading politicians who opened up their good offices for him to acquire as much information as possible for his purposes, visited the steel towns of America and hired the best engineering consultant money could buy. He wanted to get started immediately and an American consultant, C.M. Weld, arrived in India not too long after he was hired by Tata to help find adequate ore deposits for an iron and steel mill. Dorab, Jamsetji's son, joined Weld and Burjorji Saklatvala to carry out the investigations in the sometimes wild underbrush of the Central Provinces. A couple of years would pass before discouragement set in. Dorab and Weld prepared to hand in the concessions and visited the offices of the local government official to do so. While waiting for him to arrive, Dorab wandered into a display room across the hall from the official's office and noticed a report by a Bengali geologist, P.N. Bose, about some promising ore hills. Some samples from the area mentioned looked very good. Weld was called over and when the official arrived, Dorab and Weld asked for a new concession which they set about immediately to investigate. While Bose's information was not perfect, it led the team in the right direction and before long Weld came upon the hills of ore he had suspected existed all along. The hills of Dhalli and Rajhara were rich with the raw material they had been searching for. The British officials were brought in to see for themselves and the Tatas now concentrated on pinning down the most favorable coal deposits. They already knew that the Jharia coal-fields had been identified as adequate by Major Mahon. Coal samples were sent off to Germany and America to test for its cokeability.

The coal testing positive, now adequate water supplies had to located and transportation links to bring all the resources together had to be considered. While what the team felt were final surveys were taking place, P.N. Bose stepped onto the stage again. He was now a consultant to the Maharajah of Mayurbhanj who wished to attract industrial development to his state. While there were many feudal maharajahs in India at the time and right through independence, other royal rulers were instrumental in providing the necessary resources to India's industrialists to enable them to realize their sometimes ambitious ventures (see Bajaj, Kirloskar and Modi chapters for differing examples).

At the turn of the century, the Maharajah of Mysore had offered Tata land and capital to help Jamsetji realize his plans for what finally became the Institute of Science after his death in 1904.

After several more pleas, the team finally travelled to Bengal to meet the Maharajah and Bose who promised that even richer ore deposits existed in his kingdom. The party was taken through some remote areas inhabited by wild elephants and tigers, but the ore deposits were far beyond the party's expectations. The plans had to change no doubt. New surveys had to be taken, but the location of the ore was more ideal as it was closer to the coal and closer to the vast water resources of the Bay of Bengal. Government concessions were crucial to any project of this sort. The Maharajah offered four years of free royalties. A site near the town of Sakchi was staked out and the project began in earnest.

Jamsetji Tata died in 1904 in Nauheim, Germany before the great discoveries of the ore which would lead to the realization of his iron and steel project. His health had been deteriorating. Though he was just 65, he had ignored pleas by his physicians to slow down and allow others to supervise his food and exercise. He advised his children simply, upon his death, to carry out his projects if they could. If they could not, he advised them not to lose hold of what he had accomplished to date.

The Tata Iron and Steel Company was incorporated in 1907 with Tata and Sons appointed managing agents. Because capital could not be raised on the London market after several months of negotiations, Dorab and Padshah, Jamsetji's right hand men, returned to Bombay very discouraged. It is odd that the Tatas did not cross the ocean to the USA, the country from which they were obtaining all the technical expertise for the project. Jamsetji had many admirers in America and capital might have been raised there. Nonetheless, with London unenthusiastic, the Tata team had to come up with something new. A.J. Bilimoria, Jamsetji's personal assistant since the mid 1880s who quickly became indispensable, Dorab and Padshah brainstormed

J.N. Tata late in life

and came up with the idea of inviting investments from the Indian public in what could be seen as a patriotic undertaking by an Indian business house. Because of India's status as a colony, it was natural that an undertaking of this magnitude would seek capital from the capital markets of London. Thrown back on their own soil, however, there was no choice but to make the project an all-India deal. Since nationalist spirit was on the rise and Indians had money to invest, the idea, thought initially to be risky, was tried. Eight thousand Indians responded from all walks of life and the subscription was sold out in no time.

The Maharajah Scindia of Gwalior subscribed to a debenture issue worth four hundred thousand pounds to provide working capital to the project. Given the opportunity, Indians were willing to invest in their own industrialist's ventures. TISCO opened its doors in 1911 with the first steel ingot rolled out in 1912. Electricity, town planning, schools, hospitals, housing and other facilities came up around Sakchi, renamed Jamshedpur by government

Shapurji Saklatvala   Burjorji Padshah

officials who felt Jamsetji should be so honored. The industrial revolution
had reached into one of the remotest parts of India. Since those first days,
seven other companies have been acquired or promoted by the Tatas in
related lines in and around Jamshedpur, with the Tata Engineering and
Locomotive Company (TELCO) providing as pioneering a tale as that of
TISCO in some respect.

Sir Dorabji Tata Takes the Helm

Dorabji, Jamsetji's elder son, had some early twinges of independence
even as his father kept him busy with his enormous plans. Dorabji was
always able to hold his own, however. The Taj Mahal Hotel went up under
his supervision. TISCO could not have been realized without his direct
involvement. The Indian Institute of Science was not sanctioned by the
government during Jamsetji's lifetime, but Dorab and his younger brother,
Ratan, persevered until it became a reality. A slight glimpse of his self-
confidence could be gleaned from his early post-graduate days in
Pondicherry where he was on his way to setting up a textile mill and settling
in quite successfully in his new home. There lingers a question as to
Jamsetji's motivation in calling him back to Bombay, but the son obeyed.

Dorab had attended Cambridge where he excelled in sports and won
colors for cricket, rugger and soccer. He returned to Bombay in 1879 and did
his B.A. at St. Xavier's. His love for sports led him to get India to participate
in the Olympic Games and he personally scouted the country for sports
talent. He was an adventurer as his early involvement in surveying the ore
country of the Central Provinces and Bengal showed. He also believed as
much in his father's industrial visions as Jamsetji did. Otherwise he could not

have carried them out no matter how much he had promised Jamsetji he would do so.

As was not unusual with the younger brother in an industrial family, Ratanji did not have as central a role in the industrial undertakings promoted by Jamsetji. Frail of health, more inclined toward the arts and worthy causes, Ratanji was also more sensitive to the inequities he saw around him. It was a mark of difference between himself and his brother and father that the causes Ratan supported dealt more with the downtrodden, while Dorab and Jamsetji felt that the most talented in society had to be encouraged and supported. Ratan died when he was only 48. Neither of Jamsetji's sons had any children.

TISCO's Troubles Challenge Dorabji's Commitment

The iron and steel project had just opened its doors when the kinks started showing up. Coal was not of uniform quality, furnace designs were not perfected, labor needed extensive training and the Germans hired to operate the furnaces were not impressive. Tigers and elephants roamed the neighboring area of Sakchi keeping everyone on guard. Most tragically, dealers would not stock the products rolling off TISCO's lines except at a large discount because they distrusted Indian products. World War I and its demands for home-grown products to take the place of goods which could not get through to India ended the dealers' prejudices and TISCO got a chance to get its head above water. Profits were made which led management, principally Dorab, to plan a large expansion after the war. The Tata executives, however, failed to see the depression coming down the road in the 1920s and were caught short of funds when the market turned down. Not only was the expansion stalled, but a series of natural and man-made disasters knocked TISCO on its back. Raw material prices shot up, labor and transport became difficult and Japan, the company's biggest pig iron client, suffered a major earthquake.

As one director was recommending that TISCO sell out to the government and R.D. Tata, Jamsetji's cousin and partner, raised a mighty objection to such a proposal, the Tata head office was advised that TISCO could not meet its payroll. Dorab and R.D. Tata had to put up guarantees to save TISCO. Dorab pledged his entire fortune to obtain a loan from the Imperial Bank even though he owned less than ten percent of TISCO. The government also obliged by putting up a protective tariff on steel products in 1924 which kept TISCO afloat.

The expansion went forward and TISCO's operations returned to health. The next impetus for growth came with the onset of World War II. With a ready supply of iron and steel in India, the Allied Powers' war machine did not have to depend on essential shipments of materiel being torpedoed on their way from America. Indian companies like TISCO could supply equipment and provisions much more cheaply as well. The Tata management did not take advantage of its position by raising prices. They accumulated good profits nonetheless and once the war ended, they started

Dorab Tata (1859-1932)

on another expansion. A technological collaboration would be arranged with American industrialist, Henry J. Kaiser, and a large World Bank loan was made, the largest that the Bank had yet granted to any single industrial concern.

Dorab and Ratan, The Last of the Direct Line

Dorab Tata died in 1932, one year after his wife, Meherbai, had died of leukemia. Lady Mehri, as she was known, was from the South, Mysore, and had married Dorab when she was 18 and he was 38. She had been a favorite of Jamsetji. An award-winning sportswoman, accomplished pianist and a champion of women's rights in national and international fora, Meherbai was a thoroughly modern Indian woman who complemented her husband's interests well. She had encouraged Dorab to fulfill all Jamsetji's dying wishes. After her death, Dorab, who died within the same year, placed all his

Lady Meherbai, Dorab's wife

Ratan Tata (1870-1918)

wealth in a trust to be used for the advancement of learning and research, for the relief of distress and other charitable purposes without regard to place of birth, nationality or creed.

Sir Ratan Tata, the younger brother, had also set up a trust prior to his death. Before that he had contributed to many political causes including a Rs 125,000 grant to Mahatma Gandhi for his campaign for racial equality in South Africa. The names of people and causes which have benefitted from the Tata trusts down the ages fill several books. Almost singlehandedly, one family's belief in the talents and worth of its countrymen placed India far ahead of other countries who had also yet to receive their independence from the colonial powers. Ratan's art collection was donated to the Prince of Wales Museum in Bombay. Ratan's widow, Lady Navajbai, adopted Naval Hormusji Tata, a grandnephew of Jamsetji's wife, Heerabai, while the boy was studying in an orphanage. He would join the Tata organization after his graduation from Bombay University and a short stint in accountancy in London.

Naval Tata went on to become an internationally recognized authority in labor relations, becoming a member of the International Labor Organization's governing body in 1949. He would come to manage the firm's textile mills and the electric companies which were also established under Dorab after Jamsetji's death.

Hydro-electric Power: Another of Jamsetji's Projects Comes Alive

In searching for a site for his first industrial venture, Jamsetji Tata had been aware of the virtue of hydro-electric power. It was only in 1910 after his death that his son Dorab was able to promote the Tata's first power project, one year after the stone was laid for TISCO. The Tata Hydro-Electric Power Supply Co. Ltd. was registered in 1910. The firm was convinced of the utility of providing clean power to Bombay's industries, but customers were few in the beginning. Large pipelines were built attached to the slopes of the Western Ghats to bring the water from artificial reservoirs which would be constructed at the edge of the Ghats to the power stations at the foot of the Ghats. A few textile companies agreed to buy the power and eventually others joined in to make the effort viable. The Andhra Valley Power Supply Co. Ltd. was put up in 1916 and the Tata Power Co. Ltd. in 1919. All three provided 606 megawatts of electricity to the Bombay region which includes railway electric traction, textile mills, chemical and fertilizer factories and refineries. Today there are three hydel power stations in the Western Ghats and five thermal power units in Trombay.

A new 500 megawatt thermal power plant was commissioned in the first half of the 1980s at a cost of Rs 180 crore. Government approval for the new station was delayed for a number of reasons, not the least of which was the fact that power generation and transmission was a preserve of the government since independence. The Tatas have a government approval to operate their power plants through the year 2000. Naval Tata believes that as long as the Tata electric companies are doing their job, there is no need to fear government intervention. The choice of fuel for the new plant was also an issue. Designed to operate on coal and gas, it is expected to use coal for the most part. This feature disturbed environmentalists, especially scientists at the Bhabha Atomic Research Centre, who prepared a report saying that pollution emissions were far beyond safe norms for the area in which the plant was located. Company officials assured citizens that millions of dollars worth of pollution control devices would be installed at the site.

Financing was another hurdle. The companies floated a public issue and the World Bank also joined in with 50 percent of the financing. With a growing shortage of power throughout India as industrialization speeds forward, the success of the Tata power ventures should encourage the government to support similar efforts in private industry, especially since the Tata plants operate at an 89 percent load factor compared to the government facilities' national average of 48.5 percent.

The Tata Electric companies have paid uninterrupted dividends and

Naval Tata   K.M. Chinnappa

have undertaken turnkey power projects in the Middle East and Africa in conjunction with Tata Consulting Engineers. The R&D division of the power conglomerate has developed equipment to ensure the monitoring and reliability of electronic power systems in the country.

Until 1910 when the Tata Hydro-Electric Power Supply Company was established, India had only natural hydel power. Jamsetji's visits to the US and Niagara Falls, his meetings with George Westinghouse, all encouraged him to revive his original thoughts of bringing artificial hydel power to India's citizens.

Management of the electric companies has been the responsibility of K.M. Chinnappa, Vice Chairman and Managing Director. An internationally recognized expert on power, Chinnappa is also a director of Tata Industries, Vice Chairman of Tata Consulting Engineers and has been the power behind the overseas projects carried out by Tata Electric. Chinnappa serves on numerous advisory boards and is a member of the Government's Committee on Power.

Jehangir Ratanji Dadabhoy Tata—JRD

After Jamsetji's death, Dorab ran the empire with the assistance of Ratan Dadabhoy Tata, a relative. R.D. operated a trading company out of Paris and had connections in East and West. He had married a Frenchwoman, Suzanne Briere, and they had a son, Jehangir Ratanji Dadabhoy, on July 29, 1904. R.D. had studied at Elphinstone College and in Madras. His knack for finance had attracted Jamsetji early on and he was brought into the latter's schemes. But Dorab was running the show and R.D. preferred his trading business in Paris which specialized in pearls and Lyon silks. His only son was slated to become the new head of Tata Sons and its affiliate interests.

JRD grew up in France and Bombay. He attended Bombay's Cathedral School and did not go on to higher education. Drafted into the French army, he served in an Algerian regiment. At 25 he became one of the first Indians to qualify for a commercial pilot's license. Since he was raised in an industrial family, it was only natural that he would try to do something commercial with his great love for flying.

JRD's summer home in France was located near the home of French flying ace Louis Bleriot. One day JRD was offered a ride by Bleriot's chief pilot. Blue and white would be his favorite colors from then on. By 1930 he was ready to compete for the Aga Khan trophy being offered to the first Indian who could fly from India to England and back. He lost to Aspy Engineer to whom he had given a spark plug to enable the latter to finish the race. But JRD did not give up his flying interests. He went on to form India's first airline with the help of an Englishman, Neville Vintcent, who was touring India offering rides to anyone who wanted to fly. After Uncle Dorab's reluctance was overcome by the intercession of John Peterson, JRD's mentor at TISCO, Tata Airlines was off the ground with a capitalization of Rs 200,000. Two single-engine planes, three pilots and three mechanics were hired. Tata Airlines offered mail service from Karachi to Bombay and Madras as the British Imperial Air Service stopped its service in Karachi. JRD recalled the maiden voyage:

> *On an exciting October dawn in 1932, a Puss Moth and I soared joyfully from Karachi with our first precious load of mail, on an inaugural flight to Bombay. As we hummed towards our destination at a 'dazzling' hundred miles an hour, I breathed a silent prayer for the success of our venture and for the safety of those who worked for it. We were a small team in those days. We shared successes and failures, the joys and heartaches, as together we built up the enterprise which later was to blossom into Air-India and Air-India International.*[5]

JRD repeated the maiden solo flight in 1962 and again in 1982.

While he was accumulating miles in the sky, JRD had also started an apprenticeship at TISCO in 1924 under the direction of a Scotsman, John Peterson. Every paper which passed to Peterson was sent through JRD first who had a desk in Peterson's office. JRD was obviously being groomed to take over. When Dorab died in 1932, Sir Nowroji Saklatvala, a Tata relative, took over the chairmanship of Tata Sons, the managing agency which acted as the holding company for the Tata's interests in their ventures. JRD became Nowroji's right hand man and when Saklatvala died suddenly in Europe in 1938, JRD, then 34, was voted chairman by the directors of Tata Sons. One of his first actions on becoming chairman was to make the

Tata companies more autonomous, giving the senior Tata executives more authority to run their own show. All the directors were senior to JRD. The move helped them all work together more democratically.

JRD believed that there was a need for a strong human development plan in every organization. When in 1943 he became seriously ill, he wrote some thoughts on the subject:

If we have 30,000 machines, we would have a special staff or department to look after them, but when employing 30,000 human beings, each with a mind of his own, we seem to have assumed that they would look after themselves.

JRD Tata on repeat of solo flight on 30th anniversary of Tata Airlines' maiden flight

An Air India Boeing 747

R.D. Tata, father of JRD

JRD Tata

JRD with Tata executive, J.J. Bhabha

He was the first industrialist in India to set up a braintrust of talent to direct the operations and culture of the Tata companies. Sir Ardeshir Dalal, a J.N. Tata scholarship winner in 1905, joined the Tata group as Managing Director of TISCO in 1931 after a distinguished career in the civil service. Dr. John Matthai, an eminent economist and chief author of the Bombay Plan, joined the Tatas in 1940 as Director in Charge of Tata Chemicals. Matthai had served as Nehru's Finance Minister until 1950 when he resigned over differences on the implementation of the Five Year Plans. He rejoined the Tata group as Vice Chairman of TISCO. A.D. Shroff, a stockbroker, left his firm to join the Tatas and a well-known attorney, J.D. Choksi, came on board as well and served as a director of TISCO. Jamsetji Tata had always been quick to recognize the talent necessary to help him in his many proejcts. If JRD wanted to spend time developing his airline idea, he would need to have people to oversee the development of his group. As government was so involved in industrial development before and after independence, it made sense to solicit the talent of renowned civil servants who had cut their career teeth on the intricacies of the bureaucracy.

Tata Airlines Goes Public, Then International

In 1946, JRD took Tata Airlines public and the new public company was named Air-India Ltd. It was also now a passenger airline. The mail service planes had been able to carry one passenger, but on top of the mail bags. By 1947, JRD was ordering three Lockheed Constellations and

Air India plane over the Himalayas

Air India's symbol: The maharaja

JRD with wife, Thelma

proposing to the government an air service to London. He offered the
government a 49 percent interest in the new venture, the Tatas would take 20
percent and the public the balance. It was India's first joint sector (public and
private) company to be proposed. Surprisingly the government approved the
idea in ten days even though the Subcontinent was locked in a communal battle which killed hundreds of thousands overnight. Air India International was
born with Air India Ltd. providing all the personnel, equipment and
management.

After the war, planes were available at surplus prices and the
government had sanctioned no fewer than eleven other airlines. Because of
the glut, all but Air India lost money. By 1953 the government was talking
nationalization of the airlines and JRD was asked to become chairman of the
newly nationalized entity. He advised that two separate entities be created
for domestic and international lines. The government agreed and JRD
headed the international company as chairman and served on the board of the
domestic line known as Indian Airlines.

Some say that JRD devoted too much time to his airlines and not enough
to the growth of the Tata companies after independence. A man should
always be able to do what he loves best. The Tata group had taken up some
pioneering projects under JRD. Some, like Tata Chemicals, took years to
prove themselves while others, like TELCO, were modestly successful at the
start but went on to become a flagship of the group by the end of the 1960s.

Darbari Seth

Tata Chemicals

In 1939 Tata Chemicals was established at Mithapur, a city on the sea-coast of Gujarat, also known as the city of salt. It was a desolate terrain on which to locate any industry. A chemical engineer by the name of Kapilram Vakil had studied at Manchester University and had a dream about raising salt and other basic minerals from the sea to feed India's basic chemicals' industries for use in such products as glass, pesticides and textiles. The Tatas were invited to support Vakil's project by the Maharajah of Barod, Sayaji Rao. They accepted and Tata Chemicals was born in 1939. The formula for soda ash was the well-guarded secret of a few companies and Tata Chemicals was able to crack the formula and successfully set up an 80 ton per day plant.

Soon they were going in for expansion to 200 tons per day and the firm asked a young engineer on his way back from America to stop in Germany to discuss the expansion plans with the German firm which was providing the technical assistance. Darbari Seth (b. 1920) stopped in Germany as he was asked. He arrived home with a message that "the emperor has no clothes" and naturally there were few who were willing to risk their necks to agree.

Seth advised the directors of Tata Chemicals that American technology to which he had had exposure was far superior to the German technology and that, furthermore, 400 tons per day was the optimal efficient soda ash plant, not 200 tons as planned. Fifteen board members disagreed. The lone voice of support was that of JRD Tata. Seth, a graduate of the University of Punjab and the University of Cincinnati, was given the task of the entire expansion. The twenty plant complex was put up and Seth's future at Tata Chemicals was assured. Capacity was increased quickly beyond the 400 tons per day to 545 tons.

After the failure of a monsoon, the company was faced with the total shutdown of its operations as the two fresh water lakes which fed the complex were almost dry. Seth and his team came up with a technique for recycling sea water and the town of Mithapur stayed on the industrial map of India. For sixteen years, Tata Sons and Tata Industries, the managing agents of Tata Chemicals, did not take any managing agent fees. Even when the government decontrolled prices, moreover, in 1963, the company did not raise its price much to the disgust of its competitors. Even when there was a glut of soda ash later on, though, customers lined up at Tata's doors as the company had proven itself a friend earlier on.

Darbari Shah Seth is chairman of Tata Chemicals, among a host of other Tata concerns and unrelated organizations. He is chairman of Tata Oil Mills, Tata Fertilisers, Tata Tea, Rallis India Ltd., Ahmedabad Advance Mills, and Tata Energy Research Institute.

From Railways to Diesel Trucks: A New Boy on the Block

After the entry into the airlines business, the Tatas decided to return to earth for what would become their biggest undertaking yet. Starting out to manufacture steam locomotives, the Tatas set up Tata Locomotive and Engineering Company and purchased an old railway workshop in Jamshedpur to fashion its first engineering products. In the first decade of its existence, it manufactured locomotives, wagons, boilers and related products, but as the age of steam locomotives was quickly fading and its market was narrow because of its single customer, the Indian railways, a search was started for a new product. A new form of transportation was appearing in India. It took little imagination to look down the road and see a new mode of transport for goods. Tata trucks.

Daimler Benz was looking for a partner to set up a commercial vehicle plant somewhere in Asia. While there was no market yet in India (the automobile had just begun to be manufactured in the 1940s and demand was not great), the Tatas took up the deal and within a year, the first truck was

Sumant Moolgaokar

assembled from imported parts. A new foundry and forging shop were soon being added to the firm's facilities in Jamshedpur to make ancillaries and to perform some minor R&D. The Daimler-Benz truck had to be adapted somewhat to India's road conditions and the R&D unit proved itself with this first task. By 1957 TELCO was producing 6000 diesel trucks and bus chassis a year. By 1960 production of steam locomotives was phased out altogether and Tata Locomotive became Tata Engineering and Locomotive Company (TELCO). Today TELCO is producing approximately 70 percent of India's total medium and heavy commercial vehicles. It also produces a line of heavy equipment such as excavators, shovels, draglines, clamshells, back-hoes and crawler cranes. It has developed over 800 ancillary suppliers throughout India and brought into existence more than 100,000 entrepreneurs owning one to three Tata trucks. One Tata truck or bus creates employment for an additional twelve persons. In terms of sale, TELCO is the number one company in India's private sector.

The man behind TELCO's success is identified as the principal developer of India's heavy engineering industry: Sumant Moolgaokar, born in 1906 in Bombay. Moolgaokar graduated in engineering from the Imperial College of Science and Technology in London, the MIT of the UK. He started his career in 1930 as an engineer in the cement industry and joined the Associated Cement companies in 1938. Moolgaokar was put in charge of production of eleven Associated Cement companies. When World War II cut off machinery imports, Moolgaokar undertook the production of heavy machinery for the cement industry in a factory set up for this purpose in Shahabad in Hyderabad State. By 1949 he had been appointed Director-in-Charge of TELCO and also served as a Director to Tata Industries and the cement concerns. Moolgaokar was also with Tata Steel for several years and served as TISCO's Vice Chairman.

TELCO today is the largest engineering complex in the non-government sector and is totally self-reliant in machine tooling for mass production. By 1969 the collaboration with Daimler-Benz had expired. TELCO had plans for a completely indigenized product and with this in mind had purchased a large tract of land in Pune, in western India, for the expansion of its facilities. The first buildings to go up in Pune were the apprentice training facilities. Machine tool and press tool divisions as well as an Engineering Research Center were built. By 1979 the first of 9000 trucks that year was produced. The Jamshedpur plant had a capacity of 27,000. Total TELCO capacity is now 56,000 commercial vehicles. TELCO's chief competitor is Ashok Leyland which analysts feel is a more efficient company. But companies with large market shares can operate many times without regard to analysts' comments. Though the shareholders have not seen an appreciation in share value commensurate with the company's status, the financial institutions which hold 25 percent of TELCO's equity have been happy in the past because of the healthy reserves. But Tata trucks are still the preferred trucks by Indian drivers.

In 1980 TELCO planned to go to the market with Rs 48 crore convertible debenture issue for the expansion of its capacity of vehicles and spare parts. It would also replace some of its machine tools. One financial advisor warned that the Rs 48 crore issue was too ambitious. Nimesh Kampani, Managing Director of J.M. Financial and Investment Consultancy Services, proved to be correct. The market fell and TELCO had to call a meeting of stockbrokers to determine what to do in the face of market conditions. Nimesh Kampani, who had originally recommended that the firm float a Rs 20 crore issue, came back into the picture. Kampani convinced the Managing Director of TELCO, J.E. Talaulicar, in a half-hour discussion, that he could raise the entire $47.5 million. Talaulicar was convinced that Kampani's means of raising the money would work. It was a matter of marketing. At the time, only $100 million or so was being raised in the market. Kampani was convinced that an organized campaign both in and outside India could sell the issue.

The TELCO issue was the start of the non-resident investment scheme in India. In addition to arranging a nationwide campaign to educate the

TISCO blast furnace

public and the brokers as to TELCO's virtues, Kampani organized twelve conferences in the Middle East, Southeast Asia, and London where many Indians are resident. Kampani had earlier been glancing over the guidelines for public issues and saw that non-resident funds could be invited on a repatriable basis. TELCO officials were doubtful that the government would allow this. Kampani flew to New Delhi and got a Cabinet level approval to raise $10 million abroad on a repatriable basis to non-resident Indians. He collected $12 million from overseas Indians. Domestically, he had sent brochures to 250,000 people asking, "Would you buy this bond?" He started a sub-broker system in India to help in the sale and collection of monies in remoter areas. The TELCO issue was a success and Kampani went on to raise Rs 44 crore for Gujerat Fertilisers. The $100 million average annual monies raised in public issues quickly jumped with a more dynamic Controller of Capital Issues in New Delhi, Nitish Sengupta, and financial consultants like Nimesh Kampani. The marketing techniques which Kampani came up with were being watched with great interest by one of India's quickest rising industrialists, Dhirubhai Ambani. It was Ambani who was to pick up on Kampani's mass marketing approach of public issues. He also took great note of the offshore investment funds which the government was now allowing to come in on a repatriable basis. Such funds would not be subject to all the wealth and other taxes which domestic investments were heir to. When a market raid on Reliance shares occurred in 1982, non-resident investments were to play a key role in Ambani's ability to keep control of the market in Reliance shares (see Ambani chapter).

TELCO and Reliance Textile have something else in common. Neither pays any taxes if it can help it. Constantly expanding and upgrading capital equipment, both companies accumulate enough investment credits to keep taxes something which someone else pays. Both companies have had Kampani as an advisor and both companies are unrivalled leaders in their respective fields. Where they differ is that TELCO had the considerable clout of the Tata name and the help of financial institutions along the way. Reliance was built up in a short fifteen years by a small businessman with his own trading profits. Many see Reliance passing TELCO's sales by 1990. There is no doubt that Ambani's aggressive use of the stock and bond markets has helped him grow very fast.

TELCO has been criticized for taking the most generous tax deductions under every possible law provision. And the same critics have remarked that the government's policy of treating TELCO most generously in these matters smacked of too cozy a relationship. Without regard to the latter remarks, there is something to this observation. It may be found in a man named Nani Ardeshir Palkhivala, Vice Chairman of TELCO and a director of Tata Sons. Palkhivala, born in 1920 in Bombay, studied English and Law in Bombay and established his reputation as an income tax expert earlier in his career, authoring a seminal treatise, *Law and Practice of Income Tax.* Palkhivala clerked for Sir Jamshedji Kanga, one of the most brilliant income tax lawyers of his time whose chambers monopolized most of the income tax work in the courts in the late 1940s. Palkhivala put himself through school after age 16 by offering private tutoring and he was also able to contribute to his family's household. His father was a small businessman. Palkhivala, like his mentor Kanga, has represented some of the biggest companies in India, and also some of its well-known politicians.

He was an outspoken opponent of the Emergency declared by Prime Minister Indira Gandhi in 1975 (JRD Tata was supportive of the Emergency) and he was named Ambassador to the United States by the Janata government which succeeded the Emergency. Palkhivala is an Indian institution who draws crowds of 25,000 people every year to a stadium in Bombay to discuss his reaction to the annual budget pronouncements. The budget of 1985 was the first one he had favored in decades. As an income tax and constitutional counsel, author and economist, Palkhivala has contributed several lifetimes to his country and his clients. And he is the reason why TELCO knows how to enjoy tax breaks. Palkhivala is a good man to have on your side.

The Future of TISCO and the Tata Group:
Russi Mody and Ratan Tata

The company which made Tata a household word throughout India and the industrialized world has survived some rough times for the steel industry. In the 1950s and 1960s, it is said that TISCO failed to modernize. Labor troubles and low productivity were part of the problems which TISCO suffered. A sympathetic manager was in the making which would allow TISCO to realize its potential once again, however. In 1939, Rustomji Hormusji Mody, son of Sir Homi Mody, joined TISCO after graduating with a degree in ancient history from Oxford. Mody had attended Harrow before that. When he returned home, he was not permitted to linger and contemplate history, but was sent immediately to the Tatas for employment. He began by working in all areas of TISCO, starting on the shop floor at Rs 100 per month. The union at Jamshedpur was weak and struggling into the 1930s, not yet so militant as it was when Mody returned to Jamshedpur in the 1940s.

Mody, as it turned out, though not a laborer, did not get along too well with some of the managers and he was sent off to the coal fields for three years. Productivity increased and it was there that he started his love affair with the workers of TISCO. He was "noticed" and sent to the coal department in TISCO's Calcutta office. One day he was summoned by JRD Tata

Russi Mody

and asked to verify the rumor that the men (20 or so) under his supervision had not joined the recently formed Mercantile Employee's Union. Russi simply had to say that his men did not feel it necessary to join the union as he met their needs and they got along quite well. So JRD had him transferred back to Jamshedpur where things were not going well. In the late 1940s, Mody's presence at Jamshedpur staved off a potentially bloody crisis at the steelworks. Just as workers were clotting around the factory doors and shouting angry words at management, Mody came along and jumped into the fray, asking the workers what the problem was and how he could help. From that day, Mody was in charge of the men at Tata Iron and Steel Works. In the 1950s he convinced management to spend money to improve facilities for the workers and productivity took an immediate leap. TISCO had had a good history of progressive worker policies. Mody was just reminding the upper Tata echelon that those policies were being forgotten. An eight hour work day had been introduced in 1912 (before the US and Europe introduced it), and leave-without-pay, accident compensation and provident funds were established in 1920. Mody's natural affinity with the workers (there are 65,000) leads others to say that "the workingmen at TISCO worship him."

"He holds open house on his verandah every morning from 7 am to 9 pm when anybody can walk in and talk about anything he likes—a practice which Mody has now instituted for all his vice presidents. Every single day, he visits a different department or office, and meets 20 to 50 people individually."[6]

Mody took TISCO into expansion via acquisition of several companies in fields related to TISCO, in part to give his managers a chance to head their own companies. His oneness with his employees probably saved TISCO from being nationalized in 1978 when George Fernandes, then Minister of Industries, threatened to take it over. The Tata Workers' Union voted unanimously to oppose the government. It also saved TISCO's physical plant in 1979 when communists who were trying to organize TISCO's contract (non-payroll) workers and incited them to threaten to destroy the plant. The TISCO employees held them off successfully.

K. Krishnamoorthy, an expert on the history of India's iron and steel industry, remarked:

> It is an acknowledged fact that it is not technological excellence, but industrial peace that has enabled the company to make both ends meet while public sector steel plants have generally failed to obtain the best of their installed capacity, despite their better equipment.[7]

In 1984, JRD stepped down as chairman and Russi Mody took his place. (He had been managing director since 1974.) Mody attributes his straightforward dealing and compassion for others to his mother who taught him the lessons of objectivity and credibility. He had an austere upbringing, learned the habit of punctuality from his father who was a stickler for time and he was allowed to see only one movie a year. While he is a Congress Party man, his brother Piloo Mody was a member of the opposition (an independent) in the Rajya Sabha (Upper House) in New Delhi.

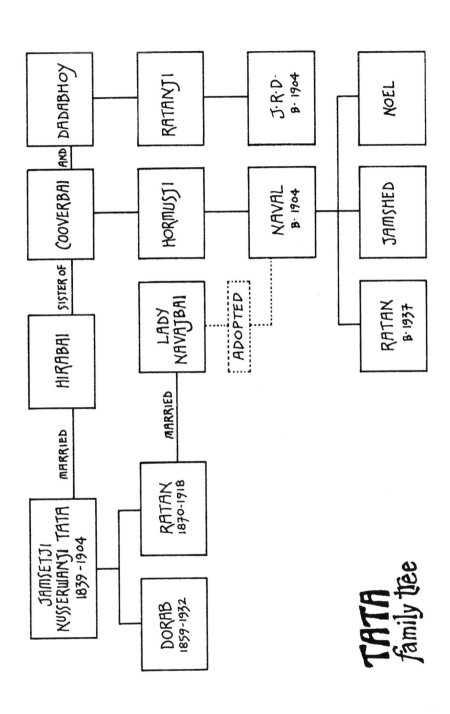

TATA
Family Tree

Mody is taking TISCO along an expansionary road which will increase its product lines. He is on the lookout for new companies or products to help double TISCO's capital investment in the next several years. Admitting that TISCO failed to adopt good technology in the 1950s, he feels that it has made up for it in the 1980s by completing the first phase of its modernization plans within the time schedule and without cost overruns. Mody is one of the most positive forces in the Tata organization and in Indian industry. But he is also frustrated many times by the inefficiency which he sees around him. He knows instinctively that his country is capable of getting more out of its people.

Sometimes we Indians are very callous to our surroundings—we take it and accept it. This is one thing I cannot understand—if we can stage a CHOGM and an Asiad that require great organizational abilities, why can't we organize ourselves to see that we are provided with adequate electricity? It does not seem that we are the same people.[8]

TISCO is Mody's life. He flies his own plane and plays the piano. He is a good cook and likes Michael Jackson. He is a leader who motivates his organization to do its job well and if it is done well, his job is to see that the rewards are there at the end of the day. The Tata companies were the first Indian companies to invite professional men onto the boards of their companies and into the chief executive officer's chair. A scarcity of Tata

Executives of Tata Consultancy Services

Air India Building, Bombay

progeny is one obvious reason for what is something of an anomaly in Indian family promoted businesses. It also makes sense, however, if one goes back to Jamsetji Tata's plans for his country's industrialization. His primary motivation was for India and its people to grow, not just the Tata corporate empire. Thus, professional managers such as Russi Mody, Sumant Moolgaokar, Darbari Seth, J.E. Talaulicar and K.M. Chinnappa are products of J.N. Tata's hopes that Indians could and should run their own country. No matter how much Jamsetji Tata kept public adulation of his accomplishments to a minimum, the more modest he tried to be, the greater was the public respect for him and anyone with whom he shared his firm's name. This is perhaps why another Tata has ascended to the highly honorary, but still commanding, role of head of Tata Industries.

Ratan Tata

Ratan Tata, Naval Tata's son, was educated at Cornell University in architecture and engineering and started his apprenticeship at TISCO as JRD had. At 48, he is Chairman of Tata Industries which, along with Tata Sons, the former group holding company, was the flagship of the group. While the company wields no legal power over the individual Tata companies, it has traditionally served as the moulder of overall policy for the group. As Ratan's father once explained about the erstwhile holding companies, Tata Sons and Tata Industries, "At the apex body as far as the members of the Tata family are concerned they will always be there by virtue of the fact that they represent the Tata Trusts' share." Today 81 percent of Tata shares are held by public charitable trusts. The Tata family holds 1.53 per-

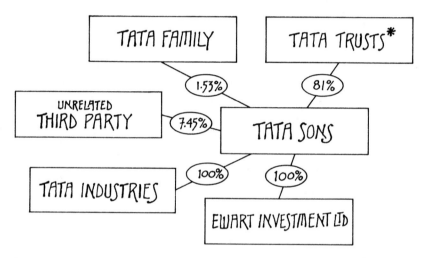

* Voting power rests with government trustee per Companies Act of 1963

Shareholdings in Tata Sons and its wholly-owned subsidiaries

cent of the shares of Tata Sons and Tata Sons in turn holds less than 20 percent of each of the major Tata companies for the most part. Ratan Tata admitted that the Tata Industries board had become somewhat moribund, but he believes it can serve a purpose once more, especially in these days of industrial and economic liberalization when new sectors are opened to large companies. He sees Tata Industries as a scout for new projects for all companies in the group and he feels that the institutional draw of the name Tata will continue to bind the independent companies together. He thinks the Tatas have lost out in certain fields because it has not had a mechanism to follow up new proposals among its members:

We have had situations where someone comes along with a project, some foreign manufacturer, asking if the Tatas would be interested in this or that. Believe it or not, there isn't a mechanism in the Tatas to say we are or we aren't interested. So we assign it to an individual company who may have other things on their mind—and maybe the proposal surfaces with the Kirloskars or the Mahindras.[9]

Ratan Tata has headed some of the troubled Tata firms, National Radio and Electronics and the Central India Spinning and Weaving Company. Though he was able to stem the bleeding in both firms, the industries were hit with recessions and it was difficult to make them profitable. He has had his entrepreneurial baptism by fire. He is interested in taking Tata companies not into dying or troubled industries, but into very high technological industries which have a long future and a short past. On February 11, 1985, *The Economic Times* of Bombay reported the following:

Tatas are planning sizeable investments in new high technology areas like telecommunications, super computers, contract oil drilling, biotechnology, advanced materials, process control systems and alternative energy sources. This, along with the outlay on approved projects like a gas-based fertiliser unit in U.P., expansion of power generation at Trombay, modernisation of the steel mill at Jamshedpur, production of light commercial vehicles and passenger cars at TELCO, and additional capital expenditure on the several on-going projects in other Tata companies, will bring the group's total fresh investments in the next five years to about Rs 2,000 crores.

Mr. Ratan Tata, chairman of Tata Industries, feels that the Tata group would continue to play a pioneering role in the development of new industries in the country.[10]

Asked what the Tata culture really adds up to, Ratan Tata states simply: "To a great extent, perhaps, it has been a little more selfless, has paid more attention to the community and to national issues."[11]

Ratan Tata, Chairman
Tata Industries

Principal Tata Companies

Company	Product
Tata Sons Ltd.	Holding company, consultancy services
Tata Iron & Steel (TISCO)	Steel and steel products
Tata Engineering & Locomotive (TELCO)	Heavy trucks, earth-moving equipment, light vehicles
Voltas	Air conditioners, marketing of engineering and food products
Tata Chemicals	Soda ash
Tata Power Company	Power generation
The Andhra Valley Power Supply Co.	Power generation
Tata Hydro-Electric Power Supply Co.	Power generation
Tata Oil Mills	Detergents, soaps, toiletries
Tata Exports	Exporting
Tata-Finlay	Tea
The Indian Tube Company	Welded tubes
Unitata Berhad, Malaysia	Palm oil

Thapar

Paper
Pulp
Chemicals
Electrical engineering equipment
Construction services
Synthetic fibers
Glass
Textiles
Sugar
Coal trading
Mining

Sales
Rs 850 crore
($708 million)

Headquarters
Thapar House
124, Janpath
New Delhi, India   110 001

Head of Group
Lalit M. Thapar

Karam Chand Thapar (1900-1962)

THAPAR

When Karam Chand Thapar, founder of the Thapar group, died in 1962 at the age of 62, he left a conglomerate of more than 25 companies spanning a dozen industries. Beginning as a coal trader in the 1920s in and around Calcutta, Thapar steadily diversified his activities to include sugar, paper, chemicals, textiles, engineering products and services as well as insurance and banking. Thapar's empire grew principally through acquisition of floundering businesses or assets still in packing crates for want of capital or competent management. Concentration on efficiency and product innovation has kept the group profitable in times of recession and very profitable in times of economic growth.

From sales of just over Rs 100 crore ($83 million) in 1962, the four sons of Karam Chand Thapar took the group to Rs 850 crore ($708 million) in turnover by 1984, placing it among India's top ten groups in the private sector. The founder's penchant for growth through diversification saved the group in the early 1970s when nationalization hit the coal industry, one of its key cash-spinning activities. Today, the group's flagship company, Ballarpur Industries Ltd. (paper, chemicals, glass) accounted for 25 percent of the group's total turnover in 1984. Three other companies in the group, Greaves Cotton & Company Ltd. (engineering products), Crompton Greaves Ltd.

(electricals and electronics) and Jagatjit Cotton Textile Mills Ltd. (cotton and man-made textiles) contributed another 47 percent to total turnover in 1984. Sugar, coal distribution, real estate and a variety of other smaller interests in mining and trading make up the balance of the Thapar group's turnover activities.

The day Karam Chand Thapar died of a heart attack he was to have delivered a speech as outgoing president of the Federation of Indian Chambers of Commerce & Industry. A distinguished audience which included Prime Minister Nehru awaited the words of this leading Indian industrialist. The speech contained enough criticism of the government's investment policies to prompt colleagues to urge KC to tone it down. Even though KC fell ill before the speech was to be delivered, he asked that it be read as written. In retrospect, KC's words were a gentle and reasoned appeal to the newly elected officials to loosen the noose around the neck of a restless business community. It revealed more about KC's own business philosophy than his powers of persuading politicians to give the private sector a more prominent role in India's economic development. KC said:

> *Economic emancipation is a long drawn out struggle in which all sections of the community must participate—businessmen more than perhaps any other single group—with unfettered devotion. Our courage and ability will be continually tested. So long as we have confidence in the value of the goal and excitement at the prospect of setting forth into unfamiliar territory and the will to do new things, think in new ways and entertain new ideas, I have no doubt in my mind that the future of India and the future of Indian enterprise are both safe and glorious.*

A pioneer who "set forth into unfamiliar territory" by demanding a share in his country's industrial process when few Indians dared, Thapar soared over colonial barriers constructed to keep local entrepreneurs hungry for the crumbs of India's foreign-dominated economic activity. His courage and ability in doing so helped assure India that it would have a formidable nucleus of home-grown industrialists to help carry out it post-independence industrialization.

Known throughout his lifetime as the "king of coal", Karam Chand Thapar was born in 1900 in Ludhiana, Punjab. He had his early schooling in Aya High School where he was popularly known as Karmon. His old schoolteacher recalls:

> *From very childhood he was volatile by nature and would not put up with any nonsense. Fearless, always ready to jump into the fray, his companions accepted him as their natural leader . . . too much enthusiasm for sports had its consequences: he failed to be admitted to the degree.*

He attended Forman Christian College in Lahore and after failing his B.A., he returned home. His father, Lala Mansa Ram Thapar, was a smalltime landowner who took a prominent part in the civic life of the city as a municipal commissioner and president of the Hindu Baradari. His father intended him to join the Punjab police. But KC's schoolteacher pointed out to

K.C. Thapar during college days

Lala Mansa Ram "that a police career may not quite suit his son, since he was possessed of a fiery temperament." KC's father gave up the idea. While it did not offer KC too much scope for his own career development, a cousin, Lala Shamlal Thapar, operated a small hosiery factory. It was here that KC put his entrepreneurial instincts to a first test. But family tensions intruded on the arrangement. KC was accused of siphoning funds from the business. To deflect his relatives' attempts at derailing him, KC proposed that he be allowed to manage the firm and that the others handle the cash flow. This was not an acceptable solution to what were deep-seated family enmities.

KC's family had also married him off without consultation. When the wife died after childbirth, the family moved to arrange another marriage. But this time KC insisted on meeting the bride-to-be beforehand. More intrigue would have ensued no doubt had not a family friend, Lala Sagar Chand, invited KC to accompany him as a junior partner to eastern India to work in the coal business. The two men opened an office in Calcutta. KC invested about Rs 12,000 of his own in the venture. The partnership did not last for more than a year. It did, however, yield KC a profit of Rs 42,000 and experience.

Modern coal mining had got its start in India in the early nineteenth century with the arrival of a Britisher in the early 1800s. When his effort failed, the property passed into the hands of Dwarkanath Tagore, grandfather of Rabindranath Tagore, and it was Tagore who floated The Bengal Coal Company in 1835 to carry on the activities. Between that time and the turn of the twentieth century more than fifty other collieries were working the well-endowed coal mines of eastern India. By the 1920's, with the discovery of new reserves, well-known British managing agencies such as Andrew Yule, Shaw Wallace, Jardine Henderson and MacNeill and Barry were deep in the coal business. Karam Chand Thapar would not hesitate to move in on this scene.

It was about 1922 when KC and Lala Sagar Chand arrived in the Jharia coal fields. Major discoveries of coal reserves were being made at the time, but it was by and large the British companies which were reaping the profits. KC began by selling coal for the British. He realized fairly quickly that his friend had wanted him to do the dog's work involved in selling coal. KC cycled 20 to 60 kilometers a day through the coalfields to coordinate suppliers and buyers. But he learned the coal business from scratch, gaining enough confidence to begin working for himself. It was not long before he began buying up coal properties at fire sale prices and making them profitable.

At the time KC entered the coal business, premium coal was exported to Burma, Thailand and Ceylon, while inferior coal remained for sale in the domestic market. KC would stand in a long queue with other Indian coal traders waiting for the inferior quality handouts from the British coal companies. KC marched to the head of the line and demanded that he be allocated better quality coal on better terms. His powerful personality apparently made it difficult for anyone to question his demands. A classmate, Lala Shamlal Dosaj, recalls: "We spent four years in college together . . . our main objective in those days appeared to be body-building . . . all these activities naturally generated heat in the blood, which would welcome the slightest pretext for engaging in a row or a brawl resulting in free fights to establish ascendency." KC started a revolution. Soon other local coal traders began demanding access to better coal. KC also began to organize a better distribution network throughout the country with the cooperation of his fellow Indians. KC soon had about fifty-six outlets all over India. Buying up coal properties was a logical step and KC jumped in with the purchase of the Sirka mines. Next, he eyed the lucrative export market, but could not find a firm to accept shipment of his coal. Finally, even an offer from one British company to ship KC's coal under the condition that he not ship to their markets was rescinded at the last minute. He eventually found some space for his first export order.

In 1929 the firm of Karam Chand Thapar & Bros. Ltd. was established (there were no brothers). Its founder had little to fall back on except for some hard-earned experience. But he had already displayed a remarkable capacity for sustained work. He now showed the ability to absorb and adapt to varied business methods. His company was housed in a building that looked neither like a modern office nor like an oriental establishment, but something between the two.

The lift was rickety but any elevator, however bad, was recognized at the time as a symbol of modernity. His staff, though seated on chairs with tables in front and typewriters noisily clicking in the background, were attired in a wide variety of dresses ranging from dhotis and kurtas, turbans and pyjamas, to the white collared shirts, ties, and pants . . .

recalls one of the earliest employees of the company, Mr. J.N. Sardana. KC himself wore a neatly tied turban with a flamboyant tie on a collared shirt: the whole organization was a sort of grafting of East on West, a queer amalgam that was becoming increasingly common as Indian entrepreneurs tried to imitate the success of the British colonists.

KC did very well. By all accounts he had in a very short period amassed a small fortune. But a few years later KC began speculating in the commodities market, principally in jute. The speculation was a disaster and when KC faced bankruptcy, he had to approach a colleague in the British firm of Byrd & Company to request funds to bail himself out of his troubles. The friend came through and KC vowed never to speculate in unfamiliar markets again. KC took the lesson to heart. "I am not a speculator, but an investor," KC wrote some years later when advised to shut down an uneconomical unit of his reborn empire. These bad years apparently did not phase KC at all. When a colleague, Lala Shyam Lal Dosaj, met KC in Calcutta, he noticed: "To my surprise he showed no signs of dismay or dejection. I recollect so vividly when he said at that time, 'I made all the money which I have foolishly lost. I can make it again and there is no manner of doubt about it.' " For the most part, however, KC had stuck to the coal business in the first decade of his residency in eastern India. But by 1932, his first opportunity to diversify arrived, albeit via the coal connection.

KC's Move Into Industry

KC's coal agent in Uttar Pradesh, L. Aurora, had been selling coal to a family there which ran into financial difficulties and did not have enough funds to keep its fledgling sugar mill going. Aurora cabled KC to ask him if he were interested in acquiring Shree Sitaram Sugar Company. KC travelled to U.P. to look over the proposition. It is said that KC stood looking over the sugarcane fields from the site of the mill and knew at that point that his ambitions were those of an industrialist, not just a coal merchant. "I now see only factories and factories," KC told Aurora. It was a time when many local entrepreneurs were entering the sugar business because of the favorable protective tariffs which had been placed on sugar imports. Nevertheless it was a major step for Thapar who by now had the funds and experience to diversify quickly and successfully.

A second sugar mill was added in 1936, the Deoria Sugar Mills Ltd., and the New Savan Sugar & Gur Refining Company Ltd. was added in 1949. The acquisition of Malwa Sugar Mills followed in 1954. With four sugar mills, the Thapars are a significant supplier to the Indian consumer. Currently looked after by B.M. Thapar, all the mills have plans for substantial expansion and modernization. To return to 1936, KC made a more important acquisition that year, that of Shree Gopal Paper Mills. The paper mill had gone into receivership to a British bank and was auctioned. KC won the bid over the British firm of Byrd & Company which grew worried about the growing success of KC's business skills. Byrd moved to cut off Gopal's

Sugar cane field ("I now see only factories . . .")

raw material supply as it was supporting a rival mill, Star Paper, owned by the Bajoria family. The British firm was successful in convincing the local government to cancel Gopal's lease of certain nearby forestlands in favor of Star and KC was forced to look as far away as Burma and Thailand for raw materials for his plant.

In the meantime, the strong-willed Punjabi did not take the local government's decision as the final word on the matter. He approached the government to make a deal. He promised that Star Paper would have first rights to the forest for its plant, but KC requested that in return the government allow Shree Gopal access to the lands as well. It was a clever proposal which showed Byrd's move for what it was. The government was too embarrassed not to agree to the more than fair proposal. But the lessons of access to raw materials were never lost on KC. His paper mills were eventually to begin vertical integration by going into production of chemicals needed in paper production. But the problem of sufficient raw materials for paper-making has been a perennial one in India, whose forestlands have declined over the decades with the rising population and urbanization. Shree Gopal consequently began to use the widest variety of raw materials ever fed a paper plant. Its production has increased well over thirty times since its acquisition by the Thapar group.

In 1937/38, Thapar ran short of cash as demand for coal, paper and industrial goods declined in a general economic downturn. Fortunately for Indian industry, World War II proved to be very good for business. Companies with even modest production know-how and established trading connections with the British reaped wartime profits and ensured a cash flow adequate to begin an impressive post-war expansion. The profits were the subject of an inquiry by the government after the war and KC along with many other business leaders of the time came under scrutiny for possible accumulation of unrecorded profits. When KC's case came up in court, he was upbraided by the judge. Never one to be cowed, KC shouted back at the judge in an unprecedented courtroom scene which left his colleagues believing that KC's life as an industrialist had ended. But KC's indignation surprised the judge and caused him to back away from pressing the court's case against the businessman.

Thapar had been steadily adding to his coal properties throughout the 1930s and 1940s. In the mid-1940s, however, he undertook another major diversification for his group, this time into textiles. In 1946, Jagatjit Textile Mills Ltd. was set up in Thapar's native state of Punjab. At first producing common cloths, it moved into finer blended fabrics and now exports its products worldwide. Sales have doubled in just a few years and the Rs 120 crore ($100 million) turnover achieved in 1984 is a result of continual expansion and technical innovation under the management of Man Mohan Thapar, the youngest of KC's sons. Another mill was added in 1963 when the Thapars acquired the seventeen-year-old Shree Sadul Mills, which was turned around and now exports well over a million square meters of cloth a year. Man Mohan Thapar attended the Philadelphia Institute of Textiles in the USA and is taking Jagatjit into a major expansion in industrial fibers over the next few years. In what has been traditionally a difficult industry, the Thapar group swam against the current to keep Jagatjit's technology up to date and its operation profitable. In fact, it is one of the few mills in India—barring Reliance and Orkay—to consistently make profits in some of the worst years of the Indian textile industry. While the share prices of other textile mills tumbled, those of JCT rose from Rs 20.25 to Rs 56.50. Man Mohan Thapar has also taken JCT abroad. The company is providing technical and managerial expertise for the modernization and expansion of a textile mill in Thailand, the Thonburi Textile Mills Ltd. In 1983 a Rs 32 crore plant at Hoshiapur went on stream producing nylon filament. Though Man Mohan plans to plough back Rs 12 to 14 crores on modernizing the textile mills, he admits that gradually the group will move out of cottons.

Man Mohan Thapar   Karan Thapar, Brij's son

Post-War Expansion

Coal, sugar, paper and textiles were now the key industrie= into which the Thapar group had expanded. After the war, many British companies could not sustain their operations in India due to economic hardship back home or the parent company's fears for their futures in an independent India. The cash flush business houses of India entered post-wa. ust-independent India ready to buy up properties from the departing colonialists. Thapar, like so many of his colleagues, was already experienced in the acquisition game. He spotted a well-known British engineering trading firm, Greaves Cotton & Company, which was interested in selling out. Just prior to the war, Greaves Cotton had begun the manufacture of a small number of oil engines and electrical equipment (the Ruston & Hornsby horizontal engine which Greaves had begun manufacturing in 1939 in India became a strategic product in the development of India's irrigation system which helped effect the Green Revolution). KC had learned of Greaves' being up for sale from a man named Tom Sturgiss, who was managing director of one of his companies, Indian Trade and General Insurance Company. The sale was negotiated with Sir John Greaves for Rs 90 lakh (well over a million U.S. dollars at the time), a price which was rather high considering that the nature of its business at the time was principally that of trading. But the prestige and goodwill connected with the Greaves Cotton name was thought to be worth the price.

Sir John Greaves was keen to sell the company to the Thapars. He was so sympathetic to the prospective Indian owners that he placed a condition on the sale. Many of the Britishers working for the Bombay based company at the time were concerned about their futures under Indian ownership and decided to quit in anticipation of the assumed misfortune which would befall them under "backward" locals. Sir John was aware of this and said he would sell the company to Thapar only if the latter would not hire back any of the employees who had fled in fear of Thapar management. (The attitude was one which would persist long beyond the period of transition to independence. Foreign firms selling out to Indian ownership in the 1980s experienced similar phenomena when Indian employees feared they would experience less than fair treatment by their own country's industrialists. Often the change of ownership provided new opportunities for promotion, however).

After the acquisition of Greaves Cotton, KC had to decide whether to retain the Greaves Cotton name and permit it to operate under the existing management. Ordinarily KC liked to put his imprint on his companies, making his formidable presence felt by executives and employees alike. According to executives who knew of his dilemma, KC was agitated for quite some time before he decided in favor of letting Greaves Cotton retain its own name and management. What factors KC weighed in making his decision can only be surmised at this stage, but the decision clearly showed a certain confidence on the part of KC. The broader corporate objectives of growth would take precedence over imposition of any one person's personality, even

Greaves Cotton Headquarters, Bombay

if it were the founder's. There were also sound reasons for retaining the well established name of Greaves Cotton. But overall KC's moves were a proof of his coming of age as a modern industrial leader.

Greaves Cotton had been started as a cotton trading firm in 1859 by a Britisher, James Greaves. He was joined in 1868 by another Britisher, George Cotton, and from cotton they began trading in engineering goods for the textile industry until the eve of World War II when they went into the manufacture of the Ruston & Hornsby horizontal engines. The 1947 takeover by Thapar began a new era for the firm's activities as the Thapars took Greaves into a wide variety of manufacturing activities in the engineering sector—diesel generating sets, centrifugal pumps, precision gears, aviation and electronics, construction and oil exploration equipment, many of these produced in collaboration with well-known names around the world. India's need for every possible type of industrial product and process in 1947 provided great scope for growth.

Another British firm, Crompton Parkinson (Works) Ltd., had been established in India in 1937 and came into the Thapar fold as part of the Greaves Cotton acquisition. Crompton Parkinson initially manufactured motors for the textile industry and had gone into the design and manufacture of electrical equipment for industrial exhausts and generating sets. But a new joint venture between Crompton Parkinson of the UK and the Thapar group came into being in 1969 with both partners holding 37½ percent of the new company, Crompton Greaves, and the balance held by the public. This new entity continued manufacturing electricals and electronics and soon moved into the export arena. Among India's top exporters of electrical equipment and technology, Crompton Greaves' products are in use in over seventy countries. Together with Greaves Cotton, Crompton Greaves offers a diversified base of engineering services and products to every major industrial sector. In 1984, sales of Crompton Greaves reached Rs 172 crore ($143 million) while its sister company, Greaves Cotton, had a turnover of Rs 108 crore ($90 million).

Thapar's companies are linked with leading foreign firms in the engineering and contractors' fields. Rolls Royce, Redifon, Marconi Space Defence Systems, Selenia, Beech Aircraft, Raytheon joined with Greaves Cotton to make a significant contribution to India's aeronautical industry. Greaves' aviation division was set up in 1949 to cater to the large demands of a new country's aero-space manufacturing activity. A Rolls Royce engine powers some of India's jet aircraft and an air traffic control system was fabricated in collaboration with Selenia of Italy. New mining methods acquired via a link-up with Intrafor of France helped one of the Thapar companies, Karam Chand Thapar and Bros. Ltd., expand into the heavy construction and civil engineering field. The Thapar-Intrafor joint venture has constructed airport runways, bridges, water treatment plants and a complex system of dams, reservoirs and tunnels for a hydroelectric project in southern India.

In the 1950s, a major opportunity for expansion in paper came along. In Madya Pradesh, the state government and the Bedi family had come together to promote Ballarpur Paper and Straw Board Mills Ltd. But the plant and equipment remained in packing crates for lack of capital on the part of the Bedis. Thapar made a bid to the government for the assets. Another industrial group, the Birlas, battled Thapar for the Ballarpur assets, but the Finance Minister at the time opted for the Thapars. The plant was set up on the periphery of Maharashtra's forests and was one of the first mills in the world to use bamboo as its exclusive raw material. In 1969 under the direction of Lalit Thapar who took over leadership of the group following KC's death, Ballarpur and Shree Gopal were merged. Advised by colleagues to keep the two operations separate as it was thought wise not to grow too large in any one industry, Lalit Thapar moved ahead with the merger. Centralization of certain common activities proved itself on the bottom line of Ballarpur in no time. In the three decades following independence, paper production had increased tenfold in India with Ballarpur accounting for 15 percent of total production. Every type of paper is produced by Ballarpur from packaging materials to fine writing papers.

Under Lalit's direction, Ballarpur expanded into chemicals, a natural outgrowth of the need to supply caustic soda and chlorine to meet Ballarpur's paper production process. At first the plants were for captive purposes, but were later expanded to cater to the general market. A major expansion of its chemicals complex at Karwar where caustic soda, chlorine, sodium tripolyphosphate and hydrochloric acid are manufactured, will service the growing needs of industries such as paper, textiles, aluminum and others. About 20 percent of Ballarpur's sales are accounted for by sales of chemicals.

During the period 1946 to 1955, two more sugar mills were added and three coal mines. In all, KC set up or acquired eight projects in nine years. He rarely borrowed except for working capital purposes. He always paid his debts, though sometimes by necessity a little late.

The Hind Strip Mining Corporation Ltd. was KC's last purchase before he began to consolidate his activities and devote more time to general activities touching the business community. He did not live to see his coal empire dissolved by nationalization. No doubt he would have fought it as vigorously as he had confronted the judge in the Calcutta court or the British merchants in the mid-1920s when he was trying to break into the coal business. KC had been offered the title of Rai Bahadur which the British were handing out to prominent Hindu citizens. He was not overwhelmed with the thought of favors from the British. At the time KC was engaged in carrying out the biggest road operation in the Arakan in Burma with a band of well-trained personnel. The job assumed great significance in view of the onset of World War II. In appreciation for this service, the British colonial government sounded him about a knighthood. KC snapped back, "I have done my work

Ballarpur Industries Ltd. (Insets: unloading bamboo for paper-making, and checking of coated paper)

and have got my price for it. There is no need for any additional reward." His
decision was perhaps influenced by national events. The same year (1942),
Gandhi launched the Quit India movement. KC did his share of harboring
nationalist political activists who were being hunted by the colonial government. But he did it quietly. It was only his fear that Mahatma Gandhi would
ask him to give up business which kept him from accepting an invitation from
Gandhi for the two to meet.

K.C. Thapar with college cricket team

Lalit Mohan Thapar, KC's Heir

KC was a tough master, according to his son Lalit, but he was also fair.
A workhorse who expected the same dedication from those around him, it was
no surprise when he suffered a heart attack at the young age of forty. KC's
strength was in his marketing ability and in his knack for training people. He
had an enormous ability to get loyalty from people despite his foul temper
and sometimes harsh tongue. He was not free with compliments to his family
or his workers as an incentive to better work performance. Rather KC would
sometimes fire people who were performing well just to keep his organization
from becoming slack and complacent. His first son, Inder, who heads the coal
trading concerns, grew up in Ludhiana with his grandfather who had asked KC
to leave the boy with him when KC had gone off to eastern India. Thus, Inder
was not with KC during the growth years of his group. Brij Mohan, the second

son, was of a quieter and more sensitive nature than KC. Pressure from the top was so great at one point that Brij Mohan went off to Switzerland to escape the hard-driving KC. (Brij Mohan almost aligned himself with the Moral Re-Armament Group in Caux. KC travelled to Caux. Though he was sympathetic to the cause, he steadily got Brij back into his fold, recalls an old associate of the family.)

It was KC's third son, Lalit Mohan, a graduate of the University of Southern California in engineering, who inherited KC's throne. Lalit was only 32 in 1962 when KC died. He says he was scared out of his wits. He had barely four years of apprenticeship in managing the group's activities as joint managing director of the group's managing agency, Karam Chand Thapar & Bros. Ltd. before KC's death. In Lalit, there was no question of doing other than what KC wanted. The family was far too disciplined, Lalit relates. For him rebellion was out of the question. Following graduation in the USA, Lalit went to England where he worked for two years in two Thapar affiliates, Ruston & Hornsby and Crompton Parkinson. Following KC's death, the family held a conclave and determined that their greater strength was in staying together. With Lalit already having been placed in an heir apparent posting by

Lalit Mohan Thapar, Head of Group

KC, the question of leadership of the group was not a difficult one. All four sons had a particular industry group to look after in any event. The question of family rivalry was kept to a minimum.

When he assumed control in 1962, Lalit's first actions were to make no immediate changes. He sat back and tried to absorb as much of the business as possible. He did not take the company on a further binge of expansions. He did not tamper with the system which had been established by those in power before him. This tack was crucial because when nationalization did hit, the group had spent the better part of the 1960s consolidating its activities and growing stronger in the industries in which they were already established.

Lalit is a rapid decision-maker as his father was. A tough taskmaster who is in his element in complex negotiations, Lalit's personality is, however, less threatening that that of KC. The sharp temper of the father has given way to a more subtle management style, a confident delegation of responsibility, especially in comparison with the management pattern of other family business houses in India. He takes time to enjoy the pleasures of travel and foreign cultures and is perfectly at home in his own as well. Unlike KC, Lalit can compliment someone on a job well done without fear of a breakdown in efficiency. The real test for his leadership must have come with the nationalization of the coal industry, however.

In the early 1960s, about 60 companies dominated the coal industry in India, producing 60 percent of the coal. Thapar's company was among the largest. Government five year plans were projecting an increased demand for coal, still the principal source of energy in India. But price controls in the industry made it difficult for companies to generate sufficient investment capital to undertake the expansion necessary to meet the projected demand. A slump hit the industry in the mid-1960s as industrial output fell and companies which had borrowed heavily to expand were caught in a cost/price squeeze which threatened their survival.

The government eventually agreed to a decontrol of coal prices, but the actual price was left to the coal companies and their chief client, the Indian railways, to work out through negotiation. The compromise price was not adequate to put the destabilized industry on its feet. Government's fear of a decline in coal output just when its large steel plants were coming on stream led to widespread calls by politicians for takeover of the industry. In the general deterioration of the state of affairs and increasing populist sentiment, wholesale stripmining occurred, adding fuel to the calls for takeover of the country's vital natural resources. Thus, by 1973, the government had assumed control of private coal mining operations. The only exception was that of Tata Iron and Steel Company (TISCO) which was spared because its coal properties directly fed its steelmaking operations in Jamshedpur in Bihar.

At the time of nationalization, the Thapar group was raising two and a half million tons of coal and selling another four million tons. No compensation was paid to the owners of the nationalized companies, but they were permitted to continue distributing coal, the business in which KC had started out in the early 1920s. Distribution outlets which numbered 56 during KC's heyday now number 130 as the Thapar reputation for knowing its coal business continues to attract customers, including government entities.

1975 saw BILT's entry into its third major activity: glass. As part of its diversification drive, the company took over Jg Glass Industries Ltd., Jg Glass Ltd., and Jg Moulds Ltd., to become the second largest glass container manufacturer in the country. Jg Glass factories at Poona and Rishikesh were set up to meet domestic glass container requirements as well as those of the pharmaceutical and beverage industries. The acquisition of Jg Glass Industries Ltd. brought with it a substantial interest in Jg Containers (Malaysia) Sdn Bhd, a unit in Malaysia. Once the first step in a new direction is taken, Ballarpur goes the whole hog. The company's interest in glass is on the increase: they tied up with Corning of the USA to bring Indian house- wives labor-saving, heat resistant cooking ware and specialized laboratory glassware for scientists. A move to take over Hindustan Pilkington Glass in the 1980s was dropped when a government decision one way or the other was not forthcoming, according to Lalit Thapar.

Inder Mohan (eldest son of K.C.)

Vikram, Inder's son

Two paper plants in Indonesia, textile and paper collaborations in Thailand, a glass plant and palm oil project in Malaysia, trading activities in the Middle East as well as performance of turnkey contracts—all have earned the group an international image and provided an outlet for the Thapars' rest- less natures. A total of Rs 11 crore ($9 million) has been invested overseas, but political turmoil, currency devaluation or other factors beyond the control of the Thapars or their influential joint venture partners abroad taught the group that foreign investment opportunities must be scrutinized much more carefully than domestic business deals.

While always open to new proposals, the Thapars do not hesitate to drop out of a venture if it is not proving itself. A joint venture with Taiyos of Japan, a leading fisheries company, was sold quickly as soon as it was clear that government policies were not going to permit the new company to get off the ground. A Rs 40 crore ($33 million) joint venture with the Andhra Pradesh government to produce pulp, A. P. Rayons, also ran into trouble at first when the state government failed to supply the raw materials promised for the project and management lines were not clearly observed. The group stuck with the project, however, and is now planning to merge its operations into Ballarpur to achieve some economies which can hopefully place A. P. Rayons on a sounder basis.

An attempt to take over the Scindia Shipping Company in 1983 was thwarted by the management of Scindia. With the depressed state of the shipping industry over the past several years, Thapar's interest in seeking a foothold in the shipping industry might have been fortuitously delayed. In August 1984, the group entered further into the electronics field with the acquisition of an Andhra Pradesh company, Solid State Devices Ltd. Thapar also announced its application to the government for the right to manufacture PABX telephone exchanges and electronic telephone instruments. Government spending plans promised the allocation of billions of rupees for the modernization of India's communications system.

Along the way, the Thapar group has also established real estate and management consultant operations, expanded into leather exports, and manufactures vegetable oil, mines China clay, manganese, iron ore, dolomite and limestone in a modest way.

There is much discussion over the cautious nature of the Thapar group and its low-key approach to business. Some say the nationalization of its coal, insurance and banking operations taught it the value of staying well outside of the politician's view. But the group's low-key intensity has deeper roots. The modesty and "sticking to business" attitude of its current chairman is more inborn than imposed from external socio-political circumstances. First, the powerful personality which the founder possessed did not lead to the development of similar larger-than-life personalities in his sons. They were expected to listen and learn first, not strike out on their own as KC had done. What did carry through from KC's era was the penchant for independence, a lack of fear for the unknown and an intuitive feeling for building a professional organization, no matter the particular endeavor.

The growth in the group's sales in the last two decades by more than eight times, from $83 million to $708 million in 1984, has not been achieved through cautious behavior, but by taking calculated risks. There is also a delegation of ideas-development and decision-making to appropriate managers in the individual companies which leaves the top management free to direct the group's growth and assess new projects. This is not to say that Lalit or Man Mohan Thapar, for example, do not command their managers and workers the same respect that their father did. Simply, there is more psychic energy in the second generation for a more relaxed approach to life in general. But it is a mark of the professionalism begun by KC that two of their four largest companies, Greaves Cotton and Crompton Greaves, have all along been headed by non-family members, executives of the caliber of Govind Mathrani, N.M. Wagle, and S.G. Padhye. Profitable initiatives can be taken up with a minimum amount of internal administrative anxiety.

Product innovation from their own R&D efforts has made the group

Soda/chlorine plant, and tanks

industry leaders in paper, chemicals and electricals. Ballarpur Industries won the 1982 Indian Chemicals Manufacturing Association award for "forward development of technology" when it succeeded in substituting hydrochloric acid for sulphuric acid to obtain phosphoric acid from a low-grade indigenous rock. The citation praised Ballarpur's breakthrough as an "elegant way to produce a high value-added and high quality product of considerable importance to India." The process eliminated the need for costly imports of sulphuric acid as well as found a way to use indigenous materials to lower overall costs.

After acquisition of Greaves Cotton in the late 1940s, the Thapars established an R&D unit which had also resulted in some technological breakthroughs. The first 220 kva capacity transformer was invented, the first short-circuit testing transformer and the first flame-proof motor for use in the petroleum industry were also Thapar innovations.

The chairman of the Thapar group has offered his services to the general business community by serving as president of a number of industry and business associations. Though Lalit Thapar does not wear his thoughts on his sleeve, he is deeply interested in the progress of his country's economy and the status of the business community in Indian society. He not only inherited the mantle of leadership from his father, but his father's interest in world affairs and economic trends which affect his country's progress. In his speech to the Federation of Indian Chambers in 1962, KC had revealed a clarity of vision with which few could argue, whether on the left or right. Applied to his own business, it is easy to see how he might have succeeded where others could not. Applied to his country, it is not difficult to understand that if he had been given the reins of power for a few years, India's economic progress could have taken certain broad strides.

> *Our basic problem is one of growth. We have many impediments, but these are within our capacity to overcome. What is necessary is not merely blind effort, but conscious appreciation of the situation and a careful formulation of policies founded on correct values and inescapable economic laws.*

The Thapar family (ca. 1946)

First row (*seated*): Rani, Neena (K.C.'s first grandchild), Man Mohan; second row (*seated*): Mrs. Inder Mohan Thapar, Raj Srivastava, Mr. Srivastava, Mrs. K.C. Thapar, Mrs. Prem Lall; third row (*standing*): Inder Mohan, Lalit Mohan, K.C., Brij Mohan

Thapar's Calcutta office

TTK

Consumer products distribution/manufacturing
Kitchenware
Pharmaceuticals
Condoms
Textiles
Readymade garments
Printing, publishing
Packaging
Chemicals

Sales
Rs 102 crore
($85 million)

Headquarters
6, Cathedral Road
Madras, India 600 086

Head of Group
T.T. Narasimhan

T.T. Krishnamachari (1899-1974)

TTK

In 1928 Tiruvallur Thattai Krishnamachari (TTK) took over the accounts of an indenting firm in Madras for which he worked for seven years without pay. The firm booked orders in south India on behalf of the illustrious British multinational, Lever Brothers, and Beecham's, the British food company. TTK inherited these accounts when the owner died. He then set up his own company, TT Krishnamachari & Company, to expand his business activities. From the mere booking of orders, TTK began a warehousing and distribution operation in south India. His dogged journeys throughout the South to market a wide variety of consumer goods brought him the affection of his customers and success in business. His business exploits even won the admiration of his social set in Madras which had almost by decree questioned what a Brahmin boy was doing selling Lever's soaps in the hinterlands.

After a decade and a half of enjoying business, TTK turned to politics, leaving his son, TT Narasimhan, in charge of the family firm. Narasimhan was fortunate to have accompanied his father all over south India to learn the art of personal selling. When the firm lost the lucrative Lever's agency in the early 1940s and the war years cut off the importation of most of their products, TT Narasimhan faced an uncertain future. Fortunately, the TTK group linked up with an American firm after the war, L. D. Seymour and

Company, to represent the American agent in south India. More than 150 products would eventually be sold by TTK on behalf of Seymour. The Seymour connection also led the Indian firm into its first manufacturing ventures in the 1950s. TTK & Company was to establish a proliferation of small and medium-scale industries in the south to manufacture many of the products it had originally imported.

With one of the widest distribution networks in the southern half of the Subcontinent and an inventory of prestigious products, the growth which should have ensued for the group in the 1950s and 60s—an era of rapid growth for most of Indian industry—was not realized. During this period, the founder of the group was serving in the Lok Sabha and as Nehru's Minister of Industries and Commerce and then as Finance Minister. While TTK presided over, and was in great part responsible for, the most dynamic period of post-independence industrialization, his sons' firm in Madras diversified into manufacturing, but did not venture too far or wide from its initial business of representing other manufacturers' products in the south. Any bold moves to grow fast or big would have required political clout. To obtain funding, licenses and other industrial approvals could always lead to criticism that the group was misusing the influence of its founder who now moved in the inner circles of power. Thus a low profile was maintained for more than twenty years or so. TT Narasimham nonetheless set about to do for consumer goods, an area of little attention at the time, what TTK was making possible for India's hard core industrialization in Delhi. (The era of consumerism in India would not arrive until the 1980s.)

The group's goal of reaching Rs 500 crore ($417 million) in sales by 1990 from 1983 sales of Rs 102 crore ($85 million) tells a new story. Such exponential growth reflects a growing confidence among the TTK partners that the fifty years of experience they have in satisfying hundred of millions of loyal consumers can mean big sales in the not too distant future. One reason for the group's optimism is the government's interest in permitting Indians to buy consumer goods at cheaper prices than was hitherto possible because of high excise taxes. Introduction of television into tens of thousands of villages is also expected to raise expectations of the viewers for the goods which companies like TTK are advertising now on television. TTK & Company will do everything it can to see that these expectations are met. The imposed reticence of the 1950s and 60s while the founder was in the thick of Delhi politics has ended. TT Narasimhan's own vision can now be recognized as the basis for the group's ability to meet its 1990 sales target.

TTK: His Origins

TTK was born in Madras in 1899, the only son of a Brahmin High Court judge who expected his son to follow in his footsteps. Graduating from Madras Christian College, TTK entered government service for a brief time before startling his family and friends by going into business. Joining A. R. Doraiswamy Iyengar in his indenting firm in Madras, TTK worked unpaid in order to learn the agency business first hand from the man who represented the biggest industrial names worldwide, Lever's and Beecham's of the UK. When Doraiswamy fell ill in 1926, five years after TTK had joined him, TTK ran the business himself, still without any compensation (his well-to-do background luckily permitted him to do so and also helped minimize any anxiety a Brahmin father might feel because of his son's involvement in trade). When Doraiswamy died in 1928, TTK was in Cochin to establish a branch office. While many companies sought to win the Lever Brothers' agency and the government even got into the act by suggesting a few names, TTK carried on Doraiswamy's business. Lever's was so impressed with TTK's perserverance in face of uncertainty that they awarded him their agency.

TTK as a young businessman

With Lever's continued patronage under his arm, TTK set up his own firm in 1928, TT Krishnamachari & Company. He immediately set about changing the way Doraiswamy had been doing business. Rather than just book orders and pass them on to the manufacturers, TTK set up his own warehousing and distribution network, selling directly to the dealers all over south India. He implemented an entirely modern approach to selling, trying new techniques such as skywriting, point of purchase displays (in which the group still excells) and modern market surveys to learn first hand what consumers wanted. He preceded many of his salesmen's footsteps throughout his territory. Sometimes he followed in their footsteps, studying the effects of their salesmanship. TTK's success in business helped make business fashionable among conservative Madras society.

TTK's first office, 111 Armenian Street, Madras

In business, TTK was always courteous, never uttering a single harsh word except in jest. He was generous to a fault, according to his friends, and there was nothing he would not do for them. He dressed in the height of fashion during his entrepreneurial days—silks, tweeds and gossamer cottons. His taste in food, books and friends was always exquisite and his success made him a much sought after young man about town.

By 1937, after a decade of his self-launch into business, TTK became restless. His interests broadened. He was propelled toward local politics. TTK had once explained to a friend from his sickbed toward the end of his life that he had strayed into politics in 1937 after casually perusing the list of members of the Chamber of Commerce constituency of the Madras Legislative Assembly. He won a seat in the Assembly as the Chamber's representative shortly thereafter.

Turning away from his life of creature comforts as quickly as he had left his government career to join business, TTK began wearing homespun clothes in solidarity with the millions of participants in the freedom movement. He gave away his silks and tweeds to less dedicated colleagues and spurned the British government in bold speeches to his colleagues at the Madras Chamber and in the local Assembly. Through his constant reading, thinking and personal exchanges with people from every walk of life, TTK honed his political views to a fine point. He became adept at treating problems in their broadest frame of reference. Always anxious to discourage actions which he felt would prove unwise for his country in the long run, TTK persuaded others of his point of view with an eloquent debating style admired as much by his enemies as his friends.

TTK was elected to the Central Legislative Assembly from Madras in 1942 against the powerfully backed Congress Party opponent, Jamal Mohamed. Immediately following the election, TTK distanced himself from the special interests which were instrumental in putting him in office. From his lone seat of opposition, TTK eventually switched over to the Congress Party. He became a member of the Drafting Committee of the Constituent Assembly to take part in drafting the Indian Constitution. His work on the Committee attracted the attention of India's first Prime Minister, Jawaharlal Nehru, and the two soon struck up a lifelong friendship.

TTK with Prime Minister Nehru

In the crucial period of nation-building in India, TTK served in the Lok
Sabha in new Delhi. More importantly, Nehru appointed TTK Minister of
Industries and Commerce (1952-1956) and Finance Minister (1956-1958
and again from 1963-1965). As Industries Minister, TTK almost
singlehandedly laid the groundwork for India's first major industrial
development program, putting flesh on Nehru's vision for a modern scientific
and technologically-oriented society. To those who knew him, TTK seemed
dominated by a sense of urgency. The pleasant nature which won him success
in business seemed to evaporate as the tasks at hand became all-consuming.
The outcome of India's experiment in independence was a matter of life or
death for hundreds of millions. TTK's impatience with bureaucratic
cowardice and obstructionism became legendary. He ignored the rising tide
of anti-TTK sentiment.

TTK with Congress Party Secretary and strong man, Kamaraj

Painting in the industrial canvas of post-independent India, TTK steamlined industrial licensing procedures (sometimes his word was sufficient for a company to move forward with a project), argued for and oversaw construction of three public sector steel plants which would feed a wide variety of small, medium and large scale industries he envisioned as downstream producers of finished goods. Automobile, engineering, electricals, chemicals, plastics, cement, aluminum, transport and communications industries were assisted under TTK's ministership. He helped secure foreign collaborations for a number of sophisticated industries, overhauled the import/export system and later on in the 1960s set up several development finance institutions to fund increased industrial activity in both the private and public sector. Small entrepreneurs were not forgotten as programs were designed to assist them as well under TTK's stewardship. Along the way, TTK insisted that the foreign companies doing business in India promote Indians into managerial positions. This was no time to argue with TTK. His determination to pursue the goal of total independence in industrial management helped assure the growth of a formidable managerial class.

His business experience had given TTK an empathy with entrepreneurs and, as Industries Minister, he was to give his support to anyone if he felt they could put together a successful venture. When the Birla group was frustrated in its attempt to set up an iron and steel mill because the sector had been reserved for the state, TTK helped them set up an aluminum plant in Uttar Pradesh in collaboration with Kaiser Aluminum of the USA. TTK knew that if India pushed for self-development of her people and her economy, there would be interest from the rest of the world in joining hands with her. He told a young journalist once:

> *Building up an army of skilled people will take a long time . . . a long, long time . . . Our Western aiders and advisers did not wish us to become men of steel. They would prefer us to grow timber, bamboo or even weak stalk like jute and mesta. What we should do is to engineer a big change from trading to manufacturing. That's what planning is all about—getting out of the jute swamps. Funny thing is that, despite all their views on what India should and should not do, the European businessmen have come running to do business with us when it became clear that we mean business. They will always come if we play our cards well.* [1]

TTK & Company Madras: 1940–1955

Except for a few years' break, TTK & Company had maintained its relations with Beecham's (it was to end in 1960), but the money-spinning Lever Brothers agency ended in the early 1940s when the British multinational decided to sell its products without benefit of a middleman. TTK & Company had done so well in marketing Lever's products, it was no longer necessary to retain the south Indian firm as agent. The loss dealt a big blow to TT Narasimhan and his company. Fortunately, the Beecham's connection and the Cadbury agency which had come to TTK in 1936, remained. At the time Lever's pulled its business away from TTK & Company, the latter was grossing about Rs 75 lakh ($625,000) a year. The loss of the big account would be exacerbated by World War II. While the war was very good for many Indian companies, at least those who were able to manufacture goods at home based on indigenous materials, for TTK & Company the war cut off supplies of many of the items which formed the basis of the firm's trading business. With his father more and more involved in politics, TT Narasimhan had taken control of the company after 1939 when it was located at 111 Armenian Street in Madras. With the end of the war, however, the picture soon brightened when TTK & Company came into fortunate contact with an American firm.

T.T. Narasimhan, Head of Group

Lawrence D. Seymour was the son of Henry Seymour, an American businessman who had formed a partnership with V. A. Dodge to represent a number of prominent American firms in India. The elder Seymour had been operating in India for some time when he died in the mid 1940s. His son, Larry, split up the partnership with Dodge after his father's death and set up his own firm in Bombay in 1945. Seymour was therefore in need of an Indian firm to represent him in south India. The TTK group was put in touch with Seymour by the man who had been dealing with the elder Seymour's partnership. He also happened to be a friend of the Indian group. After three days of exchanging telegrams, Seymour appointed the TTK group its agent in south India. They had not yet met.

The first product to be handled as a result of the Seymour connection was Pond's face cream. More than 150 products would follow. TTK & Company was to distribute Westclox alarm clocks, Kraft cheese, Kellogg's cornflakes, Schaeffer pens, Aqua Velva aftershave lotion, among a host of items which became household words around the world. TTK & Company used its marketing skills to make them household words in India as well.

By 1953 the last American had left the Seymour office in Bombay. TT Narasimhan, who by now had spent eleven years as head of TTK & Company, became managing director of L. D. Seymour & Company. This put TTN in direct touch with the American manufacturers and led to the first TTK manufacturing ventures. Soon he met Mr. Kellogg who was prepared to franchise the manufacture of his cornflakes in India provided that the corn would be purchased from the USA. The condition could not be met and the deal fell through. TTK & Company did begin manufacturing the powder which went into Pond's face cream (Pond's eventually set up its own manufacturing operation), but the first product to be manufactured was Waterman's ink. A small company, Right Aids Orient (P) Ltd., was set up in Dooravaninagar, outside Bangalore, to manufacture the inks. The group had not located the plant in its home town of Madras because of an inadequate power supply base and a Chief Minister who was less than sympathetic to production of unessential items such as ink and pens. As the manufacturing unit got off the ground, TT Narasimhan was buying up more shares in the L.D. Seymour agency in Bombay and eventually came to hold a majority interest in the company.

The year 1955 saw the group erecting another plant on the premises at Dooravaninagar. TT Private Ltd. was founded with an initial capital of Rs 50,000 ($4,170) as a dairy engineering firm. TT Narasimhan and C. V. Chandrasekhar were its Founder-Directors. The Indian company collaborated with leading dairy firms in Denmark, Holland and Germany and bid on erection of dairy plants around India, while manufacturing components for these products as well as for other engineering industries.

Dairy plants were erected by TT Private Ltd. in Trivandrum, Gaya, Bhavnagar, Hyderabad and Ambala. The company also provided plans for plants in Calcutta, Madras and Bangalore—all against international competition in global tenders. Transistor covers, reflectors for cycle lamps, vane pumps for water motors were among the products manufactured for a large number of clients. R. V. Krishnamurthy, the company's purchase manager, recalls that none of the projects was easy. He said that since the quality of the milk and water varied from area to area, equipment had to be specially made to suit each area. This was the genesis of the company's famed toolroom.

In the meantime, the group had been importing small quantities of *Prestige* cookers which found ready buyers in India. TT Narasimhan recognized an immense potential for the product and envisioned correctly that one day pressure cookers would become an item of everyday use in Indian households. He initiated negotiations with the Prestige Group Ltd. of the UK and a collaboration agreement was signed November 1, 1955. The Indian government gave permission for the agreement with the unique proviso that TT Private Ltd. should not produce fewer than 2000 cookers per month. After the agreement was signed, it took a lot of convincing of the pro-dairy types within the company to make the switch to pressure cookers. By 1959 the equipment had been imported and the factory completed.

At first, the problems presented by having to install the 250-ton imported deep drawing press caused those involved to doubt whether the project could get off the ground. A crane was brought from Calcutta, the Electricity Board provided trailers, the Highways Authority gave special permission to move the press by road and, finally, hundreds of persons from a private company were pressed into service to erect the giant press. But because of power shortages even in Bangalore, the plant had initially to operate at night. Since the power was insufficient, the toolroom, die-casting and compression moulding had to be shifted elsewhere until 1963 when power supplies improved. Eventually, the demand for the cookers was so great that other products being manufactured at the Bangalore site had to be moved to make room for the *Prestige* expansion. The key to TTK's success with its pressure cookers was its attention to "demonstration" marketing. Sales would stall unless dealers and customers were instructed in the use of the new gadgets. The "mass" demonstrations organized by TTK & Company proved immediately successful.

TTK: New Delhi: The Popular Industries Minister Turns Tax Man

In Delhi, TTK's popularity with industrialists was to end abruptly when he was appointed Finance Minister by Nehru in 1956. The 1956 Industrial Policy drafted by the government in which TTK had a large role had made clear the government's intent to reserve a large chunk of strategic industrial development for the public sector. This had followed on the heels of a resolution introduced in Parliament in 1954 which declared that the pattern of economic policy must be a socialistic one. Accumulation of private wealth and conspicuous consumption would have to be curtailed. The vehicle was taxation. The 1957 budget presented to Parliament by TTK as Finance Minister poured a mountain of ice over the heady ambitions of India's private businessmen. Wealth taxes, gift taxes, expenditure and capital gains taxes, recommended by the Kaldor Committee, were to number the days of legal accumulation of wealth and were to make it difficult for industrialists to retain private control of the enterprises they were erecting with heretofore untrammeled dynamism. Needless to say, the budget brought down the wrath of India's industrialists. The government was playing hardball with TTK as starting pitcher. In defense of the budget, the Minister had said:

> There are many moments in the history of every nation when it must advance on a great many fronts at the same time . . . Sacrifice on a nationwide scale and injustice and excessive inequality go ill together. . . that is why I have endeavoured in this budget to snatch . . . an opportunity for imparting a new turn . . . toward greater . . . equity.

With the Congress Party's goal of democratic socialism reasserted in Nehru's 1957 budget, the private sector was on notice that it would have to toe the line and play an increasingly subtle (and more sycophantic) game with politicians who could be persuaded to interpret the new rules liberally. The industrialists, politicians and bureaucrats would adjust, but avoidance of tax and growth of a formidable unregistered economy were to follow. TTK had given some hints of what he thought the private sector's role would be in a socialist economy in a 1955 article in the *Commerce Annual Review Number:*

> *Institutionally, the private sector in a composite economy will be judged, inter alia, by its ability to assist in capital formation, by the ease and rapidity with which it can socialize its management and by the degree of restraint it will exercise on the operation of the profit motive, while the individual in the private sector will be judged mainly by his utility as an actor materially contributing to the process of the economy. The place of the private sector in the economy of the future of this country is in its hands to decide.*

It was an opaque statement uncharacteristic of the clear-thinking former businessman who had kicked over family tradition to follow his own dreams, reaped the benefits unencumbered by excessive government interference, all the while maintaining a certain sense of independence. His goals as Minister no doubt had to be loftier than those of an individual businessman. But an earlier statement about economics made to a journalist in 1949 sounded more like TTK:

> *We have great master craftsmen in politics, but alas, there is not proper economic leadership for the country. If India had leaders in the field of economics and finance as dynamic as Pandit Nehru and as powerful as Sardar Patel, then her future would be assured.*

Some in the business community did not choose to split hairs. They struck back at the Finance Minister. A scandal broke out in the Ministry of Finance over the questionable allocation of funds. Though TTK was not involved in the Mundhra affair, as it was known, he ended up handing in his resignation. Industrialists had had their temporary revenge. In the process, they alienated a man who had been their friend. The breakdown in communication over the means by which to achieve a greater social and economic equity in the system pitted two important segments of that society against each other. The socialists in Parliament and the bureaucracy looked upon private capitalists as no better than the western firengis who had finally been shown the door in 1947. Indian industrialists, on the other hand, were ready to become full-fledged nationalist businessmen in their own right after independence, regardless of what they had been before. They came to resent the politician's holding them at arms length while expecting support around election time. Rather than build a grass roots campaign to head off a confrontation, however, some business leaders took a shorter route via schemes such as the Mundhra affair, deepening the growing enmity between what should have been an overt alliance in the struggle for economic independence.

TTK & Company: Madras: 1955-1965

With their father bringing down the house in New Delhi, TT Narasimhan had been joined in business by his youngest brother, TT Vasu, in 1954. TT Vasu had started his career in journalism, founding two magazines, "U" and "The Movies," and then had worked with the *Indian Express* group in Delhi. Vasu became the group's valued liaison in the capital, serving as spokesperson and salesman for the group's corporate goals. While Narasimhan kept out of the limelight, TT Vasu travelled around the world, representing Indian industrialists in a variety of fora. Like his father and brothers, TT Vasu is a talented musician. TTK had often surprised early morning visitors to his government office in New Delhi with recitals to his own accompaniment. TT Vasu's active participation in the company's activities helped several strategic projects get off the ground.

T.T. Vasu, Partner, TTK & Co.

By 1958, a pharmaceutical project was following closely on the preparations for the *Prestige* cooker manufacturing unit. Orient Pharma Private Ltd. (now known as TT Pharma Private Ltd.) was established to manufacture the world famous *Woodward's Gripe Water,* a product of Sanitas of UK. The group's pharmaceutical activities had begun in 1953 when TTK & Company became agents for Robopharm of Switzerland, and then Kali-Chemie of West Germany and A. Menarini of Italy in 1954 and 1955. At that time pharmaceutical manufacturing plants were virtually non-existent. Nearly 95 percent of the medicine sold in India was imported. The situation changed rapidly thereafter, in every industry, and TTK began its processing and manufacturing in 1958. First importing bulk drugs to be repackaged in a small factory started at 3 Cathedral Road in Madras, the company had nine employees. A second-hand tabletting machine was bought next to stamp out pills from imported granules. Construction of Orient Pharma's factory to produce *Woodward's Celebrated Gripe Water* followed in 1958 at Pallavaram, outside Madras. Operations commenced in 1959 with 38 employees at the helm.

In 1962, Kali-Chemie products began to be manufactured from imported raw materials and sold under Orient Pharma's name. Robapharm sent a man from Switzerland to help Orient Pharma begin manufacture of some of its products. Orient had also begun to produce a toiletries line of Williams products for L. D. Seymour and Company. Soon a division had to be set up to monitor the quality of the growing list of pharmaceuticals being manufactured by Orient. Pharma Research and Analytical Laboratories was established in 1969 for this purpose and, in time, it began to develop new products of its own.

By 1970, the firm felt it was time to get into the manufacture of basic chemicals. So by 1974 it had opened a basic chemicals division to synthesize intermediates and chemicals which were being imported. The first product to be synthesized was Bronidiol which was being imported from Boots, England for use as a preservative and bactericide in the gripe water. The synthesis was accomplished by using Indian-made machinery and local raw materials.   TT Pharma is the only other company worldwide, aside from Boots, to

Model with Prestige Pressure Cooker

manufacture this item. In 1984, more than 75 percent of the company's sales were accounted for by new products developed in its own R&D laboratories. A herbal division has developed a number of successful formulas acclaimed in both domestic and export markets. In less than three decades, the Indian pharmaceutical industry had begun exporting its own products from a situation of total import dependency in the early 1950s.

The next factory to go up was an assembly plant for Westclox alarm clocks. Timers for *Prestige* cookers were also manufactured at Time-Aids (India) Pvt. Ltd. as well as an assortment of kitchenware which has since become as popular as TTK's *Prestige* cooker. Time-Aids, which was set up just outside Madras at Chromepet, eventually designed and marketed its own time pieces. 1963 saw the establishment of a corrugated paper and board container company under the direction of T. R. Batra and his brother, A. K. Batra. Packwell Industries Private Ltd. has three factories in Pallavaram, Bangalore and Cochin, and serves several major industries including automotive components, light and medium-heavy engineering goods, pharmaceuticals, cosmetics and ready-made garments.

London Rubber Company (India) Ltd.

TTK had been importing condoms since the mid-1950s when in 1963 it signed an agreement with the London Rubber Company in the UK to manufacture the product in India. With the Indian government placing greater emphasis on family planning programs at the time of the TTK collaboration, the move looked right. The British company took a 51 percent equity interest and TTK & Company the remaining 49 percent. The joint venture, called London Rubber Company (India) Ltd., or LRC (I) Ltd., was established with an initial capacity of 37 million units per year at Pallavaram (current capacity is 225 million units per year).

The British partner had begun production of condoms in 1932 in a small, primitive factory in London. Earlier it had distributed a condom manufactured by a number of other British companies, but by giving the condom a trade name, *Durex,* Lionel Jackson, president of London Rubber, popularized its use and increased his sales. From the back of a barber shop in London's East End, Jackson expanded his operations steadily. By the 1950s he was automating his facilities and had expanded into other rubber products as well. The TTK-London Rubber venture progressed successfully and led to a continual upgrading of the Indian firm's technology based on international developments in the industry. LRC (I) Ltd., the Indian firm, eventually would be capable of erecting an entire plant within India based on indigenous resources.

The early years of the project were not studded with profits. Even with increased support from the government for family planning, it was a while before the still conservative society could accept the national objective to promote smaller families. Thus LRC (I) Ltd. did not turn a profit for almost a decade. In 1971, however, TT Vasu's salesmanship paid off when the first government order for 15 million *Nirodh* condoms was received. In 1972, sales were further enhanced when the TTK product received the endorsement of a Swedish development agency which contributed aid to India specifically for the dissemination of TTK's condoms. From modest initial sales to the government under its "free supply" program, LRC (I) Ltd.'s annual sales average 150 million pieces a year.

LRC (I) Ltd. also developed various condoms for the commercial market and backed up their sales efforts with an advertising blitz which pushed, some felt, propriety to the limits. The *Fiesta* condom ads moved TTK's products to the top of the charts. It featured a young couple engaged in conversation over the color of the week, the mood it reflected. The ads were meant to sell condoms, birth control and pleasure all rolled into one. The Indian firm's British partner even found the ads daring. But certain official circles' nerves were put on edge with the clever ads conceived by Advertising Associates (South) in Bangalore, headed by Bunty Peerbhoy.

In the early 1980s, as the public joint sector company concept became popular, LRC (I) Ltd. decided to go into business with the State of Maharashtra, one of India's most populous states. A joint venture, Lorcom Protectives Ltd., was set up in Aurangabad to manufacture 200 million condoms annually. The State Industrial Corporation of Maharashtra was the partner in a project which was put up in record time with no cost overruns. Again, orders expected from the central government did not materialize immediately. Imports of condoms continued at a brisk rate, at times reaching 150 million a year, discouraging the new joint venture partnership further. But in 1983, Lorcom received its maiden order for 10 million condoms from the government. In the meantime, however, LRC (I) Ltd. further determined to supplement its direct sales campaign by offering turnkey technology to other states and to foreign governments as well. A Rs 6 crore ($5 million) project was signed with the state of Rajasthan in 1984. It was a deal struck between the state and both the Indian and British affiliate, LRC Overseas Ltd. LRC (I) Ltd. also completed an agreement in late 1984 to set up a turnkey condom plant in Ho Chi Minh City for the Government of Vietnam. TTK has received similar inquiries from China and introduction of TTK products in Indonesia was also being negotiated in early 1985.

Just as TT Narasimhan had believed in the potential market success of the *Prestige* cooker in the absence of any hard market data, he had been just as confident in the early 1950s when he began importing *Durex* condoms that one day the condom would become the popular family planner it has. He was convinced, he said, that if India could become flooded with tens of millions of simple and cheap contraceptives such as condom protectives, many of its problems would be overcome. It was fortunate that the government felt similarly. India was the first country to make family planning an official part of its national development policy. LRC (I) Ltd., promoted by the TTK group, was a pioneering effort on the part of Indian industry to help meet the country's fundamental development needs.

Another of these needs was literacy and information dissemination. A printing and publishing unit, established with German collaboration in 1965, Tamilnad Printers and Traders Pvt. Ltd., became a wholly owned unit of the TTK group in 1972. Originally incorporated as Maps & Atlases Publications Pvt. Ltd., the company began with an offset press in its facilities in Bhromepet, just outside Madras, in 1968. It is the leading publisher of maps and atlases in the private sector in South Asia today.

TTK and Textiles

Next the group went into the manufacture of hosiery (underwear) with the founding of TT Investments & Trades Pvt. Ltd. in 1969 in Thajavur in Tamil Nadu. *TanTex,* a household name in south India, is the largest selling brand of hosiery in the country. Numerous auxiliary units had to be established in the neighboring area to meet the high demand. (Even the seconds, or reject, market in *TanTex* grosses over a million dollars a year.) Again, with eye-catching advertising, the latest *TanTex* products for women were an instant hit and orders could not be filled fast enough. The *TanTex* technology is going overseas to Mauritius as a result of an agreement the TTK group has signed with the Dookun group there. A Rs 2 crore ($1.6 million) hosiery plant whose output will be exported will provide employment for 1000 Mauritians.

T.T. Raghunathan
(T.T. Narasimhan's youngest son)

The growing popularity of the *TanTex* products pushed the group to set up TT Textiles Ltd. to ensure a steady supply of quality cotton yarn to TT Investments & Trades. Located at Nargari in Andhra Pradesh, in the heart of an important yarn market which supplies the surrounding handlooms and powerlooms industry, TT Textiles has 25,000 spindles and expects to expand to 50,000 by 1986. Production began only in 1982. By 1984, TT Textiles was merged with an older company in the group, Indian Textile Paper Tube Company Ltd., in which the group had acquired an equity interest in 1968.

Indian Textile Paper Tube had been founded in 1955 by A & F Harvey & Sons in collaboration with a British firm, Textile Paper Tube Co. Ltd. of Romilly, Cheshire, UK to manufacture paper cones and tubes to replace the traditional wooden bobbins in the textile industry. Production began in 1956 near the railway station at Virudhunagar in Tamil Nadu. Related products such as wound paper tubes, cheese tubes for winding yarn and sewing thread tubes began to be produced at the facility in the 1960s. Principally producing for its own captive spinning and weaving mills, the plant also threw off some excess production which TTK & Company offered to market for the Harvey company. A sole selling agency was worked out in 1964 and sales climbed throughout India for Harvey's products. When Harvey's decided to divest its ancillary units in 1967, TTK was there to make an offer. In 1968, TTK & Company also negotiated to assume management of the day-to-day operations of the company. Harvey's continued to be an important buyer of the firm's products. Sales increased more than seven times by 1983 from fifteen years earlier when TTK & Company had taken it over.

TT Textiles, the newly merged company, is now the largest company in the group by asset base and it has started to produce sophisticated tube packaging for the defense industry. Further consolidation of the group's activities is expected to continue throughout the 1980s, helping the group to expand its product line as well as deepen penetration of the domestic and international markets.

It has been argued that the Monopolies Restrictive Trade Practices Act (MRTP) which was ushered in during one of TTK's tenures as Finance Minister hindered indigenous R&D efforts in India. With production restricted, licenses sometimes difficult to obtain and, for many companies, the lengthy torture of obtaining MRTP approval, a company could not afford to spend additional time or money developing technology which already existed in the world. TTK & Company had taken a different route, perhaps not by design. Staying small, it avoided coming under the MRTP rules and thus was able to expand into many new product areas without going through the time-consuming defense under the MRTP act. It thus had time and funds to begin R&D efforts required to adapt the technology it obtained from abroad. This was particularly true in its pharmaceuticals division, but every major company in the group, TT Investments & Trades, TT Private Ltd., TT Textiles, and others have developed new products from internal R&D as an ongoing part of operations. Most private companies now have in-house R&D cells, but the amount of corporate funds spent on R&D points to a future of dependence on foreign technology. (The 1985 change in the MRTP legislation defining a monopoly company as one with Rs 100 crore in assets, rather than a mere Rs 20 crore, may encourage many companies to strengthen internal R&D.)

TTK: A Second Time Around as Finance Minister, Then a Leave-Taking

When TTK became Finance Minister for a second time following Nehru's re-election in 1962, he set about building the financial institutions which have proven over time to be a successful basis of the democratic/socialist capitalism which the nation's founders had envisioned. The National Industrial Development Corporation, the Industrial Development Bank of India and a host of organizations to stimulate growth in small-scale industries were promoted by TTK. But he could not turn back the tide of government domination of the economy which was picking up steam in the 1960s. The Monopolies Enquiry Commission which resulted in the promotion of the MRTP act was formed around this time to look into restrictive trade practices. The Commission itself did not find that monopolies had to be suppressed, but a Select Committee of Parliament introduced the draft bill prepared by the Commission. The conclusion of the Commission was that mere size had to be controlled irrespective of whether large houses actually exercised monopolistic powers or not.

The view from the industrialist's corner was not encouraging. They saw the mounting criticism of business as a portent of an uncertain future at best. S. L. Kirloskar recalled in his autobiography that the confusion of the latter part of the 1960s was foretold in the previous years when TTK was both helpful and then, in Kirloskar's view, catastrophic to the private sector:

> The 1960's were a period of considerable expansion and diversification for us along with growing export promotion. In all this we received help and encouragement from the two ministers with whom we were particularly concerned, Mr. T. T. Krishnamachari and Mr. Manubhai Shah. These two would frequently go out of their way to cut through the normal procedures, so that often their mere assurance was sufficient for us to go ahead with our work." He continued: "How little I foresaw, in those years of optimistic progress, how the picture would change after 1965! The Dark Ages of confused planning, legal restrictions, the switching of Government's interest from large to small industries, the infighting among the politicians culminating in the splitting of the once monolithic Congress Party—all these were still in the future, destined to create a situation in which industrial enterprises could not get off the ground. As if all these obstacles were not enough, the same Mr. T. T. Krishnamachari who had been so helpful as Commerce and Industry Minister, would as Finance Minister bring in taxation so crippling that funds otherwise available for investment or savings were completely siphoned away by Government, leaving industries starved for capital. [2]

TTK handed in his resignation in 1965 to Prime Minister Lal Bahadur Shastri who had succeeded Nehru in 1964. There was little of the rapport between the new Prime Minister and the able administrator that had existed between Nehru and TTK. The salesman turned politician/minister served as Nehru's alter ego so much so that it would have been almost impossible for him to serve under anyone else. TTK retired to his farm in Tambaram outside Madras. He continued to travel, write and study. And until the end of his life, he would drive into Madras almost daily in his little Herald to meet friends and reminisce. His brilliance and independence won the admiration of the

TTK

highest public officials at home and abroad. The humblest citizens in his own country received hope from TTK's vision and energy. The impressions he left on his friends and acquaintances were startingly diverse, painting the portrait of a practical-minded idealist, loyal, engaging, acerbic, aloof, yet warm. His name still sets industrialists' teeth on edge. Newer industrialists who got their start in the 1960s and 1970s might have had a more instinctive appreciation for the possibilities of growth under a more regulated system. They grew quickly while older industrial families resisted the "new politics" which required business to take a permanent genuflected posture before politicians, and vice versa. It is clear from interviews given toward the end of his life that TTK felt the full weight of India's complex approach to development. His friendships with people of every political persuasion proved his lack of sympathy for hardline slogans and ideologies. His results-oriented nature offended ideologues because their theories could not keep up with his accomplishments. In the end, TTK stood alone.

TTK & Company: Stepping Out From the Shadow of the Founder

While the TTK group grew during its founder's days in Delhi, emphasis was still on its agency businesses for the most part. The 1970s brought a cash crisis and management problems. TT Narasimhan and his wife, Padma, placed a call to their son, TT Jagannathan in the USA in the early 1970s to get him home. He was finishing up his Ph.D. in operations research at Cornell University and was planning to remain in the USA. They needed him home to help in the reorganization of the business which by now was in a rolling crisis. He returned home and eventually moved his headquarters to Bangalore to manage TT Private Ltd., the pressure cooker company. As heir apparent to TT Narasimhan, Jagannathan assumed responsibility for the group's entire marketing operations in 1984. Earlier he had become managing director of the group's parent company, TTK & Company. The 1977 loss of the Cadbury agency resulted in an immediate cash drain of five million dollars a year. The new management team which now included TT Jagannathan and his mother, Padma, helped turn the company around. The successful reorganization of the business inspired a new corporate family spirit in the group's widely diverse activities. If unprofitable operations had to be shut down, the employees were absorbed elsewhere in other TTK companies.

Mrs. T.T. Narasimhan, Partner, TTK & Co.

T.T. Jagannathan, Partner, TTK & Co. (Narasimhan's eldest son)

Today, more and more authority is being placed in the hands of the professional managers, many of whom have been with the group for over 25 years. TT Jagannathan confirmed that the group's partners believe in delegation of authority. Two non-family members, K. Kuppuswamy and V. Gopalan, responsible for a large part of the group's successful ventures, serve on the corporate board along with the members of the TTK family. TT Narasimhan's younger son, TT Ragunnathan, has also joined the family business and heads one of the group's flagship companies, TT Textiles.

As the group moves confidently forward, it is taking on an increasingly international image. New joint ventures with London Rubber Company Ltd. of the UK are planned in India and in third countries. Collaborations have been

TTK Headquarters, 6 Cathedral Road, Madras

announced with leading industrial groups of other countries in Mauritius, Sri Lanka and Indonesia. From the days of being an agent for foreign products within India, it has begun appointing agents abroad to market TTK products in the East and West. TTK is growing big in an era when it may not necessarily be inauspicious to do so. Its growing success after three decades in the shadow of its founder is proof in part of the increased prosperity of the country for which its founder had worked with such dedication. In the 1980s, the shadows of TTK and TTK & Company merge once again, nearly fifty years after they last separated.

T.T. Rangaswamy (third son of TTK), Manager, T.A. Taylor's

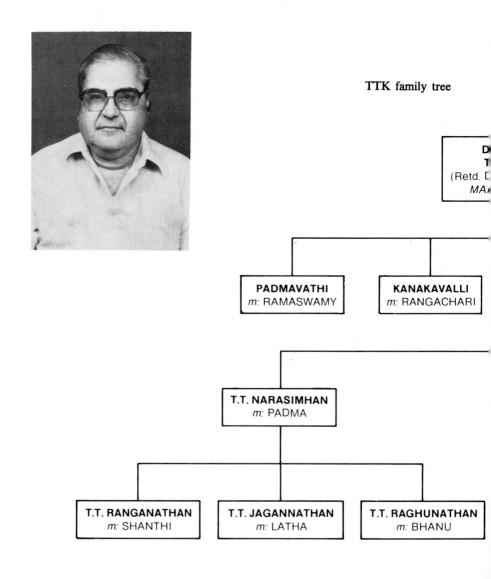

TTK family tree

TTK with President John F. Kennedy

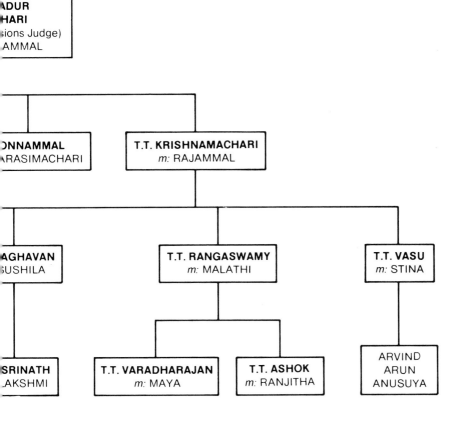

T.T. Varadarajan, Managing Director,
Maya Appliances

T.T. Ashok, General Manager,
T.A. Taylor's

T.T. Srinath, Partner, Lakshmi Metal Caps

Walchand

Automobiles
Construction
Cement
Sugar
Heavy machinery for nuclear reactors,
space vehicles, fertilizer and
chemical plants

Sales
Rs 475 crore
($396 million)

Headquarters
Construction House
Walchand Hirachand Marg
Ballard Estate
Bombay, India 400 038

Head of Group
Lalchand Hirachand

Walchand Hirachand (1882-1953)

WALCHAND

Along with Jamsetji Tata, Walchand Hirachand is perhaps the foremost industrial pioneer in modern Indian history. The story of his life is also that of the origin and development of several strategic Indian industries: aircraft, automobiles, construction and engineering, shipping and ship-building. Walchand's successes also exploded the myth that Indians were not capable of promoting technologically sophisticated companies. Along with the Tatas, Walchand stepped into the core industries in the teeth of fierce foreign competition supported by the ruling foreign government. Not only did his companies have to step among the land mines of foreign competition, but the family became deeply involved in the freedom movement which set the colonial government on their trails for long periods of time.

Two of Walchand's greatest industrial achievements, Hindustan Aeronautics Ltd., set up in Bangalore, and Visakhapatnam Shipyard, were nationalized as the government felt them to be too important to be left in private hands. The flagship company of the group, Premier Auto Ltd., the country's first automobile manufacturer, and Hindustan Construction Company, one of India's largest private sector construction firms, have remained in the Walchand group's hands. Within the space of a half century, beginning modestly, Walchand built his group into one of India's largest private sector business houses. He took his group into agricultural development as well.

After his death the Walchand group sank into conservatism and failed to modernize its thinking or its operations. Walchand's brothers lacked his ability to make profits and his flare for taking risks. Bahubali Gulabchand, who often accompanied his uncle Walchand on the latter's trips abroad, analyzes:

> *Lalchand could keep pace with Walchand on his adventures, but he could never make his companies show good profits. On the other hand, Gulabchand was more conservative–he did not like to take on more work than he could comfortably handle. He was a very good administrator, however, and he could earn profits.*

Crippling labor strife at the Premier Auto plant and a takeover attempt by the R.P. Goenka group pushed the group to open the door to the younger generation of managers who were only too anxious to test their entrepreneurial skills. Vinod Doshi, Arvind Doshi, Ajit Gulabchand and Chokar Doshi are out to prove that the spirit of Walchand Hirachand is in their blood.

Origins of the Group

Gujarat is often called the cradle of Indian industrial enterprise since many of India's capitalists trace their roots there. The Parsis and Gujaratis who migrated from Gujarat to Bombay in the early nineteenth century laid the foundations of Indian ventures which were to successfully rival European (and particularly British) enterprise by the end of the century. Among those who left Gujarat was Nihalchand Bhimji Doshi who left the small village of Wankaner in North Gujarat to settle in Satara district (now part of Maharashtra) which was already under British rule.

The early years of the nineteenth century were ones of great insecurity in Western India. The Maratha kings were locked in the death throes of their struggle against the British, piracy was rampant, and Gujarat, divided into a number of petty kingdoms, was daily witness to murder and assault. In comparison, British India, particularly the city of Bombay, was an oasis of peace and stability. Thus began an exodus to Bombay, a movement of people which continues even today, making it one of the world's most populous cities.

Seeing the turmoil round him, Doshi took the decision to migrate to British India. He reached Phaltan where he set up a shop in Tailor's Lane in the Wednesday Quarter of the town. The shop did well, selling grain and general provisions. Along with the business expansion, the Doshi family grew to include six sons and a daughter. To cope with the extra expenses, Doshi decided to open a branch in neighboring Sholapur. Soon the branch was doing better than the main shop, and the whole family shifted to Sholapur.

Though Doshi and his son Nemchand (d. 1869) were responsible for the

Hirachand Nemchand

migration of the family to British India where they could take advantage of trade and stable business conditions, it was Nemchand's sons, Sakharam (1852-1923) and Hirachand (1856-1937) who are credited with elevating the family to a position of financial stability, public recognition, and social status. Sakharam and Hirachand were given only a smattering of formal education. Their father died when Hirachand was only 13. Even during their father's lifetime, there was an uneasy co-existence between Sakharam and Hirachand and their half-brothers, Gautamchand and Jyotichand. This was soon to flare up into open antagonism. The resultant decision by Sakharam and Hirachand to leave the family when they were in their early 20s must have been a traumatic one. To break away from the traditional Indian joint family even today is difficult. It must have been even more so a century earlier when social ties were far stronger.

Despite their isolation from their extended family and their youth, the two boys did extremely well. A large measure of their success was due to

Sakharam Nemchand

Hirachand's mastery of languages – Hindi, Marathi, English and Sanskrit.
His reading of English dailies like the *Times of India* and English books
created within him an awareness of business opportunities and enlarged his
knowledge of Western business practices imported into India by her

colonizers. As the only Jain in his community to know English, he had a definite business advantage. It enabled him to acquire several profitable agencies, among them that of the Sholapur Spg. & Wvg. Mill, set up in 1880 by a Bombay textile magnate, Morarjee Goculdas.

This contact with the Goculdas family was to have far-reaching consequences for the Walchand group. Apart from the continuous help which the Morarjee family extended to Walchand Hirachand (1882-1953), it enabled the Walchands to make commercial alliances with the powerful Bhatia community—a sect of Gujaratis which came to dominate Bombay's business scene from the middle of the nineteenth century until the Depression years. Morarjee Goculdas was one of the community's acknowledged leaders.

The progressive tendencies exhibited by Hirachand, which had brought the group business and profits, all too soon began to peter out. In 1891, Hirachand's eldest sons, Manikchand and Jivraj, had established a profitable money-lending business in Bombay. In 1905, disaster struck when not only did a large creditor default, but also bubonic plague caused the death of four members of the Doshi family: Manikchand and his wife, Jivraj, and Sakharam's wife, Umabai, one after another within the space of a year. These losses unnerved Hirachand and he closed down the Bombay office. He was 53 and he became increasingly conservative in his business practices. He turned away from the new avenues of business to the steady, traditional one of money-lending while his brother, Sakharam, continued to be principally concerned with yarn and cotton trading.

It was in this highly conservative household that Walchand Hirachand – the third son of Hirachand and unquestioned founder of the Walchand group – received his earliest business training.

The Early Years

I detest the politics of Walchand, but his efficiency as a contractor I respect.

–A British official.

Born in 1882, Walchand enjoyed several advantages denied his ancestors. Though his early schooling at Aurangabad and Sholapur was makeshift, he was subsequently sent to Bombay's prestigious St. Xavier's College. The plague epidemic in Bombay, however, forced him to move to Poona where he enrolled in the equally respected Deccan College. The premature deaths of his two brothers precipitated Walchand's entry into business immediately after he obtained a bachelor's degree in history and economics.

Besides education, the young Walchand had also the security of a healthy financial background and a large network of carefully nurtured social and business contacts. With these advantages, and endowed with remarkable entrepreneurial spirit, Walchand combined a stubborn will which refused to give in to obstacles. He never allowed his own financial limitations to prevent

Jivraj Walchand

him from dreaming of and then planning for what seemed unobtainable projects. Walchand's first construction contract was for Rs 80,000 ($16,600) (including cost, his partner's share and his own profit) in 1904. Fifty years later, he had established India's first modern shipping company, her first

Manikchand Walchand

automobile plant and her first airplane plant besides several engineering and construction companies.

Entry into the construction and engineering field was not easy, however. Walchand had to face considerable disapproval from his father who felt that undertaking contract work was a loss of face. His uncle, Sakharam, tried to change Walchand's mind. Walchand refused to be diverted and set up a small construction company in partnership with one L.B. Phatak, Messr Phatak and Walchand, in 1903, which undertook work for the railways.

Domestic disapproval was not the only negative element which Walchand had to face. Under colonial rule, the construction industry was largely in the hands of European firms because of two factors principally. On the one hand, most Indians were like Hirachand—uninterested in construction, considering it a demeaning activity; on the other hand, British officials preferred to give government contracts to established firms who had their headquarters in Europe and subsidiaries in India.

Walchand's firm began by undertaking minor railway contracts for which there was less competition. It was a period of great railway construction activity in India as elsewhere in the world. Proving itself capable, the partnership firm flourished. With the outbreak of World War I, opportunties for other forms of construction materialized. Phatak & Walchand went public and diversified somewhat by buying a small foundry in Bombay, interests in a small colliery in the Central Provinces, as well as investing in new equipment.

Soon the firm had established an enviable record for promptness and efficiency which often surpassed that of rival European firms. Moreover, by minutely scrutinizing every detail and maximizing time efficiency, Walchand was able to offer substantially lower estimates for comparable quality. Thus, though a small firm, it had carved out a fine reputation in a very competitive field. By 1917 the pace became too fast for Phatak and he retired. The company carried on its activities, even more vigorously than before.

Tie-up with the Tatas

Walchand's rapid growth was helped enormously by the bouyancy in the economic climate of India. Usually war conditions are followed by a depression, but in India after World War I the upsurge in business activity continued until the mid-1920s. The stock markets were more active than at any time in their history. Every business house worth its salt was planning new ventures, and Walchand was no exception. He threw himself into no fewer than three separate fields of activity: shipping, sugar and expansion of his now traditional metier, construction.

Fortunately for Walchand demand for construction services continued at a brisk pace after the war. In Bombay there was a tremendous post-war boom during which an ambitious reclamation scheme was proposed. As with many land deals, this one triggered off a nasty scandal in which Indians accused British policy makers of giving plum contracting works to British firms while Indians were thrown morsels of sub-contracting work and menial labor contracts. The outcry was so great that the British Government hastily looked around for a capable Indian construction company to blunt the outrage of the locals. They focussed on a new partnership.

Another pioneering industrial family, the Tatas, had foreseen the potential in the construction industry as well. They had the financial resources, but not as much experience in the field as Walchand. They offered to tie up with him after Walchand's partner retired. Though friends and relatives warned him of being swallowed by the big Tata fish, Walchand did not hesitate. It was an opportunity for rapid growth and he realized that if he wanted his dreams to be fulfilled, he would always need a partner. Few of his ventures were without one and most were with many. Thus Phatak & Walchand was dissolved and a new company, the Tata Construction Company was formed in 1920.

Under Walchand's management, Tata Construction was awarded several prestigious contracts. Several of these were, and remain essential

to Bombay's survival, and most of these projects have withstood the
elements with only minor modifications. Two projects are particularly notable:
the extension of the Bhor Ghats which enabled trains to run directly
between Bombay and Poona, and the Tansa Completion Works which supply
Bombay her water.

Bhor Ghats (Walchand is second from left)

During this period the company was perhaps at its largest, employing
about 30,000 workers. It also spawned five subsidiaries. While three were in
related fields, two were quite diverse, the Indian Hume Pipe Company and the
Marsland Price Company.

The collaboration with the Tatas was not destined to last very long. The
Tatas were uneasy with Walchand's impetuousness which often bordered on
foolhardiness. When offered an opportunity, he would make a decision
instantaneously, almost blindly. One can only presume that the group he
established survived because of the painstaking attention to detail which he
gave to the project *after* completely committing himself. This ability to take
quick decisions and risks served him well and badly in almost equal
proportions.

It was this rash trait which plunged him into the shipping industry. As
Scindia Steam Navigation Co. Ltd. grew stronger, so did British hostility to
the Walchand group. The more moderate Tatas, with their strong affiliations
with leading Britishers, began to feel the delicate pinch of their connection with
Walchand. Further, though Walchand held only a minority share in Tata

Construction, and had been made its managing director as late as 1929, he was undoubtedly its most dominant figure, both because of his dynamism and technical expertise. By the 1930s, however, the Tatas were becoming engrossed in their big ventures such as Tata Steel and Tata Hydro-Electric. Tata Construction was also feeling the effects of the Great Depression which cast its wide net from the shores of America. Sir Dorab Tata decided to sever links with a company in whose policy decisions the Tatas played little role.

Construction House, Bombay, Walchand group headquarters

In 1932 Walchand bought all the promoters' shares and management rights from the Tatas. Three years later Tata Construction was renamed Premier Construction and became the flagship company of the Walchand group. Gradually the company developed into that of a holding concern* as most of the construction activity was diverted to Hindustan Construction and the Walchand group diversified into sugar, automobile production, engineering, aircraft manufacture, among other businesses. In 1938 Walchand built Construction House on a prime piece of Bombay land which continues to serve as the group's headquarters.

Birth of Walchandnagar

Opium, cotton cloth and sugar have been the basis of some of the largest Indian fortunes. The Walchand family still resided in the interior of India when trade in opium filled the coffers of those living on the coast who had the

---

* The Chairman of Premier Construction is traditionally the head of the Walchand group.

guts to sail to China and sell their opium there. The Walchands had too little money to take advantage of the textile mill building boon of the 1870s which was ushered in by Indian entrepreneurs whose names are fading fast with the passage of time. But, by the 1930s, the Walchands had accumulated sufficient capital to reap the benefits from the government's new sugar policy and, in 1933, Walchand promoted the Ravalgaon Sugar Farm Ltd., leaving management of the construction business in the capable hands of his brother, Ratanchand.

Ratanchand Hirachand

Unlike other sugar barons, Walchand did not have to look far for land on which to build his factory. He had always dreamed of channeling India's vast agricultural resources in some profitable way and in 1923 had bought about 1500 acres of land at Ravalgaon, near the Girna Canal in Nasik district, Maharashtra. There he experimented, often at outrageous expense, with a wide variety of crops, from mango trees to sugar cane, cotton to groundnut. In 1933 these experiments were halted and he began to cultivate sugarcane to feed his new sugar factory.

As profits swelled, the factory expanded, gradually drawing upon cane grown by other farmers. The farm came in handy for other reasons also. Walchand's brother, Gulabchand, was in hot water with British authorities for his political activities. Walchand sent him to Ravalgaon to cool his heels and expend his excess energy. It proved to be a fortuitous decision. Gulabchand threw himself wholeheartedly into the project. As the farm and factory crystallized, a new township emerged, Walchandnagar.

It was home not only to sugar but to a host of ancillary industries as Gulabchand tried his hand at practically everything: sugar candy and confectionery, wax from sugar's waste scum, cardboard and paper from sugarcane trash, alcohol from molasses. Like the Modis in the north, Gulabchand challenged the giant Lever Brothers. Copying Lever's brand "Dalda," he began to market ghee and vanaspati under the brand "Valda." The vanaspati factory led him into the manufacture of soap and tin containers. By the end of World War II, Walchandnagar was a highly diversified complex of agriculture-based industries.

Politics and the Walchand Group

"Gulabchand belongs to the Hindu Sabha, Lalchand belongs to the Congress, Ratanchand to no party, and Walchand belongs to every party," Sardar Vallabhbhai Patel once jokingly remarked. The description of the Walchand brothers was apt, and highlighted the complex role played by Walchand Hirachand in Indian politics during the turbulent pre-independence years.

As an industrialist, Walchand could not afford a head-on collision with the British Raj. Co-operation with the administrative authority was necessary and unavoidable. Yet social, cultural, and even religious ties bound him to participate in the freedom movement. Moreover, as his industrial empire grew, so did economic antagonism from British groups hurt by his competition, giving Walchand another reason for joining hands more firmly with the nationalist movement.

While talking to Edgar Snow, Walchand described the humiliating conditions in which Indian industrialists had to operate. Recounting his meeting with Walchand in his book, *Glory and Bondage,* Snow quotes Walchand as saying:

I positively do not want the British in India. When I went to Japan, the Japanese treated me on terms of equality; they looked after me right royally in smart high-class tourist shelters like the Imperial Hotel; wherever I went, I was entertained with honour and respect. In England on the other hand, every hotel I went to would be found "full-up". Big merchants and industrialists had no desire to invite me to their homes. Even in America, hoteliers would tell me that they "didn't allow blacks". So what sort of feelings are men like me going to have, about people like those?. . . . . Look at me. Today, am I free? I'm a slave, I say, a slave!

However, as a businessman, first and foremost, Walchand had to co-operate with the Raj in order to preserve and expand his business. This not so subtle pattern of conflict and co-operation with the foreign government in India was not Walchand's problem alone. It was shared, in varying degrees, by all Indian capitalists, especially after the outbreak of World War I.

As an entrepreneur with seemingly preposterous dreams for setting up Indian shipping, Indian automobile and Indian aircraft industries, Walchand soon clashed with British vested interests. In 1906 Dadabhai Naoroji's speeches at the Calcutta session of the Indian National Congress stirred Walchand's patriotic feelings. As his clash with the British business houses worsened, Walchand's thoughts crystallized on the issues and actions involved if India were to attain her freedom. Walchand became convinced that economic independence was the key to political and social freedom.

Lalchand Hirachand

To attain such an end, Walchand fought hard, constantly varying his methods. He began to secretly fund Congress activities and provide shelter for those who had to go underground for a while. He refused, in spite of tremendously heavy losses and intense pressure from all sides – even some of his directors – to allow Scindia Steam Navigation to be sold to British shipping interests or to be closed down. As president of business associations such as the Maharashtra Chamber of Commerce, the Indian Merchants Chamber, FICCI, he lashed out at British government policies prejudicial to Indian business. When Gandhi was arrested in 1930 during the salt satyagraha, Walchand renounced the British titles awarded to him and refused to accept others in later years. All his business ventures were inaugurated by down-and-out Congress leaders rather than top British dignitaries.

Walchand stopped short of openly identifying himself with any nationalist party though. Reminiscing about his uncle, Bahubali Gulabchand tried to explain:

> Walchand was closely associated with Congress. However he disliked the revolutionary traits which developed soon after the mid-1930s. He was a businessman and he could see no point in jeopardising all the gains he had made. Thus he disapproved of civil disobedience and other such revolutionary acts.

It was this respect for the law and capitalism which prompted WH to sign, along with 20 other "Mercantile Leaders of Bombay," a manifesto denouncing Jawarharlal Nehru's socialism. Reacting sharply and swiftly against the manifesto, G.D. Birla wrote severely to WH:

> Do you think you were right in signing that manifesto against Jawaharlal? If its merits are to be judged by the results then I must say that you have been instrumental in creating further opposition to capitalism. You have rendered no service to your castemen. It is curious how we businessmen are so short-sighted. . . . It looks very crude for a man with property to say that he is opposed to expropriation in the wider interests of the country. It goes without saying that anyone holding property will oppose expropriation. . . . .our duty does not end in simply opposing socialism. Businessmen have to do something positive to ameliorate the condition of the masses. I feel that your manifesto, far from helping, has done positive harm to the capitalistic system.

The debate would pick up steam after independence—whether business-men should speak their minds openly, or fall in line with a system which left them philosophically on the peripheries of their own country's development. Comparing the growth and progress of groups such as Birla and Walchand, one is forced to acknowledge that opposing the powers that be for any reason ultimately proves unwise if one wishes to achieve material success in an economy heavily controlled by government.

Though WH was not a member of any political party, his brothers, especially Gulabchand, were very much in the forefront of political agitation. When Lokmanya Tilak visited Sholapur in 1918, Gulabchand was the leader

Gulabchand Hirachand

of a band of youngsters who presented him with an address. During his stay in Sholapur, Gulabchand interested himself in an activist newspaper, the *Karmayogi,* in founding a national school, and in establishing peace when Hindu-Moslem riots broke out in the town. He held various official posts in the Congress organization and even had to go underground soon after the 1930 non-co-operation movement was launched. He was jailed twice for his political activities, the first time for two months in 1932. He was released after the term only on condition that he would not leave his house in Sholapur. However, learning that one of his daughters was ill in Bombay, he jumped parole and went to Bombay for eight days. On his return to Sholapur he was sentenced to eighteen months rigorous imprisonment and a fine of Rs 20,000. A few months later his term was reduced, but his prison term only served to anger him further. He now redoubled his political activities and his speeches became more "fiery and critical of imperialist tendencies."

By 1933, Gulabchand was almost as disillusioned with Gandhi and the Congress Party as with the British Government. In the Karachi Congress session, Gandhi wanted all Congressmen to wear khadi. The khadi-clad Gulabchand rejected the enforced wearing of the material. Why not swadeshi cloth? he questioned. Why boycott the entire cotton textile industry, a large part of which is in Indian hands? The contradictions in Gandhian thinking put him off so much that he left the Congress Party to join the Swaraj Party. The disillusionment went deep and antagonism to the Congress continued. In the 1967 elections, the Walchand group was among the important contributors to the conservative Swatantra Party.

Gulabchand's activities soon became a source of anxiety for the group. Walchand had been playing the delicate balancing act between the British and Indian nationalists. The Tatas with their strong pro-establishment attitude were still his partners. Already in deep water with Scindia, he could not afford to lose business in his other companies by being branded as an activist. Their father, Hirachand, was even more anxious to save the group from any stigma which could harm the business and proposed to the brothers that they split up. Walchand would not endorse this. Though he was the force behind the group's growth, and it was his brother's actions which were jeopardizing the group, he would not sanction a split. WH persuaded Gulabchand to develop

Car caravan: The family returning to Bombay from Calcutta by car in the 1920s: a harbinger of their pioneering role in India's automobile industry

the group's sugar interests at Kalamb (later Walchandnagar), hoping that by engrossing Gulabchand in the difficulties of setting up a sugar plantation and mill in barren wasteland, Gulabchand's high profile with the British government would die down.

By the 1940s, however, even Walchand's patience was wearing thin as government apathy thwarted almost every business plan conceived by the group. He now openly began to declare: "the sooner this Government is destroyed, the sooner will the destruction of India cease and happy days dawn for the country."

HCC Reaps the Benefits of The Gulf Construction Boom

Over the years, the Walchand group's interest in construction which had sprung from a small railway contract, has developed into one of India's premier civil construction companies. Reported to be the sixth largest company in the Indian private sector in terms of sales ($103 million in 1983), HCC is ninth among a few large private Indian construction companies* and as such is well positioned to bid for contracts in the burgeoning construction boom which Ajit Gulabchand, managing director of HCC, thinks will generate $58 billion of business in the next few years.

How much of this business Gulabchand will be able to drum up for HCC in the face of stiff competition, not only from Indian firms but also western construction companies (who, with the downturn in Gulf business, have set their sights on India), is anybody's guess. But there is no denying that HCC is in a very strong position indeed with a tradition of performance built up by capable engineers like Shiv Chandra Banerjee, Alexander Burn Lawson and Bapusaheb Sardesai. They worked under Walchand Hirachand and later Ratanchand Hirachand (Walchand's younger brother). In recent years, men such as Nagobhushana Rau have similarly sustained HCC's growth.

Under Nehru, when independant India embarked on monumental construction works through the five-year plans, HCC boldly accepted many important contracts and involved itself, in varying degrees, in projects of national importance, among them the Koyna Dam in Maharashtra, Le Corbusier's new capital city of Chandigarh, and Bhilai Steel Works and the Damodhar Valley Project,

As growth began to slow down in India, fresh jobs loomed on the horizon from another quarter. While the rise of the oil-producing nations jeopardised HCC's sister concern, PAL, for HCC the emergence of OPEC meant a new

---

* The Indian construction industry is dominated, on the one hand, by large public sector undertakings, and on the other by small and medium-sized private companies. There are, however, a few large private construction firms, which though pigmy by international standards, are well regarded. Among these can be mentioned: HCC, Dodsal Pvt. Ltd., Continental Construction Pvt. Ltd., Essar, Jaiprakash Associated Ltd., Afcons, Gammon India Ltd., Cemindia Ltd., Shapoorji Pallonji & Co. Pvt. Ltd., Engineering Construction Corporation (ECC) of Larsen & Toubro, Coromandel Engineering Co. Ltd. of the TI group.

lease on life. Flush with funds, the Gulf countries embarked on a massive construction spree and HCC went international.

Apart from good profits, HCC benefited enormously from its activities in the Middle East. Faced with its first international competition in a long time, the company streamlined itself and made an effort to understand it strengths and weaknesses. It learned to work under a completely different system. For example, while the Indian government, which is the main domestic source for large contracts, tends to contract out in small parcels, the Arabs were inclined to float complete tenders. Thus, HCC for the first time was exposed to

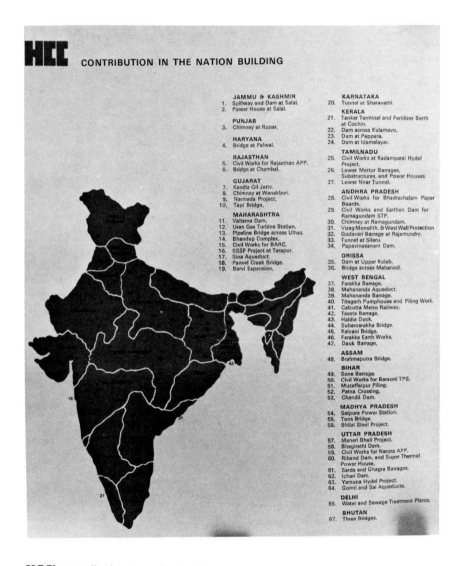

HCC

CONTRIBUTION IN THE NATION BUILDING

JAMMU & KASHMIR
1. Spillway and Dam at Salal.
2. Power House at Salal.

PUNJAB
3. Chimney at Ropar.

HARYANA
4. Bridge at Palwal.

RAJASTHAN
5. Civil Works for Rajasthan APP.
6. Bridge at Chambal.

GUJARAT
7. Kandla Oil Jetty.
8. Chimney at Wanakbori.
9. Narmada Project.
10. Tapi Bridge.

MAHARASHTRA
11. Vaitarna Dam.
12. Uran Gas Turbine Station.
13. Pipeline Bridge across Ulhas.
14. Bhandup Complex.
15. Civil Works for BARC.
16. SSSF Project at Tarapur.
17. Sina Aqueduct.
18. Panvel Creek Bridge.
19. Barvi Expansion.

KARNATAKA
20. Tunnel at Sharavathi.

KERALA
21. Tanker Terminal and Fertilizer Berth at Cochin.
22. Dam across Kulamavu.
23. Dam at Peppara.
24. Dam at Idamalayar.

TAMILNADU
25. Civil Works at Kadamparai Hydel Project.
26. Lower Mettur Barrages, Substructures, and Power Houses.
27. Lower Nirar Tunnel.

ANDHRA PRADESH
28. Civil Works for Bhadrachalam Paper Boards.
29. Civil Works and Earthen Dam for Ramagundam STP.
30. Chimney at Ramagundam.
31. Vizag Monolith, & West Wall Protection
32. Godavari Barrage at Rajamundry.
33. Tunnel at Sileru.
34. Papavinasanam Dam.

ORISSA
35. Dam at Upper Kolab.
36. Bridge across Mahanadi.

WEST BENGAL
37. Farakka Barrage.
38. Mahananda Aqueduct.
39. Mahananda Barrage.
40. Titagarh Pumphouse and Piling Work.
41. Calcutta Metro Railway.
42. Teesta Barrage.
43. Haldia Dock.
44. Subarnarekha Bridge.
45. Kalyani Bridge.
46. Farakka Earth Works.
47. Dauk Barrage.

ASSAM
48. Brahmaputra Bridge.

BIHAR
49. Sone Barrage.
50. Civil Works for Barauni TPS.
51. Muzaffarpur Piling.
52. Patna Crossing.
53. Chandil Dam.

MADHYA PRADESH
54. Satpura Power Station.
55. Tons Bridge.
56. Bhilai Steel Project.

UTTAR PRADESH
57. Maneri Bhali Project.
58. Bhagirathi Dam.
59. Civil Works for Narora APP.
60. Rihand Dam, and Super Thermal Power House.
61. Sarda and Ghagra Barrages.
62. Ichari Dam.
63. Yamuna Hydel Project.
64. Gomti and Sai Aqueducts.

DELHI
65. Water and Sewage Treatment Plants.

BHUTAN
67. Three Bridges.

HCC's contribution to nation-building

the exigencies of total project planning and execution. Efficient management systems were *de riguer.* Moreover, though Walchand himself had always invested in prime up-to-date equipment, after his death the group entered a phase of cautious spending. This, combined with the availability of cheap labor, resulted in HCC's neglecting to mechanise adequately. But with the huge amounts involved in Gulf contracts, where speed and efficiency were the bywords, HCC had to adjust overnight with purchases of the latest technology. It benefitted enormously from the experience and is now in a position to take advantage of the domestic construction boom.

HCC also learned the hard way about the problems a large labor force can cause a company. As HCC found to its cost, reliance on the human factor can, on occasion, be disastrous. The Idukki Dam project, India's first and highest arch dam, nearly brought ruin on HCC. The firm sustained a direct loss of Rs 5 crore on a Rs 17 crore contract, as well as the intangible costs of a tarnished reputation. With men, equipment and cash flow tied up until the company could resolve its conflicts with labor, the project, which should have taken five years to complete, took ten.

In the face of such problems, HCC's management made a determined effort to improve the company. On occasion in the past, HCC had successfully collaborated with various world-renowned firms like Nikex of Hungary, Waagner Biro of Austria and KWU of West Germany. To restore confidence in its name, HCC now tendered for various important national projects in collaboration with Bechtel of USA, Taylor Woodrow of UK, Christiani and Nielson of Denmark, and Taisel of Japan. To expedite the backlog of Rs 200 crores worth of work on their books, HCC also went public. Until the public issue, 99 percent of HCC's equity had been held by Premier Construction (the Walchand group's main holding company which is itself very closely held).

With increased exposure to new techinques and more money to play around with, HCC is poised for growth. To some extent, the results have already come in. The company's turnover has in a period of five years (1978-79 to 1982-1983) jumped from $27 million to $93 million, representing an increase of 249 percent. Gross profit has also shown a very healthy increase during the same period, going from $1.4 million to $7.8 million.

The Struggle to Set Up India's First Automobile Factory

Though the first successful car was designed, manufactured and driven by Karl Benz of Mannheim in 1885, it took sixty years for the automobile industry to come to India. In 1944 the Walchand group established the Premier Automobiles Ltd. (PAL). One of the earliest automobile ventures in India, PAL began by assembling and repairing models of Plymouth, Dodge, De Sota and Fiat cars. Soon after India achieved independence in 1947, the company went into actual production of automobiles in collaboration with the Chrysler Corporation of the U.S.A. and the Fiat Company of Italy.

The idea of an Indian automobile industry, first conceived in 1934 by Sir M. Visvesvaraya, Dewan of Mysore State, appeared as folly to most industrialists of the time. "Under present conditions," they opined, "importing foreign-made cars and selling them pays better than manufacturing them in India." Moreover, several American companies, Ford and General Motors particularly, had their own Indian companies which imported components from the U.S.A. Their assembly business was large and profitable.

Nevertheless, by 1936 the Dewan of Mysore had drawn up a proposal for an Indian car company and circulated it among Indian industrialists. In 1939 the Government of Bombay, at that time under the control of the Indian Congress Party, showed interest in the scheme. It was prepared to support its establishment on certain conditions and only with the involvement of an experienced and reputable business house. Walchand's interest was sparked and he immediately set about to mobilize support for the project under his banner. Because of World War II and the political turmoil within India, however, his efforts over the next five years were largely fruitless.

The profits made by foreign car traders proved to be the major obstacle to the manufacture of cars in India. The *Bombay Sentinel* of April 18, 1941 reported under the headline "General Motors find India a Gold Mine":

> *The news recently published in newspapers that India is to have its own car factory at Bangalore has caused quite a flutter in the dovecotes of some of the foreign manufacturers who have built flourishing factories for the assembling of American cars and trucks. Their uneasiness is quite explained by the fact that the production and selling of cars is a real 'money-spinner', even judged by the American standards.*

Walchand, however, was not deterred and he began attempts, through personal meetings and correspondence with both the Governments of India and of Bombay Province, to get encouragement for his plant by way of contributions, concessions in taxes and transport dues and tariff protection. A new company was formed, Indian Motors Ltd., Bombay, with a managing agency of three partners: Walchand Hirachand, Dharamsey Mulraj Khatau and Tulsidas Kilachand. Proceedings were also afoot to get technical collaborations with either the Ford or Chrysler Companies of the U.S.A. and to purchase suitable land for the plant.

The new project faced mounting difficulties. Walchand was convinced that the new plant would have to have some form of government help to succeed. He also saw the help given to the German and Russian automobile industries by their respective governments and felt that since the automobile industry was a core industry in industrial development, it should receive some help from the Indian government. Unfortunately, the Indian government did not quite see Walchand's point of view. In any case the Indian government was in no position to take on additional burdens during a World War and growing domestic political turmoil.

Since World War II created several demands, however, Walchand tried to capitalize on the situation. Before the war the government had accepted the idea of mechanizing the Indian Defense Force and thus needed all types of motor vehicles (in 1940, 60,000 such vehicles were supplied to the Services). If Walchand could get the job of supplying even a fraction of these vehicles, he would have no cause for anxiety about the success of his factory. Walchand thus proposed to the Government that he would undertake to construct 5,000 motor vehicles a year and supply them to the Defense Force within nine months from receipt of the order. In return he asked for help in opening the factory by way of its being designated a "War Efforts" project. This would facilitate purchases of scarce commodities through access to even scarcer foreign exchange which could in turn be used to pay Chrysler for an automobile collaboration. But the exigencies of the war meant that the government needed vehicles now, not nine months hence. Ford and General Motors were more than capable of meeting the Army's demands. Moreover, the Army was not keen on having three companies, each with its own vehicle model, supplying the Defense Force.

Such problems were compounded by the fact that the Government of Bombay was no longer controlled by an Indian ministry. By November of 1939, the Indian cabinet had resigned and the government was in the hands of Governor Sir Robert Lumley. Though personally sympathetic to Walchand, the Governor regretfully maintained that they could not honor the pledges made by the previous Government in view of the war crisis.

Stopped cold in his efforts to get the support of the British government, Walchand turned to Mysore, an independant state within British India, where he was already putting up his aircraft factory. Though the Dewan, Sir Mirza Ismail, was in favor of the scheme, the British government (perhaps due to pressure brought on them by certain American companies who had vested interests in continuing their import and assembling trades) prevailed on the Nizam to stop the proposals. Walchand next turned to Madras State, then Baroda State, but to no avail.

Competition with the Birlas

Meanwhile time was running out. The Birlas were pushing towards opening their own automobile plant. This finally moved Walchand Hirachand to forego seeking government aid which, in any case, did not appear to be forthcoming. His plant was finally established in 1944.

It was felt by some leading businessmen such as Sir Purushottamdas Thakurdas that it would be quite wasteful for two Indian business groups to invest so much capital in similar products when the market was likely to be limited. In 1942 negotiations were held between the Birlas and Doshis with a view to merging the two automobile schemes, but no agreement could be reached. The Birlas formed the Hindustan Motors Ltd. in Calcutta in 1942 with a paid-up capital of Rs 4.96 crore ($4.1 million) and Walchand

Harlow trainer of Hindustan Aeronautics Ltd., Bangalore

Hirachand formed the Premier Automobiles Ltd. in Bombay in 1944 with a paid-up capital of Rs 2.2 crore ($1.8 million).

Though the Birlas had a head start on the Walchand Group, neither group was able to start production until 1947 in the absence of the necessary import permits from the Government of India. But both groups prepared to meet the predictable increase in the post-war demand for cars. Premier Automobiles completed their works and commenced operations for the assembly of cars in March 1947. Due to the threat of partition in eastern India, Hindustan Motors could not decide on the location of its factory until 1947. Both companies installed plants on a scale which was much in excess of potential demand in the immediate future, anticipating that demand would expand considerably in the coming years. Both companies would enjoy a complete monopoly of the market for almost 40 years.

Ancillary Industry

In advanced countries, automobile manufacturers produce only major components and buy remaining materials from ancillary units. In India, the automobile industry was established largely as a result of aggressive and pent-up desires on the part of two business houses to be independent and to acquire power in relation to foreign interests. There were no ancillary units to rely on and PAL had to set up its ancillary industries unit which increased cost of production markedly. Following independence, however, several ancillary industries did develop and this period saw PAL production and profitability take off at a very good rate.

Walchand with his family members on his 71st birthday celebrated at Bombay (standing from left) Bahubali Gulabchand, Arvind Daftari, Ushakant Ladiwala, Mrs Nalini Popatlal, Mrs Jayashri Ushakant, Mrs Leelawati Vidyachandra, Miss Shobhana, Mrs Kamalini Bahubali, Mrs Sharayu Arvind Daftari, Miss Nirmala Ratanchand, Miss Rajani Motichand, Miss Trishala Gulabchand, Mrs Leelavati Bharat, Popatlal Shah, Vidyachandra Shah, Bharat Gulabchand ; (on chairs, from left) Lalchand Hirachand, Mrs Lalitabai Lalchand, Motichand Goutamchand, Mrs Kusumabai Motichand, Walchand Hirachand, Mrs Kasturbai Walchand, Gulabchand Hirachand, Mrs Shantabai Gulabchand, Mrs Vimalabai Ratanchand, Rajas, Ratanchand Hirachand, Govindji Raoji ; (on the ground, from left) Upendra Abhayakumar Shah, Chakor Lalchand, Miss Nanda Motichand, Shashank Lalchand, Miss Chhaya Motichand, Arvind Raoji Doshi, Ajit Gulabchand, Miss Aruna Ratanchand, Miss Anjana Gulabchand, Vidyut Mehta.

Walchand family on Walchand's 71st birthday

Gradual Decline

These years, however, were the only good ones for the company. Profits were a result more of generally rapid economic growth of the country than of good management or good workmanship. This poor performance began to show when general conditions began to deteriorate in the 1970s. The first hints of the problems in store for PAL came with the oil crisis of the early 1970s. In 1972-73, major ancillary suppliers to PAL could not provide components, thereby disrupting over three months' production. Power cuts aggravated the problem and the company had to lay off its workmen. The loss of production was estimated at Rs 10 crore. This set the pattern for the next decade: increasing costs of production and slack demand led to low volume of production and in 1976, consequently, losses all around. Efforts were made to improve matters. The government tabled a Finance Bill which reduced the excise duty on automobiles from 20 percent to 15 percent. The company passed on the benefit to the consumers and demand immediately improved, though the respite was short-lived. The next year, 1977, the militant union leader, Datta Samant, joined the PAL labor unions, provoking prolonged labor unrest, frequent go-slows, lock-outs and even violence at all the company's plants. It was only towards the end of March 1981 that all the issues with labor were sorted out and normal production could be resumed.

Improved Conditions

Since 1981 conditions at PAL have improved. Sales turnover increased by 59 percent to Rs 165 ($138 million). Profits recorded a much larger improvement. Production and sales in terms of units both for passenger cars and commercial vehicles showed considerable increases.

Silver plaque given to 300,000th
buyer of Premier automobile

WALCHAND
family tree

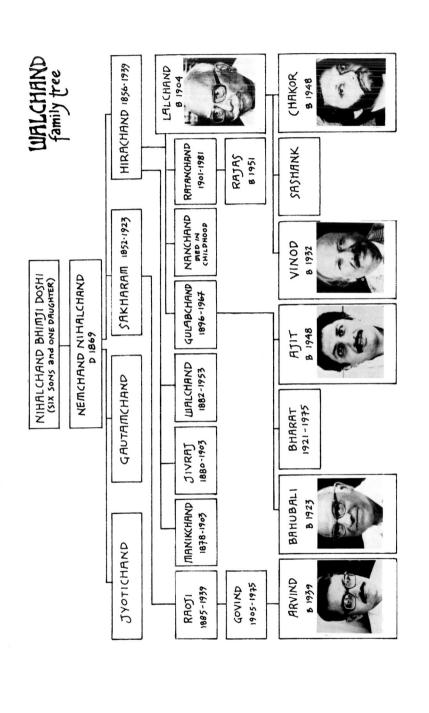

NIHALCHAND BHIMJI DOSHI
(SIX SONS and ONE DAUGHTER)

NEMCHAND NIHALCHAND
D 1869

JYOTICHAND

GAUTAMCHAND

SAKHARAM 1852-1923

HIRACHAND 1856-1939

RAOJI 1885-1939

MANIKCHAND 1878-1903

JIVRAJ 1880-1903

WALCHAND 1882-1953

GULABCHAND 1896-1967

NANCHAND DIED IN CHILDHOOD

RATANCHAND 1901-1981

LALCHAND B 1904

GOVIND 1905-1975

ARVIND B 1939

BAHUBALI B 1923

BHARAT 1921-1975

AJIT B 1948

VINOD B 1932

RAJAS B 1951

SASHANK

CHAKOR B 1948

Principal Companies of Walchand Group

Company	Products
Acrow India Ltd.	Acrow steel formwork used in construction
Bombay Cycle & Motor Agency Ltd.	Automobile, airconditioner sales, service & repairs
Cooper Engineering Ltd.	Combustion engines, castings, machine tools
*Hindustan Construction Co. Ltd.	Construction
Indian Hume Pipe Co. Ltd.	Hume pipes & special pipes
*Premier Automobiles Ltd.	Passenger & commercial vehicles
Premier Construction Co. Ltd.	Investment & consultancy, leasing
Ravalgaon Sugar Farm Ltd.	Sugar, confectionary, sugar wax, sugar mill machinery, confectionary machinery
Tiwac Industries Ltd.	Clocks
Vikhroli Metal Fabricators Ltd	Design, fabrication & erection of all kinds of structural steel works
*Walchandnagar Industries Ltd.	Sugar & cement plant machinery, equipment for nuclear reactors, space vehicles, fertilizers & chemical projects

* Over $50 million in sales

The better results can be ascribed to a number of tangible factors, not the least of which was the improved labor situation. PAL has always had the advantage of a popular product: demand has generally been more than supply and their model, the Premier Padmini, has always sold at a premium. The management has also undertaken several modernization schemes which include the import of capital goods for improving the fuel efficiency of the engine as well as upgrading their model through adoption of the Italian Fiat 124 model car body on the existing power train. By 1982, 80 percent of the modernization plans was completed. The most potent factor in the rejuvenation of the company was perhaps the veiled threat by financial institutions to replace the management of the founding family by that of a senior professional within the group if the company's results did not improve very soon. Another factor may have been the corporate raid on PAL in 1983 by the R.P. Goenka group which was foiled as the Doshis marshalled support from fellow industrialists to resist the takeover. The inner conflicts can only be guessed at, but the end result is there for all to see: the Doshi family remains very much in control of the company and PAL's performance is much improved.

There seems little doubt that the improvements brought about by the crises faced by PAL's management has placed it in a much better position to diversify and expand its operations.

END NOTES

Bajaj

1 T.V. Parvate, *Jamnalal Bajaj* (Ahmedabad: Navajivan Publishing House, 1962), p. 29.

2 Letter from Rahul Bajaj to authors dated September 21, 1983.

3 V. Kulkarni, *A Family of Patriots* (Bombay: Hind Kitabs Ltd., 1951), p. 2.

4 Shriman Narayan, *Jamnalal Bajaj* (New Delhi: Ministry of Information and Broadcasting, Government of India, 1974), p. 1.

5 Kulkarni, p. 30.

6 Letter from Viren J. Shah to authors dated January 30, 1985.

7 *Ibid.*

Birla

1 The Birlas and Tatas have been running neck and neck in the industrial rankings for several decades now. But while the Tatas have been among the industrial elite for over one and a half centuries, the Birlas are relatively recent entrants in comparison. In 65 years they have risen to the premier position in terms of assets and profits though they are second in terms of sales. When the Tatas established their first cotton mill, the Empress Mill in Nagpur in 1874, Shiv Narain was earning Rs 10 a month as a clerk. A decade after the Tatas started their steel plant in Jamshedpur and the vast hydro-electric complex in Bombay, the Birlas were able to put up their first industrial venture—a jute mill.

2 G.D. Birla, *In the Shadow of the Mahatma* (Bombay: Orient Longman, 1955), p. xiv.

3 During the days of the freedom movement, all four brothers participated in varying degrees. After independence, they came under strong criticism for growing too fast by a government leaning increasingly toward anti-capitalist policies. This caused the Birlas to retire into their own business circles. The only member of the family to take interest in politics now is KK Birla who, after trying unsuccessfully in 1967 and 1971 to win a seat in Parliament, was elected in 1984 to the Upper House of Parliament, the Rajya Sabha.

4 FICCI Proceedings of the 27th Annual General Meeting (1954) cited in Stanley Kochanek, *Business and Politics in India* (Berkeley: Univ. of California Press, 1974), p. 218.

5 *Ibid.*

6 P.C. Rao, *B.M. Birla—His Deeds and Dreams* (New Delhi: Arnold Heinemann, 1983), p. 3.

7 T.N. Ninan et al, "Empire in Transition," *India Today* (July 15, 1983), 99.

8 For a very interesting exposition, see N.K. Sengupta, *Changing Patterns of Corporate Management* (New Delhi: Vikas Publishing, 1983), p. 188f.

9 Dilip Thakore, "Legend in his Lifetime," (details unknown).

10 Interview with authors.

Goenka

1 Battle of Plassey, 1857. Victory over French forces ensured British hegemony over large parts of India.

2 Not to be confused with Ramnath Goenka, chairman of the *Indian Express* group.

3 Sir Hariram, Sir Badridas and Ghanshyamdas.

4 Now part of Duncans Agro Industries Ltd.

5 Renamed Woolcombers of India Ltd. (in JPG group).

6 *Bombay Magazine* (March 22, 1984), 88.

7 Interview with authors.

8 *Ibid.*

9 Jugnu Rama-Swamy, "The Changing of the Guards at Kamani's," *Sunday Observer* (Dec. 11, 1983).

[10] Now known as Centron Industrial Alliance.
[11] Wilkinson Swords produced shaving systems worth an estimated $66.6 million for the British market in 1980 and is the second largest manufacturer in the field after Gillette of the USA.

Kirloskar

[1] S.L. Kirloskar, *Cactus & Roses* (Pune: C.G. Phadke, 1982), p. 178.
[2] *Ibid.,* p. 62.
[3] *Ibid.,* p. 21.
[4] *Ibid.,* p. 50.
[5] *Ibid.,* pp. 78-79.
[6] *Ibid.,* p. 114.
[7] *Ibid.,* p. 126.
[8] *Ravi,* unpaginated booklet published in memory of Ravindra Kirloskar, n.p., n.d.
[9] *Ibid.*
[10] Dilip Thakore, "The Uncompromising Economics of S.L. Kirloskar," *BusinessWorld* (July 2-15, 1984), 36-54.

Mafatlal

[1] Interview with authors.
[2] *Ibid.*

Modi

[1] Dr. P.P.S. Chauhan, *A Vision of Karmayogi Gujar Mal Modi* (Modinagar: Allied Publicity Bureau, 1977), p. 11.
[2] Interview with authors.
[3] *Ibid.*
[4] Chauhan, p. 52.
[5] *Ibid.,* p. 58.
[6] *Ibid.,* p. 74.
[7] *Director Digest* (July/August, 1982), 17.

Oberoi

[1] M.S. Oberoi, *A Vision Come True,* pamphlet (January, 1978), unpaginated.
[2] *Ibid.*
[3] *Ibid.*
[4] *Ibid.*
[5] Interview with authors.
[6] Spencer & Co. used to be one of the largest chains in India. Over the years, however, it has declined to seventh place. The top four groups are all Indian-owned entities: ITDC, a government entity; Indian Hotel Company owned by the Tata group; East India Hotels Ltd., the Oberoi chain, and Welcomgroup, a division of ITC. Two other Indian hotel companies are number five and six in size: UP Hotels and Hotel Corporation of India.
[7] This was an isolated case. The Tata's Taj Group of hotels did not get into an expansionary phase until the mid-1960s and ITC did not go into hotels until the 1970s.
[8] S.L. Kirloskar, *Cactus & Roses* (Pune: C.G. Phadke, 1982), p. 283.
[9] Oberoi, n.p.
[10] *Ibid.*

Tata

[1] Raymond Chapman, *The Victorian Debate* (New York: Basic Books, 1968), p. 7.

[2] R.M. Lala, *The Creation of Wealth* (Bombay: IBH Publishing Company, 1981), p. 86.

[3] Chapman, p. 4.

[4] Frank Harris, *Jamsetji Nusserwanji Tata* (Bombay: Blackie and Son (India) Ltd., 1958), p. 64.

[5] Lala, p. 61.

[6] Subrata Roy, "Businessman of the Year 1983," *BusinessIndia* (December 19, 1983-January 1, 1984), 54-64.

[7] "Mody, JRD and TISCO," *Gentleman* (February 1985), 139.

[8] "The New Man of Steel," *Gentleman* (February 1985), 136.

[9] Chander Uday Singh, "The Tatas Changing of the Guard," *India Today* (December 3, 1981), 101.

[10] Anil Mehta, "The Tata group plans massive high-tech investments," *The Economic Times*, Vol XXIV, NO. 228 (Bombay, February 11, 1985), 1.

[11] Chandrika Hariharan, "The heir apparent to the house of Tata," *BusinessIndia* (December 21, 1981-January 3, 1982), 51.

TTK

[1] K. Krishna Moorthy, "Management, Like Music, is a Concerted Action," *Director Digest* (August 1984), 57-58.

[2] S.L. Kirloskar, *Cactus & Roses* (Pune: C.G. Phadke, 1982), p. 174 and p. 179.

LIST OF ILLUSTRATIONS

Goenka

Kirloskar

Mafatlal

Mahindra

Tata

APPENDIX

Principal Companies/Executives/Sales/Products

AMBANI

Reliance Textile Industries Ltd.
Chairman: Dhirubhai H. Ambani
Jt. Mg. Dir.: Ramniklal H. Ambani
Sales: Rs 605 cr ($504 mn)
Products: Polyester filament yarn, textiles, petrochemicals

BAJAJ

Bajaj Auto Ltd.
Chairman: Rahul Bajaj
Sales: Rs 225 cr ($186 mn)
Products: Motor scooters, motorcycles, three-wheelers

Mukand Iron & Steel Works Ltd.
Chairman: Viren J. Shah
Chief Exec.: Rajesh Shah
Sales: Rs 95 cr ($79 mn)
Products: Steel and alloy castings, construction, engineering

Hindusthan Sugar Mills Ltd.
Chairman: Ramkrishna Bajaj
Mg. Dir.: R.P. Nevatia
Exec. Dir.: Shishir Bajaj
Sales: Rs 52 cr ($43 mn)
Products: Sugar, cement, alcohol

Bajaj Electricals Ltd.
Chairman: R.P. Nevatia
Chief Exec.: Shekhar Bajaj
Sales: Rs 47 cr ($39 mn)
Products: Markets fans, lamps, electricals

BIRLA

I. L.N. Birla

Jiyajeerao Cotton Mills Ltd.
Chairman: K.K. Birla
Sales: Rs 100 cr ($83 mn)
Products: Textiles, chemicals

II. K.K. Birla

Central India Machinery Mfg. Co. Ltd.
Chairman: D.P. Mandelia
Sales: Rs 65 cr ($54 mn)
Products: Textile and cement plant machinery

Texmaco Ltd.
Chairman: K.K. Birla
CEO: R. Maheshwari
Sales: Rs 99 cr ($83 mn)
Products: Wagons, textile machinery

Zuari Agro Chemicals Ltd.
Chairman: K.K. Birla
CEO: H.S. Bowa
Sales: Rs 116 cr ($97 mn)
Products: Chemical fertilizers

III. B.K. Birla

Century Enka Ltd.
Chairman: D.Y. Gaitonde
Sales: Rs 119 cr ($99 mn)
Products: Nylon and polyester filament yarn

Century Spg. Mfg. Co. Ltd.
Chairman: B.K. Birla
CEO: B.L. Jain
Sales: Rs 242 cr ($202 mn)
Products: Cloth, yarn, cement, tyrecord, chemicals, engineering, paper, shipping

Gwalior Rayon Silk Mfg. Co. Ltd.
Chairman: Aditya Birla
Sales: Rs 372 cr ($310 mn)
Products: Viscose staple fibre, rayon grade pulp, paper

Hindustan Aluminum Corp. Ltd.
Chairman: Aditya Birla
Sales: Rs 286 cr ($238 mn)
Products: Aluminum ingots, rolled products

Indian Rayon Corp. Ltd.
Chairman: Aditya Birla
Sales: Rs 103 cr ($86 mn)
Products: Viscose filament, rayon yarn, cloth

Jayshree Tea & Industries Ltd.
Chairman: B.K. Birla
Sales: Rs 85 cr ($71 mn)
Products: Tea, plywood, superphosphates

Kesoram Industries & Cotton Mills
Chairman: B.K. Birla
Sales: Rs 143 cr ($119 mn)
Products: Cement, viscose filament, rayon yarn

IV. Gangaprasad Birla

Hindustan Motors Ltd.
Chairman: G.P. Birla
Sales: Rs 298 cr ($248 mn)
Products: Automobiles

Hyderabad Asbestos Cement Products Ltd.
Chairman: C.K. Birla
Sales: Rs 95 cr ($79 mn)
Products: Asbestos products.

Orient Paper Industries Ltd.
Chairman: G.P. Birla
Sales: Rs 86 cr ($72 mn)
Products: Pulp, paper and board, caustic soda

V. M.P. Birla

Birla Jute Industries Ltd.
Chairman: M.P. Birla
Sales: Rs 233 cr ($194 mn)
Products: Cement, jute

VI. Ashok Birla

Tungabhadra Industries Ltd.
Chairman: Ashok Birla
Sales: Rs 72 cr ($60 mn)
Products: Vanaspati, refined and hardened oils

Zenith Steel Pipes Industries Ltd.
Chairman: Ashok Birla
Sales: Rs 85 cr ($71 mn)
Products: Steel pipes, ingots, billets, sockets

GOENKA

I. R.P. Goenka

Ceat Tyres of India Ltd.
Chairman: R.P. Goenka
Mg. Dir.: Harsh V. Goenka
Sales: Rs 263 cr ($219 mn)
Products: Automobile tyres and tubes

Dunlop India Ltd.
Chairman: Manohar Chabria
Chief Exec.: Sanjiv R. Goenka
Sales: Rs 320 cr ($267 mn)
Products: Automobile tyres and tubes

Bayer (India) Ltd.
Chairman: R.P. Goenka
Sales: Rs 85 cr ($71 mn)
Products: Pharmaceuticals, rubber products

KEC International Ltd.
Chairman: N.L. Hingorana
Sales: Rs 78 cr ($65 mn)
Products: Power transmission towers

II. G.P. Goenka

Duncans Agro Industries Ltd.
Chairman: Gouri P. Goenka
Sales: Rs 166 cr ($138 mn)
Products: Tea, cigarettes

National Rayon Corp. Ltd.
Chairman: J.P. Thacker
Sales: Rs 70 cr ($58 mn)
Products: Rayon yarn, caustic soda, tire cord, sulfuric acid

Herdillia Chemicals Ltd.
Chairman: J.N. Guzder
Sales: Rs 53 cr ($44 mn)
Products: Heavy organic chemicals

III. J.P. Goenka

Duncans International Ltd.
Chairman: J.P. Goenka
Sales: Rs 30 cr ($25 mn)
Products: Garments

Anglo-India Jute Mills Co. Ltd.
Chairman: J.P. Goenka
Sales: Rs 38 cr ($32 mn)
Products: Jute

Swan Mills
Chairman: Kantikumar R. Podar
Sales: Rs 45 cr ($38 mn)
Products: Cotton textiles

KIRLOSKAR

Kirloskar Cummins Ltd.
Chairman: C.S. Kirloskar
Vice Chairman: Arun Kirloskar
Sales: Rs 115 cr ($96 mn)
Products: High horse power diesel engines

Kirloskar Electric Co. Ltd.
Chairman: S.L. Kirloskar
Vice Chairman: Dr. C.A. Phalnikar
President: Vijay R. Kirloskar
Sales: Rs 91 cr ($76 mn)
Products: Electrical engineering equipment

Kirloskar Oil Engines Ltd.
Chairman: S.L. Kirloskar
President: Arun Kirloskar
Sales: Rs 86 cr ($72 mn)
Products: Diesel engines

Kirloskar Bros. Ltd.
Chairman: S.L. Kirloskar
President: P.D. Gune
Sales: Rs 62 cr ($52 mn)
Products: Pumps

MAFATLAL

I. Arvind Mafatlal (The Classic Group)

Mafatlal Fine Spg. & Mfg. Co. Ltd.
Chairman: Arvind N. Mafatlal
Chief Exec.: Padmanash A. Mafatlal
Sales: Rs 116 cr ($97 mn)
Products: Textiles, chemicals

Mafatlal Industries Ltd.
Chairman: Arvind N. Mafatlal
Sales: Rs 90 cr ($75 mn)
Products: Textiles, chemicals

National Organic Chemical Industries Ltd.
Chairman: Arvind N. Mafatlal
Chief Exec.: M.S. Patwardhan
Sales: Rs 172 cr ($143 mn)
Products: Agrochemicals, petrochemicals

Polyolefins Industries Ltd.
Chairman: Arvind N. Mafatlal
Chief Exec.: N.M. Dhuldhoya
Sales: Rs 98 cr ($82 mn)
Products: Polyethylene, rubber chemicals

II. Yogindra Mafatlal (The Sungrace Group)

Indian Dyestuff Industries Ltd.
Chairman: Yogindra N. Mafatlal
Sales: Rs 98 cr ($82 mn)
Products: Vat dyestuffs

III. Rasesh Mafatlal (The Stanrose Group)

Standard Mills Co. Ltd.
Chairman: Rasesh N. Mafatlal
Sales: Rs 153 cr ($126 mn)
Products: Textiles, caustic soda

MAHINDRA

Mahindra & Mahindra Ltd.
Chairman: Keshub Mahindra
Mg. Dir.: B.R. Sule
Sales: Rs 420 cr ($350 mn)
Products: Jeeps, tractors, electronic components

Mahindra Ugine Steel Co. Ltd.
Chairman: Harish Mahindra
Sales: Rs 50 cr ($42 mn)
Products: Alloy and specialty steels

MODI

Modi Rubber Ltd.
Chairman: K.N. Modi
Vice Chairman: V.K. Modi
Sales: Rs 241 cr ($201 mn)
Products: Automobile and truck tires and tubes

Bombay Tyres International Ltd.
Chairman: K.N. Modi
Vice Chairman: V.K. Modi
Sales: Rs 124 cr ($103 mn)
Products: Automobile and truck tires and tubes

Godfrey Phillips India Ltd.
Chairman: R.A. Shah
President: K.K. Modi
Sales: Rs 133 cr ($111 mn)
Products: Cigarettes

Modipon Ltd.
Chairman: K.N. Modi
President: K.K. Modi
Sales: Rs 99 ($83 mn)
Products: Synthetic yarns and fibers

Modi Industries Ltd.
Chairman: K.N. Modi
Sales: Rs 97 cr ($81 mn)
Products: Vanaspati, sugar, oils, gases, paints, soups, alcohol, steel, welding electrodes

OBEROI

The East India Hotels Ltd.
Chairman: M.S. Oberoi
Deputy Chairman: P.R.S. Oberoi
Sales: Rs 50 cr ($42 mn)

Mercury Travels (India) Ltd.
Chairman: M.S. Oberoi
Mg. Dir.: Gautam Khanna
Sales: Rs 2.5 cr ($2 mn)

Oberoi Hotels (India) Pvt. Ltd.
Chairman: M.S. Oberoi
Sales: unknown (privately held)
(Holds 35% in East India Hotels and 100% of Oberoi International Pvt. Ltd.)

TATA

Tata Iron and Steel Co. Ltd.
Chairman: R.H. Mody
Sales: Rs 781 cr ($651 mn)
Products: Steel, steel products

Tata Engineering and Locomotive Co. Ltd.
Chairman: S. Moolgaokar
Chief Exec.: J.E. Talaulicar
Sales: Rs 755 cr ($629 mn)
Products: Trucks, buses, heavy equipment

The Tata Power Co. Ltd.
Chairman: Naval H. Tata
Chief Exec.: K.M. Chirnappa
Sales: Rs 175 cr ($146 mn)
Products: Electricity generation and distribution

The Tata Oil Mills Co. Ltd.
Chairman: D.S. Seth
Sales: Rs 155 cr ($129 mn)
Products: Soaps, synthetic detergents, cattle/poultry feeds

Tata Chemicals Ltd.
Chairman: D.S. Seth
Sales: Rs 105 cr ($88 mn)
Products: Soda ash, chemicals

Tata Tea
Chairman: D.S. Seth
Sales: Rs 105 cr ($88 mn)
Products: Tea, bulk and packaged

Voltas
Chairman: A.H. Tobaccowalla
Sales: Rs 280 cr ($233 mn)
Products: Marketing of consumer goods, manufacture of air conditioners, engineering goods

Indian Hotels Co. Ltd.
Chairman: J.R.D. Tata
Mg. Dir.: A.B. Kerkar
Product: Five-star hotels

The Tata Hydro-Electric Power Supplies Co. Ltd.
Chairman: Naval H. Tata
Vice Chair: K.M. Chinnappa
Sales: Rs 71 cr ($59 mn)

THAPAR

Ballarpur Industries Ltd.
Chairman: Lalit M. Thapar
Sales: Rs 211 cr ($176 mn)
Products: Paper, pulp, chemicals, vanaspati

Crompton Greaves Ltd.
Chairman: N.M. Wagle
Sales: Rs 172 cr ($143 mn)
Products: Electrical engineering equipment, international trade

Jagatjit Cotton Textile Mills Ltd.
Chairman: Man Mohan Thapar
Sales: Rs 120 cr ($100 mm)
Products: Textiles, nylon filament yarn, polyester fiber

Greaves Cotton Ltd.
Chairman: Lalit M. Thapar
Mg. Dir.: Govind Mathrani
Products: Engineering, aviation equipment

TTK

T.T. Krishnamachari & Co.
Chairman: T.T. Narasimhan
Mg. Dir.: T.T. Jagannathan
Sales: Rs 31 cr ($28 mn)
Products: Marketing and distribution

T.T. (Pvt.) Ltd.
Chairman: T.T. Narasimhan
Mg. Dir.: T.T. Jagannathan
Sales: Rs 18 cr ($15 mn)
Products: Pressure cookers, domestic appliances

TTK Pharma Pvt. Ltd.
Chairman: T.T. Narasimhan
Mg. Dir.: K. Kuppuswamy
Sales: Rs 15 cr ($12.5 mn)
Products: Pharmaceuticals, processed foods

London Rubber Co. (India) Ltd.
Chairman: T.T. Narasimhan
Jt. Mg. Dir.: T.T. Vasu
Chief Exec.: K. Kuppuswamy
Sales: Rs 6 cr ($5 mn)
Products: Condoms

WALCHAND

Hindustan Construction Co. Ltd.
Chairman: Lalchand Hirachand
Chief Exec.: Ajit Gulabchand
Sales: Rs 110 cr ($92 mn)
Products: Construction

Premier Automobiles Ltd.
Chairman: Vinod L. Doshi
Chief Exec.: P.N. Vencatesan
Sales: Rs 169 cr ($141 mn)
Products: Automobiles

Walchandnagar Industries Ltd.
Chairman: Lalchand Hirachand
Chief Exec.: Chakor L. Doshi
Sales: Rs 127 cr ($79 mn)
Products: Sugar, cement, machinery for nuclear reactors, space vehicles, fertilizer and chemical projects

GENERAL BIBLIOGRAPHY

Anon. *Report of the Monopolies Inquiry Commission* (Government of India), 1965, Vols. I and II.

Anon. *The Stock Exchange Official Directory* (Annual). Bombay.

Bagchi, A.K. *Private Investment in India 1900-1939*. Cambridge: Cambridge University Press, 1972.

Gadgil, D.R. *The Industrial Evolution of India in Recent Times.* Calcutta: Oxford University Press, 1959.

Hazari, R.K. *The Structure of the Corporate Private Sector: A Study of Concentration, Ownership and Control.* London: Asia Publishing House, 1966.

Kochanek, S.A. *Business and Politics in India.* Berkeley: University of California Press, 1974.

Lamb, Helen B. *Studies On India and Vietnam.* New York: Monthly Review Press, 1976.

Majumdar, R.C., and A.K. Majumdar (eds.). *The History and Culture of the Indian People.* Bombay: Bhavitya Vidya Bhavan, 1969. (11 volume series.)

Ray, R.K. *Industrialization in India – Growth and Conflict in the Private Corporate Sector 1914-1947.* Calcutta: Oxford University Press, 1979.

Sen, S.P. (ed.). *Dictionary of National Biography.* Calcutta: Institute of Historical Studies, 1972. (4 volumes.)

Sengupta, N.K. *Changing Patterns of Corporate Management.* 2nd Revised Edition. New Delhi: Vikas Publishing House Pvt. Ltd., 1983.

GROUP BIBLIOGRAPHIES
AND SOURCE MATERIALS

AMBANI GROUP

Articles, Brochures, Reports

Anon. "Reliance: A Success Story," *Imprint* (Jan. 1984).

Balance sheets (1979-1984) and company pamphlets.

Director Digest Portfolio 1983: "Reliance Textiles—How Multiple Strategies Led to Phenomenal Growth," pp. 99 f.

Narayan, Rajan. "Reliance: A Story of Astonishing Growth," *Business India* (April 28–May 11, 1980).

Ninan, T.N., and Chander Uday Singh: "The Reliance Mystery: Non-Resident Investment," *India Today* (Dec. 31, 1983); "The Investment Maze: Reliance Textile," *India Today* (Jan. 15, 1984); "Reliance Roulette," *India Today* (May 31, 1982).

Pednekar, Vandana. "How Many Times Can the Finance Minister Lie?," *Illustrated Weekly of India* (Jan. 29, 1984).

Radhakrishnan, N. "The Way of the Manipulators," *Bombay* (June 22–July 6, 1982).

Vidyadharan, Aravind. "A Rejoinder to Vandana Pednekar: Much Ado About Nothing," *Illustrated Weekly of India* (Feb. 26, 1984).

Interviews

Interview with Dhirubhai Ambani and senior executives (Oct. 1984).

BAJAJ GROUP

Books and Articles

Anon. "The House of Bajaj and Ethics in Business," *Business India* (Jan. 22–Feb. 4, 1979).

Anon. "Viren Shah: The Businessman Politician," *Business India* (March 13-26, 1978).

Bajaj, Jankidevi. *Meri Jeevan Yatra* (Hindi, Marathi).

Bajaj, Kamalnayan. *Kakaji-Bapu-Vinoba* (Hindi).

Bajaj, Ramakrishna: various. *Atlantic ke Uspar* (Hindi). New Delhi: n.d.; *Challenges to Trade; Jamnalalji Bajaj ki Diary,* Parts I-V (Hindi); *Patravyavahar,* Parts I-VIII (Hindi); *Rusi Yuvakon ke Beech* (Hindi); *Social Role of Business.* Maharashtra Chamber of Commerce: 1970; *Vinoba ke Patra* (Hindi); *Young Russia.*

Birla, G.D. "Jamnalalji" (Hindi, Gujerati). New Delhi: n.d.

Ganguly, Sabyasachi. "Testing Time for the King of the Road," *Business World* (Oct. 11-24, 1982).

Jain, Yashpal (ed.). *Kamalnayan Bajaj – vyakti aur vichar* (Hindi).

_____. *Shriman Narayan – vyakti aur vichar* (Hindi).

J.B. Seva Trust. *Smaranjali* (Hindi).

Kamath, M.V. and Shrirang Pingle (eds.). *Ramkrishna Bajaj,* Felicitations volume. Maharashtra Chamber of Commerce: 1983. There is also a Hindi edition.

Kasbekar, Kiron. "Bajaj Auto vs. Piaggio," *Business India* (Aug. 30–Sept. 12, 1982).

Kulkarni, V. *A Family of Patriots* (Hindi, English). Bombay: 1951.

Mishra, Bhavaniprasad and Yashpal Jain (eds.). *Samarpan aur Sadhan* (Hindi). Published on Occasion of 80th Birthday of Jankidevi Bajaj.

Narayan, Shriman. *Jamnalal Bajaj* (Hindi, English). Publications Division, Ministry of Information and Broadcasting, Government of India (n.d.).

Kalelkar, Kakasaheb (ed.). *Bapur ke patra* (Hindi). Jamnalal Bajaj Seva Trust. Benares: 1957.

_____. *To a Gandhian Capitalist.* Bombay: 1946.

_____ (ed.). *Panchwen Putrako Bapuke Ashirwad* (Hindi, Gujerati).

Parvate, T.V. *Jamnalal Bajaj Nav Jeevan* (Gujerati). Ahmedabad: n.d.

Oza, Suresh Dutt. *Jamnalal Bajaj aur unka rashtriya jeewan me yogdaan* (Hindi). Unpublished Ph.D. diss., Lucknow University, 1982.

Ranke, Rishabdas. *Jeevan Johri* (Hindi).

Shah, C.H. and C.N. Vakil (eds.). *Agricultural Developments of India.* Orient Longman: 1979.

Shikhare, D.N. *Kritarth Jeewan* (Marathi).

_____. *Nagpur se Nagpur* (Hindi, Marathi).

Thakore, Dilip. "The Firodias Move to Prove a Point," *Business World* (Sept. 12-25, 1983).

Thomas, Binoy. "Rahul Bajaj – The Scooter King in Top Gear," *Society.*

Tripathi, R. *Seth Jamnalal Bajaj* (Hindi). Allahabad: 1932.

Upadhya, Haribhau. *Shreyarthi Jamnalalji* (Hindi), in two editions, one complete, one abridged. New Delhi: 1951.

Vakil, C.N. (ed.). *Industrial Development of India.* Orient Longman: 1973.

Viswanathan, S. "Getting Out of the Mini-Mould," *Business India* (Dec. 7-20, 1981).

Brochures, Reports, Pamplets

Annual Reports.

Brochure on Hindustan Sugar 1932-1982. Published by Bajaj Group, Bombay: n.d. (anon.).

"The House of Bajaj—A Profile," published by Bajaj Auto Ltd., Bombay, 1982.

"I Had Him in Mind," published by Bajaj Auto Group Ltd., Bombay, 1982.
Interviews with Ramkrishna Bajaj, R.P. Nevatia, Rahul Bajaj, Viren Shah, 1984.

BIRLA GROUP

Books and Articles by GD Birla

Atulanada Chatterjee. Calcutta: 1956.
Bapu (Speech delivered at Sangir Kala Mandir, Calcutta, Dec. 24, 1981.)
Bapu – A Unique Association (4 Volumes). Bombay: Bharatiya Vidya Bhavan, 1977.
Bikhere Vicharon ki Bharoti. New Delhi: 1975.
Dayri kee pannee. New Delhi: 1957.
India's March Towards Freedom 1935-1947. New Delhi: 1981.
In the Shadow of the Mahatma. London: 1953 and Bombay: Orient Longman, 1955.
Krishnam Vande Jagadguru. Bombay: Bharatiya Vidya Bhavan, n.d.
Kuch Dekha, Kuch Sunna. New Delhi: 1966.
Rup aur swarup. New Delhi: n.d.
Shri Jamnalal Bajaj. New Delhi: n.d.

Books

Anon. *The Path to Prosperity* (A Collection of Speeches and Writings of GD Birla: A Birla Group Publication). Bombay: n.d.
Anon. *Modern India – Heritage and Achievement* (Shri GD Birla's 80th Birthday Commemoration). New Delhi: Hindustan Times Press, 1977.
Burman, Debajyoti. *The Mystery of Birla House.* Calcutta: 1950.
_____. *TTK and Birla House.* Calcutta: 1957.
Parekh, Kishore. *G.D. Birla—A Photobiography.* Bombay: n.d.
_____. *The Glorious 90 Years.* Bombay: 1984.
Rao, P. Chentsal. *B.M. Birla – His Deeds and Dreams.* New Delhi: Arnold Heinemann, 1983.

Articles

Anon. "After G.D. What?," *Surya India* (July 1-15, 1983).
Anon. "Century: The Bluest of the Blue Chips," *Business India* (May 15-28, 1978).
Banerjee, Sumita. "G.D. Birla: I'm Trying to Be a Good Guy," *Society* (July 1983).
Banerjie, Indrani. "Kesoram Rayon Factory: The Invisible Menace," *India Today* (June 30, 1984).
Behara, Meenakshi. "The Quiet Rise of Aditya Birla," *Business India* (May 7-20, 1984).

Dagli, Vadilal, and others. "A Maker of Modern Industrial India," *Commerce* (June 25, 1983).

Goradia, Praful, Anirban Chakraborty, GD Birla and others. "The Empire that GD Built," *Capital* (April 16-29, 1984).

Jack, Ian. "The King is Dead," *Sunday* (June 26–July 2, 1983).

Roy, Subir. "The House that G.D. Birla Built," *The Telegraph* (June 26, 1983).

Thakore, Dilip. "How Century Plans to Keep Flying High," *Business World* (March 26–April 8, 1984).

_____. "A Legend in his Lifetime," *Business World* (March 20–April 12, 1981).

Brochures, Reports, Pamphlets, etc.

Company brochures, press releases, pamphlets.

We Keep the Wheel Moving Nationally and Internationally (Brochure of B.K. Birla Group), Bombay: n.d.

Words to Remember (Published by G.D. Birla Group), Bombay: 1983.

India Developing (Published by G.D. Birla Group), Bombay: 1983.

Partners in Progress (Published by Ashok Birla Group), Bombay: n.d.

Interviews

Interviews with Aditya Birla, Ashok Birla, and with senior and junior executives.

GOENKA GROUP

Books and Articles

Anon. "The House that Goenka Built," *Business Standard* (May 10, 1981).

Anon. "The Front-Line Aspirations of G.P. Goenka," *Business World* (March 15-18, 1982).

Kasbekar, Kiron and Subrata Roy. "The Goenka Split," *Business India* (Jan. 18-31, 1982).

Katiyar, Arun. "Kamani Engineering Corporation – The Plot Thickens," *Bombay* (Dec. 7-21, 1983).

Kochanek, Stanley. *Business and Politics in India.* Berkeley: University of California Press, 1974.

Kottary, Sailesh. "The Goenka Connection: Ceat's Turning Point," *Business World* (May 9-20, 1983).

Singh, Chander Uday. "The Goenkas – Corporate Raiders," *India Today* (Aug. 15, 1984).

Singh, Kushwant. *The Power and the Sword: Asian Cables – The First 25 Years: 1959-1984.*

Thakurta, Paranjoy Guha. *"The Dunlop Takeover,"* Update (Jan. 22, 1985).

Timberg, Thomas A. *The Marwaris.* New Delhi: Vikas Publishing House Pvt. Ltd., 1978.

Anonymous Pamphlets and Brochures

Duncan Group Profile (Pamplet published by J.P. Goenka Group and Companies, anon., n.d.)

The Duncan World of Textiles (Published by Swan Mills, Ltd., n.d.).

Indira Priyadarshini (Published by R.P. Goenka). Bombay, 1985.

"Life: Sketch of Rai Bahadur Sir Baridas Goenka."

"Romance of the Road – Ceat Tyres of India" (Brochure published by Ceat Tyres).

"Write-up on the G.P. Goenka Group of Companies."

"Write-up on the late Shri K.P. Goenka."

Reports, Enquiries, Directories etc.

Balance sheets and P.R. materials.
Monopoly Inquiry Commission Report.
Stock Exchange Directories.

Interviews

Interviews with Harsh Goenka, R.P. Goenka, and various executives.

KIRLOSKAR GROUP

Books and Articles

Anon. "Kirloskar Poised For a Great Leap Forward," *Business India* (Oct. 30–Nov. 12, 1978), pp. 22-37.

Kirloskar, S.L. *Cactus and Roses.* Pune: C.G. Phadke, 1982.

Kottary, Sailesh. "The Success Formula of India's Most Profitable Company," *Business World* (July 4-17, 1983), pp. 33-48.

Valluri, Madhu. "S.L. Kirloskar: The Old Man and His Oil Engines, *Society* (January, 1982), pp. 40-43.

Company Brochures

"The Inner Force."
"Ravi."
Annual Reports.

Interview

Interview with S.L. Kirloskar and senior executives.

MAFATLAL GROUP

Writings of Arvind Mafatlal

"Banking and Industry – The Role of Banks in National Life."
"Business Community and Social Justice."
"Business in Egalitarian Society."
"Economic Growth with Social Justice."
"In Search of Social Peace."
"Social Responsibilities of Business and Industry."

Books and Articles

Anon. "The Cow and the Tractor," *Time* (Asian Edition: May 10, 1963).
Anon. "The House of Mafatlal" by a special correspondent, *Indian Management* (July-Aug. 1968).
Anon. "The Mafatlal Split," *Business India* (May 14-27, 1979).
Hazari, R.K. *The Structure of the Corporate Private Sector.* London: Asia Publishing House, 1966.
Hill, Roy. "Running a $250-million Family Firm," *International Management* (July 1973).
Joshi, L.A. *The Control of Industry in India.* Bombay: Vora & Co. Publishers, Pvt. Ltd., n.d.
Rele, Subhash J. "The Success Story of the Mafatlals," *Industrial Times* (Aug. 20, 1973).
Tripathi, Dwijendra, and Makrand J. Mehta. *Business Houses in Western India* (mimeograph), esp. Chapter VI: "The Mafatlals."

Reports, Directories etc.

Balance Sheets of Mafatlal Group Companies and P.R. material.
Monopoly Inquiry Commission Reports
Stock Exchange Directory

Interviews

Interviews with Yogindra Mafatlal, Rasesh Mafatlal, Atulya Mafatlal, and senior and junior executives.

MAHINDRA GROUP

Articles

Hariharan, Chandrika. "Mahindra & Mahindra: Making Up for Lost Time," *Business India* (March 15-28, 1982).
Roy, Subrata. "The Biggest Merger of All," *Business India* (Dec. 6-19, 1982).

Pamphlets, Booklets, and Directories

Published by Mahindra:
Mahindra and Mahindra Limited
The Mahindra Group
Mahindra Corporate Profile
Stock Exchange Directory

Interviews

Interviews with B.R. Sule, Keshub Mahindra, B.K. Khare, and junior executives.

MODI GROUP

Books and Articles

Anon. "On Rough Roads," *Femina* (Aug. 23–Sept. 7, 1984).

Anon. "Raizada Seth Madan Lal Modi," *National Investment and Finance* (July 27, 1980).

Anon. "Takeover of Firestone Puts Modis at the Top," *Delhi Recorder* (Dec. 15, 1981).

Aggarwal, R.S., and C.M. Gupta. *Charitavali – Modinagar Sansthapak* (Hindi). Published by Modi Industries, Modinagar, 1967.

Chauhan, Dr. P.P.S. *A Vision of Karmayogi Gujar Mal Modi.* Modinagar: Allied Publicity Bureau, 1977.

Chenan, D., and P. Balakrishnan. "The Modi Blues," *Business India* (Oct. 22–Nov. 4, 1984).

Deas, Ross. "Vinay and Bhupendra Modi's Grand Strategy," *Director Digest* (July-Aug. 1982).

Mathai, P.G. "The Modis: Rough Weather," *India Today* (Oct. 31, 1984).

Ninan, T.N. "The Growth Impulse of the House of Modi," *Business World* (July 20–Aug. 2, 1981).

Thakore, Dilip. "Managing the House of Modi," *Business India* (Oct. 15-28, 1979).

Miscellaneous Pamphlets

Anon. "Shradhanjali" (Hindi), by Dayawati Modi Public School, Modinagar, 1976.

Anon. "Modinagar ka Nirman" (Hindi), Modi Group, n.d.

Gupta, C.M. "Geetanjali" (Hindi), Meerut, 1976.

———. "The Light of Modinagar," Meerut, 1976.

Modi, Rai Bahadur Gujarmal. "Approach to Uttar Pradesh's Fourth Five-Year Plan" (Hindi and English), Lucknow (July 27, 1968).

———. "Presidential Address at the Oil Technologists' Association of India," Kanpur (Oct. 27, 1951).

_____. "Presidential Address at the 8th Annual Convention of the Oil Technologists' Association of India," Kanpur (Jan. 1, 1953).

Shant, Lakhan. "Aao Baccho Ser Kerau" (Hindi), published by S. Gupta, Meerut, 1976.

_____. "Rashtra Seva Kaavya" (Hindi), published by G.P. Gupta.

_____. "Seth Gujarmal Modi Thirth Yatra Kaavya" (Hindi), published by G. Prakash Gupta, Modinagar, 1977.

Tyagi, V.S. "Amar Vani" (Hindi), Meerut, n.d.

Reports and Documents

Annual Reports.

MRTP Reports.

Stock Exchange Directories.

"Gujarmal Modi Hospital and Research Centre for Medical Sciences, New Delhi," a Modi Group publication, n.d.

"Modi Group of Industries," a company brochure published on the 50th anniversary of Modi Group Enterprises, 1983.

"Rai Bahadur Gujarmal Modi," a four-page advertiser's supplement issued to most national newspapers on Feb. 4, 1976.

Interviews

Interviews with K.N. Modi and senior and junior executives (1984 and 1985).

OBEROI GROUP

Books and Articles

Anon. "India's Oberoi Lights Up," *Hotel and Restaurants International* (April, 1983).

Cherian, Dilip. "Oberois: Going Places," *Business India* (Aug. 3-16, 1981), pp. 36-47.

Oberoi, M.S. *A Vision Come True.* Autobiographical sketch, January, 1978.

Sahai, Ratna. "Oberoi Spearheads the Growth of Hoteliering in India," *Harijana Tourism Annual Newsletter,* 1982.

Company Publicity Materials, Annual Reports, and Hotel Brochures.

Interviews

Interviews with M.S. Oberoi, P.R.S. Oberoi, Gautam Khanna, Allan Fernandes, Ratna Sahai, and other executives.

TATA GROUP

Books

Harris, F.R. *Jamsetji Nusserwanji Tata.* Bombay: Blackie and Son (India) Ltd., 1958.

Karaka, D.F. *History of the Parsees,* Vols. 1-11. London: 1884.

Keenan, John. *A Steelman in India.* New York: 1943.

Lala, R.M. *The Creation of Wealth: A Tata Story.* Bombay: P.C. Manaktala for IBH Publishing Company, 1981.

_____. *The Heartbeat of a Trust.* Bombay: Tata-McGraw Hill, 1984.

Menon, Aubrey. *Sixty Years: The Story of the Tatas.* Oxford: Oxford University Press, 1948.

Wacha, D.E. *The Life and Life-Work of J.N. Tata.* Madras: Ganesh and Co., 1914.

Articles and Pamphlets

Anon. "The Tata Iron and Steel Company," pamphlet issued by TISCO, 1966.

Elwin, Verrier. "The Story of Tata Steel," privately printed, 1958.

Naidu, Leila and Binoy Thomas. "Interview with J.R.D. Tata," *Society* (July, 1981).

Annual Reports

Interviews

Interviews with Tata executives.

THAPAR GROUP

Books and Articles

Anon. "Greaves 1983-84," Greaves Cotton & Co., 1984.

Anon. *A Century of Progress.* Published by Greaves Cotton & Co., 1960.

Cherian, Dilip. "Keeping a Firm Grip," *Business India* (March 26–April 8, 1984).

Datta, Asoke (ed.). *The Thapar Group – In India and Overseas.* Published by Ballarpur Industries Ltd., New Delhi, n.d.

Thapar House Magazine, Founder's Memorial Number, Vol. I, No. 2 (July-Sept. 1962).

Annual Reports

Various, of Thapar Companies.

Interviews

Interviews with Lalit Thapar, senior directors and executives, 1984.

TTK GROUP

Books and Articles

Anon. "Homage to T.T. Krishnamachari," *The Indian Review*, Vol. 69, No. 12 (March, 1974).

Ravindranath, Sushila. "TTK: Dark Horse from the South," *Business India* (Feb. 13-26, 1984), pp. 62-72.

Company Brochures

TTK Spectrum, house journal of the TTK group of companies.

Interview

Interview with T.T. Vasu.

WALCHAND GROUP

Books and Articles

Behara, Meenakshi. "Winds of Change at Walchands," *Business India* (May 23–June 5, 1983).

Doshi, Hirachand Nemchand, "Jainadharmachi Mahiti" (Marathi), pamphlet published by author, Sholapur, 1901.

Ganguly, Sabyasachi. "PAL Gears for the Maruti Challenge," *Business World* (July 19–Aug. 1, 1982).

Hazari, R.K. *The Structure of the Corporate Private Sector*. London: Asia Publishing House, 1966.

Hirachand, Lalchand. *"Indian Sugar Industry," Bombay Investor's Year Book, 1940*. Bombay: 1940, pp. 71-72.

Hirachand, Ratanchand. "Construction Engineering in India," *Bombay Investor's Year Book, 1940*. Bombay: 1940, pp. 75-77.

Hirachand, Walchand. *"Why Indian Shipping Does Not Grow," Bombay Investor's Year Book, 1940*. Bombay: 1940, pp. 58-66.

Khanolkar, G.D. *Adhunik aud Yogik Bharatache Shilpakar: Walchand Hirachand, Vyakti, Kala va Kartrutva*. Published by Walchand Group, Bombay, 1965.

_____. *Walchand Hirachand: The Man, His Times and Achievements*. Bombay: 1969. (Marathi edition also: *Valchand Hirachand Vyakti*

Kala ane Karya. Published by Walchand Group, Bombay, 1967.)

Magudkar, Dinanath Bapuji. *Seth Hirachand Nemchand* (Marathi). Published by Ratanchand Hirachand, Bombay, 1967.

Piramal, Gita. "Entrepreneurship in Bombay," *Economic Times* (Feb. 18, 1984).

Sardesai, B.D. *Walchand Diamond Jubilee Commemoration Volume.* Published by Walchand Group, Bombay: 1942.

Tripathi, Dwijendra, and Makrand J. Mehta. *Business Houses in Western India* (mimeograph), esp. Chapter 9: "The Walchands."

Pamplets and Special Papers (by the Walchand Group)

Anon. "The Walchand Group."

Anon. "The Spirit of Enterprise 1882-1952" (Bombay: 1953.)

Pandit, Ramu. "Walchand Hirachand" (Gujerati).

Balance sheets.

Stock Exchange Directory

Monopoly Inquiry Commission Reports.

Interviews

Interviews with Arvind Doshi, Bahubali Gulabchand, junior executives.

Product Index[1]

Index